Uyless Black

Sams **Teach Yourself**

Networking

in **24**
Hours

 800 East 96th Street, Indianapolis, Indiana, 46240 USA

Sams Teach Yourself Networking in 24 Hours

ISBN-13: 978-0-768-68576-3
ISBN-10: 0-768-68576-1

Library of Congress Cataloging-in-Publication Data

Black, Uyless D.
  Sams teach yourself networking in 24 hours / Uyless Black. — 4th ed.
       p. cm. — (Sams teach yourself in 24 hours)
  Previous ed.: Sams teach yourself networking in 24 hours / by Joe Habraken. 3rd ed. 2004.
  Includes index.
  ISBN 978-0-7686-8576-3 (pbk.)
  1. Computer networks. I. Habraken, Joseph W., 1954- Sams teach yourself networking in 24 hours. II. Title.
  TK5105.5.H385 2009
  004.6—dc22
                                        2009013953

Printed in the United States of America
Second Printing July 2009

Trademarks

Warning and Disclaimer

Bulk Sales

Sams Publishing offers excellent discounts on this book when ordered in quantity for bulk purchases or special sales. For more information, please contact

U.S. Corporate and Government Sales
1-800-382-3419
corpsales@pearsontechgroup.com

For sales outside of the U.S., please contact

International Sales
international@pearson.com

Editor-in-Chief
Mark Taub

Acquisitions Editor
Trina MacDonald

Development Editor
Songlin Qiu

Managing Editor
Kristy Hart

Project Editor
Jovana San Nicolas-Shirley

Copy Editor
Karen A. Gill

Indexer
Erika Millen

Proofreader
Sheri Cain

Publishing Coordinator
Olivia Basegio

Cover Designer
Gary Adair

Compositor
Jake McFarland

Table of Contents

About the Author

Uyless Black has written 35 books on computer networks. He was one of the first writers to publish a book on Transmission Control Protocol/Internet Protocol (TCP/IP) and related Internet protocols. His book *Voice over IP* (VoIP) remains a best seller in the field of data communications texts. Uyless has many years of experience as a programmer and in creating and managing data communications networks.

His educational credentials include a B.S. from the University of New Mexico, an M.S. in computer systems from the American University, and a graduate degree from Rutgers' Stonier Graduate School of Banking.

Dedication

This book is dedicated to Milli Second.

Acknowledgments

I want to thank Joe Habraken and Matt Hayden, who wrote and revised the first editions, for their contributions to this book. I was given an easier task of revising this Fourth Edition. I also want to thank my acquisitions editor, Trina MacDonald, for her guidance and support throughout this project. Holly Waters performed her usual great job of reading the manuscript, editing, and formatting it, as well as suggesting changes that made for a better book.

I have gone through the process of writing and producing a book more than 50 times. By producing, I mean the process of working with subject matter experts and editors to make certain the material is correct and readable. Before I sent the manuscript for this book to Sams, I proofread the material over and over, maybe as many as ten times. Did I find all my grammar errors and typos? Not by a long shot. But, I would wager that the Sams editing team found most of them. I can safely state that they are one of the best editing crews to have ever worked on one of my books.

Reviewing and editing someone's book manuscript is not an easy task. It requires almost superhuman attention to detail and a great deal of tact. Writers are known to have big egos, and editors must often tread cautiously when infoming the author that a sentence or paragraph is gibberish.

I want to thank the Sams staff for how they handled the editing of this book. I know from experience that they are top-notch. First, Ravi Prakash reviewed the manuscript from the technical standpoint. He offered several ideas that I put into the book. He made suggestions for changes; most of which I included. And he did all this with grace. I want to single-out the editors who helped make the book so much better than the manuscript I sent them. They are Songlin Qiu, Jovana San Nicolas-Shirley, Karen A. Gill, and Sheri Cain. The art department, including Laura Robbins, did a terrific job of redoing my original submissions.

We Want to Hear from You!

As the reader of this book, *you* are our most important critic and commentator. We value your opinion and want to know what we're doing right, what we could do better, what areas you'd like to see us publish in, and any other words of wisdom you're willing to pass our way.

You can email or write me directly to let me know what you did or didn't like about this book—as well as what we can do to make our books stronger.

Please note that I cannot help you with technical problems related to the topic of this book, and that due to the high volume of mail I receive, I might not be able to reply to every message.

When you write, please be sure to include this book's title and author as well as your name and phone or email address. I will carefully review your comments and share them with the author and editors who worked on the book.

Email: networking@samspublishing.com

Mail: Mark Taub
            Editor-in-Chief
            Sams Publishing
            800 East 96th Street
            Indianapolis, IN 46240 USA

Reader Services

Visit our website and register this book at informit.com/register for convenient access to any updates, downloads, or errata that might be available for this book.

Introduction

This book provides a reference guide for anyone who wants to get up to speed on computer network concepts and networking technologies. Because each piece of networking hardware and software operates differently, it would require a book the size of the New York City white pages to cover all aspects of the subject. Thus, this book concentrates on fundamental concepts. Emphasis is placed on understanding how the major components of a computer network function and how to use proven practices to deploy, upgrade, and maintain the network.

What's New in This Edition

This book has been overhauled for this Fourth Edition, including scores of references to commercial products and websites. New coverage has been added related to Microsoft Windows Server software. Updated information on the Linux platform and wide area networks (WANs) is also included. The wireless material on Wi-Fi and Bluetooth has been updated and expanded. As well, the latest Internet security protocols have been added to Hour 20, "Security."

Organization of This Book

The book is divided into six parts. Each part provides a body of information that covers a specific area pertaining to computer networks.

▶ Part I, "What Is Networking?," introduces networking, including an overview of the primary components of computer networks. This part explains the broader issues of how hardware and software function to support the interworking of computers, servers, routers, and other devices.

▶ Part II, "The Basics," focuses on the concepts underlying data networks. We examine how packet-switching operates and look at the operations of local area networks (LANs) and WANs. This part discusses computer network protocols and explains a widely used conceptual model that depicts how a sending computer transfers data to a receiving computer. Because of the impact and importance of wireless networks, the hour on this topic has been moved from Part VI (of the previous edition) to this part of the book.

▶ Part III, "Building Networks," walks you through the process of planning and building a network from conception to implementation. Issues related to planning network capacity, creating the network, and then connecting to the Internet are included as part of the discussion. For this latter discussion, the information of TCP/IP and related, supporting protocols has been expanded.

▶ Part IV, "Network Operating Systems," provides an overview of network operating systems, the major network servers, and Microsoft Windows Server 2003/2008, UNIX, and Linux.

▶ Part V, "Network Administration," examines the issues related to administering a network. This part includes discussions on both troubleshooting and management.

▶ Part VI, "The Future of Networking," examines future possible implementations of wireless technology, operating systems, and other aspects of networking. This part discusses the issues related to the future of Linux, the emerging network "cloud," nationwide wireless hotspots, and the extraordinary field of protein-based computers.

For these 24 hours, you will be the designer of a computer network, as well as its implementer. After you have successfully created a plan for the system, you will undo the shrinkwrap and assemble the components. Next, you will take over the role of the network administrator and make sure the users are happy with your creation. Don't worry—you've been blessed with a competent project team; you can delegate a lot of the work to them.

Conventions Used in This Book

Each hour starts with "What You'll Learn in This Hour," which is a brief list of bulleted points highlighting the hour's contents. A summary concluding each hour provides similar though more detailed insight reflecting what you should have gained from the hour.

This book has several unique elements to help you as you're learning networking. Throughout the book, you'll see the following elements:

Did you Know?

This element offers advice or teaches an easier way to do something.

By the Way

This element provides additional information that's directly related to the surrounding discussion.

Watch Out!

This element advises you about potential problems and helps you steer clear of disaster.

I look forward to hearing your comments about this book and learning about your ideas. Please feel free to communicate with me at UylessBlack.com.

HOUR 1

An Overview of Networking

What You'll Learn in This Hour:

▶ Definition of a computer network

▶ Why we need computer networks

▶ Components of a network

▶ Different types of networks

▶ Importance of the Internet

Computer networks have become part of our everyday lives. We use them to take cash from the local ATM. Whenever we send email or browse the Web, we rely on the world's largest computer network, the Internet, to be our electronic mailman. Telemarketers, usually during dinner hour, use computer networks to sell us their wares. Our cable television stations rely on computer networks to transport programs onto our TV screens. What is a compelling example of their presence in our lives? Without computer networks, our cellular phone is little more than a battery powering-up a meaningless screen.

To provide these extraordinary services, computer networks transfer data to and from our TV sets, personal computers, cell phones, and other modern machines. This data is then translated by applications into video TV images, icons on PC screens, and text messages on cell phones. These network tasks take only a second or so (often less) to be completed—even if the network must fetch data from around the world. Why watch a science fiction movie? A computer network is equally impressive.

Although data networks, like computers, have become an integral part of our lives, most people consider computer networks too complex a subject to even consider setting one up. Usually, we resort to a nearby geek squad to help us, or we bring in specialists from our company's networking department.

But let's leak a secret—one these technical "whizzes" would like not to be known: Networking is not all that complicated. It doesn't require a membership in a secret society. Unless you choose to become a software programmer or a hardware designer, unless you choose to build a network from scratch, you have no need to devote years of study to be able to set up and manage your own network.

In the past, managing networks did indeed require in-depth experience and training. And make no mistake: This book will not give you sufficient information to manage the Internet! But now, with the proliferation of millions of networks and network users, the industry provides tools to allow you to not only understand computer networks but to set them up and manage them effectively.

Gaining the ability to create a computer network requires an understanding of a few fundamental concepts, the nuts and bolts of data communications. Coupled with the pliers of common sense—and reading this book—you can assemble your own network.

Reading to Learn More

The more you read about networking concepts and issues related to computer networks, the easier it will be to implement and maintain your own network. The website www.informit.com is a good way to get started. After reading this book, go to that site. You might be surprised to learn how familiar the concepts are to you. Also, I recommend the Wikipedia entries on the subject at http://wikipedia.org. For the more advanced reader, I suggest studying the Internet specifications, available at http://www.isoc.org.

What Is a Network? What Is Networking?

In simplest terms, a computer network consists of two or more connected computers. This connection is twofold: (a) physical, through wires, cables, and wireless media (the atmosphere with, say, cell phones), and (b) logical, through the transport of data across the physical media. We discuss the components required to make the physical connection in several parts of this book; notably, Hours 4, 10, and 23. The logical connections are discussed throughout the book.

In the context of this book, what is networking? If I say to someone, "I'm networking!," what does this declaration mean? For starters, it doesn't mean I'm socializing with co-workers or mingling with parents at the local PTA. It means I'm sitting at a computer, communicating with someone or something via a computer network. Fine, but you don't need to do 24 hours of reading to teach you how to sit at a terminal and play online Scrabble.

Thus, *Sams Teach Yourself Networking in 24 Hours* is a shorthand title for teaching you how to *build* a network so that you can later *do* networking.

As suggested, there's more to networking computers than physical connectors, such as electrical plugs in the wall and ports on a PC. Several basic rules must be followed if the computers are to exchange data with each other.

▶ The machines in the network must use the same procedures for sending and receiving data. These procedures are called *communications protocols*. If these devices do not (or cannot) use the same protocols, conversions must take place, usually with services called *protocol converters*. The idea is akin to someone who translates between a person speaking Spanish and a person speaking English. For computer networks, I can send my son an email from my wire-based computer to his Internet cell phone.[1] For my son (Tommy) to read this message, conversions are performed at the physical level (wire-based images to wireless-based images) and at the logical level (email format to text format). Fortunately, you will not have to deal with protocol converters. They are provided for you automatically.

▶ The data must be delivered without corruption. That is, if I key-in "Hello, Tommy" in my email, it must (and will) be received at his cell phone as, "Hello, Tommy," and not, say, "Hello, Mommy."

▶ A method must be in place whereby the receiving computer (By the way, a modern cell phone contains at least one computer) can acknowledge the receipt of uncorrupted data and inform the sending computer if the data was indeed received in error. Thus, if Tommy's machine receives "Hello, Mommy," Tommy will never see this error appear on his screen. Unbeknownst to Tommy, a piece of software will check the data and return a message to my computer asking for a retransmission. I also will not know about this wonderful service. What is more, because *all* these dialogues are taking place so quickly (in a few fractions of a second), Tommy and I are unaware of the short delay in our ongoing dialogue.

▶ Computers on a network must be capable of determining the origin and destination of a piece of information, such as an email or a text message. After all, if Tommy wants to send a response to me, the network must be able to route it to my computer, and Tommy's device must provide the address to the network. Once again, you usually don't need to be concerned with these tasks. Addresses are often assigned to you automatically. As we shall see, it is yet another service provided to network users.

▶ Obviously, standardized addresses are required for the correct exchange of data between computers. Because millions of computers around the world can be

[1] *As of this writing, not all cell phones support Internet sessions, but the trend is in this direction.*

networked, these addresses must be "scalable" to accommodate a large computer population.

▶ For security and management, there must be a method for identifying and verifying the devices connected to a network. Hackers must be prevented from damaging computers and files.

This list is not an exhaustive set of network requirements and, as stated, to obtain most of these services, you need not lift a finger to your keyboard or keypad. We've listed them to give you an idea of some of the issues faced when computer networking gurus tackle the task of exchanging and sharing data between computers. As seen earlier, for data transfer among computers to take place, rules must be followed. Otherwise, the process is akin to people attempting to speak to each other in different languages.

Networks can be as simple as a point-to-point connection between two computers transferring files to each other. Networks can also be quite complex. One example that comes to mind is the Federal Reserve's system, which allows us to electronically transfer funds between accounts. Another is the cellular network. It tracks us as we move across a terrain and hands off our connection to the next wireless tower in a "cell" where we have recently moved.

Despite the fact the point-to-point example is much simpler than the bank and cellular examples, each has to follow the same basic rules to permit users to communicate with each other. We will explore both simple and complex networks in this book.

However, before we delve into the details of a computer network and how to set one up, we should pause and answer this question: Why would we want to build a network in the first place? I suspect you have your own answer; otherwise, you would not be reading this book. Permit me to offer some thoughts on the matter; perhaps they are the same as yours.

Why Build a Network?

If we're happy with receiving or sending information by hand, we can resort to the postal service. But hard copy correspondence is called "snail-mail" for good reason. It's far too slow in today's accelerated world. By the time a letter arrives, its contents are often old news.

▶ In contrast, a computer network enables faster communications between parties. In so doing, it leads to more efficient use of time.

▶ By sharing electronic data among perhaps thousands of people, a computer network encourages (requires!) the use of standard policies and procedures. After all, our personal computer and our text-proficient cell phone have no inferential power as we humans do. We can just respond with, "Say again please," if we don't understand a transmission. But a computer network must be laboriously programmed to perform this one simple task. However, and once again, these standardized procedures lead to more efficient communications.

▶ Networks provide backup and recovery support for our data. If the postal service's mail truck breaks down, our letter might be delayed for a day—at least. Not so for a computer network. It's designed to provide near-instantaneous recovery from a failure—all *without a loss* of a single character or number in our (electronic) mail.

▶ "I've lost that file!" "I've lost the letter!" These lamentations are no longer true with computer networks. If networks are properly designed, it's easy to store copies of our data. Be it mail, photographs, files, or video, we can keep copies safe and sound on another computer in another part of the country—if we take the time to instruct the network to do so.

▶ Shared resources lead to less expensive communications. Take the Internet, for example. It's an expensive public network (in reality, millions of interconnected networks), but we use it for a few dollars a month, and its performance is such that we might consider it our own private network. That is, we think we have this network for ourselves, but we don't. A term to describe this fine service is *virtual private network.*

As many reasons exist for using computer networks as there are people sharing them and organizations building them. One person might have a bunch of computers at home—one for her, one for him, several for the kids. She may want to hook all the computers together so the family can have a common calendar and email, which, as we know, the kids will more readily read than the note on the fridge. Another person may want to connect his small office or home network to the Internet to use the Web. Yet another person in Texas may to play Texas Holdem with his friends living in New Jersey.

Computer networks have transformed the way we work and play. For better or worse, they've changed our lives. I trust that you think the change is for the better. I do. But we've said enough about why we use computer networks. Let's now see how they're used, and more to the point, how we can use them to improve our personal and professional lives.

How Networks Are Put Together

To repeat an important point, if we were to break down a network into its simplest components, these components would be identified as one of two categories. One is the physical network. It consists of the wiring or wireless medium; the network cards inside the computer that interface with the "plugs" on the computer; and, of course, the computers themselves (which might take the form of mail servers, file servers, and other machines discussed later). The other category is the logical part of the network. Usually implemented in software, it provides the means to build those parts of the network with which we "interface." Examples are email, text messaging, web pages, videos, and the images on our computer screen. We introduce these components during this hour, and they are covered in more detail in coming hours.

The Network Architecture: Combining the Physical and Logical Components

When computers are connected, we must choose a network architecture, which is the combination of all the physical and logical components. The components are arranged (we hope) in such a way that they provide us with an efficient transport and storage system for our data. The network architecture we choose dictates the physical topology and the logical arrangements of the system. For example, if I say, "I'm building a Switched Ethernet network," this statement implies the overall architecture of my future network. Let's now examine these physical and logical components.

The Physical Network

The physical network is easy to understand because it's usually visible. Mainly, it consists of hardware: the wiring, plugs such as computer ports, printers, mail servers, and other devices that process and store our data. The physical network also includes the important (read: vital) signals that represent the user data. Examples are voltage levels and light pulses to represent binary images of 1s and 0s—strung together in many combinations to describe our data.

I say "usually visible" because we can't see wireless connections. Although more ethereal than copper wire connections, wireless connections are nonetheless physical, taking the form of electromagnetic radio waves.

Quite rare only a few years ago, wireless networks such as Wi-Fi are now common. If you have a broadband connection in your home, chances are good your computer is connected to your broadband hardware device with a wireless arrangement. How we explain the layout (also called a *topology*) of a wireless network is no different from that of a wire-based network.

Physical Layout—Network Topologies

As mentioned, the physical aspect of the network consists of the components that support the physical connection between computers. In today's networks, four topologies are employed: (a) star, (b) ring, (c) bus, and (d) cell. They are depicted in Figure 1.1.

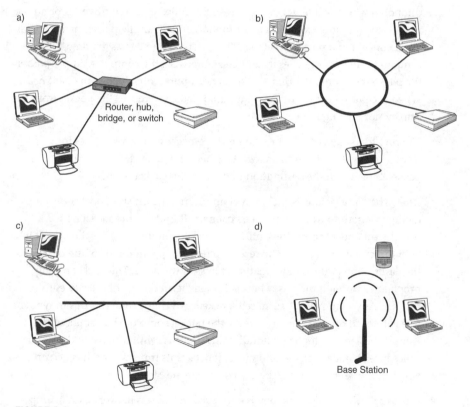

FIGURE 1.1
Network topologies: (a) Star topology, (b) Ring topology, (c) Bus topology, (d) Cellular topology

▶ **Star**—The *star* topology employs a central connection point, called a *router, hub, bridge*, or *switch*. The computers on the network radiate out from this point, as seen in Figure 1.1(a). The job of the central point is to switch (relay) the users' data between user machines and perhaps other central connection points. The terms router, hub, bridge, or switch are used interchangeably by some people. Generally, the terms hub and bridge are associated with devices of a somewhat limited capacity. The term switch has historically been associated with telephone networks (with the exception of the 1970's computer network message switches and 1980's packet switches). The term router found its way into the industry in the 1980s and is now used more frequently than the other terms. Whatever we call these machines, they manage *traffic* on the network and relay this traffic back and forth between our computers.

▶ **Ring**—The *ring* topology, shown in Figure 1.1(b), connects the computers through a wire or cable. As the data (usually called a *packet*) travels around the ring, each computer examines a destination address in the packet header (similar in concept to a postal envelope's "to" address) and copies the data if the computer's address matches its address. Otherwise, the computer simply passes the packet back onto the ring to the next computer (often called the next *node*). When the packet arrives at the originating node, it removes the packet from the ring by not passing it on.

The ring topology is the first example of a *broadcast* network: Nodes in the network receive all traffic in the network. Whether a node chooses to accept the packet depends on the destination address in the packet header.

▶ **Bus**—The *bus* topology is shown in Figure 1.1(c). It consists of a wire with taps along its length to which computers connect. It is also a broadcast network because all nodes receive the traffic. The sending node transmits the packet in both directions on the bus. The receiving nodes copy an image of the packet if the destination address matches the address of the node. The packet rapidly propagates through the bus, where it is then "terminated" at the two ends of the bus. As you may have surmised, packets traveling along this bus may interfere with each other if the nodes relay the packets onto the bus at about the same time. The bus topology handles this situation with a collision detection procedure. A node keeps sending until it detects its transmission has occurred without interference (by checking its own transmission).

▶ **Cellular**—The *cellular* topology is employed in wireless networks, an arrangement shown in Figure 1.1(d). Cellular networks use broadcast protocols; all nodes (cellular phones) are capable of receiving transmissions on a control channel from a central site. A wireless control node (called the base station) uses this common channel to direct a node to lock onto a specific (user) channel for its connection. During the ongoing connection, the cell phone is simultaneously communicating with the base station with the control link and the user link.

The Logical Network

The previous section explained the physical layout of networks, such as the star topology. In explaining how packets of user traffic are moved across these topologies, we have also explained the logical aspects of a network. Again, the logical parts of computer networks entail the invocation of software to "propel" the packets across the physical media and to receive them at the other end.

Unlike the physical network, the logical network is not visible. It uses the physical network for transport of data. We defer describing the details of the logical network here, as it is described extensively in almost every subsequent hour.

Two Varieties of Networks: Local and Wide Area

The topology of a computer network is an important feature of its composition. Another is the geographical composition: the network's coverage. That is to say, how far does it extend? The span of a network—its physical girth—often dictates how it goes about sending, receiving, and otherwise managing data.

The Word "Link" Is Used in Two Ways

Often, the word "link" is used to describe a computer network communications channel, such as a satellite link or a cellular telephone link. Other words for link are line and channel. Be aware that the Web use of "link" is different. For the Web, "link" means a connection to something else, such as another web page or another web site.

By the Way

LANs

A local area network (LAN) is so-named because the nodes are in close proximity to each other, usually within a building or inside a home. In the past, the procedures (protocols) employed to manage a LAN depended on the nodes being close to each other—within a kilometer or so. The older Ethernet bus topology is an example of this distance-limited idea. Another way to describe a LAN is that it is usually a private network. It is owned, operated, and used by a company or an individual, to the exclusion of other companies and individuals.

Also, in the old days (a couple decades ago), a LAN was noted for its "high-speed" capacity. The original Ethernet LAN sent and received data at 10 million bits per second (bps)—a phenomenal transfer rate in those days. Today, this capacity and beyond is enjoyed by both LANs and wide area networks (WANs), discussed next.

"High-Speed" Networks Are No Faster Than "Low-Speed" Networks

All computer networks operate at the same speed. They send and receive data at roughly 186,000 miles per second. So, what makes those wonderful "broadband" Internet connections seem so "fast"? After all, the transmission speed is limited by the laws of physics. The answer is that computer networks use various methods to represent data on the communications link. For example, the character "U" in my name could possibly be represented by a code of eight bits (binary 0s and 1s). However, for "high-speed" links, data is coded and compressed in such a way that large data streams are represented by far fewer bits. Therefore, a broadband link, operating at millions of bits per second, is using clever coding and compression techniques to put more bits per second onto a communications channel.

The term "speed" to describe (1) a high-capacity system (2) offering fast response times is just fine. Speed in this context describes the rate at which data is transmitted or the measurement of how long it takes for a function to be performed.

WANs

As their name implies, wide area networks (WANs) are geographically scattered. They are usually connected to local networks with a router. This machine relays the packets between computers, which often reside on LANs, as seen in Figure 1.2. Access to a WAN is obtained with a dial-up telephone line or with a broadband link, such as a Digital Subscriber Line (DSL), a cable TV link, or a satellite link. The dial-up option, although widely used, is quite limited in its capacity, perhaps operating at only 56,000bps. In contrast, broadband links transport data in the megabit per second (Mbps) range. Once you've used broadband, you likely won't be happy with dial-up. Downloading a web page on a dial-up line might take several minutes, in contrast to a broadband link, which takes a few seconds.

FIGURE 1.2
LANs and WANs

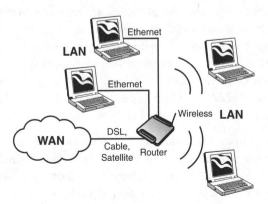

The term "broadband" can be confusing. Strictly speaking, it refers to the frequency spectrum with a broad band of frequencies, but it also describes a network or communications link that sends and receives data at a high bit rate, such as 4,000,000bps. If eight bits are used to comprise a character, such as the letter A, this broadband link can accommodate 1/2 million alphabetic characters per second (4,000,000/8 = 500,000). It's easy to understand why broadband is so popular.

WANs are often public networks. That is, they're available to anyone who wants to use them and pay for their use. The telephone system is a WAN public network facility. So is the Internet. Some WANs are private networks, owned and operated by companies or other enterprises. An example of a private WAN is a bank's ATM network. Typically, the bank leases communications links from a communications carrier, such as AT&T, and then installs its own ATM machines and routers, configuring them for its own unique requirements. As a bank customer, we can use the ATM network, but we can't connect our computers to it. In this regard, it's a private network.

Examples of Network Topologies, LANs, and WANs

Insofar as possible, we've avoided using buzz words to describe network topologies. It might be helpful to associate specific names with these topologies, but you can skip this section if you prefer. Here's a list of common computer networks and their associated topologies; all will be examined in subsequent hours:

- ▶ **Star networks**—Switched Ethernet (LAN); Asynchronous Transfer Mode (ATM) (LAN or WAN); Frame Relay (WAN); the Internet (WAN); Synchronous Optical Network (SONET) (WAN)

- ▶ **Ring networks**—Token Ring (LAN); IBM Token Ring (LAN); Fiber Distributed Data Interface (FDDI) (LAN); Synchronous Optical Network (SONET) (WAN)

- ▶ **Bus networks**—Ethernet Bus (LAN); Token Bus (LAN)

- ▶ **Cellular networks**—The cell phone networks (WAN); Bluetooth (LAN); Wi-Fi (LAN)

How the Internet Relates to Your Network

The most widely used data network in the world is the Internet, which is a public WAN. We gain access to it by paying a monthly fee to an Internet service provider (ISP) such as AOL or Verizon. Our interface with the ISP is with a dial-up link or a broadband connection. The ISPs have contractual arrangements with each other for the purpose of exchanging traffic with their respective customers.

The Internet owes its origin to the pioneering endeavors of the U.S. Department of Defense. During the 1960s, the Advanced Research Projects Agency (ARPA) was tasked with creating a government network to facilitate the exchange of information between various agencies and universities. Eventually, the ARPANET evolved to the Internet of today. This extraordinary network consists of millions of connected networks, such as the LAN in your home or office. According to www.internetworldstats.com/stats.htm, 1.5 billion people are now using the Internet (sometimes called the Net for short).

The ISPs manage their respective part of the Internet with routers, servers, and firewalls and play the vital role of informing other networks and providers about their customers. This procedure is elegantly simple. An ISP advertises its customers to the Internet by sending out information. For example, a packet, sent to practically any ISP in the world, states, "Uyless Black can be reached through me." In so doing, the ISP advertises my name (such as UylessBlack.com) and an address to reach me (such as a network ID and an end user ID).

> ### An Email Address Is Not an Address
>
> When we say, "Send me your email address," we don't mean what we say. Our so-called email address is an email name. One of mine is UylessBlack.com. It is the job of the ISP to correlate this name into a routable address. Chances are you've come across an Internet address. It might appear as 192.99.3.4, for example. Internet addresses are similar in concept to postal addresses (street, city, state, and ZIP code) and are explained in Hour 3, "Getting Data from Here to There: How Networking Works."

Connecting to the Internet

Until a few years ago, the prevalent method for connecting to the Internet was through POTS (plain old telephone services). These dial-up connections are still popular, but they are of limited capacity. Increasingly, Internet users are migrating to broadband services provided by the telephone and cable TV companies, as well as satellite and cellular companies.

Figure 1.3 shows an example of a machine that can connect users' computers to the Internet. It is called by various names because it provides a multitude of services. First, it is a modem. A modem (from modulator/demodulator) provides the physical transmissions for the connection, such as voltages and frequencies. Second, it acts as a firewall; that is, it attempts to block unwelcome visitors from intruding into users' computers and files. Third, it performs the functions of a router. For example, this machine can support several computers' Internet sessions with both remote and local computers. It "routes" traffic back and forth by examining addresses in each packet. Fourth, it is a wireless (cellular) machine. The antenna and associated components in the machine send and receive traffic within a LAN—in this situation, our home or office.

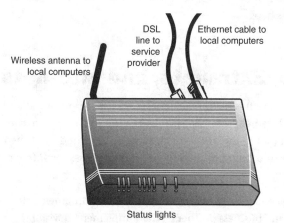

DSL line to service provider

Ethernet cable to local computers

Wireless antenna to local computers

Status lights

FIGURE 1.3
A router and attached links

Why the Internet Matters

At the risk of stating the obvious, the Internet has transformed the way we do business. Prior to its inception, it was quite difficult to transfer data from one computer to another—unless that computer toed the line and used the same proprietary procedures as the sending machine. For example, IBM marketed its own suite of protocols, as did other vendors. None of them could communicate with each other. The data communications industry was operating in a Tower of Babel. It was suffering from serious compatibility problems, with the resultant loss of productivity.

To their credit, many international organizations had standards used by hardware and software vendors. The modem and fax standards, published by the International Telecommunications Union (ITU), were adapted by all modem and fax manufacturers. But this is not the situation for data communications protocols. For example, the ITU's Open Systems Interconnection (OSI) protocols never caught on. The OSI protocols suffered from unnecessary complexity and from the fact that the standards (the documents) were "owned" by the ITU. But, as discussed in Hour 3, the OSI model itself is still widely used and cited by the industry.

In contrast, the Internet's protocols are designed for simplicity. What's more, they're "open." Anyone can use the Internet specifications without paying a red cent for them. These standards are codified in the Request for Comments (RFCs). They are the Bible of the Internet and the bedrock of data communications networks.

Later we will examine several of the Internet data communications protocols. I suspect you've already come across many of them. Does TCP/IP ring a bell? You may not know, but these communications protocols run in your computer each time you log on to the Internet. We won't get ahead of ourselves but will return to the Internet several times in this book.

Intranets, Extranets, and internets

The Internet (uppercase *I*) is the public network we use to send email and browse the Web. If we use the Internet protocols (such as TCP/IP) in a private network, we have created an internet (notice the lowercase *i*). Some vendors and associated literature use the term intranet to describe a private network that uses the Internet protocols. (Another term is extranet.)

Today, many businesses use the Internet to connect their internets with their customers, suppliers, and business partners. When implemented with proper security measures, Internet-internet associations provide a tremendous value to an organization. They dramatically reduce the costs of "doing" networking. The open, noncopyrighted standards of the Internet have been an extraordinary technical and financial blessing to the data communications industry and to our wired world. The virtual private network, introduced earlier, owes its existence to the Internet.

Summary

In this hour, we've learned about what computer networks are and how they operate. We've also come to know a bit about bits, bandwidth, and bits per second (bps). We've explored network topologies, local and wide area networks, and the Internet and internets.

Q&A

Q. *What is a computer network?*

A. A computer network is an organized collection of computers linked together for the purpose of exchanging data with each other.

Q. *What are the different topologies used on computer networks?*

A. The topologies are star, ring, bus, and cellular.

Q. *Given the information gleaned from the previous question and answer, what is another variety of a computer network?*

A. The composition of a computer network is further distinguished by its geographical situation: local or wide area; and its "openness": private or public.

Q. *What is the relationship of the Internet to an internet?*

A. The Internet is a public network. An internet is a private network that uses the same procedures (protocols) as the Internet. By using common protocols, internets can readily communicate with each other through the Internet.

HOUR 2

The Benefits of Networking

What You'll Learn in This Hour:

- ▶ Computing before the advent of computer networks
- ▶ The first computer networks
- ▶ How packet-switching transformed data networking
- ▶ The downsides of not networking computers
- ▶ The advantages of using computer networks

It is interesting to speculate how life would be if we humans did not have—what Alexis de Tocqueville proclaimed—a natural propensity to organize things at the drop of a hat. But we *do* organize. This trait helps make us the dominant large-body species on earth. What's more, our comfortable lot in life depends on our highly organized networks—from the postal service, to the world's electronic funds transfer system. Without networks, many of the luxuries we take for granted in our daily lives could not exist. In this hour, you will learn more about the extraordinary benefits of computer networking.

Computing Before Computer Networks

Assume that you have a time machine and can go back 40–50 years to examine the computers that existed during those years. Chances are you wouldn't recognize much about them. The computers that businesses and governments used were huge water-cooled behemoths the size of rooms. In spite of their bulk, they weren't powerful by today's measures; they could process only small programs, and they usually lacked sufficient memory—that is, the physical part of the computer where the computer stores the 1s and 0s of software and data—to hold a whole program at one time. That's why pictures of these older machines are often depicted with huge reels of magnetic tape, which held the data the computer wasn't using at that moment. This model of computing is antiquated, but only 40–50 years ago, it was state of the art.

In those days, computers offered little interaction between the user and the system. Interactive video display screens and keyboards were for the future. Instead of sitting at a terminal or PC typing characters and using a mouse, users submitted the work they needed the computer to do to a computer operator, who was the only person allowed to directly interact with the computer. Usually, the work was submitted on punched paper tape or punched cards.

A great deal of the time, computers were kept in climate-controlled rooms with glass walls—hence the slang name "glass house" for a data center. Users submitted their jobs on punch cards that were executed (run) in batches on the computer—one or two batches per shift—from which we derive the term batch processing. Batch processing was common in early environments in which many tasks were scheduled to run at a specific time late in the evening. The user never directly interacted with a batch-processing computer. Debugging (correcting) programs was much more difficult because a programmer had to wait for the machine to print the results of the program's "run," debug the code, and then resubmit the job for another overnight run.

Computers at that time couldn't interact with each other. An IBM computer simply couldn't "talk" to a Honeywell or Burroughs computer. Even if they had been able to connect, they could not have shared data—the computers used different data formats; the only standard at that time was ASCII. ASCII is the American Standard Code for Information Interchange, a way computers format 1s and 0s (binary code) into the alphabet, numerals, and other characters that humans can understand. The computers would have had to convert the data before they could use it, which, in those prestandard days, could have taken as long as reentering the data.

Even if computers had been capable of understanding each other's data formats, the data transfers would have been slow because of the inability to link computers directly together. Even between computers made by the same manufacturer, the only method to transfer data was to carry a tape or a large hard disk to the recipient of the data. This meant physical delivery of these storage devices to each location needing a copy of data—a snail's pace when compared to modern networks.

Fortunately, the U.S. government's Advanced Research Projects Agency (ARPA) funded several programs based on a set of memos written at MIT in 1962 about interconnecting computers. These ideas found support at ARPA, which then funded the creation of an ARPAnet: a network of interconnected computers communicating with each other with "packets." In 1968, ARPA published a Request for Comments

(RFC) for the development of a packet switch called the Interface Message Processor (IMP). The RFC was awarded to Bolt, Beranek, and Newman (BBN), the company who designed some of the first successful packet switches.

Networking's Breakthrough: Packet-Switched Data

This section provides an explanation of packet-switching, a technique used in all computer networks to transport traffic between nodes. Regardless of the scope and size of the network, it uses packet-switching operations.

Packet-switching was invented to solve several problems pertaining to the methods used by emerging data networks to transmit data. In the past, a communications link used a technique called circuit switching to allot resources to traffic. For voice traffic, circuit switching was effective, because it dedicated a channel to a voice conversation for the duration of the conversation. Generally, the link was effectively utilized because the two people on the telephones talked most of the time.

This situation was not the case for data dialogues. Because of the stop-and-go nature of keying in data on a computer keyboard (keying in characters, backspacing to correct mistakes, thinking a bit more about the "transmission"), a circuit-switched network, like that of the telephone system, experienced frequent periods when a dedicated link was idle—waiting for the two correspondents to actually correspond. Packet-switching solves this expensive problem by providing these benefits:

▶ More than one user stream of data can be sent over a link during a given window of time.

▶ Packet-switching does not set up a connection through a network. Thus, it does not require dedicated end-to-end channels. If problems occur in one part of network, user data can be dynamically rerouted to those switches that are operating satisfactorily. In the past, a failed circuit switch required the tedious and time-consuming job of reestablishing a dedicated end-to-end connection.

▶ Because many user sessions (such as email and text messaging) entail a slow introduction of data into the network, packet-switching "packages" this data into small bundles and sends it on its way to the destination. (By the way, even "faster" sessions, such as file transfer, do not fully utilize a high-capacity communications link.) While the packet switching software is waiting for more data to spring forth from our cumbersome fingers and thumbs, it shifts its attention to an active user and for a brief time, it allots network resources to this user. Later, when we are keying in data, it turns its attention back to us.

▶ In other words, expensive network resources are used only when users need these resources. It's an ideal arrangement for "bursty" data communications in which facilities are used intermittently.

At first glance, packet-switching might be a bit difficult to understand. Nonetheless, to grasp the underpinnings of computer networks, we must come to grips with packet-switching. To that end, here's a brief experiment that should help explain packet-switching networks. We will compare packet-switching networks to a postal network.

Assume you are an author writing a manuscript that must be delivered to your editor, who lives far from you. Also assume (for the purposes of this experiment) that the postal service limits the weight of packages it carries, and the entire manuscript is heavier than the limit. Clearly, you're going to have to break up the manuscript in a way that ensures your editor can reassemble it in the correct order without difficulty. How are you going to accomplish this task?

First, you break up the manuscript into standard sizes. Let's assume a 50-page section of the manuscript plus an envelope is the maximum weight the postal service will support. After assuring your manuscript pages are numbered, you divide the manuscript into 50-page chunks. It doesn't matter whether the chunks break on chapter lines or even in the middle of a sentence—the pages are numbered, so they can be reassembled at the receiving node. If any pages are lost because of a torn envelope, the page numbers help determine what's missing.

Dividing the large manuscript into small equal-sized chunks with a method of verifying the completeness of the data (through the use of the page numbers) is the first part of packetizing data. The editor can use the page numbers, which are a property of the data, to determine if all the data has arrived correctly. He can use other procedures to verify the correctness of the received data.

Next, you put the 50-page manuscript chunks into envelopes numbered sequentially—the first 50 pages go in envelope number 1, the second 50 pages go in envelope number 2, and so forth until you've reached the end of the manuscript. The sequence numbers are important because they help the destination node (your editor, or a computer) reassemble the data in proper order.

The number of pages in each envelope is also written on the outside of the envelope, which describes the data packet's size. (In computer networks, the number of characters (bytes) is used, not the number of pages.) If the size is wrong when the packet arrives at the destination, the destination computer discards the packet and requests a retransmission. Another approach is for the sending and receiving parties to agree on the size of the packets before they are sent.

Last, you write your editor's address as the destination and your address as the return address on the outside of the envelopes and send them using the postal service. Figure 2.1 illustrates the hypothetical envelope and the relationship each element has to a data packet in a computer network.

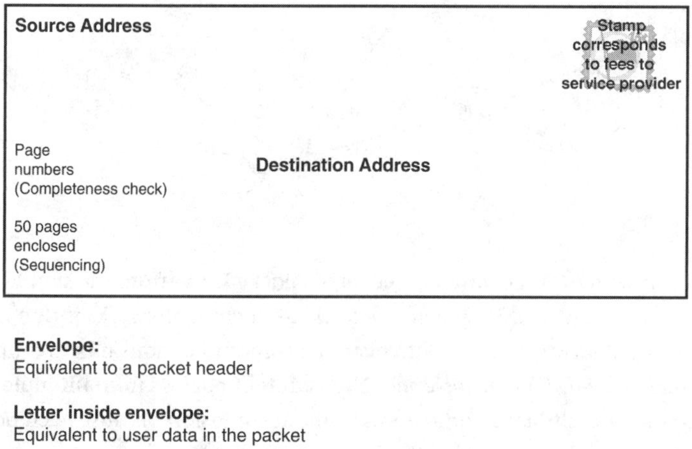

Source Address

Stamp
corresponds
to fees to
service provider

Page
numbers
(Completeness check)

Destination Address

50 pages
enclosed
(Sequencing)

Envelope:
Equivalent to a packet header

Letter inside envelope:
Equivalent to user data in the packet

FIGURE 2.1
The various parts of the envelope and how they correspond to the parts of a data packet

The route the envelopes take while in transit between your mailbox and your editor's desk is not important to your editor and you. As shown in Figure 2.2, some of the envelopes might be routed through Chicago; others might be routed through Dallas—it's not important as long as all the envelopes arrive at your editor's desk. If the number of pages your editor receives does not match the number of pages written on the outside of the envelope, the editor knows that something is wrong—the envelope came unsealed and pages fell out, or someone tampered with the contents. If you had sent your editor this (electronic) manuscript over the Internet, the process would work the same way—the sections of the book (inside the packets) could have been routed through many machines (routers) before arriving at your editor's computer.

In networking terms, each complete envelope is a packet of data. The order in which your editor—or a computer—receives them doesn't matter because the editor (or the computer) can reassemble the data from the sequence numbers on the outside of the envelopes.

For each correct envelope your editor receives, he sends you an acknowledgment. If an envelope fails to arrive or is compromised in some way, your editor won't acknowledge receipt of that specific envelope. After a specified time, if you don't receive acknowledgment for that packet, you must resend it so the editor has the entire manuscript. Packet-switched data does not correspond perfectly with this example, but it's quite close, and it's sufficient for us to proceed into more technical details.

FIGURE 2.2
Data packets
can follow sev-
eral paths across
the Internet.

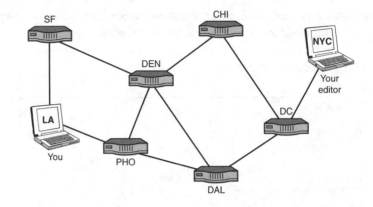

Any data you send over a computer network is packetized—from the smallest text message to the largest file. The beauty of packet-switching networks is that more than one computer can transmit data over one communications link at a time—a concept called *time-division multiplexing*. Thousands of packets from multiple machines can be multiplexed onto a link without confusion because each packet (like the postal envelope) contains the following elements:

▸ **A source address**—The return address or origin of the packet

▸ **A destination address**—Where the packet is headed

▸ **A sequence number**—Where the packet fits in with the remainder of associated packets

▸ **An error check**—An assurance that the data is free of errors

Because each computer has a different address or set of addresses (as explained in Hours 3 and 15), transmitting data through computer networks is similar to sending mail through postal networks.

The importance of standards with respect to packet switching specifically (and computer networks in general) cannot be overstated. The success of packet-switched networks depends on the widespread adoption of standards. Networking rewards cooperation. No matter how elegant and efficient a system is, if it does not adhere to a community-accepted standard, it will fail. Several organizations exist to create these standards. For packet-switching, the authoritative bodies are the International Telecommunications Union (ITU) and several Internet working groups and standards bodies.

Benefits of Networking

As explained at the beginning of this hour, before computer networks came about, transferring data between computers was a time-consuming and labor-intensive task. As local area networks (LANs) were coming into existence in offices, a person who wanted to exchange data with someone whose computer was located on another LAN copied the data onto a disk, walked to the other machine, and transferred the data file to the other computer. This technique earned the name Sneakernet.

File Management

Obviously, Sneakernet is not an efficient way to move or manage files. It's time consuming and unreliable. Moreover, the data is decentralized. Each user can conceivably have a different version of a particular file stored on her standalone computer. The confusion that ensues when users need the same version of a file and don't have it can create serious problems for an organization. With computers connected through a network, data can be shared among them. We take this capability for granted today, but it didn't exist until LANs were connected in the late 1970s.

Sharing Software

Disconnected computers also suffer from another malady: They can't share software applications. Every application must be installed on each computer if data passed by Sneakernet is to be effective. If a user doesn't have the application that created a file stored on her computer, she can't read the file. Of course, if we can't share applications, no one can share, say, calendars or contact lists with other users, let alone send them email. Sharing software has just the opposite effect of nonshared software. For example, we need not load all the software on our computer to have our traffic routed from our LAN in Los Angeles to a LAN in New York. Our computer shares *some* of its software with a *lot* of software on a local router to provide this service.

A *groupware* application (also called collaborative software) is an application that enables multiple users to work together by using a network to connect them. Such applications can work serially, where (for instance) a document is automatically routed from person A to person B after person A is done with it. Groupware might also enable real-time collaboration. IBM's Lotus Notes software is an example of the former, and Microsoft's Office has some real-time collaborative features. Another example is the help desk of software vendors. Often, when a customer calls for assistance, the technician connects to the user's application with troubleshooting software routines to analyze the problem. The user's computer is sharing the powerful investigative software, but the user's computer doesn't have to download it to use it.

Other examples of shared applications are group calendaring, which allows a staff to plan meetings and tasks using a centralized schedule instead of 20 different ones; and email, or electronic mail, which is often called the killer application (killer app) of networking. Email and other network applications are discussed in more depth in Hour 13, "Network Applications."

In on the Kill

The term killer app is not a negative term. In spite of what might be a sensible conjecture about its meaning, it does not refer to viruses or other malicious software. Instead, a killer app is an application so useful it affects the operations of an organization and likely increases the demand for computer resources. Email is the killer app of networking because it allows users to hold conversations in a common workspace without exchanging cumbersome paper files and memos. With the popularity of cell phones, text messaging became an associated killer app. And the Web is the mother of all killer apps.

Sharing Printers and Other Peripheral Devices

Printers and scanners are expensive. If they can't be shared, they become an enormous capital expense to organizations and even a household. You can imagine the strain on a budget if each computer in a home or enterprise had to have a dedicated printer or scanner.

Centralized Configuration Management

As personal computers found their way into the mass marketplace, software manufacturers faced a major problem: The correction and improvement of their products, which resided on millions of machines. Before computer networks became commonplace (abetted by the Internet), a correction to, say, a bug in Microsoft's DOS software required the sending of a disk to users, or the users having the means to dial up a Microsoft site to download the patch on a low-capacity telephone line. Many users didn't keep their systems tuned to these updates, resulting in dissimilar versions of software throughout a product line. The Microsofts of the world faced a complex situation when trying to keep their changes compatible with customers' software.

With high-capacity computer networks, the vendors can automatically download their changes to millions of users, all in a few seconds. In today's environment, with each logon to the Internet, it isn't unusual for a user's PC to have enhancements and corrections made to several of a machine's thousands of software programs.

What is more, network administrators use their own networks to manage those networks. For example, in a large corporation, hundreds or even thousands of servers and routers are positioned across a country, a continent, or perhaps the globe. With a variety of software utilities, an administrator can diagnose and fix problems, as well as install and configure software. These utility suites allow a network administrator to collect and standardize computer configurations and to troubleshoot problems in the network.

Learning about network management and its initial setup requires a lot of work on the part of the administrator, but when the initial installation is finished, the administrator's life becomes easier. Centralized management saves time and money (two things accountants appreciate). It also engenders the goodwill of the users and the credibility of the administrator (two things the users and administrators appreciate). To find out more about managing networks, look at the network administration hours in Part V of this book, "Network Administration."

Speed and Economy

In a nutshell, computer networks allow us to perform our jobs more quickly and more efficiently and lead to greater productivity in the workforce. It's fair to say they have been an important cog in increasing the wealth of a country, as well as its citizens.

And we shouldn't omit the fact that these wonderful systems allow us to play Texas Holdem and Scrabble online well into the hours when we should be sleeping.

Summary

When computer resources are shared through a network, its users reap a variety of benefits ranging from reduced costs, to ease of use, to simpler administration. The financial savings and worker productivity gains represented by networks will be appreciated by companies trying to economize. From the worker's viewpoint, an employee does not have to chase down information anymore. If applications such as email, calendaring, and contact management are added to the mix, the network begins to establish synergistic relationships between users and data. A well-designed computer network allows us to accomplish a great deal more than we could do without it.

Q&A

Q. *Name the technology that enhances the utilization of network resources.*

A. Packet-switching is the technology that does this. It improves the utilization of communications links and provides a means for dynamic, adaptive routing through the network.

Q. *What sorts of computer resources can be shared on a network?*

A. Networks facilitate the sharing of data, software applications, printers, scanners, computers, and those vital tools for productivity and creativity: human minds.

Q. *What are some of the reasons for using centralized management?*

A. Centralized management of a network promotes more efficient administration of computing resources, effective (automated) installation of software on network users' desktop computers, easier computer configuration management, as well as troubleshooting and recovery from problems.

HOUR 3

Getting Data from Here to There: How Networking Works

What You'll Learn in This Hour:

▶ Network protocols and the OSI model for computer networks

▶ Network addresses (IP and MAC)

▶ Introduction to Ethernet, IP, and ATM

In the preceding hour, we learned why packet switching is important to data networking and the transport of data between computers. In this hour, we learn more about how networks transport data. The first part of this hour expands on the concept of protocols, with an explanation of the famous Open Systems Interconnection (OSI) model. Next, network addresses are explained, followed by introductions to Ethernet and ring networks. The Asynchronous Transfer Mode (ATM) protocol is highlighted, as well as a protocol operating in almost all computers today: the Internet Protocol (IP). In subsequent hours, we return to these networks and protocols with more detailed explanations.

Network Protocols

To briefly review points covered in Hour 1, "An Overview of Networking," computers communicate with each other with network protocols—rules governing how machines exchange data. We learned that *physical protocols* are employed to describe the medium (a copper wire, for example), the connections (a USB port, for example), and the signal (the voltage level on a wire, for example). We also learned that logical protocols consist of the software controlling how and when data is sent and received to computers, via the supporting physical protocols. In summary, protocols embody the rules—executed in various combinations of hardware and software—for sending and receiving data across a network.

To grasp the full concept of network protocols and the method by which data moves through computer networks, you need to understand their functions in relation to each other and a computer network. To begin, let's examine the most popular conceptual model for networking: the OSI model.

The OSI Model (and Why You Should Be Familiar with It)

During the 1980s, two international standards bodies (the International Telecommunications Union [ITU] and the International Organization for Standardization [ISO]) created a model by which data communications protocols could be designed, executed, and maintained. In conjunction with the model, the ITU and ISO also published numerous protocols that followed the rules of the OSI model. The model provides a tremendously useful paradigm of how functions can be distributed among the various parts of a network.

Because the Internet protocols (such as TCP/IP) came into existence at about this time, the OSI protocols never found a wide following, but the OSI model became the archetype for computer networks. Interestingly, the Internet protocols developed somewhat separately from the OSI model, yet they closely parallel its structure.

As seen in Figure 3.1, the model is organized into seven layers. The layers are worth memorizing for debugging network problems—ranging from design issues to snafus with connections. The model is also helpful when conversing about a network. For example, Tommy might say to me, "I'm working on a Web application in Layer 7 of the model." With that information, I know immediately the nature of the application and the underling features (protocols at Layers 6 through 1) that *can* be used (or *must* be used) to support his application.

Each layer communicates only with the layer directly above or below it within the same computer. These communications take place with software *function* or *library* calls. If you have a background in software, you know these calls are also known as *application programming interfaces* (APIs). If you are not a software programmer, don't be concerned about them; just remember that one layer invokes another layer by invoking the software residing in that layer. The good news is you won't have to deal with this level of detail for bringing up your own network. But, as mentioned, it's a good idea to know the model's general structure.

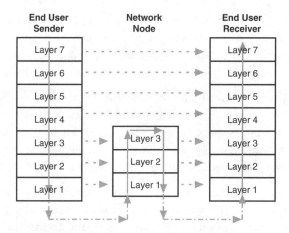

FIGURE 3.1
The OSI model shows how data is transported through a network.

The *sole* purpose of the layers' communications is for one end user machine to transmit data to another end user machine, as seen in the left and right protocol stacks in Figure 3.1. The transport of this data is in the form of packets. In the figure, the solid-lined arrows depict how the data, along with each layer's control information (headers), is physically passed between layers (vertically). The dashed-lined arrows depict how the data and headers are logically exchanged across peer layers (horizontally). Finally, the dashed/dotted lines show the data as it is transmitted across the communications links.

The *principal* purpose of the vertical process is to execute the horizontal process. Of course, the actual transmission across the communications link or links only occurs at Layer 1, again as depicted by the dashed /dotted lines.

Take a look at the middle of Figure 3.1. All layers need not be executed in every machine in the network. For the relaying of packets through a network between two end-user computers, only Layers 1–3 are needed. Thus, when Tommy sends an email to me, the traffic only passes through Layers 1–3 of the routers in the Internet. Even though these routers contain all seven layers, for ongoing relay support, they are not concerned with the activities of Layers 4–7, which are usually end-to-end activities. The router passes these headers (and Tommy's email) transparently to a next node. Consequently, by executing fewer layers and their associated functions, the routers relay the packets more quickly.

With this background, we'll examine Figure 3.1 in a bit more detail. In so doing, we'll explain the major functions of each layer and provide examples of prominent protocols residing in each layer. As well, we'll compare the model to postal service operations.

▶ **Layer 7 (application)** contains the applications most familiar to users, such as email, text messaging, and file transfer. Applications such as the File

Transfer Protocol (FTP) and Telnet reside in Layer 7. In the postal model, the application layer corresponds to writing or reading a letter. Products such as Microsoft Word and Excel operate in this layer, as does the widely used Hypertext Transfer Protocol (HTTP).

▶ **Layer 6 (presentation)** deals with the way different systems represent data. For example, Layer 6 defines the syntax of the data, such as IBM's convention of coding characters entered from the keyboard. This layer can also make code conversions, such as displaying UNIX-style data on a Windows screen, or translating a Photoshop-specific image to a JPEG image.

Layer 6 does not have an analogue in the postal model, but if it did, it would be similar to the rewriting of the letter so anyone could read it. A fitting analogy is to a translator; using the postal model again, assume your letter written in English is being sent to Mexico. A translator (equivalent to presentation layer software) translates the data in your envelope into Spanish. Similar to the letter in the example, data can be "rearranged" to fit the kind of computer and software on which it executes.

An array of Layer 6 products are on the market, many of which are stored inside your computer or on your hard disk. You never see them directly, but you invoke them when prompted to, as in, "Choose from this list which program you wish to use to open this file."

▶ **Layer 5 (session)** handles the dialogues between systems. This layer handles bidirectional (two-way) or unidirectional (one-way) communications. In the postal metaphor, the session layer is similar to a letter writer instructing a recipient to respond immediately to the letter, to not respond at all, or to respond at any time. In a text messaging application, one user might be keying in text on a cell phone and sending the message at about the same time another user is performing the same operation. In this situation, Layer 5 allows the users to send and receive data at the same time. In a file transfer application, one user may not be allowed to send files while she is sending a file. Layer 5 often forbids you to enter and send email when it is busy with other tasks.

▶ **Layer 4 (transport)** can be compared to the registered mail system. It is concerned with ensuring mail arrives safely at its destination. If a packet fails to reach the end user, the sending Layer 4 resends the packet. In effect, Layer 4 recovers from any errors at Layers 1–3. For example, if a router in a network suffers a temporary failure and loses traffic, the transport layer comes to the rescue. The sending machine's Layer 4 must hold a copy of each packet it sends and can only discard this packet when it receives an acknowledgment from the receiving machine. If it is notified to resend, it does so. If it does not receive such an acknowledgment, it assumes something is amiss and resends anyway. If the receiving machine happens to receive duplicate packets, it uses sequence numbers in the packet to discard the redundant data.

It's all rather extraordinary, wouldn't you say? All these activities (sending packets, checking for errors, acknowledging the data, perhaps resending one or more packets) take place so quickly that they usually remain transparent to end users.

For the postal service, an end-to-end integrity service takes several days. For computer networks, it takes several fractions of a second, even if the end user session spans the globe. Chances are, you have come across the Transmission Control Protocol (TCP). It operates at Layer 4 inside your computer—without your intervention—to provide this wonderful end-to-end service.

▶ **Layer 3 (network)** provides addressing and routing services. When we send someone a letter, we use a street address and a ZIP code to identify the location of the recipient. When a computer sends data, it also uses addresses. For this operation, Layer 3 places two addresses in the packet: its own address (source address) and the address of the recipient of the packet (destination address). Thereafter, as Figure 3.1 shows, only Layers 1–3 need be executed in an internet until the packet arrives at its final destination.

Layer 3 is similar to the mail-sorting clerks at the post office, who aren't concerned about the mail reaching its final destination. Instead, their concern is sorting and relaying the envelope to the next node (post office) toward the destination. Of course, the mailperson at the end office does indeed deliver the mail to the recipient.

This layer contains the Internet Protocol, the IP in TCP/IP, and the Internetwork Packet Exchange (IPX), an IP-like protocol used in older NetWare products.

▶ **Layer 2 (data link)** defines a set of rules for transporting traffic on *one link* (link is a physical communications channel or line) from one node to another node. Layer 2 has no awareness of conditions beyond this one link. In our postal model, Layer 2 represents conventions controlling the delivery of a postal envelope, such as dropping off the letter at a mail box, without knowledge that the letter might have to go to another mailbox. This layer contains the rules for the behavior of several widely used protocols, such as Ethernet and ATM.

The layer is concerned with finding a way for Layer 3 components to communicate *transparently* with Layer 1 components. In so doing, it keeps Layer 3 independent and unaware of the details of Layer 1—an extraordinarily useful service. For example, IP operating at L_3 never cares if its packets are sent over, say, a wireless cellular phone channel or a wire-based copper cable. Layer 2 performs the mediation needed to create this veil. IP sits in front of this veil, not caring if its packets are to be placed onto satellite, copper, cable, radio, or optic links. It is a brilliant way for conceiving this part of the model.

Layer 2 may place packets inside *frames*, which are used by hardware devices to send and receive traffic below Layer 3. This operation is akin to placing one postal envelope (a conventional envelope) inside another postal envelope (an overnight delivery envelope).

A Short but Important Diversion

Why is it necessary to place packets inside frames? A partial answer is that local area networks (LANs) are not designed to work with packets and Layer 3 addresses. LANs operate *only* at Layers 1 and 2 of the model and use another address. You might have heard of this address; it's called a MAC or Ethernet address. You'll learn more about this address later in the section, "MAC or Layer 2 Address: That Is to Say, Ethernet Addresses."

Consequently, after the packet has traversed the Internet or an intranet, the network Layer 3 address is correlated to a Layer 2 address for use on the LAN. Thereafter, it is the job of the LAN Layers 1 and 2 to deliver the frame and packet to the final destination computer.

This aspect of computer networks can be confusing to a newcomer. For that matter, many people who are well versed in this subject do not understand the relationship of Layers 2 and 3 (and especially their addresses). Let's pause to examine Figure 3.2. It should help us understand the relationship of packets to frames, Layer 3 to Layer 2, and the addresses used in these two layers.

FIGURE 3.2
Relationships of the lower layers of the model

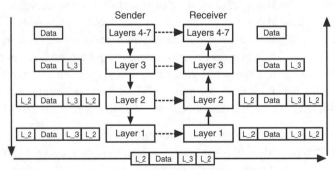

Through networks and communciations links

Note: Only Layers 1, 2, and 3 need to be executed in networks.

The lower layers are not concerned with the meaning and syntax of the user's data. As seen in Figure 3.2, this data (which also contains control information—headers and maybe trailers—appended by Layers 4–7) is passed to Layer 3. This layer appends source and destination network addresses and other control information into a part of the packet, called the packet header, which is labeled L_3 in the figure.

Next, the data is passed to Layer 2, which adds both a header and trailer to the Layer 3 packet (labeled L_2 in the figure). This entire data unit is called a Layer 2 frame, which contains all the data from the upper layers, including the Layer 3 packet. In addition, this layer adds a source and destination address in its header. But these addresses play a different role than the Layer 3 addresses. Shortly, we'll examine the functions of these two sets of addresses.

Finally, Layer 1 receives the complete frame and sends it onto the link and into the network with electrical, electromagnetic, or optical signals. The vertical arrow on the left side of Figure 3.2 and the long horizontal arrow at the bottom illustrate these operations.

At the receiving computer, the process just described is reversed. The traffic is now passed up the layers, and the various headers and trailers created at the sending site are used by the receiving site to tell it what to do with the user's data. If the data is email, the headers will so indicate; the same is true for text messaging, video, and so on. After the respective layer examines the headers and trailers, it discards them.

Notice how symmetrical the operations are. Although the data is *physically* passed down and up the layers and the sender and receiver respectively (usually in the form of software function calls), the purpose of the model is to *logically* pass the data between peer layers of the two nodes. This idea is shown in Figure 3.2 with the dashed arrows in the middle of the figure.

▶ **Layer 1 (physical)** is similar to the trucks, trains, planes, and rails that move the mail. This layer is concerned with the physical aspects of the operation, such as electrical, electromagnetic, and optical signals; the network interface cards (NICs); and the wire and cable. The modem is an example of a Layer 1 device. Also, many of the operations of broadband services operate at Layer 1. As examples, the Digital Subscriber Line (DSL) service from the telephone companies and the cable broadband service from the cable TV providers mainly operate at Layer 1 of the OSI model.

A Better Term for "Packet"

By the Way

We've just introduced the term "frame," the unit of data operating at Layer 2. Previously, the term "packet" was introduced for use at Layer 3. Later, we must introduce two more terms describing self-contained units of data passing through computer networks. (You may have come across "datagram" and "cell" in other literature.) Sorry for all these terms. I promise I didn't make them up. The ITU and ISO have created a generic term to encompass all these buzz words: the *protocol data unit (PDU)*. If you aren't sure which of these terms to use, just resort to "PDU."

How to Identify the Type of Packet in an Ethernet Frame

In today's networks, different kinds of packets *may* be exchanged between computers on an Ethernet link. In the past, the previous sentence with the words "may be" would read "are." Times have changed and, with rare exceptions, the data inside the Ethernet frame is an IP packet.

Nonetheless, the Ethernet header contains a field called EtherType, which is filled in by the sending node to identify the specific packet being carried in the Ethernet frame. As examples, IPv4 is EtherType 0800, and IPv6 is EtherType 86DD. This field is quite valuable for organizations that are migrating to IPv6 but still have IPv4 components to support. In effect, dual stacks of software are maintained, and the EtherType field is used to pass the IP packet to the process in the appropriate software protocol stack.

As mentioned, before IP became so pervasive, IBM, Novell, DEC, Apple, and other vendors deployed their own proprietary L_3 protocols, and some machines, such as routers, had to support all of them. The EtherType field was used to pass the packets to the correct process in a protocol stack.

The Internet Model

The Internet also uses a protocol model, which is similar to the OSI counterpart. However, it is a five-layer scheme and does not include the presentation or session layers. Does this mean that the services associated with these layers aren't available for Internet operations? No, it means the services exist in vendors' products, and with some exceptions, they aren't defined in the Internet standards.

In later hours, we examine many aspects of the Internet's use of this model, as well as the standards and protocols published by the Internet Engineering Task Force (IETF). These specifications are now embedded into practically all vendor's products. In just two decades, they have transformed the computer network industry.

Addresses: Network or Layer 3 Addresses

Continuing our postal service analogy, we now focus on those all-important addresses. Computer networks have a source and destination address appended to each packet header, similar to the postal envelope shown in Figure 2.1 (Hour 2, "The Benefits of Networking"). These addresses are embedded in the L_3 header, as seen in Figure 3.2. The principal job of a router (aptly named) is to use the destination address to route the packet toward its final destination. Because this operation takes place in Layer 3 of the OSI model, these identifiers are called network addresses.

The most widely used network address is the IP address. It is 32 bits long, which conceptually allows for 2^{32} addresses (4,294,967,296). When this address was conceived, the first 8 bits identified a network, and the remaining 24 bits identified a host (such as a computer) attached to that network. This convention assumed an IP address would not have to identify more than 256 networks! Hindsight is twenty-twenty (LANs had not yet made their presence known), and we will learn shortly that the Internet standards bodies have modified this structure and published other protocols to allow the 32 bits to identify many more networks and hosts. For now, let's examine the conventional IP address format.

IP addresses are written in dotted decimal notation, with one byte (eight bits) between each dot. A dotted decimal IP address appears as 192.168.100.25.

Because each number is described by one byte, and because each byte is 8 bits (of binary 1s and 0s), each number can have a value ranging from 0 to 255. Because there are 4 numbers with 8 bits each, the total address space is 32 bits long (4*8 = 32). So the preceding address, in binary, appears as 11000000.10101000.01100100.00011001.

In the past, IP addresses were allocated to organizations in address blocks. Address blocks come in different sizes, based on the class of address. This scheme is explained here for background information. Because of its limitations, it was replaced by Classless Inter-Domain Routing (CIDR), described next.

▶ **Class A** addresses use 24 of the 32 bits in the address space for host addresses. A Class A address appears as X.0.0.0, where X is the network address.

▶ **Class B** addresses use 16 bits each for the network and host. A Class B address appears as X.X.0.0.

▶ **Class C** addresses use 24 bits for the network address space. Here's an example of a Class C address: X.X.X.0.

▶ **Class D** addresses are used for *multicasting*: sending messages to many systems. Some 911 systems use multicast because it helps ensure that the systems receive all messages. Online teaching applications often use multicast for delivery of the lecturer's voice and video packets to a wide audience.

Private addresses can be used when traffic does not leave a private network. Thus, they can be reused in each private network. The Internet authorities have allocated these values for private addresses:

10.0.0.0	through	10.255.255.255
172.16.0.0	through	172.31.255.255
192.168.0.0	through	192.168.255.255

Alternatives to the Conventional Address

In the previous section, we learned the IP address is only 32 bits long, and that its structure of four eight-bit boundaries restricts how the 32 bits are used. In this section, we examine three conventions published by the Internet authorities to compensate for the restrictions of the original IP address length and format. They are CIDR, NAT, and IPv6.

CIDR

The Internet standards bodies recognized the "classful" address described earlier would not meet future needs. Consequently, in 1993, CIDR (pronounced "cider") was introduced. Instead of using the rigid 8-bit boundaries, CIDR specifies arbitrary (variable-length) boundaries of the 32 bits in the IP address. It also specifies a method to group network addresses with the same sequence of bits in the network "space" as only one entry in a router's routing table. This technique, called address aggregation, greatly reduces the size of routing tables and speeds up routing table lookups.

By the Way

IP Addresses Are Often Called Prefixes

With the use of CIDR and aggregation, the 32-bit (four decimal digits) number is now described as a prefix. For example, the prefix 128.7/16 is a shorthand notation that means to use the first 16 bits of the 32-bit IP address of 128.7. As a consequence, all traffic with an IP address beginning with 127.7 belongs to one entry in a routing table. Thus, 128.7.444.666 would match this table entry. So would 128.7.33.11, but 128.8.222.111 would not.

The idea is for the forwarding software to find a match that has the longest routing prefix. With this approach, it's possible to substantially reduce the number of entries in a router's routing table (also called a forwarding table or a routing information base).

> Route aggregation and prefixes are simple in concept, albeit complex in implementation. If you want more details, you can find some fine ideas at www.patentstorm.us/patents/7027445/description.html.
>
> Hereafter, the terms IP address and prefix are used interchangeably.

NAT

The Network Address Translation (NAT) Protocol allows multiple hosts on one network (say a private LAN in an office) to use the Internet with only one public IP address. A router sits between the private network and the public Internet. The router is assigned a public IP address to communicate with the Internet. However, behind the router, on the local LAN, all computers (hosts) use private addresses. What is more, these private addresses are never revealed to the public Internet, which results in a valuable security service to a user. It is the router's job to maintain a table that tracks and converts private addresses on outbound packets to the public address. Conversely, for inbound packets, the router converts the public address to a corresponding private address. Other identifiers, beyond this discussion, are used to help the router keep the traffic properly tagged.

IPv6 Addressing

IPv6 (version 6) is intended to be the successor to the current IP (IPv4). IPv6's header contains larger address spaces, thereby eliminating the need for CIDR and NAT. Each address is 128 bits in length, compared to 32 bits for IPv4. Thus, IPv6 supports 2^{128} addresses. This huge number is often compared to the number of people living today, which is about 6.5 billion humans. IPv6 provides 5×10^{28} addresses for each of these people! A 128-bit address supports thousands of billions more addresses than a 32-bit address.

It's reasonable to assume the IPv6 source and destination address fields will suffice for the foreseeable future. That stated, because of the effectiveness of CIDR and NAT, IPv4 continues to be the dominant IP version deployed in both public and private networks. Some governments have established deadlines for equipment and software to be IPv6 capable. The U.S. Government's deadline is 2008. Time will tell if IPv6 becomes the prevalent version for running IP.

MAC or Layer 2 Address: That Is to Say, Ethernet Addresses

Each device on a LAN is identified with a Media Access Control (MAC) address. As mentioned earlier, it is also called a Layer 2 address. Originally, this identifier was called the Ethernet address. When the Ethernet specification was folded into the IEEE 802 standards, its name was changed to the MAC address because it is associated with the IEEE 802 Layer 2, which is called the Media Access Control layer. Some people refer to this value as a hardware address as well, because manufacturers might place the MAC address on a logic board (such as an NIC) inside the computer.

As with the source and destination IP addresses at Layer 3, a LAN PDU (a frame) contains Layer 2 source and destination MAC addresses. They are coded in the L_2 header, shown in Figure 3.2. (This layer contains a header and a trailer.) The address is 48 bits long and must be used on all LANs if they are to operate correctly. In the past, the Xerox Ethernet Administration Office assigned these values to LAN equipment manufacturers. Now the IEEE takes care of this responsibility.

Using Addresses to Relay Traffic

When Ethernet was coming into existence, so too was the Internet. Both were created by their inventors without these men knowing how often their creations would interact with each other in the future. Thus, two sets of computer network addressing standards found widespread use in the industry. When it became apparent that Ethernet-addressed networks would have to interact with IP-addressed networks, the question became: How?

As mentioned, a MAC (aka Ethernet) address is usually configured by the vendor on the NIC in each computer. Let's assume you have two PCs attached to your router via Ethernet cables. For this discussion, we amplify a previous figure to that shown in Figure 3.3. Notice that the Ethernet LAN operates with IP at L_3 and with Ethernet MAC at Layers 1 and 2.

Also, notice that PCs C and D use wireless protocols and interfaces (W1 and W1) at Layers 1 and 2. In some wireless networks, this Layer 2 is similar to Ethernet's Layer 2.

PCs A and B and the router use MAC addresses to ensure traffic is sent to the correct node on this local network. Let's assume PC A is sending data, via the router, to PC B. It creates the frame with a MAC source address of A and a MAC destination address of B. The router is configured to pass this data unit to PC B by examining the MAC destination address of PC B. The router does not pass the data up to its L_3.[1]

---

[1] *Some people identify a machine that routes based on MAC addresses (and not IP addresses) as a bridge. High-end routers can be configured to operate with either MAC or IP addresses.*

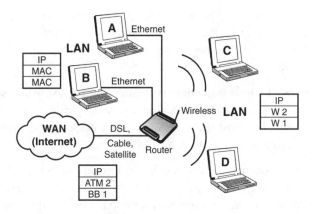

FIGURE 3.3
LAN and WAN
layers

Upon receiving this frame, PC B determines the destination MAC address in the L_2 header of the frame is the same as the address of PC B, so PC B accepts the traffic and passes the packet to IP at L_3. (Because of some other control fields in the frame header, PC B knows it must pass this packet up to its L_3, which it does.)

PC B's IP then looks at the L_3 destination address in the IP header. Lo and behold, this address is the same address as the IP address of PC B. Thus, PC B knows it must perform a number of IP services. It then passes the data up to Layer 4. Eventually—actually almost instantaneously—the data is presented to an end user application in Layer 7, such as email.

Alternatively, let's assume that PC A wants to send a packet to a remote computer, somewhere in the Internet. In this situation, the destination MAC address is *not* that of the PC B, but that of the router. By previous agreements, PC A and the router have agreed that any nonlocal traffic will be sent to this router, but the final IP destination address has been placed in the IP L_3 destination address field by PC A. Thus, the router examines the L_3 header and its destination IP address. It learns that this packet is intended for a nonlocal computer.

The router then makes several forwarding decisions, which result in the packet being sent to the wide area network (WAN)—that is, the Internet—toward its journey to the destination user.

In this situation, the router no longer deals with the MAC L_2 address, which is *strictly a local address*. It strips off Ethernet's L_1 and L_2 and sends the L_3 IP packet to its external link to the Internet (the WAN cloud in Figure 3.3) via DSL, broadband cable, satellite, or conventional dial-up. (For the dial-up option, and not shown in Figure 3.3, a router is not installed at the local site. The telephone company at its end office assumes the responsibility of providing a router interface into the Internet.)

Ethernet MAC is not designed to operate on a WAN link. Therefore, at this WAN interface, the IP data unit is placed inside at ATM data unit (shown as "ATM2" in the figure). ATM is designed for use in different kinds of computer networks. It has found a wide niche in WANs because it specifies procedures for negotiating services such as higher throughput and faster response time. It is a common L_2 protocol on locally attached routers, as seen in Figure 3.3.

The notation of "BB 1" (broadband at L_1) means Layer 1 is DSL, cable, satellite, or nonbroadband dial-up. IP and ATM don't care about the physical media at L_1. Of course, network designers must take these options into account when they place assorted L_2 protocols over various L_1 interfaces.

To conclude this introduction on how data moves through computer networks, hereafter, the IP traffic is relayed through the Internet, using the L_3 IP addresses to aid in this operation. ATM also plays a major role in this partnership, which we examine in Hour 6, "Extending LANs with Wide Area Networks (WANs)." At the other end of this session, the processes in this example are reversed, all with the goal of delivering the email (the data) to the end user.

Fortunately, you won't have to be concerned with these details. For certain, when you bring up your own network, you will come across terms such as IP, MAC addresses, and ATM. Therefore, knowing their functions will help you to better operate and manage your own network. But with some exceptions, the service provider is responsible for installing and configuring all these protocols and addresses, all to your benefit.

Overview of the Principal Protocols

In Hours 8, 14, and 15, we return to the principal protocols employed to "move data from here to there." For the remainder of this hour, we examine several keys aspects of these protocols, which will allow us to proceed into subsequent hours.

Ethernet

The Ethernet standards are designed for LANs. The original Ethernet protocol was developed at the Xerox Palo Alto Research Center (PARC) in the early to mid 1970s.[2] Originally, Ethernet ran over a shared coaxial cable, as seen in Figure 1.1(c) in Hour 1. The LAN nodes are allowed to send frames at any time, without prior arbitration process. Consequently, traffic on the shared channel might cause a "collision." Each node is capable of monitoring its own transmission. Therefore, when a node notices

---

[2] I had an opportunity to visit PARC in the early 1980s to evaluate Ethernet for possible use by the Federal Reserve Board. We did not choose this LAN at this time, but I was impressed with Ethernet's architecture. I was even more impressed with PARC's use of computer screen icons (trash cans, and so on) that Apple and Microsoft later put into their products.

interference, it initiates a procedure to make certain all other nodes are aware of the problem, and then it resends the frame.

Such a procedure entails wasted resources during periods of high activity, resulting in more collisions. As well, a break in the cable, or a malfunction of a cable termination point, brings down the network. Consequently, the industry has migrated to Ethernet Star topologies (Figure 1.1(a), Hour 1). A variety of "Switched Ethernet" standards and products are available, which we examine in Hour 11, "Selecting Network Hardware and Software."

To conclude this introduction to Ethernet and to set the stage for subsequent hours, the following facts are germane. Ethernet:

- ▶ Does not require an association (a logical connection) to be set up before frames (data) are exchanged

- ▶ Does not provide an acknowledgment for the successful receipt of a frame

- ▶ Does not check for out-of-sequence or duplicate frames

- ▶ Performs an error check for corrupted data; if corrupted, the frame is discarded

- ▶ Does not provide for the negotiation of services

- ▶ Is not designed for WANs

FDDI and Token Rings Diminish in Use

During the 1970s and 1980s, Ethernets had competition from the Fiber Distributed Data Interface (FDDI) and IBM's Token Ring. These LANs have taken a back seat to the Ethernet products and are no longer a major factor in the industry.

By the Way

The Internet Protocol (IP)

IP is the most widely used Layer 3 protocol in the computer network industry. Originally developed for use in WANs, today it operates over Layers 1 and 2 in practically every data (and even voice) communications device in existence. Even cell phones, if Internet capable, employ IP. As mentioned earlier, IP carries the ubiquitous IP addresses in its header, which is the main reason for its popularity. Be aware that specific IP implementations might not use the header fields to perform these services:

- ▶ **Type of Service (TOS)**—Requests various levels of delay and throughput of packet delivery.

- ▶ **Time to Live (TTL)**—Time the packet can remain active as it finds its way to the destination. Often implemented with a maximum permissible hop count (number of nodes that can be traversed). This option is used to ensure IP packets do not "thrash around" in the network indefinitely.

▶ **Fragmentation**—Allows an IP packet larger than the permitted L_2 frame size to be reduced to fit into the frame and then reassembled at the receiving IP node.

▶ **Options**—Provides for other optional services; some are defined in the IP standard.

By the Way

> ### Packet = Datagram
>
> For the sake of accuracy and to avoid confusion, we must introduce another term for an L_3 PDU (packet). Much of current literature, as well as the original specifications, called the IP PDU a "datagram." In the 1970s, the term packet was associated with a Layer 3 protocol that set up a connection before the exchange of traffic. The term datagram was associated with a Layer 3 protocol that sent traffic at any time, without a prior connection set up. Today, most people use the terms interchangeably.

To conclude this introduction to IP and to set the stage for subsequent hours, the following facts are germane. IP:

▶ Does not require an association (a logical connection) to be set up before packets are exchanged

▶ Does not provide an acknowledgment for the successful receipt of a packet

▶ Does not check for out-of-sequence or duplicate frames, unless an IP option is supported

▶ Performs an error check for corrupted data; if corrupted, the packet is discarded

▶ Provides for limited negotiation of services

▶ Is not aware of the nature of the underlying Layers 1 and 2

The Asynchronous Transfer Mode (ATM)

ATM is a relative newcomer to the world of network protocols. It has not seen much use in LANs, at least in comparison to Ethernet. However, it's employed extensively in WANs. If you have a home network with a DSL link to the Internet, chances are good that your router is running ATM at Layer 2 for communicating with your Internet service provider (ISP).

For the transport of traffic through the Internet, the use of IP addresses has proven to be excessively cumbersome and time consuming. Here is where ATM comes into play. Before IP packets are transported into the Internet, their IP addresses are correlated with other identifiers called *virtual circuit/path IDs*. These values are not addresses, but simple labels that identify the traffic. A "routing" table (which is called a label switching table) of these values can be accessed quickly, without resorting to the inefficient IP operations. Indeed, IP packets are transported transparently through an ATM-based network. Thus, ATM networks are noted for their efficiency and low delay. Much of the ATM logic can be executed in hardware, which further reduces the time to process traffic. In addition, ATM was designed to allow the network provider and network users to negotiate and provide an array of services.

The ATM PDU Is Called a Cell

ATM does not use the terms frame, packet, or datagram. It uses the term *cell* to describe its data unit. Because it is a Layer 2 protocol, it carries a Layer 3 IP packet inside its cell. Don't confuse a mobile network cell, which is a defined geographical area, with that of an ATM cell, which is a unit of traffic. It is not unusual for an ATM cell to be sent through the cells of a cellular network.

To conclude this introduction to ATM and to set the stage for subsequent hours, the following facts are germane. ATM:

▶ Requires an association (a logical connection, called a virtual path or virtual circuit) to be set up before cells are exchanged

▶ Does not provide an acknowledgment for the successful receipt of a cell

▶ Does not check for out-of-sequence or duplicate cells. Protocols at higher layers assume this function (for example, TCP, discussed in Hour 14, "Connecting to the Internet: Initial Operations")

▶ Performs an error check for corrupted data; if corrupted, the cell is discarded

▶ Provides for a rich set of services and extensive traffic management tools

▶ Is not aware of the nature of the underlying Layer 1

IPX

The IPX protocol is derived from a Xerox Network Services (XNS) product and is part of Novell's NetWare operating system. IPX uses an address similar to the conventional IP classful address, but it makes some adjustments for the sake of efficiency. IPX was widely used in the 1980s and 1990s, but it has seen diminishing use as the industry has migrated to IP. A survey on the Internet[3] revealed that 44% of companies using Windows Server did not run IPX; 34% ran IPX but were migrating away

---

[3] Go to *http://articles.techrepublic.com.com/5100-10878_11-5026038.html.*

from it. In addition, Windows Vista does not support IPX, nor does any Mac OS later than version 9.2.2. We bid farewell to IPX, but we also assure IPX customers that Novell is now supporting them with its migration to TCP/IP.

And Farewell NetBIOS and NetBEUI

Let's also put to rest two other systems. The Network Basic Input/Output System (Net-BIOS) is—in computer network time—an ancient protocol. Developed in 1983 for IBM PC networks, it provides services similar to the session layer of the OSI model. If used, NetBIOS runs over TCP/IP principally for some naming services.

The Network BIOS Extended User Interface (NetBEUI) has been used in small LANs, the old LANManager; as well as Windows 3.x. It isn't routable. Computers attached to a nonlocal network can't use it. Thus, IP has replaced most NetBEUI installations.

Summary

We've covered a lot of material in this hour. The information is important and will be a great aid for grasping many concepts in the next 21 hours. The topics in this hour are vital to the network or networks you have in your office and home. With the concepts presented in this hour, you should have the basic tools to begin setting up your own network.

Q&A

Q. *In a typical data network, which layers of the OSI model are executed?*

A. Only Layers 1, 2, and 3, which translates into faster relaying of traffic through a network.

Q. *IP operates at which layer of the OSI model?*

A. Layer 3.

Q. *To deal with the limited address space of IPv4, the industry has devised three solutions. What are they?*

A. Classless Inter-Domain Routing (CIDR), the Network Address Translation (NAT) protocol, and IPv6 are the three solutions devised by the industry.

Q. *Why have IP "classful" addresses fallen into disfavor?*

A. The use of rigid network and host bit boundaries restricts the number of addresses that can be obtained from a 32-bit address space.

HOUR 4

Computer Concepts

What You'll Learn in This Hour:

▶ How computers work

▶ The varieties of computer hardware

▶ Functions and operations of software

▶ Operating systems

Networks are made of computers in the same way a band is made of musicians. Each computer—and each band member—is unique, and in the right circumstances, they all work together to produce a fine performance. If they don't, the result is chaos for the computers and cacophony for the band.

Similar to bands, networks require certain conventions be observed when computers are networked to interplay with each other. Although each computer is unique, it operates the same way as other computers on the network. If you understand how a computer works, you'll be better prepared to understand how networks work. The analogy ends here, as I have never found a musician who operates the same way as another musician.

Anyway, keep in mind you're not being asked to become a computer guru, but given that networks hook computers together, a basic understanding of a computer's architecture helps to achieve a better understanding of networking.

Numbers, Magnitudes, and Fractions

Of necessity, this book uses terms such as "giga," "tera," "nano," and "pico" to describe the magnitude and precision of numbers. They can't be avoided because computer networks are often described by their capacity, or the number of bytes (characters) or number of bits (0s and 1s) sent per second. For example, vendor literature about a high-capacity network cites a transmission "speed" of 10 gigabits per second, or 10Gbps and storage vendors refer to terabytes when discussing large file systems. Also, computers are often compared to how long it takes to perform a task. For example, access time for a disk might be 10 milliseconds, or 10ms. To help with these translations, Figure 4.1 lists common terms associated with the base 10 numbering system.

FIGURE 4.1
Common terms

Multiplication Factor	Prefix	Symbol	Meaning
1 000 000 000 000 000 000 = 10^{18}	exa	E	Quintillion
1 000 000 000 000 000 = 10^{15}	peta	P	Quadrillion
1 000 000 000 000 = 10^{12}	tera	T	Trillion
1 000 000 000 = 10^{9}	giga	G	Billion
1 000 000 = 10^{6}	mega	M	Million
1 000 = 10^{3}	kilo	K	Thousand
100 = 10^{2}	hecto	h	Hundred
10 = 10^{1}	deka	da	Ten
0.1 = 10^{-1}	deci	d	Tenth
0.01 = 10^{-2}	centi	c	Hundredth
0.001 = 10^{-3}	milli	m	Thousandth
0.000 001 = 10^{-6}	micro	μ	Millionth
0.000 000 001 = 10^{-9}	nano	n	Billionth
0.000 000 000 001 = 10^{-12}	pico	p	Trillionth
0.000 000 000 000 001 = 10^{-15}	femto	f	Quadrillionth
0.000 000 000 000 000 001 = 10^{-18}	atto	a	Quintillionth

Computer Hardware

Computers consist of two components: hardware and software. Hardware is the physical part of a computer. Software executes on the hardware. The hardware is usually stable and is infrequently altered. In contrast, software changes often. For example, as Internet users, we frequently receive alerts on our screens about a vendor wanting to download changes to a software product.

The two terms are self-descriptive: Hardware implies somewhat rigid components—not easily changed. Software implies flexible components—easily changed. Hmm, make that easily changed in comparison to hardware. Some software programs contain thousands of lines of code (which are instructions, such as "print," "copy," and "delete") with many interdependent instructions. They may be easy to change, but they may not be easy to change *correctly*.

Firmware is a special type of software that rarely changes. It's stored in hardware called read-only memory, or ROM. As its name suggests, ROM can only be "read" and not "written." It can be changed, but only with special operations and procedures. Therefore, it's neither "hard" nor "soft"; it's "firm."

Hardware, as you've probably guessed, makes up the physical components of a computer. It includes but is not limited to the following:

▶ CPU (central processing unit)

▶ Screen and keyboard

▶ Memory

▶ Disks

▶ Add-in components, such as network interface cards (NICs)

▶ Sockets, slots, and ports

In the next few pages, we take a high-level tour of a PC. Although the descriptions will focus on an IBM-compatible PC (the most common kind of personal computer), the concepts presented here also hold for Macintoshes or any other computer designed with a modular, expandable architecture. Don't be concerned about your specific PC, such as a Dell or an HP. Our descriptions are appropriate for any computer. Figure 4.2 will be helpful as we survey the innards of the computer.[1]

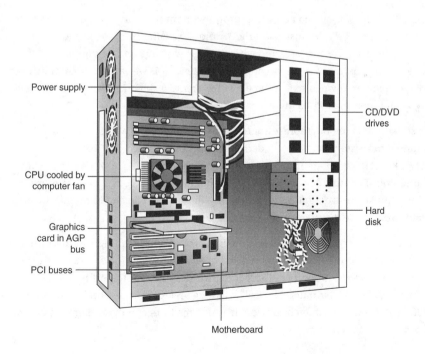

FIGURE 4.2
Major hardware components in a PC

---

[1] *Source: Wikipedia, The Free Encyclopedia, subject: "Computer Hardware."*

The CPU

When you remove the cover from a personal computer, the first thing you might see is a section of metal and ceramic, mounted on a circuit board. This component is the CPU, also often called the processor. The basic purpose of a CPU is to execute software programs, which are instructions the CPU uses to manipulate data stored in computer memory. The data may be an email, an Excel spreadsheet, a PowerPoint graphic, and so on. Whatever it is, the CPU, a powerful microprocessor, is the focal point for processing the data—as dictated by the software.

Motherboard

The CPU is usually placed on a circuit board mounted into a socket on the motherboard. A motherboard also provides connections through which internal components of the computer communicate. For example, it's configured with ports to which memory is attached. It may also connect external peripherals, such as a printer.

The motherboard is aptly named because it's the focal point for the "family" of hardware components inside the computer and those attached to the computer.

The CPU is the *sine qua non* for computing—without it, a computer is absent its oar and tiller. The CPU administers all the 1s and 0s coming from the keyboard, the mouse, the disk, the network, and whatever else we have on our computer. It then processes this data so we can accomplish whatever it is we want to accomplish—to see a display on a video screen, type a letter, create a spreadsheet. Whatever we do on a computer, the CPU is involved.

As stated, CPUs are microprocessors. The earliest microprocessors had only a few hundred transistors per chip. Modern microprocessors, such as Silicon Graphics, Inc.'s POWER4, contain more than 170 million transistors on a square the size of your thumbnail. The next generation of processor chips are projected to have more than 1 billion transistors—an enormous capability that will likely lead to architectures different from those discussed in this hour.

Microprocessors quickly execute instructions. For example, as I key in this sentence on my PC keyboard and perhaps execute a Save command for the text, my computer's CPU is executing lines of software code designed to support my input—my commands to the computer. The CPU will take several-to-many cycles (iterations) to fulfill this task. It must fetch software instructions from computer memory, decode them, execute them, and store the results.

The CPU performs these rather prosaic operations at astounding speeds. The PC I'm using to explain this feature has a clock rate of 1.73GHz. This figure means the CPU is operating (cycling) at 1,730,000,000 times a second. Granted, multiple cycles may be needed to, say, save this sentence in memory. Nonetheless, a 1.73GHz CPU can perform thousands of operations—such as fetching a Web page, displaying a photo on a screen, and so on—in one second. Even more, modern computers are capable of executing multiple instructions per clock cycle, which translates into an even faster CPU than described previously. Consequently, "clock speed" alone is not used much nowadays to describe the actual processing power of a computer.

Let's make a few more points about computer processors and their capacity. Other terms are used to describe the processing power of a CPU, such as instructions per second (IPS) and floating point operations per second (FLOPS). Experts who analyze computer capacity exercise caution in using these statistics alone for evaluating and comparing performances. Nonetheless, for our analysis, it's instructive to note that in June 2008, a CPU achieved a 1 teraflop rate. That's 10^{12} FLOPS!

A typical human spends several seconds (minutes?) performing numeric addition with pencil and paper, depending on the magnitude of the number. In computer terms, the human executes this addition at roughly 0.0119 IPS. One of Intel's 3.2GHz processors performs 59,455,000,000 IPS for a comparable numeric addition. Needless to say, this CPU can do a lot of work in a short time.

What is more, a computer does not demand health benefits or ask for a pay raise. It doesn't leave work early to pick up the kids. While we humans continue to raise the overhead incurred by businesses, computers continue to lower these costs. You think we will see fewer automated voice services and Web sites and more human interactions for our airline reservations and other purchases? Think again. We humans have flopped! Just consider:

- **1961**—About $1,100,000,000,000 ($1.1 trillion) per GigaFLOPS
- **1997**—About $30,000 per GigaFLOPS
- **2008: May**—About $0.13 per GigaFLOPS

Memory

A microprocessor integrates most or all of the CPU on an integrated circuit (a silicon chip). However, not all chips are microprocessors. Some chips, called memory chips, are built as arrays holding the 1s and 0s the CPU is processing. Their purpose is to provide a place in the computer for the storage of data. The data can be accessed in any order (nonsequentially)—thus, the name random access memory, or RAM.

By the Way

> ### Memory Modules
>
> When these chips are arranged into groups, the resulting memory devices are called Single Inline Memory Modules (SIMMs, which is an older technology), or Dual Inline Memory Modules (DIMMs). When you buy memory from a retailer, you're buying memory modules instead of individual memory chips.

RAM is usually associated with volatile types of memory (often called dynamic, or DRAM), where data is lost after the power is switched off. However, some types of memory can keep a charge (and maintain the data) after the computer is turned off.

In spite of the differences in terms, all computer memory works in a similar fashion: Put a charge across memory, and it holds 1s and 0s for the CPU to access. The key point with respect to memory is to make certain the memory you purchase is the type your computer requires. Your user manual should provide this information. If you can't find it, personnel in computer stores can help you. Of course, the manufacturer's website can also provide this information. Should you call the vendor's telephone for help? Good luck! Remember our recent discussion on the cost/performance differences between human and computer activity. Chances are, you'll talk to a computer about computer memory.

Anyway, memory is also used to provide CPU access to data. If the computer had to read data from tapes or disks each time it needed the next batch of data or instructions, computers would be far too slow to be useful. But the use of memory, specifically RAM, has led to extraordinarily fast computers.

However, RAM is no match for the pace of the CPU because of the relatively slow speeds by which memory is accessed for data and instructions. CPUs can process code in 3 nanoseconds (ns). Memory access is roughly 100ns, a huge difference in speeds. Therefore, small memories, called caches, are located close to the CPU to provide data and instructions faster than conventional memory.

Memory is great for helping computers to operate efficiently. However, there's one thing memory can't do, which the next section explains.

Watch Out!

> ### Be Smart—Add Memory!
>
> Analysts from think tanks, such as the Gartner Group and the Meta Group, claim memory is often more important than CPU power: Memory is fast storage. Typically, a computer can access memory chips quite quickly; access speeds are measured in nanoseconds (millionths of a second). Contrast this with the hard drives, which have millisecond (hundredths of seconds) access times. Even if a computer has a powerful processor, it will run slowly if it's short on memory. By

contrast, a less powerful CPU armed with a lot of memory may out-perform a more powerful but memory-starved CPU.

Disks

Memory abets computer speed. However, RAM is volatile, which means that it only functions when the computer is turned on. Because RAM is made of chips depending on an electrical power source to store data, when the power is cut, it can no longer store anything. I doubt you want to retype everything every time you turn on the computer. There ought to be a way to store data so that it can be retrieved the next time you turn on your machine.

External storage devices were invented to store data, regardless of the state of the computer. One such device is called the disk (or hard disk). Disks fulfill two of the most common needs of the computer: They store data in a nonvolatile state (that is, the data stored on disks doesn't disappear when the power is cut), and they act as additional (albeit slower) memory when the computer needs more memory (RAM) than is physically installed.

Disk storage is so named because data is recorded on round, rotating surfaces called disks. Prior to the invention of disks, almost all data was stored on cardboard (punch) cards or magnetic tape. For cards and tape, access to the data was sequential. Record 1 had to be accessed before record 2 could be obtained, and so on. The disk technology permits random access, which greatly facilitates the searching for a specific record. You can imagine the delay if a directory assistance operator in Los Angeles had to sequentially search a computer file to find the phone number of XYZ Corporation.

Disks and Magnetism

Did you Know?

Magnets have two poles: north and south. Remember that computers use only 1s and 0s. The values of 1s and 0s are binary—that is, they're either 1 or 0; there's nothing in between. Fortunately, north and south on magnetic particles are also binary, and the computer can exploit the orientation of microscopic magnetic particles to correspond to the 1s and 0s. A magnetic particle with the north pole facing up might be a 0, and a particle with the south pole facing up might be a 1—just what we need to store data.

For many years, disk storage had a limited capacity. At the risk of dating myself, I cut my programming teeth on an ancient IBM 2311 disk. It stored 7.25 million bytes on one disk pack (six platters rotated as a single unit). The data transfer rate from the disk into computer memory was only 156 kilobytes per second (Kbps). The newer units in operation today store roughly 250 gigabytes (GB) of data. Their data transfer rate is 61.4 megabytes per second (Mbps).

Varieties of Disks

Modern disks for personal computers generally come in one of two varieties: IDE and SCSI. These variations entail different methods by which hard drives connect to computers. Because devices of one type are incompatible with devices of the other type, it's important to know a bit about both of them.

Integrated Drive Electronics (IDE) (also known as Advanced Technology Attachment, or ATA) is a connection standard for hard drives that places the electronics that control the drive directly on the drive itself. IDE/ATA supports up to two drives connected to a single cable and disk sizes up to 528 megabytes (MB). A more recent version of the IDE standard, called Extended IDE (EIDE), can support larger disks; it is now common to see EIDE disks with capacities of up to 120 gigabytes (GB). EIDE is often called "Ultra DMA." You'll usually find these drives sold as ATA these days, but they're just IDE with a different name, because the interface is the same as IDE. You might also come across the term SATA, for Serial Advanced Technology Attachment, which is an enhancement to ATA in offering faster transfer rates.

Solid State Drives (SSDs)

You should also investigate the possibility of using solid state drives (SSDs). They use solid state memory for the storage of data. As of this writing, they are more expensive than conventional disk units, but for some applications the extra cost may be justified. They are much faster than rotating disks and emit no sound. For applications needing very fast response times, SSDs might be worth their expense.

Small Computer System Interface (SCSI)

The small computer system interface (SCSI, pronounced "skuzzy"), shown in Figure 4.3, is a standard for connecting peripheral devices to a computer. SCSI enables 8 to 16 devices to be connected to the computer in a chain (that is, on a single bus).

FIGURE 4.3
The SCSI
connector

Each device on a SCSI chain has a number called (not surprisingly) a SCSI ID, which enables the computer to locate that device when needed. Each end of the SCSI chain must be terminated, which means that a special device called a terminating resistor must be plugged in to the end of the cable. The terminating resistor ensures the electrical characteristics of the cable remain consistent along its length. SCSI comes in a variety of speeds ranging from 5Mbps to 300Mbps. With some exceptions, SCSI is backward compatible, which is a fancy way of saying that old devices can connect to newer SCSI controllers and still work (although the entire SCSI bus slows down to the speed of the slowest device to which it's connected).

Of course, peripheral devices, such as disks, don't operate on their own; they must connect to something in the computer, which is the subject of the next section. Also, in Hour 11, "Selecting Network Hardware and Software," this subject is revisited with some recommendations on which disk technology might fit your network.

Expansion Cards

At the beginning of this hour, we learned the CPU fits into the motherboard through a socket. In addition to the socket for the CPU, the motherboard provides interfaces for after-market devices. These devices, which fit into expansion slots on the motherboard, are called expansion cards (as well as expansion boards, adapter cards, or accessory cards).

Whatever they are called, they are electronic assemblies connecting to a computer through a standard interface called a card slot. Adapter cards provide a variety of services to the computer, including video, network, and modem operations.

It is safe to make the claim that without IBM's decision to adopt a modular design for its initial personal computer, and the computer industry's following suit, modern personal computers would not have become the powerful and adaptable machines that they are today. The modularity and adaptability of the IBM PC drove the personal computer's explosion of popularity in the early 1980s. In fact, the computer industry's rapid growth can be attributed to the adapter-card standards promulgated by IBM for the early PC.

Adapter cards handle an array of functions, including the following:

- ▶ Network adapters connect computers to the network.
- ▶ Video adapters provide a way for the computer to display images on a video monitor.
- ▶ Drive controllers connect hard drives to the system.
- ▶ SCSI controllers connect any devices that use the SCSI interface to the computer.
- ▶ Sound and video cards enable a variety of media types—from CD to MP3—to be played on a computer.

This list is not comprehensive; it doesn't include all the different types of adapter cards. Nonetheless, it does cover the devices you're likely to encounter in a common computer.

Although most motherboards have expansion slots, the expansion slots on all motherboards are not the same. Various computer manufacturers have devised different interfaces for cards used in their systems. For Intel-based computers, the most common slot designs are, in order of age from oldest to youngest, ISA, EISA, and PCI. ISA stands for Industry Standard Architecture, which was what IBM called this interface when it created it in the early 1980s. As of this writing, ISA, EISA, VESA-Local Bus, and several other slot interfaces are considered to be obsolete technologies.

Peripheral Component Interconnect (PCI)

PCI is the current interface standard, supplanting several older interfaces. PCI came about from an initiative by Intel to allow add-in adapters to run almost as fast as the system in which they're installed. The interface into the motherboard can be an integrated circuit fitted onto the motherboard, or it can be an expansion card that fits into a socket.

Typical PCI cards used in PCs include network cards, sound cards, modems, USB or serial ports, TV tuner cards, and disk controllers. In the past, video cards were PCI devices, but growing capacity requirements for video have outgrown the capabilities of PCI. However, PCI cards are widely deployed in devices such as modems. The chances are good that the modem in your PC is PCI based.

Status of Expansion Cards

Many devices that have been implemented on expansion cards are now part of the motherboard. However, PCI is still used for certain specialized cards, although many tasks that have been performed by expansion cards may now be performed by USB devices (explained later in this hour).

Network Cards

To connect a computer to a network, a network card is installed into the computer. Other terms used for this hardware are network adapter card or network interface card (NIC); the terms are synonymous. Network cards are available from a variety of manufacturers and in a variety of interfaces including Ethernet and Asynchronous Transfer Mode (ATM), which you might recall from Hour 3, "Getting Data from Here to There: How Networking Works." Thus, an NIC operates at Layers 1 and 2 of the OSI model. What is more, every LAN NIC contains a MAC (Ethernet) address.

Because of the near-universality of Ethernet, most companies now offer a network interface as part of the motherboard, either with a dedicated Ethernet chip (connected through a PCI) or with the Ethernet protocol integrated into the motherboard hardware. A separate network card is not required unless multiple interfaces are needed or some other type of network, such as ATM, is used. Newer motherboards sometimes have dual network (Ethernet) interfaces built in.

You will find network cards easy to install. Typically, just turn off the power to the computer, open the case, find a slot that matches the card's interface (usually ISA, EISA, or PCI), center the card above the slot, and press the card firmly into the slot to seat it. Mission accomplished; turn the computer back on. When the computer is fully running, you can install device drivers. These software components (described in the second part of this hour) enable the computer to communicate with the device. After the device driver software is installed, you usually have to restart your computer one more time to connect to the network. When in doubt, read the accompanying manual!

Video Adapter Cards and Monitors

If you ask people to identify "the computer," some will point to the monitor on their desks rather than the casing containing the CPU. Although they would be incorrect in defining a monitor as the computer, they would be making a point that we do well to heed. Human beings are visually oriented creatures. In general, visually striking images garner more attention than drab impressions. The computer box beside your desk just doesn't create visual interest, which explains why manufacturers such as Apple offer the CPU in bright colors. It adds visual relevance to a machine. It also sells computers.

By contrast, the monitor is visually interesting because it's colorful and full of motion. Computer monitors get attention out of proportion to the amount of actual work they do. The keyboard and mouse are where the user's part of the work is done; the system box does the computing, but the monitor is what we see and therefore what we respond to.

Because what we see on a video monitor screen is such an important part of how we interact with computers, the video adapter card, or video card, is an important part of the system. Video cards convert the digital information the computer uses internally to a format for display on a computer monitor. The image on the screen is made up of pixels (picture elements). Think of a pixel as a small image on a grid, represented by bits (1s and 0s).

The number of bits needed to describe a pixel is called bit depth. The "shallowest" bit depth is 1. One binary bit can represent one of two states (1 and 0), a technique for monochrome monitors. A bit depth of 2 can describe four colors, and so on.

Color Depth

Color depth deals with the quality of the images produced by a monitor, which are a function of its bit depth, as well as how the bits are used.

256-color screens are sometimes called 8-bit color, because 8 bits (or eight 1s and 0s) are used to tell the computer what color to display in each pixel. Because 8 bits can be combined into 256 different combinations, 256 colors can be described with this technique. The next step up from 8-bit color is 16-bit color, and what a change! With 16 bits, a monitor can display up to 65,536 colors onscreen. A few years ago, 16-bit color was referred to as high color.

Today, many computer monitors can show an infinite number of colors in the red-green-blue (RGB) color space by changing the red (R), green (G), and blue (B) video signals in continuously variable intensities.

The minimum standard for video displays on Intel-based computers is called VGA, or video graphics adapter, which is a baseline, antiquated standard. Of more interest are the modern standards. For example, a display operating in SuperVGA (SVGA) mode can display up to 16,777,216 colors because it supports a 24-bit-long description of a pixel.

At the high end of quality are monitors with a bit depth of 32 bits (SuperVGA + Alpha Channel), a special graphics mode used by applications needing an even better picture, such as animation and video games. This procedure uses 24 bits for describing the color of the pixel and 8 bits for describing its light diffusion (the translucency of the pixel). You've seen these pixels displayed on the more expensive monitors. They produce beautiful, even stunning displays.

The Universal Serial Bus (USB)

Just a few years ago—a long time in the computer industry—computer manufacturers often designed and built vendor-specific ports on computers. (The term port is used here to describe the "plug," or the "connector" on the back or side of a computer.) For example, Apple's mouse port was Apple specific and prohibited an IBM mouse from plugging into it.

Fortunately, several influential standards groups succeeded in promoting the use of standard ports for certain interfaces. One set of prominent data communications standards was (is) the Electronic Industries Association (EIA) specifications. The EIA spearheaded the standardization of ports for data terminal equipment (DTE), such as a PC, and its connection to data communications equipment (DCE), such as a modem.

Notwithstanding these efforts, vendor-specific ports led to compatibility problems, resulting in the inability to "plug and play" various peripherals from other manufacturers. Not only were the "plugs" different, the device drivers (discussed shortly) were manufacturer specific. For a nontechnical PC user (most of the population), finding the correct driver for a peripheral was akin to diving into a technical black hole. In addition, many of these interfaces wouldn't allow a peripheral device (such as an external hard disk) to be connected or disconnected without restarting (rebooting) the computer.

In the mid 1990s, several influential computer companies participated in developing the Universal Serial Bus (USB) specification (thanks to Intel, Microsoft, Philips, and US Robotics). Apple's iMac G3 (1998) was the first computer built with USB ports. Today, the USB interface (see Figure 4.4) is commonplace and has replaced not only manufacturer-specific interfaces, but other standardized plugs and receptacles as well.

FIGURE 4.4
The USB

USB is a serial (one bit at a time) bus standard for interfacing peripheral devices with a computer. It allows hot swapping: connecting or disconnecting devices without rebooting the computer. It supports up to 127 device connections per host and can operate at a data transfer rate of 1.5 to 60Mbps. It permits a host to connect to multiple downstream USB ports though USB hubs, which is similar to a branching tree structure. The limit is five levels of tiers. A host can have multiple host controllers attached to it.

To reduce the number of manufacturer-specific interfaces, USB defines 19 classes of devices. A specific class describes how a device is to "behave"—that is, how it is to communicate with its attached computer. Consequently, the same interface (connector, cable, and software device driver) can be used by any device that adheres to the protocols for that class. As one example, Class 07h sets the behavior for printers, regardless of whether they are made by Dell, Apple, or IBM.

Furthermore, a computer's operating system (OS, discussed in the next section of this hour) is supposed to support all USB device classes. Just a few years ago, it would have been impossible to buy a digital camera without an accompanying CD, which was filled with software to allow the camera to communicate with the computer. Now, and as another example, Microsoft's Vista operating system includes support for device class 06h (digital camera). So does a Canon camera. They interwork, transparently to a user! (I use an exclamation point in the last sentence. The readers who have been in the industry for a while will understand why.)

USB and FireWire

FireWire, published as IEEE 1394 by the Institute of Electronic and Electrical Engineers, defines a high-speed serial bus to connect peripherals to a computer. So does the USB specification. The two standards differ in their technical "behavior," and we need not concern ourselves with these details. Your network can do just fine with USB unless your applications need a lot of capacity (in bits per second) and are time sensitive. Examples are advanced audio and video systems. You will pay more for FireWire because it outperforms the less expensive USB.

Operating System (OS) and Other Software

Computer hardware is an intriguing subject. But left to itself, it's little more than electrically charged, but otherwise inert assemblages of metal, silicon, and other high-tech mucilage. For this hardware to be effective, for it to "compute," it needs software.

Indeed, computer hardware is designed to operate with software, a set of instructions that informs the hardware the tasks it is to undertake to support an end-user's application, such as email. An operating system, or OS, is the baseline software enabling users and their applications to interact with computer hardware. If hardware is the body of a computer, the operating system is its brain.

There's no technical reason why each program couldn't contain an OS and control the operations of the hardware. But this approach would be foolhardy because the OS frees application designers from having to delve into the intricacies of the physical architecture of the computer, which into itself is complex.

The OS also offers consistent user and programming interfaces and standard ways of doing simple tasks such as copying data between applications, writing a memo, editing a photo, or placing a song on an iPod. Applications invoke OS services with *application programming interfaces* (APIs), also known as *system calls*. An API can pass parameters, such as data, to the OS and receive parameters informing the application about the results of the operation. For nonprogrammers, a user can invoke the

OS from a keyboard, a mouse, or by touching the screen. For the mouse and screen functions, the OS provides a graphical user interface (GUI, pronounced "gooey").

Common operating systems—those you might have come across—are Microsoft's Windows and Vista, Apple's OS X, UNIX, and Linux.

There are several types of operating systems. The following list is a general categorization. The OS on your computer may use combinations of these categories.

- **Single-tasking systems**—Performs one task at a time. (A task is also called a process. It is an instance of a software program currently being executed. An example is an addition operation or a print operation.)

- **Multitasking systems**—Can run several tasks simultaneously and allows programs from multiple users to share in the use of the CPU and other hardware. Typically, the OS gives each user or user-support program a "slice" of time. The swapping of tasks occurs so quickly that the operations are transparent to the user.

- **Single-user system**—Used by one user at a time on one machine at a time.

- **Multiuser systems**—Supports many simultaneous user sessions on one computer.

- **Multiprocessing systems**—Some computers have multiple processors (CPUs). If so, different programs might run on the different processors.

Multitasking

An operating system might use one of two types of multitasking: cooperative and preemptive. The latter approach is found in more of the prominent OSs than the former.

Cooperative multitasking prevents the OS from making all decisions about which applications' tasks are given system resources, such as the CPU. When an application is done with a task, resources are passed to another application. Preemptive multitasking has the OS making the decisions about which program gains use of the systems resources. Preemptive multitasking is the model used in Linux, UNIX, Microsoft's Windows enterprise operating systems (Windows 2000, XP, 2003, and so on), and NetWare.

What Happens When a Computer Is Turned On

When a computer is turned on, we immediately see images and text on the screen informing us our pressing the "on" button was successful, and activities are underway to allow us to use the machine. During this time, the computer is preparing its hardware and OS to support the applications we later invoke when we click on an icon.

Generally, this startup process—dubbed by the industry as "booting the computer"— entails the execution of firmware from read-only memory (ROM), often called boot ROM. This firmware first loads program code from a disk and then executes the code, which is called a boot loader. The boot loader's task is to load the most critical parts of the OS, called the kernel, and start the kernel running. The kernel's name is appropriate, because it is central to the OS and remains in memory while the machine is turned on. It is responsible for the most basic tasks, such as input/output (I/O) management of attached peripherals, memory management, CPU allocation, and regulating the processes and tasks to support users' applications.

Let's assume you're informed your machine is now at your disposal. Windows displays a colored (sort of) window. A MAC shows off an abstract smiley face. You want to log onto the Internet, so you click an icon on the screen identifying your Internet service provider (ISP). This simple action results in the loading of ISP software from your disk and scores, perhaps hundreds, of supporting software "routines." Thereafter, as you interact with this software and the Internet, the OS keeps track of all these resources by

▶ A unique identifier for each of the software processes that is executed to support your session. It is called a process ID (PID).

▶ A list of memory locations the program is using or is allowed to use. Some memory is reserved for the OS and other critical "nonapplications."

▶ The PID of the program, which requested the execution of this program. This identifier is called the parent process ID (PPID).

▶ The filename from which the program was loaded.

▶ A file containing values of all CPU storage locations for this program. This isn't conventional memory. It's implemented with special hardware called registers.

▶ A program counter, indicating which code in the program is currently running.

Complex? Yes, but it's quite logical. Unlike humans, well-designed computer hardware and software can always be understood because all of it operates...yes, logically. Let's pause for a moment and examine the items in this list and compare them to a common human activity: taking a commercial fight on an airplane. The airline keeps track of its resources (flyers) by

▶ A unique identifier for each of the people on the flight. It is called a reservation number.

▶ A list of seats on the plane that a flyer is allowed to use. Some seats are reserved for the crew and first-class passengers.

▶ The name of the person who set up the reservation. This identifier contains credit card information.

▶ The airline flight number from which the person began the journey, to check of lost luggage, for example.

▶ A list containing information on all passengers (especially, after 9/11). This is not conventional data, but privileged information.

I can't stretch the analogy to the sixth operation, but the point to this comparison is to recognize that the seemingly complex activities of a computer's OS is akin to many of our daily tasks: keeping an account of what's going on.

OS: The Transparent Workhouse of the Computer

During a session on a computer, the user should not be aware of the activities of the OS. What is more, it would be unusual if you must delve into OS operations on your computer. For that matter, this statement also holds for the OS in other machines that may be part of your network, such as the router interfacing your machine to the Internet. If error messages appear on your screen informing you of a problem with your operating system, your best move is to "move" the computer to the nearest OS expert—perhaps the nearby computer shop. Some of my nontechnical friends and colleagues have attempted to fix an OS problem. Not only were they never successful, but on some occasions they made matters worse.

That stated, the integrity of modern operating systems is quite good, especially when compared to only 10 years ago. It's no small feat for the OS to manage all the hardware and software on a modern computer. Recently, I ran virus detection software on my PC and kept a window open that informed me of the number of identifiable files the virus software examined. By "identifiable," I mean a file with a Windows name, such as "C:\Uyless Black\Networking in 24 Hours\Hour 4." After the scan was complete, I was informed 162,976 files were scanned. Bear in mind that many of the files contain programs, emails, photos, videos, slide presentations, spreadsheets, and so on. That's a lot of things to keep in proper working order.

One more point about the operating system and other software. I suggest you allow each manufacturer to download changes to its products. If you block these updates and "fixes," you'll find yourself operating with an out-of-date system. This could become a problem because an outdated OS might contain problems (bugs) and might not have the latest security enhancements.

Examples of Operating Systems

To conclude the discussion on operating systems, this section highlights several of the more widely used products. First, we discuss Microsoft's Windows and Vista.

Windows and Vista

Microsoft Windows is a family of operating systems. In November 1985, Microsoft introduced Windows as an add-on to MS-DOS in response to the growing interest in GUIs and complaints about the poor user interfaces furnished by MS-DOS—especially compared to Apple's GUI. Windows now dominates the world's personal computer OS market. Estimates vary, but most surveys claim Windows has roughly 90% of market share.

Microsoft takes the approach that an OS for the home (with inexperienced users) should not be the same as an OS for the office (experienced users or a competent support staff). Having worked extensively in both environments, I think this philosophy is sound. Most home users don't need the power and complexity of an office-oriented OS. Nor do they need the price tag associated with a richer OS.

With each release of Windows, the product has improved. (With Windows 95 (1995), Microsoft OS began supporting preemptive multitasking.) Microsoft's OSs have been criticized for many years for their "user unfriendliness" and lack of functionality. I agree with some of these complaints, but it should be noted that Mr. Gates and company began their OS work using MS-DOS and had to keep aspects of this OS as part of their future operating systems. Anyway, with the 2001 introduction of Windows XP, Microsoft gained praise for its OS.

Microsoft also entered the server market in 2003 with Windows Server 2003. Today, Windows Server 2008 is slated as its successor. Because servers play a key role in computer networks, they are discussed as separate subjects in Hours 5, 10, 14, and 15–18.

Vista is slated to replace Windows XP. It offers many new features, including a new GUI, more powerful search tools, and support for multimedia applications. It simplifies file sharing and makes it easier to install a home network. Perhaps the biggest change from XP is better security features, a subject for Hour 20, "Security."

Mac OS

In the early days of Windows, many Macintosh users complained Microsoft had "stolen" the look and feel of the Macintosh. These users apparently didn't know Apple's nifty GUI contained a lot of features first developed at Xerox's Palo Alto

Research Center (PARC). As mentioned in an earlier hour, I visited PARC in 1982 to evaluate Ethernet. I was astounded when I saw PARC's GUI, including trashcans and icons of files. I cannot say if Steven Jobs took PARC's ideas. But I can say the two were remarkably similar...and PARC's GUI came first.

Anyway, in 1984 Apple invented the Macintosh OS, also called the System. It had a clean and sparse interface, well suited to nontechnical users. These features, combined with the Macintosh's reputation for freeing the user from concern about computer hardware and obscure MS-DOS commands, led users to develop a near-fanatical devotion to Apple. (I was one of those fanatics. Unlike MS-DOS applications, Apple had—for that time—an extraordinary graphics package called Mac-Draw. I bought my first Mac because of MacDraw. The next day, I terminated contacts with graphic artists who had been hand-drawing the illustrations for my books.)

Mac OS initially came with a proprietary network called LocalTalk, which was upgraded to become AppleTalk. It was a layered architecture, quite similar to the OSI seven-layer model explained in Hour 3. With the rise of the Internet, MacTCP arrived and replaced AppleTalk. Thereafter, Mac users could connect to the Internet using the TCP/IP protocol suite.

Apple has rewritten its operating system software to create OS X, an OS constructed around the UNIX-based microkernel. It's a preemptive operating system that acts a lot like a high-end UNIX technical workstation with a user-friendly interface. It's proven quite reliable and has made further inroads into the artistic/technical community.

UNIX and Linux

The final operating systems we examine for computers and computer networks are UNIX and Linux. UNIX began as an experiment in a Bell Labs computer lab in 1969 and is now a popular server and workstation operating system. AT&T made UNIX available to anyone under liberal license arrangements. The licenses included *all* the source code, which was an unheard-of practice at that time. Early on, the Internet TCP/IP protocol stack was included in the package, which further spawned its use (and helped foster the relatively new Internet standards).

UNIX runs on almost every type of computer ranging from Intel compatibles to high-end multiprocessor transaction servers used by banks, public safety agencies, and other institutions. It bears mentioning that the owner of the trademark is The Open Group. Only systems fully compliant with and certified to the Single UNIX Specification are qualified to use the trademark.

UNIX, like its younger sibling Windows NT, is a preemptive operating system. As mentioned, unlike every other operating system we've discussed, it's often shipped with the source code (the set of instructions written in a computer language such as C). Most commercial operating system vendors don't provide source code because they believe it's proprietary. With UNIX, you often get the source code, which means that if you can program a computer, you can customize the operating system.

Since the mid 1990s, a new variant of UNIX called Linux has sprung up and received a lot of attention. Linux is a UNIX-like operating system written in such a fashion as to evade the copyright restrictions on UNIX while retaining its look and feel. From a cost/benefit perspective, Linux is an attractive operating system.

Renowned for its use in servers, Linux is supported by many companies. It operates in a variety of machines, including computers, E-book readers, DVRs, video game devices, mobile phones, and routers.

As network clients, UNIX and Linux perform quite well. Their default network protocol stack is the TCP/IP model, which is the set of protocols used on the Internet. UNIX (or Linux) servers are the foundation of most of the Internet's web servers. We'll take a closer look at UNIX and Linux in Hour 17, "UNIX and Linux Networking."

Device Drivers

A device driver is a software module operating on behalf of a device, such as a scanner, a printer, a disk unit, and so on. It permits other software programs to interact with the device and usually communicates with the device through the computer bus. When a program requests a service, say to access data on an external hard disk, the driver issues commands to the disk. Once the disk sends data back to the driver, the driver may inform the program of the activity, as well as cause the application to take other actions. Drivers are *very* hardware dependent and operating system specific. It's at the device driver level where products become the most specific to a manufacturer.

Device drivers are quite important to the overall architecture of a computer because they isolate the application programs and the operating system from the many details of a specific piece of hardware. For example, an application program might have a line of code instructing the computer to print a document. The code might be "WRITE," "PRINT," or "PRINTLN" with a parameter in the code identifying what's to be printed. A Hewlett-Packard printer requires a different command than a generic PRINTLN, as does an Apple Computer, and so forth. The driver accepts generic software commands and converts them into the specific commands the device uses.

Summary

At the beginning of this hour, we noted it's helpful to know a bit (or byte) about the computer to understand certain aspects about computer networks. This hour was written to assist you in doing just that.

If you don't have a general understanding of how a computer works, what the parts of a computer are, or what an operating system is, you can still build your own network. After all, for small networks, vendor products are often "plug and play." Nonetheless, if you've grasped the concepts presented in this hour, you'll make networking your systems a much easier task. Okay? Let's see how you did.

Q&A

Q. *Which of these components consist principally of software: CPU, OS, device drivers, Windows, RAM, ROM, disk, UNIX, memory, applications, Vista?*

A. OS, device drivers, Windows, UNIX, applications, and Vista consist primarily of software.

Q. *What is the purpose of cache?*

A. Cache provides for a higher-speed memory to reduce the speed differences between the CPU and main memory. Remember, cache is placed closer to the CPU than the memory modules, which reduces the time of the data to "travel" back and forth between these components.

Q. *Which computer component connects internal components, such as memory, as well as external components, such as printers?*

A. It's the mother of all boards: the motherboard!

Q. *Which of these computer components likely has an Ethernet address associated with it: CPU, cache, network interface card (NIC), device driver, OS?*

A. The network interface card (NIC) likely has this. The very name of this component should have given you a hint. After all, we've learned that Ethernet is a networking standard.

Q. *Fill in the blank: If hardware is the body of a computer, _____ is the brain.*

A. If hardware is the body of a computer, **the operating system** is the brain.

HOUR 5

Network Concepts

What You'll Learn in This Hour:

▶ Principal hardware and software elements of a network

▶ The need for speed in computer networks

▶ Network hardware: routers (switches, bridges, hubs), servers

▶ Network software: server operating systems

▶ Media options for the communications link

For the past four hours, we have examined the basic components of computers and how these components relate to networking. This hour expands this information and explains networking hardware and software in more depth. Some of the topics covered here were introduced earlier. For this hour, we take a closer look at them. The preceding discussions viewed them as standalone ingredients to the networking recipe. Now we mix them up a bit and discover how they interact to provide a coherent service to users. By necessity and because of their scope, we will parcel the subject of networking software into more than one hour. The latter part of this hour is an introduction to Server Operating Systems (SOS). In Part IV, "Network Operating Systems," we return to SOS with more details.

Elements of a Network

A computer, such as a PC with special software, could fulfill the roles of the hardware and software described in this hour. However, the computer's hardware and software have been designed to support an all-purpose computing environment. Thus, the conventional computer is a "generalist": It performs generic services well but is not tailored for specific tasks, such as data communications networking. To illustrate this idea, we examine two key pieces of networking hardware: the router and the server.

We follow this discussion with an examination of a key component of networking software: server operating systems. We preface these topics with a discussion about the speeds of computer networks.

The Need for Speed

We learned in Hour 1, "An Overview of Networking," that the term "speed" refers to how quickly a packet's contents are sent to a receiver. This time depends on how long it takes network machines to process a packet, such as receiving a packet from a communications link, examining its destination address, and forwarding it to another link. For our analysis here, speed does not mean the time it takes a packet to travel over the links. Traveling time, or propagation delay, is an aspect of speed governed by the laws of physics.

Whatever the definition of speed may be, users want "fast" networks. They want a quick response to their request for a new page during a Web session; they want quick turnaround to their request for a file transfer. Even if their electronic pen pal takes a while to key in a text message, they want an instant display of their partner's happenstance input.

Thus, in addition to a computer network's requirement to deliver accurate information to an end user, it must deliver this information in a timely manner. This task is no small feat. Consider the Internet, for example. It processes billions of packets 24/7, provides an average delay through the Internet of less than one-fourth of a second, and loses only about 2–3% of those billions of packets. And, don't forget: Software in your computer ensures the lost packets (if needed) are re-sent. It's an extraordinary service that most of us take for granted.

Speed Factors

Two factors contribute to speed...or the lack thereof: (a) delays in processing traffic in hardware and (b) delays in processing traffic in software. That stated, regardless of the efficiency and speed of hardware and software, ultimately they are slaves to the amount of data they must process in a given time.

For example, during certain times of the day, more users are logged on to a network than at other times, which, of course generates more traffic (packets) for the hardware and software to process. If the hardware and software cannot process each packet as it arrives, the data is placed into a queue in memory or on disk to await the availability of resources. The idea is the same as our waiting in line at a movie theater to purchase a ticket. We stay in this queue until the ticket seller can wait on us. If a lot of customers arrived before we did and are waiting in line ahead of us, we experience a delay in buying our tickets. Like data packets obtaining service from the CPU, we experience a longer response time obtaining service from the ticket seller.

This explanation also explains why you might experience longer response times when connected to a data network. There are more users logged on; they are generating more traffic; the queues are bigger. It's almost that simple. The other factor is the blend of traffic being processed by the network. If many video and voice users are active, the network must process considerably more packets, because voice and video applications require more bandwidth (in bits per second) than email and text messaging.

Hardware and software speed can be measured in several ways—some performed on paper, others performed in a lab. The best tests measure real-world performance, or how data is processed in an existent situation. Fortunately for you, by the time you have made decisions about the hardware and software components of your network, your vendors have already expended many hours in the design and testing of their products—all with the goal of providing fast processing to minimize delay.

Hardware Considerations

Unless your specialty is network performance, you're usually exempt from the need to perform tests on hardware speeds. That being the situation, what should you be aware of? What aspects of hardware performance might be a valid concern? If you have concerns, check your vendors' performances on the following components:

- ▶ Capacity of CPU(s) (measured in clock rate, bits or floating point operations per second [FLOPS], or for networking, the number of packets processed per second)
- ▶ Amount of memory and its access performance (latency to fetch data from and send data to memory locations)
- ▶ Efficiency and speed of cache (latency to fetch data from and send data to the CPU)
- ▶ Amount of disk and time to access and transfer data into and out of the computer
- ▶ Network cards' capacity in speed and buffering capabilities

Software Considerations

Likewise, given that you will usually be exempt from the need to perform tests on software efficiency, what should you be aware of? At the risk of oversimplification, other than purchasing a better-performing product, it's likely an ill-performing piece of software will be beyond most remedial actions available to you. But some options are usually available in most software vendors' products.

One option is increasing the amount of memory available to the program. This change can yield two benefits, both contributing to better performance. First, the program's code might not have to be traded in and out of computer memory to and from disk. With limited memory, the operating system might be forced into *paging* operations: moving software modules to and from disk, a situation that can lead to poor performance. Second, for some software programs, the space for their queues is increased, thus allowing the software to better service its traffic load.

Talk to Your Vendors

For hardware and software performance issues, the best approach is to talk to your vendors. It is in their interests to keep you happy. But this dialogue is usually not just a matter of the vendor maintaining a relationship with a specific customer. The vendor wants to solve the problem unto itself. Plus, and a very big plus, the vendor has in place sophisticated procedures to assist you in assessing the "speed" of your network. You're paying for the product; make the best of your contract.

Notwithstanding these caveats, many networking hardware and software components provide users with diagnostic capabilities, which are available to you. In Part IV, we delve into this topic in more detail.

For the remainder of this hour, we turn our attention to several key hardware and software elements found in many data communications networks. First, we examine two hardware components: the router and the server. Next, we highlight server operating systems, with the emphasis on Microsoft Windows Server, UNIX and Linux, and Novell NetWare. The balance of this hour concludes with an introduction to commonly used media, such as copper wire and optic fibers.

Router

A router is a specialized hardware device with a tailored operating system—all designed to relay (route) packets between nodes in a data network. Although the term "data" is used in the previous sentence, routers routinely process packets containing voice, video, photos, and music. All user traffic has been encoded into binary images of 1s and 0s. Thus, the router does not care about the specific nature of the traffic. Nonetheless, network managers have tools to place priority parameters in the packet header to inform a router it is to treat certain packets, such as time-sensitive voice traffic, with a higher priority than, say, a file transfer.

Figure 1.3 in Hour 1 is an example of a simple router situation: one connecting two small home networks to the Internet to "low-end" routers. These routers usually support only a few Ethernet interfaces and a limited number of wireless devices. In contrast, the routers deployed in enterprises, such as banks and retail stores, are much more powerful. These "high-end" machines contain multiple processors and specialized hardware called application-specific integrated circuits (ASICs). As suggested by the name, these ICs are tailored to perform specialized tasks. For a router, they assist in the tasks of (a) finding a route to a destination and (b) forwarding the packets based on this route discovery. Regardless of the possible use of ASICs, all routers engage in their most important jobs: routing and forwarding.

Routing

Routing, or more accurately, route discovery, involves the building in router memory of a routing table or routing information base (RIB). This table provides the same service as a road map. A road map shows where (which road) to drive a vehicle to the *next* city toward a final destination city. Likewise, the routing table shows where (which communications link) to forward traffic (packets) to the *next* node toward a final destination computer. Entries in the routing table are created by a process called route advertising, shown in Figure 5.1.

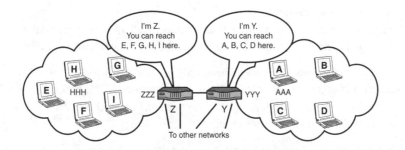

FIGURE 5.1
Route advertising to create the routing table

For simplicity, we examine the Internet Protocol (IP) and Media Access Control (MAC) addresses of four nodes with these abbreviated symbolic values. Recall from Hour 3, "Getting Data from Here to There: How Networking Works," that the IP address is 32 bits long and the MAC address is 48 bits long.

▶ Node A has an IP address of A and a MAC address of AAA.

▶ Node Y has an IP address of Y and a MAC address of YYY.

▶ Node Z has an IP address of Z and a MAC address of ZZZ.

▶ Node H has an IP address of H and a MAC address of HHH.

The router with address Y knows about nodes A–D because these machines are attached to a local area network (LAN) interface on this router. When you turn on your computer, one of the initial operations performed by its software is the sending of packets to a locally attached router to inform the router your computer is up and running and to furnish the router with the IP address of your PC. Let's assume it is IP address A. Likewise, the router informs your PC about its IP address. Additionally, the router and PC exchange their Ethernet MAC addresses. Shortly we will see why.

Another initiation operation takes place at router Y. It must inform all directly attached devices, such as computers, servers, and other routers, about its active presence (it's turned on!) and about its IP address Y. This convention is appropriately called a "Hello" in the industry.

Next, router Y is obligated to advertise IP address A to other networks' routers to which it is directly attached by a communications link.

In this example, it informs router Z the node with address A can be reached at address Y. The receiving router (Z) stores this information in a routing table. Router Z also stores which communications line (which physical port) can be used to reach A. After all, a high-end router might have scores of communications links in operation to other networks, as seen in Figure 5.1. Router Z must know the specific link to use to send packets to A.

Router Z then relays this advertisement to all the networks to which it is attached, but it changes the advertisement slightly. It informs its neighbor networks and the attached computers that address A is reachable through router Z and not router Y.

Notice this elegant subtlety. By advertising only the *next* network that can reach node A, nonadjacent networks are "hidden" from other networks. All that the router and nodes care about is the next hop toward a destination. This technique simplifies routing and provides a bit of privacy as well.

In a few milliseconds, the advertisement about A from router Y reaches router Z, which informs the nodes "behind it" about the ability to reach node A, through node Z. These computers store this information in their own routing tables.

In a matter of seconds (usually fractions of a second) the address of your computer is made known, at least conceptually, to any computer in the world. I say conceptually because security and privacy policies—as well as matters of efficiency—curtail how this advertisement is promulgated. Nonetheless, the basic operation is not much more complex than this explanation.

Forwarding

After the entry for the routing table has been created, the following operations take place. Please refer to Figure 5.2 during this discussion. Computer H wants to send data to computer A. Courtesy of route discovery, computer H has enough information in its routing table to know node A can be reached through node Z. It forms an IP packet with the packet header containing the following:

> Source IP address = H

> Destination IP address = A

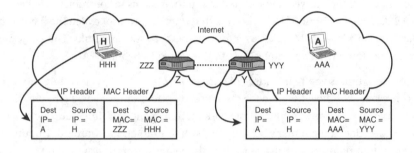

FIGURE 5.2
Forwarding operations

However, recall from Hour 3 that Layer 2 Ethernets (LANs) do not process Layer 3 IP addresses. Therefore, computer H must also place the MAC address of router Z in the Ethernet header's destination address field. Let's say it's ZZZ, even though we know it's really a 48-bit value. It also puts its own MAC address in the sending part of the Ethernet address. Let's say it's HHH. Thus, the Ethernet frame contains the following:

> Source MAC address: HHH

> Destination MAC address: ZZZ

We examine what happens between the routers in a later hour. For now, let's look at the receiving site. The MAC addresses in the Ethernet frame going from router Y to node A have changed. They are

> Source MAC address: YYY

> Destination MAC address: AAA

However, the IP addresses *have not changed*. They remain

> Source IP address = H

> Destination IP address = A

What's happened here? Look again. The MAC addresses have only local significance. They are not transported through the wide area network (WAN, or in this situation, the Internet). In contrast, the IP addresses have end-to-end significance. We see once again why Ethernet is thought of as a LAN. It isn't just because of some of its technical underpinnings, but its address structure as well.

The communications links between routers Y and Z are not configured with Ethernet, because for this analysis, we assume it is a wide area connection. So what happens to Ethernet? The sending router strips it away for a wide area transport, and the receiving router reconstitutes it at the other end with the relevant local MAC addresses. That's fine, but you could reasonably ask: What replaces Ethernet between the wide area routers? If the answer is nothing, this situation seems to contradict the OSI model discussed in Hour 3. The answer is that another protocol called the Asynchronous Transfer Mode (ATM) takes over for Ethernet for wide area links. This subject is covered in Hour 6, "Extending LANs with Wide Area Networks (WANs)."

Fortunately, unless you're in charge of a large private network, you will not have to be concerned with how these addresses are set up and maintained by a router. However, enterprise networks and their network management personnel must have a keen knowledge of the router's behavior in both routing and forwarding. Hundreds of configuration parameters must be fed into the router's operating system (OS) for the machine to go about its tasks correctly.

Other Functions of Routers

In addition to the important tasks just explained, high-end routers provide extensive support for network integrity management, traffic management, and security management, which are subjects for subsequent hours. We now turn our attention to another specialized machine—the server—and the framework by which the server operates: the client/server model.

By the Way

Switches, Bridges, and Hubs Perform "Forwarding" Operations

The router is one of several machines designed to relay traffic through networks. You might come across the terms switch, bridge, and hub. These devices also relay packets and interconnect servers and other computers. In the 1990s, the terms router, switch, bridge, and hub could be defined to identify a specific kind of hardware and its associated software. That's not so today. For example, a router can perform the functions of a so-called ATM switch, a MAC bridge, or a wiring hub. Don't be concerned with these terms unto themselves. As long as you know what they can or cannot do, the names associated with them are not all that important.

The Client/Server Model

In the early days of computer networks—back in the 1960s—most machines connected to a computer were quite limited in their capacity. They were called "dumb" terminals for good reason. They had no CPU; no memory; no disk. They depended on a large "mainframe" computer, often with an associated "terminal controller" to provide services. A terminal user keyed in a response for data, mail, and so on and received the response from a centralized mainframe.

As computers found their way into many companies in the 1970s, and as personal computers found their way into most homes in the 1980s, the mainframe's job of servicing perhaps thousands of attached computers created bottleneck and performance problems. And, after all, it made no sense to keep the now highly capable personal computers from doing more of the computing.

However, the complete distribution of all work to each computer—including responsibility for the integrity of a company's data (accounts receivable files, for example)—was viewed as too risky. As private industry migrated to electronic data and computer-based information, the industry came up with a compromise: Off-load some of the computing responsibilities to the distributed computers, but not all of them. Give freedom to the users of the computer network, but not unfettered freedom. What evolved from this situation was the client/server model, now used in many networking environments.

If you use the Web or email, your machine has client software providing this service. For example, when you click on a web page icon, your client program requests a service from a server program, located in another computer in a network. Usually, the server software fulfills the request and returns the response. The same type of operation takes place with a request to transfer funds from your bank account, or sending an email, and so on.

The client/server model provides a convenient method to place functions in distributed computers in one or many networks. The server doesn't expend resources until it's asked to do so. In addition, in many companies, all critical data and software are stored on servers, which translates to better security and control over a vital resource.

Client/server systems aren't immune from problems. Because the server (or groups of servers, called server farms) must process all clients' requests, the system is subject to bottlenecks during periods of high activity. Another approach, called peer-to-peer networking, avoids this problem by distributing the workload among multiple machines. Although this avoids bottlenecks, updating files—keeping them synchronized in a nanosecond environment—isn't trivial. Anyway, our focus here is on servers that operate with the client/server model.

Server

A server can perform a variety of operations, depending on the specific vendor product and the software loaded on the machine. Some products are specialized to perform one or few functions. For example, a network time server's only job is to provide the network with an accurate clock. At the other end of the service spectrum, some servers provide a wide set of operations, such as hosting user applications; providing mail services; supporting telephony applications, such as voice over IP (VoIP) and PBX operations; providing directories that translate between an email name and its associated address; providing authentication and security services; managing user groups; providing backup and recovery for software and data files; offering web services; and managing printer pools.

RAID

One of the most important jobs of servers in enterprises is the caring of the company's automated resources: its data and software. Most servers execute software to manage your databases. That's good news. It's even better news if you actually use the software. It does no good if you don't take the time and effort to back up your data. Mark these words: Sooner or later, if you don't take measures to protect your data, you'll lose some or all of it. To that end, let's examine an operation called *redundant arrays of inexpensive disks*, or RAID.

RAID operates using a variety of methods commonly referred to as "levels" of 0, 1, 5, and 6.

RAID 0

RAID 0 is best described as several hard drives connected to a computer with no redundancy. The purpose of RAID 0 is to increase throughput and response time. If data is spread over several drives, it can be read from and written to the drive more rapidly. However, multiple copies of data don't exist. If the data is corrupted, it's lost.

RAID 1

RAID 1 performs disk mirroring or duplexing. In disk mirroring, two small computer system interface (SCSI) drives of the same size connect to the RAID controller card, but OS sees them as one drive. For example, in a RAID 1 configuration, if you connect two 40-gigabyte (GB) drives to the computer, the computer sees only 40GB of disk space rather than 80GB. This happens because the RAID controller arranges the disks so that all data is written identically to both disks. In a RAID 1 configuration, one drive can fail and the other drive can continue working; the users never know that a drive has failed. In some systems, it's possible to connect each drive to a separate SCSI controller so that there's no single point of failure; either disk or either controller in a mirrored set can break, and no data or function will be lost.

RAID 5

RAID 5 requires a minimum of three disks of equal capacity (compared to RAID 1, which requires two disks), but the net improvement is worth the cost. In a RAID 5 configuration, all data is spread across multiple disks in a process called striping, which is the operation by which a RAID drive controller card writes data across multiple disks. Additionally, information about the file called parity data is saved on all three disks. Thus, a single drive in a RAID 5 set can fail, and the parity data on the other two drives can be used to reconstruct the data on the failed drive.

RAID 5 offers another advantage: raw speed. Because any given file is divided into smaller pieces and stored on multiple disks, any time a user requests a file from the server, three disks read it simultaneously. This means that the file is read in to memory and out to the network more rapidly, which keeps your users happy.

RAID 6

RAID 6 provides backup and recovery from two drive failures. This feature is important for large-capacity systems because the amount of disk space increases the time to recover from the failure of a single drive. RAID 6 is the latest RAID version and is sometimes called Advanced Data Guarding (ADG).

RAID controller capabilities vary widely. Some require a lot of human interaction for configuration operations, and some (such as HP's AutoRAID units) can largely manage themselves after being given some basic parameters. HP's product can be set up in a few minutes.

Vendors' products might offer variations of RAID levels 0, 1, and 5. If you become involved with this aspect of networking, ask your prospective vendors about RAID level 0+1 and 5+1. RAID 6 might be your preference if you have a very large file system and are concerned about the time taken to perform backup and recovery. They are beyond our general descriptions, but keep this idea in mind for future reference.

High Availability and Fault Tolerance

Redundant RAID systems operate without interruption when one or more disks fail. If a corrupted disk is replaced, the data on the new device is rebuilt while the system continues to operate normally. Some RAID systems must be shut down when changing a disk; others allow drives to be replaced while the system is up and running, a technique called hot swapping.

Hot swapping is important in applications needing continuous availability. The air traffic control system comes to mind. Your network might not need RAID or hot swapping, but you should know enough about the nature of your automated resources to make an informed opinion. Also, be aware that RAID will take care of some of your data backup problems, but not all of them. It's conceivable that the redundant data could be lost. On the TV program *24*, Jack Bauer and his associates regularly blow up entire computer installations.

Jokes aside, many companies archive their data to remote sites, even storing the data files and supporting computers in secure air-conditioned vaults. Even more, some companies have adopted two programs to ensure their customers and users are never (almost never) denied service of the servers. They revolve around *high availability* and *fault tolerance.*

Some computer servers run applications so critical that downtime is not an option. Examples of such systems include 911 systems, banking systems, and the air traffic control systems cited earlier. These systems must be operational around the clock; when they aren't, bad things happen.

But everyone knows that computers malfunction. So how do network and systems administrators get around the inevitability of computer failure? The answers are fault tolerance and high availability. These two terms refer to two methods to ensure that systems can stay online and active in the face of hardware and sometimes software failures.

With fault tolerance, every component is duplexed; there is two of each device. If one component fails, the other piece of hardware picks up the load and ensures users don't see downtime. Fault-tolerant systems command a premium price, which many critical-system customers are willing to pay for their peace of mind and satisfied customers.

High availability, also called clustering, is an arrangement using several computers to ensure an application never shuts down because a computer fails. In this cluster, typically two or more computers are connected to a shared disk. At any point, one of the computers is running an application stored on the shared disk. If the computer running the application fails, control of the shared disk passes to another computer, which starts the application so that users can continue to work. Unlike fault-tolerant systems, highly available systems don't run continuously through component failure. A highly available system shows a brief interruption in service and then continues.

Neither fault tolerance nor high availability is better than the other. Both are useful, and their proper use depends on the criteria brought to the network design. We'll discuss network design later in this book, including how to define the criteria for building a network.

Server Operating Systems

Just as network clients must have operating systems loaded for the client machines to function, a network server must have an operating system. (Refer to Hour 4, "Computer Concepts," for explanations of prevalent client OSs.) The chief differences between desktop operating systems and Server Operating Systems (SOS) are, not surprisingly, scale and resources.

Typically, SOSs are optimized differently than desktop operating systems. A desktop operating system is designed to provide the user at this desktop workstation with the best possible performance for the application currently being used. By contrast, an SOS's charge is to balance the needs of all users accessing the server rather than giving priority to any one of them.

Prominent features of SOSs are

▶ Support port interfaces for Ethernet and other protocols

▶ Manage traffic coming into and out of the machine

▶ Provide authentication, authorization, and logon filters

▶ Furnish name and directory services

▶ Support file, print, web services, and backup mechanisms for data (fault tolerance systems discussed earlier)

Be aware that an SOS is not the same as an OS, such as DOS, Windows XP, and Vista. The SOS is a more specialized piece of software. Certainly, Windows and other OSs offer some of the support features of an SOS, but not to the extent of those offered by the SOS. Also, some literature and vendors use the terms Network Operating System (NOS) and SOS to describe the same software. Others use NOS to describe yet another specialized OS: one concerning itself even more with the management of LAN and WAN traffic. An example is Cisco's Internet Operating System (IOS), which runs in Cisco routers. From the view of the OSI seven-layer model, the focus of an SOS is on the upper layers, whereas an IOS is concerned with the lower layers—especially Layer 3, where routing and forwarding operations take place. As one example, an IOS creates routing tables; a SOS does not. In the following sections, we will examine prominent SOSs.

Novell NetWare

Novell NetWare is the oldest PC-based product in the SOS category. In the early 1980s, Novell (founded and led by Raymond Noorda) led the charge into personal-computer networking. NetWare is a rich and complex product. In contrast with other, newer SOSs such as Microsoft Windows XP, NetWare is less intuitive.

In the file, print, and directory services arena, NetWare is a formidable performer, offering a full suite of file, print, and web services. Novell has also made forays into the Linux arena, an important move discussed shortly.

NetWare was not designed with the Internet in mind. A great many of the design choices Novell made appear to have been an attempt to simplify networking enough to make it palatable for PC users. In the first place, Novell did not build native support for Transmission Control Protocol/Internet Protocol (TCP/IP), the basic protocols computers use to communicate across the Internet. Novell had good reason for this approach: When NetWare was developed, TCP/IP was a relatively new and immature protocol standard; it required manual configuration, and maintaining it was difficult.

Given the complexity of TCP/IP and the technical skills of its target market group, Novell decided to develop a simpler protocol. Novell's proprietary network protocol is called Internetworking Packet Exchange/Sequenced Packet Exchange (IPX/SPX); in many ways, it was ideal for PC networking. IPX was and is largely self-configuring, easy to install, and simple to maintain.

As the Internet revolution picked up steam (and TCP/IP with it), Novell's position suffered some because the original NetWare was founded on IPX networking. However, current versions of NetWare natively use IP, and this has helped NetWare's popularity. Logically enough, as stated in Hour 3, NetWare's IPX user base is diminishing as customers migrate to NetWare's use of IP.

The NetWare product has been superseded by the Open Enterprise Server (OES). This system provides all the services of a typical SOS, and it can run over either Linux or a NetWare core platform. It appears the NetWare community might migrate to Linux, but as of this writing, it's too soon to read these tea leaves. Presently, NetWare has a large customer base, and Novell is unlikely to do anything to alienate this population. There's good reason for NetWare's popularity: It's a fine product.

Microsoft Windows Server 2003

Beginning in the late 1980s, Microsoft decided it needed a high-end SOS to compete with NetWare and UNIX. After a three-to-four year struggle (described in Pascal Zachary's book *Showstopper*), Microsoft had what it had set out to create: Windows NT.

Initially, Windows NT version 3.1 (the first version, but renumbered to match the existing version of 16- bit Windows) was all one product; there was initially little differentiation between versions used for servers and versions used for workstations.

By the time Microsoft released Windows NT 3.5 in 1995, Microsoft had created two versions of the operating system: Windows NT Workstation and Windows NT Server.

To date, these products have evolved into Windows XP Professional for the workstation market and Windows Server 2003 for the server market. Both operating systems are built on the same platform, but Microsoft's Server products have a rich set of utilities and tools that the Workstation product lacks. The ability to connect a variety of networks was built into Windows XP from the start. Additionally, Windows Server 2003 can handle the server portion of network application work, which makes it an ideal application server platform. It uses the familiar Windows interface that simplifies administration. Windows XP is well suited to small organizations because of its point-and-click features.

For the majority of beginning networkers, Windows Server 2003 is likely the easiest enterprise-class network OS to install and maintain. Do not construe that statement to mean that Windows SOS is simple; it isn't. But compared to other SOSs, Windows Server 2003 has a certain amount of familiarity because it uses the ubiquitous Windows interface.

Microsoft Windows Server 2008

Microsoft intends Windows Server 2008 to eventually replace its 2003 platform. It combines the features of Windows Server 2003 (Release 2) and Microsoft's new OS, Vista. It is a complex and rich SOS, and newcomers will find the learning curve steep, but worth the effort. It has many enhanced features relative to Server 2003, including increased security measures, task scheduling, firewalls, and wireless networking. Also, its diagnostics are quite good. Microsoft has made further progress with Server 2008 by fully adapting the Internet standards, notably TCP/IP, Dynamic Host Configuration Protocol (DHCP), and Domain Name System (DNS).

For both Windows Server 2003 and 2008, your network should have an experienced system administrator to handle the management of this software. Its complexity makes it unsuitable for the casual user or part-time system administrator, but in the hands of a knowledgeable system administrator, Microsoft's SOSs are quite effective.

UNIX

As mentioned in Hour 4, UNIX was developed at AT&T's Bell Labs. UNIX is a preemptive SOS with a rich user interface. However, with this richness comes a degree of complexity. UNIX can accomplish many tasks with ease and efficiency, but the initial complexity of the user interface led to UNIX being tagged as "user unfriendly."

As with Windows server products, UNIX can operate as either a client or a server on a network. For the most part, there's little difference between a client UNIX system and a server UNIX system except for the power of the hardware—the server should be more powerful than the workstation—and the tightness of the security. UNIX comes with such a rich feature set that it seldom needs third-party software to administer its users.

UNIX is designed for a multitasking, multiuser environment. It provides a large inventory of software tools to complement its OS. In spite of an undeserved reputation for difficulty (at least for professional programmers), UNIX provides fast file and print server operations.

The UNIX operating system consists of many software modules and a master program, the *kernel*. The kernel starts and stops programs and handles the file and printer systems. The kernel also plays the key role in scheduling access to a hardware component to avoid a potential conflict between contending programs.

Because of its age, UNIX is a stable platform. However, it isn't produced by a single vendor; instead, a host of vendors purvey UNIX, and each version is slightly different. As a result, there's a lack of shrink-wrapped applications or applications ready to install right out of the shrink-wrapped box. In recent years, UNIX vendors have attempted to create a standard for it. This effort has met with only limited success because several versions of UNIX are supported by various vendors and standards groups.

UNIX is best suited to networks in which an experienced system administrator is in charge. Its complexity makes it unsuitable for the casual user or part-time system administrator, but in the hands of a knowledgeable system administrator, UNIX can accomplish its tasks reliably and fast.

Linux

In the late 1980s and early 1990s, UNIX became a dominant force in the computer industry. However, the cost of UNIX was beyond many individuals' budgets and usually restricted it to running only on company machines. The few UNIX-like operating systems of reasonable cost (such as Minix, an operating system designed by a Dutch professor for teaching purposes) were judged inadequate by the user community.

In 1991, Linus Torvalds created a new UNIX-like operating system that he fancifully called Linux. The fledgling operating system was rapidly adopted by the Internet community, which extended Linus's creation.

Linux operates on a variety of computer hardware, including desktops, large mainframe computers, mobile phones, routers, E-books, and video game systems, such as PlayStation. TiVo also uses Linux.

Linux is inexpensive, it's open source (that is, when you buy the programs, you also get the source code and the rights to modify and rebuild, or recompile the programs to make them do what you want), and it's supported by a cast of an untold number of programmers who voluntarily contribute their ideas and time. In addition, Linux Users Groups (LUGs) are located in many cities to promote the use of the operating system. These groups provide training, demonstrations, and technical support to new users. Chat rooms and newsgroups are also part of the Linux community.

Where possible, Linux adheres to International Organization for Standardization (ISO), Institute of Electronic and Electrical Engineers (IEEE), and American National Standards Institute (ANSI) standards. It also has all the tools that UNIX does: shell scripts, C, C++, Java, Expect, Perl, and Eiffel. From a networking perspective, Linux has tools to hook up to most prevalent networks. It can network using TCP/IP. It can use SMB (server message block) and act like a Windows server. It can run IPX and act like a NetWare server. Linux is arguably the most popular web- and mail-server platform on the Internet, in large part because it is inexpensive and open.

As mentioned, Linux is not a proprietary product available from just one vendor. It's typically available in distributions from vendors who package the software and source code with some of their own improvements. Often, software compiled on one distribution of Linux can run on another without porting, or working on the source code to ensure compatibility. Even if it doesn't, Linux's software development tools are second to none, and debugging problems is relatively straightforward.

To gain a sense of the impact and value of Linux, consider these statistics, taken from several websites: A study of Red Hat's Linux 7.1 estimates that if this OS (with 30 million lines of source code) had been developed by the conventional vendor proprietary methods, roughly 8,000 man-hours would have been expended at a cost of about $1 billion (in 2000 dollars). This study reflects a conservative estimate. Other studies claim bigger Linux OSs, under conventional developments, would have cost $6 or 7 billion! Software developers don't come cheaply, and having *free* input from thousands of programmers gives Linux notable leverage in the server OS marketplace.

For the story of the development and rise of Linux, read *Just for Fun: The Story of an Accidental Revolutionary* by Linus Torvalds and David Diamond. It's Torvalds's first-person perspective and is a quick and entertaining read.

That's it for now for SOSs. We've touched the surface of their capabilities and operations, but we've not explained how to use them and how to get the best performance out of them. We'll do just that in Hours 16 and 17.

Media

For the installation of your network, you might be able to determine the media to be used to transport your traffic. The word "might" is noted, because some network products and protocols require a specific media. For example, switched Ethernet stipulates the use of copper wire or optic fiber. Although an enterprising engineer could install, say, coaxial cable, instead of twisted copper pairs in a LAN, it would not be a good idea to do so. First, the physical layer of the OSI model would have to be redone, entailing hardware changes. Second, the line drivers would have to be rewritten. Third, the data link layer, while remaining mostly intact, would still need some changes.

On the other hand, you often have a choice about the quality (and cost) of the media. Shop around; look for a good buy, but don't compromise quality for a few dollars saved. The difference in price between high-quality and lower-quality wire is small, and you might save yourself some headaches later by paying a bit more up front.

I grant that spending a few cents more per meter of cable can translate into a big budget item if an enterprise is pulling cable through a new skyscraper. Still, be careful about pulling low-quality cable. Keep in mind the old saw, "Penny-wise, pound-foolish."

Copper Wire

Under most conditions, your decisions on media will focus on the category of copper wire that will be installed for your network. Twisted-pair[1] wiring comes in several levels, ranging from Level 1 (or Category 1), formerly used for older telephone applications, to Level 6 (or Category 6), which is certified for data transmission up to 350 megabits per second (Mbps).

Twisted-pair cables are explained in more detail shortly.

Before we examine these categories, let's take a brief detour to discuss a LAN technology you will likely come across: 10BASE-T. (We cover variations of this technology in Hour 11, "Selecting Network Hardware and Software.") This term is constructed as follows:

- ▶ **10**—Speed in Mbps

- ▶ **BASE**—Uses a baseband signaling technique (binary, digital images)

- ▶ **T**—Uses twisted-pair cable for the media

---

[1] The wire is twisted to enhance the quality of the electrical signals.

Many Ethernet products are based on the 10BASE-T technology. Others use optical fiber. Again, in Hour 11, we examine other Ethernets. For now, let's examine the twisted-pair categories:

- ▶ **Category 1** is not rated for performance and is no longer rated by the standards groups. Previously, it was used for telephone systems and doorbells.

- ▶ **Category 2** is also no longer rated by the standards groups. In the past, it was used on token-ring LANs.

- ▶ **Category 3** is the lowest level that can be used for networking. It's used for Ethernet 10BASE-T and has a maximum data rate of 16Mbps. Although Category 3 is rated for 10BASE-T, Category 5 is now much more common because it supports both 10BASE-T and faster speeds such as 100BASE-T.

- ▶ **Category 4** is used for 16Mbps token-ring and Ethernet 10BASE-T networks. Its maximum data rate is 20Mbps.

- ▶ **Category 5 (and 5e)** is used for Ethernet 100BASE-T and has a maximum data rate of 155Mbps. This is currently the most common cable. In fact, many companies are wiring everything in their offices (both phone and data) with Category 5 cable because it can be used for everything from basic two-wire phone services to ATM.

- ▶ **Category 6** is used for Ethernet 1000BASE-T (gigabit Ethernet). It's rated for 350Mbps over 4-pair unshielded twisted-pair wire. And Category 6a, a relative newcomer, is suitable for 10GBASE-T Ethernets.

To maintain the maximum data rate, you must string and terminate the wires according to the Electronics Industries Association (EIA) 568B standards. If the wires are not correctly installed, their potential data rate can be jeopardized. Generally, the vendors provide guidance about the installation of their products, such as recommended distances for a wire span. Their specifications error on the side of caution. Follow their guidelines, and you'll be well within the EIA standards.

Install the Best Cable

If you're building a copper-wire–based network, it doesn't make sense to install cable less than Category 5 because installing Category 5 wire can extend the life of your media. Category 5 standards specify the wires in twisted-pair cabling maintain their twist within one-half inch of the final termination point. Category 5 also has strict standards for the radius of bends in Category 5 wire and other stipulations leading to enhanced performance.

Optical Fiber

Because of the huge success of switched Ethernet and its use of copper wire, it's unlikely you'll be faced with installing, using, or maintaining optical fiber cable. Exceptions to this last statement might apply to some of your nonnetworking activities. You might be tasked with assembling your optical cable Christmas tree, or your children might be tossing around Frisbees illuminated with fiber optics. But these optical products come in shrink-wrapped boxes and require none of your networking expertise for their use.

Jokes aside, optical fiber has replaced most of the wire-based media in "core" networks around the world, such as the telephone networks. Moreover, you might want to consider using fiber optics if you need very secure communications links for your network or you need extraordinarily high data rates—well beyond the Gbps rates quoted earlier.

For security, the light images carrying pulses of 1s and 0s are contained within the cable. Unlike electromagnetic signals, this media releases no stray energy. Thus, the optical cable is not subject to snoopers detecting "residual intelligence" emanating from the cable. It's generally accepted that an optic fiber cable can be tapped without detection, but this discussion assumes you aren't into the spy business. In any case, Hour 20, "Security," will explain how you can secure your transmissions.

For capacity, it's likely that your LAN will perform just fine with standard Ethernet hardware and software. To transport your data through an internet or the Internet, most of the links operate in the gigabit range, using optical fibers. For example, in Hour 6, we examine the Synchronous Optical Network (SONET) technology, which can provide an optical link operating at 389,813.12Mbps. What's more, systems are coming out of the lab that transmit at 14 terabits per second (Tbps). Consulting Figure 4.1 in Hour 4, in visual terms, this is 14,000,000,000,000 bits per second; a capacity (eventually?) needed for core networks, but certainly not for LANs and other enterprise systems.

Therefore, aside from those optical Christmas trees and Frisbees, it's likely you will not have to become proficient with this technology.

Coaxial Cable

We can make the same claim with coaxial cable. Other than its presence in the cable TV network, it has ceased to be much of a factor in networks in general, and data networks specifically. I used to deal with coaxial cable when the original Ethernet specification stipulated its use. No longer. Now it's copper wire.

Wireless Media

Unlike coaxial cable, a network manager should be versed in wireless media technologies—if not the wide area cellular system, then certainly the more localized Bluetooth and Wi-Fi standards and products. In many offices and homes, they offer attractive alternatives to copper wire. We will touch on Bluetooth and Wi-Fi with an introduction, and provide more details in Hour 7, "Mobile Wireless Networking."

Bluetooth

Bluetooth is a technology whose time (to come) was long overdue. The networking industry needed Bluetooth many years ago. It offers an inexpensive, high-capacity media and low-power consumption device for short distances, without the need to pull wire around a room. In addition, Bluetooth is not a line-of-sight medium. If the devices are close enough, the radio waves will provide correct communications. Also, Bluetooth contains an extensive protocol suite, enabling devices to discover each other, as well as discover each other's attributes.

Because of these features, Bluetooth is now used in mobile phone ear sets, laptops, printers, digital cameras, video games, telephones, and many other devices.

Wi-Fi

Wi-Fi is more expensive than Bluetooth because it operates at a higher capacity, consumes more power, and covers greater distances. Some people refer to Wi-Fi as a "wireless Ethernet" because it provides many of the services of a conventional wire-based Ethernet. Wi-Fi will present you with more challenges as a network manager, but as we shall see in Hour 20, it has more features than Bluetooth.

Summary

During this hour, we learned about the main hardware and software components that make up a computer-based network. We examined routers and the important jobs they perform pertaining to route discovery and forwarding. Server operating systems were introduced, with a highlight on those that dominate the marketplace. The importance of "speed" was emphasized because of its effects on throughput and response time. The hour concluded with a survey of the most widely used media for the communications channel.

Q&A

Q. *Although the efficiency of hardware and software is key to high-speed networks that offer fast response times, these components are at the mercy of what?*

A. Regardless of the efficiency and speed of hardware and software, ultimately they are slaves to the amount of data they must process in a given time. Thus, a network with a large population of users will not experience the performance of a lightly loaded network.

Q. *Name two factors pertaining to software you might influence to improve the performance of your network.*

A. Installing more memory in your machines and increasing the queue sizes of components such as servers and routers can improve network performance.

Q. *Two of the principal responsibilities of a router are routing and forwarding. Do they provide different services? If not, contrast these two operations.*

A. They do not perform different services; rather, they provide complimentary services. Routing, or more accurately, route discovery, is the process by which the router discovers the "best" route to a destination address. Route discovery entails the building of a routing table, or a routing information base (RIB). On the other hand, forwarding entails the router examining the destination address in a packet and matching this address to an entry in the routing table to determine the next node to receive the packet as it makes its way to the final destination.

Q. *One inexpensive way to help ensure that a company's data is protected is through a technique called _____.*

A. Redundant arrays of inexpensive disks, or RAID, can do this.

Q. *List the major services provided by Server Operating Systems (SOSs).*

A. Server Operating Systems

  Support port interfaces for Ethernet and other protocols

  Manage traffic coming into and out of the machine

  Provide authentication, authorization, and logon filters

  Furnish name and directory services

  Support file, print, web services, and backup mechanisms for data

Q. *Technically speaking, your local area network (LAN) can be configured at the physical layer (L_1) with optical fiber, copper wire, coaxial cable, infrared, and wireless. Given cost and product availability, which of these media would you "lean toward" for your LAN?*

A. For Ethernets, which dominate the industry, the coaxial implementations are pretty much a thing of the past. Optical fiber is likely overkill. Infrared might be an alternative for a line-of-sight link. But for practical purposes, copper wire and wireless Ethernets will most likely serve you the best. For short distances, a wireless connection is quite attractive, except it might not provide the through-put to that of copper wire.

HOUR 6

Extending LANs with Wide Area Networks (WANs)

What You'll Learn in This Hour:

▶ The definition of a wide area network (WAN)

▶ Components of a WAN

▶ Key network interfaces

▶ Using carrier providers for the local interface: telephone (T-carrier systems and digital subscriber line, or DSL), cable, and satellite services

▶ Broadband WAN carrier systems

▶ How the Internet can help you assemble your WAN

Networks are often distributed over a wide geographical area, which may encompass too great a distance to tie them together with local area network (LAN) hardware and software. If LANs situated in remote locations need to be connected, they are interworked with a WAN. Of course, this concept assumes the WAN components are selected, assembled, and integrated properly with the LAN components, which we will begin to do in this hour.

What Is a WAN?

In previous hours, we introduced WANs and the general reasons for their existence. We now move to the details. First, most LANs' media, such as copper wire or optical fiber, are installed, owned, and operated by individuals (such as you and me) or enterprises (such as banks and grocery stores). This Open Systems Interconnection (OSI) physical layer is located in our home or a company's office. It might be situated among rooms in our home, or in between an enterprise's office buildings—a campus, for example.

However, when connecting a LAN located in one part of the country to a LAN in another locale, we (and most companies) are not allowed to pull copper wire across the country. Even if we obtained government licenses to do so, it would be far too expensive an undertaking. Indeed, the proposition is absurd. If everyone "pulled cable," millions of communications links would be laid to connect millions of LANs. Thus, like the public telephone networks, which support the connection of private telephone networks (private branch exchanges [PBXs], for example), public data networks—spread over a wide area—support the connection of private LANs and individual computers. One such public data network is the Internet, the mother of all wide area computer networks.

At this juncture, we need to emphasize the following about the public telephone networks and the public data networks. They

▶ Are now capable of transporting any image (voice, video, data, photos, and graphics)

▶ Have migrated to packet-switching technologies to carry this traffic

▶ Are blurring their former distinctions of being a "telephone" network or a "data" network

▶ Have altered their roles; an Internet service provider (ISP) might be a telephone company, such as Verizon, or a nontelephone company, such as AOL

To understand this situation, consider the conventional telephone network of some 40 years ago. AT&T and the Bell System were America's common carriers. They built the fantastic network that carried our voice and video traffic. Their systems were not designed for data, but with the invention of one of the most important machines in history, the *modem*, data could be placed onto telephone lines. (The modem is examined in Hour 8, "Remote Networking.")

The early Internet was formed by using the telephone network and adding modems and packet switches for the transport of data. As these telephone carriers evolved and as the Internet came into existence, their facilities began to look the same. As well, their roles began to merge. Nowadays, a "telephone" company, such as Verizon, does not restrict itself to telephone calls. It's both an ISP and a conventional network provider. This situation is the reason for my comment about the "blurring" of roles between the telephone systems, the data networks, and the ISPs.

Notwithstanding this migration, WANs require someone to build and install expensive communications facilities. AT&T, the reconstituted telephone regional companies, and other enterprises are in this business. They lease their wide area communications links to anyone who will pay for the rentals, such as AOL. In turn, AOL might choose to add value to the links by installing Cisco routers and Hewlett-Packard servers to create a private internet. AOL will then enter into agreements called *peering agreements* with other companies to connect their facilities into the public Internet. For example, AOL might agree to interwork with MSN by allowing their respective customers' traffic to pass across the WAN communications lines they have leased from, say, AT&T.

The result is the availability of both public and private WANs to connect our LANs or our plain old dial-up modems. One result is also the extraordinary Internet, a collage of millions of computers, thousands of ISPs, and hundreds of WAN companies. The Internet is an amazing phenomenon. Even more amazing, it works.

Here are three examples of WANs:

▶ The automated teller machines (ATM) machines scattered around a city and connected to a bank's central processing facility. For control purposes, the bank leases lines from carriers and adds its own security and applications software.

▶ An international company with installations of groupware (shared collaborative software) at its remote locations around the world. To ensure the email and groupware messages operate reliably, the company uses leased lines instead of the Internet as a backbone. Therefore, this WAN is considered a private network.

▶ An international company with installations of groupware at its remote locations around the world. It chooses to use the Internet for its WAN backbone. Therefore, this WAN is called a *virtual private network* (VPN): It appears to be a private network, but it isn't because it's using the pubic Internet.

Components of a WAN

The main task of a wide area computer network is to transfer user traffic as quickly and securely as possible. The network is unaware of the contents of the traffic because it does not interact directly with the users and user applications software. Thus, it is not concerned with user-friendly graphical user interfaces (GUIs), mail servers, or file servers. These services are provided only when the traffic arrives at the node (say, a server) where the destination application is directly connected.

The notion of removing the WAN from direct communication with the user is of great importance, because it frees the network from repetitively executing millions of lines of software code. To see why, please refer to Figure 6.1. User packets are sent directly from a computer via a dial-up connection, a LAN, or a broadband link to a machine shown here as a LAN/WAN gateway. In practice, this device is likely a conventional router located at our home, our office, or the site of our ISP. Wherever it is placed, it is called a gateway because it does indeed provide a "gateway" from the local area to a wide area (and vice versa at the other end of the path).

FIGURE 6.1
Traversing a WAN

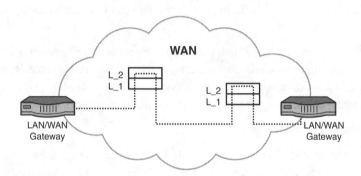

The dashed lines inside the WAN signify the packets' journey through the network. The diagrams inside the WAN labeled "L_1" and "L_2" signify the lower two layers of the OSI model that operate in the machines at the WAN nodes. As you see, only the lower two layers of the model are invoked to process user packets. With minor exceptions, the upper layers aren't executed inside the WAN for end user traffic.

Again, this design is quite significant because it keeps WANs "lean and mean." They're fast because (a) the equipment and software is optimized for speed and not user interactions; (b) the hardware nodes are connected with *very* high-speed links— orders of magnitude faster than the links you have in your home or office. The result is low delay and high throughput.

Yes, but what happens to all the wonderful services we obtain from computer networks? Where did our email windows go? Our bank account screens? Where are the text message templates? How does the WAN play our videos and our music? The answers to all these questions are the same: The data inside the packets might contain all this information, but the WAN does *not* process any of it. Its job is to ferry this data reliably and quickly to the end computer, the final mail server, the destination file manager, the receiving text messenger, and so on. At the final destination, the upper layers are finally invoked at servers and clients to provide us these services.

Thus, our email or text messages are transported transparently through the WAN only to be used at the final destination. Certainly, a WAN executes upper layer software for its own internal operations, such as network management, but it doesn't execute this code for user traffic.

An elegantly simple solution to an immensely challenging problem: transporting millions of packets through these WANs in a few milliseconds. Given the amount of data involved, the magnitude of the user base, and the requirement for very fast response times and very low delays, these operations could not be performed satisfactorily if the network nodes executed the upper layers of the model. Fortunately, the WANs have no need to examine the upper-layer headers and data.

True, but how do the WAN nodes in Figure 6.1 know how to route the traffic? After all, in Hour 3, "Getting Data from Here to There: How Networking Works," we learned that the IP addresses in the IP packet (datagram) are processed at Layer 3. We also learned the Layer 2 Ethernet addresses in the Ethernet frame are stripped away before reaching a WAN because they have only local significance. Is the WAN clairvoyant and somehow able to infer the destination address from the surrounding Ethernet ether? No. Let's place some more pieces into our puzzle by examining the major components in the WAN; then we can answer these questions.

User-Network Interface, Inner-Network Interface, and Network-Network Interface

To organize our analysis, we begin with Layer 1, followed with Layer 2. We precede these tasks with an important detour to examine the communications interfaces we have from our homes, home offices, and enterprise locations *to* and *from* the WAN. It is called the *user-network interface* (UNI). Equally important, we examine the interface between network nodes inside the WAN, called the *inner-network interface* (INI). As well, we look at the interface between WANs, known as the *network-network interface* (NNI). The positions of these interfaces are shown in Figure 6.2.

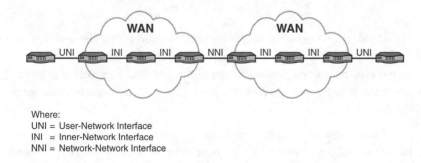

FIGURE 6.2
Positions of the interfaces

Where:
UNI = User-Network Interface
INI = Inner-Network Interface
NNI = Network-Network Interface

The prominent wide area UNIs, INIs, and NNIs are listed in Table 6.1, along with the layer or layers of the Internet/OSI models they occupy; at which interface or interfaces they reside; and the hour or hours in this book where they're explained. Please note that not all interface options are explained in this book, but we do cover the basics for those you might come across.

TABLE 6.1   Prominent WAN Interfaces

Name	Layer[1]	UNI?	INI?[2]	NNI?[2]	Hour
Residential BB	L_1	Yes	No	No	6
T-Carrier System	L_1	Yes	Yes, but diminishing	Yes, but diminishing	6
SONET[3]	L_1	Yes, but not extensive	Yes	Yes	6
ATM[4]	L_2	Yes	Yes	Yes	6
MPLS[5]	L_2/L_3	Yes, but not extensive	Yes	Yes	6
Dial-Up Modem	L_1	Yes	No	No	7
Cellular Phone	L_1, L_2, L_3	Yes	Yes	Yes	7

[1] This column lists only Layers 1–3. Some of these interfaces execute Layers 4–7, but they aren't germane to this discussion.

[2] Usually transparent to the user.

[3] SONET = Synchronous Optical Network

[4] ATM = Asynchronous Transfer Mode

[5] MPLS = Multiprotocol Label Switching

Also, remember this discussion's focus is on WAN interfaces. Consequently, Ethernet is not included but is examined in several parts of this book. As well, Bluetooth is considered to be a local interface and is not in this table but is explained in Hour 7, "Mobile Wireless Networking." Wi-Fi, also examined in Hour 7, can be deployed as a LAN or WAN.

Your need to understand the communications operations at the UNI, INI, and NNI will depend on the size of your company, your company's networking requirements, and its associated geographical scope and scale. For many installations, you will never become involved with these interfaces and you will have no way to access them for their manipulation. Your only access to them will be the passive use of their services. Here are four possibilities of your use of UNI, INI, and NNI operations:

▶ As one example, perhaps all you need is a DSL service from your home to the Internet. With this scenario, you'll have no need to use or understand systems such as SONET or MPLS.

▶ As another example, you might opt for leasing a local phone company's T-Carrier line from your clinic to a hospital facility located up-state. This UNI might be all you need to purchase, because the phone company is then responsible for any INIs and NNIs that might be used for the end-to-end service.

▶ As a third example, your company might need a combination of DSL circuits for connection to the public Internet as well as T-Carrier links to set up your own private network, with the ability to interwork these two sets of systems. In this situation, you must come to grips with INI and NNI capabilities.

▶ At the extreme, perhaps you're affiliated with a Fortune 500 company, with offices, stores, and so on placed around the globe. This scenario likely puts you in a situation in which you need to know (and use) an array of hardware and software at all three interfaces.

Whatever your situation might be, this hour will get you started in the right direction.

Residential Broadband

The term residential broadband was coined a couple decades ago to describe a collection of UNI technologies to overcome the slow speeds of dial-up modems. The word "residential" is not accurate, because these systems operate at both homes and offices. The word "broadband" is accurate, because it describes a high-speed capability. However, "broadband" links are also found at INIs and NNIs.

During the past 20 years, the telephone companies, cable companies, and satellite companies have been vying with each other to capture this market and to eventually place low-capacity modems in the dustbin. This part of the hour provides an overview of them. Be aware that most of these providers offer additional services such as email accounts, data file backups, IP address options, and security.

DSL

DSL is the offering from the telephone companies, using the current telephone wires that are laid throughout a neighborhood. DSL employs advanced hardware as well as sophisticated signaling and coding techniques to increase the line's capacity from 256 kilobits per second (Kbps) to several megabits per second (Mbps), depending on the specific offering (and price). In addition, DSL divides the bandwidth (the frequency range) to permit the simultaneous use of the link for more than one telephone call, fax session, Internet surfing, and so on. The exact capacity again depends on the specific offering and associated price.

When DSL came into the market in the 1990s, many customers found it to be complex, unwieldy, and error prone. I thought DSL problems were mainly ones of the telephone companies debugging their products, getting their staff trained with help desks in place, and having user-friendly documentation printed. Today, DSL can be installed by almost anyone who can read a two-page brochure. Therefore, we won't spend unnecessary time on DSL.

Without question, DSL was sorely needed. Its success has spurred the use of computer networks almost beyond belief. My only recommendation to you if you are a small office or residential user is to make sure you follow the instructions regarding the placement of filters on all phone devices. (They prevent unwanted signals from interfering with each other.)

For larger installations, you will likely be given more options for using the DSL links. One option that might be available in your area is called Asymmetric DSL (ADSL). This variation is so-named because it supports different data rates (in bps) on the two directions of a DSL link. If you have more data streaming down to your site than going up from your site, ADSL will likely be an effective option for your UNI connections. Also, ATM (discussed shortly) provides the potential for substantially enhanced services. DSL routers can enhance security and configuration alternatives (by using Point-to-Point Protocol [PPP] and Challenge Handshake Authentication Protocol [CHAP], discussed in Hours 8 and 20). The DSL router also runs IP and thus provides you with IP addressing, which your ISP manages for you.

Cable Modem Services

The cable TV companies offer a competitive service to DSL. Like DSL, the cable modem products have been very successful. Most of the information just written about DSL also pertains to cable modem services. One notable exception is how cable TV provides conventional telephone service.

Comcast and other CATV firms do not have access to the telephone wires and end offices. To get telephone service, a subscriber can subscribe to a third party for Voice over IP (VoIP). Other cable companies provide a VoIP product based on PacketCable, with one piece of additional equipment named the Embedded Multimedia Terminal

Adapter (EMTA). If you opt for computer networking via cable, check out these two technologies, both for price and quality of service (QoS). And if you want to know more about VoIP, take a look at another of my books, *Voice over IP*.

Satellite Services

Satellite services are available in a range of products and speeds. Two U.S. satellite carriers are in this business: HughesNet and Wild Blue. They provide several speeds from the network to your site (download) of rates from 1Mbps to 3Mbps and upload speeds ranging from 128Kbps to 300Kbps. This capacity difference in each direction of transmission is called asymmetrical bandwidth.

The lower-capacity upload speed from your site to the Internet should not pose a problem if you fit the mold of an average data communications user (receiving much more traffic than you send). However, if you have applications needing high throughput and low delay, the uplink channel might be too slow.

Roll Your Own

In Hour 7, we look at other wireless options, beyond these conventional asymmetrical channels, which you might be able to install without the intervention of a communications carrier.

By the Way

Layer 1 WAN Carrier Systems: T1 and SONET

The most prominent components at the physical layer of WANs are known collectively as the "T1" and "SONET" carrier systems. (These technologies have slightly different implementations and names in non-North American countries.) They can be deployed as user links to the WAN at a UNI, but they are more commonly used inside the network between the network nodes (INI) or between networks (NNI). Both technologies are designed to provide the following services:

▶ Define the specifications for the media, such as the dimensions of copper wire, the light reflective properties of optical fiber, and the frequencies to be used for wireless channels.

▶ Define the characteristics of the signals representing the data (1s and 0s) in the form of electrical, electromagnetic, or optical images. Examples are permissible voltages for a copper wire, frequency bands for wireless links, and light intensity for an optical cable.

▶ Establish rules for the synchronization of the signals between the sending node and the receiving node, such that the receiver "knows" exactly when a 1 or 0 is arriving.

▶ Provide conventions on how thousands of users' packets are combined (multiplexed) into a *payload* (a fancy name for a larger packet) on the media, how they are added to the payload, and how they are dropped off at the final WAN node destination.

▶ Stipulate the procedures for recovering from faulty lines (such as a backhoe severing a cable) and diverting the affected payloads to a functioning link. These payloads are not diverted based on an individual IP address. Rather, the diversion and recovery are based on hundreds of user packets, which have been multiplexed into larger packets.

▶ Notify network personnel about problems and their severity (such as sending an "alarm" packet to a network control center about a radio signal experiencing distortion because of an electrical storm).

These services are vital to the health of communications networks. Without them, computer-based business and private correspondences would cease to operate. We take them for granted, but they're essential to our professional and personal lives.

Unless you're responsible for a large network, you won't become involved in these operations. If you're in charge of your company's communications links to, say, AT&T, you should have an understanding of these WAN physical carrier systems. For home and small office networks, your principal concern is the integrity of your link to the nearby WAN gateway. That link is usually a broadband connection to a local carrier (a DSL; perhaps a T1 line). It's the responsibility of this carrier, such as Verizon, to provide you, a paying customer, a link of high integrity.

The next section provides an overview of T1 and SONET. For more details, check out *SONET and T1: Architectures for Digital Transport Networks*, written by yours truly and Sharleen Waters.

T1

The T1 carrier family has been the North American mainstay for leased (private) lines for over 40 years, which is an extraordinary span of time for a technology to stay relevant in this information age. The word "family" is used because the term T1 is the handle used to describe several options, which are explained shortly.

T1 is installed in many companies, ranging from large banks to small hospitals. It's a proven, well-understood technology. T1's staying power is also attributable to its provision for high-speed, reliable links from a company's office (say, a medical facility) to another office (say, a hospital).

One more point about T1. Some vendors and literature use the initials "DS" (for digital signaling) in place of the "T." For example, DS1 is used instead of T1. Strictly speaking, the T aspect of the technology refers to the signals themselves, and the DS refers to the way they're formatted to create units of traffic—that is, how they're "framed" on the channel. Thus, you might come across the term T1 frame. It's nothing more than a packet of bits, but with another name.

Synchronization of Signals

One of the most important functions of OSI Layer 1 is synchronizing the signal from the sending machine to the receiving machine. With proper synchronizing (or timing) the receiver knows exactly when to examine the line for the presence of an incoming 1 or 0. The T1 system was designed with the expectation that nodes in digital networks (such as multiplexers) might use different clocking sources to govern their synchronization timings. For example, one network might operate with a different clock than another network. As a consequence of this approach, T1 networks are said to be asynchronous systems, meaning the signals in the network don't necessarily operate at the same clocking rate.

Because of this design, T1 networks expend considerable resources to devise clever ways to synchronize traffic flowing between the network machines. In so doing, T1 might add or subtract extra bits to compensate for clocking disparities. These schemes make for awkward payload management. Because of the asynchronous nature of the T1 technology, the industry is migrating to an improved scheme, SONET, which is described in the next section.

The T1 Hierarchy

Table 6.2 provides a summary of the T1 family of carrier systems. Again, the more accurate term for a signal is "DS," which is used in this table. Notice the number of "conventional" voice channels each T1 hierarchy can support. The term "conventional" is used because, in the old days, 64Kbps was the nominal rate for digitized voice. Today's advanced voice digitization technology can produce a high-quality voice signal with 16Kbps. In deference to legacy, T1 is still quoted with 64Kbps rates.

TABLE 6.2   The T-Carrier Family

Signal	Bit Rate	Conventional DS Channels
DS0	64Kbps	1
DS1	1.544Mbps	24
DS2	6.312Mbps	96
DS3	44.736Mbps	28

Possible Uses for T1 Lines

Although T1 lines were designed for digital phone services, not all trunks carry data. A T1 line, for example, can carry up to 24 separate voice phone lines (or even more, if advanced coding techniques are used). Alternatively, it can carry up to 1.544Mbps of data. Another possibility is the use of 12 voice channels (half the available channels); the remaining bandwidth (about 768Kbps) is used for data.

These and other possibilities are available through your local phone provider. The difference between the kinds of services is based on their use, not from any inherent differences in T1 implementations. All the aforementioned services can be carried over the same type of line. That's why knowing a bit about T1 technology is useful before you begin to order a communications line for your WAN.

Provisioning Trunks

When you order a line (also called a trunk) from your local phone company, the technical staff will ask how you want to provision it. Depending on your applications, you might want the trunk for voice traffic, data, video traffic, or some combination of the three. For small- to medium-sized operations, you normally will be using either part of a T1 (fractional T1) or a full T1. Larger WANs or offices with high-bandwidth requirements often require T3 (DS3) lines, which can support almost 45Mbps transfer rate.

Leased Lines

When you purchase fractional or full T1 data services from a telephone company, you might be provisioned with a circuit that carries data between two specific points. Those points can be two of your offices; alternatively, one end could be your office and the other could be an ISP. As mentioned, these facilities are often called leased lines because we rent or lease them from the carrier, and no one else's traffic is allowed to be transported across these "private" lines.

SONET

T1 continues to serve the industry well. But it's an old technology and is based on communications concepts devised in the 1960s. SONET is designed to enhance (and eventually replace) T1. Think of T1 as a first-generation WAN carrier system and SONET as a second-generation system. I use the term "WAN," but nothing precludes T1 or SONET from being deployed in a local environment, such as a business or hospital campus.

In addition to providing T-Carrier services, SONET does the following:

▶ Uses clocks referenced to a common and stable reference, which obviates the cumbersome schemes of trying to synchronize different timing systems.

▶ Employs highly efficient "grooming" methods for adding, segregating, and dropping user payloads within the SONET super-packet. ("Super" meaning it contains payloads from many users.)

▶ Has successfully encouraged vendors to use the same conventions, such that a network can be set up with equipment from different manufacturers. Conceptually, T1 could do the same, but its history discouraged this convergence.

▶ Provides a rich array of network management tools as well as extensive procedures for network recovery. Again, T1 could have done the same, but vendors developed their proprietary schemes before any T1 "standards" bodies could publish such conventions.

▶ Takes advantage of the high transmission rates of optical fiber.

Like T1, SONET is organized by a multiplexing hierarchy, based on a bps rate and the number of user payloads combined into a SONET frame—the term used for a super-packet. Table 6.3 provides a summary of the SONET hierarchy. (Note: The optical carrier (OC) signal can also be an electrical or electromagnetic signal, in which case the initials of OC can be substituted for STS [Synchronous Transport Signal]).

TABLE 6.3   The SONET Hierarchy

Signal	Bit Rate	Conventional DS Channels
OC-1	51.840Mbps	28
OC-3	155.520Mbps	84
OC-12	622.080Mbps	336
OC-48	2488.320Mbps	1,344
OC-192	9953.280Mbps	5,376
OC-768	389813.12Mbps	21,504

Because of the limitations of T1, SONET is now the prevalent WAN carrier technology used inside the WAN network cloud. Typically, if you lease a T1 or T3 line from a carrier, this traffic is repackaged at the carrier's site and multiplexed into SONET frames for transport across the WAN.

Layer 2 for WANs: ATM and MPLS

The most prominent components at the data link layer (Layer 2) of WANs are the ATM and MPLS.

ATM

To understand why ATM is used in computer networks, and to understand why it has achieved wide use, please refer back to Figure 5.2 in Hour 5, "Network Concepts." Recall that the Layer 3 IP address is the most widely used address in the data communications industry. Also, the Layer 2 Ethernet address is employed only in LANs and therefore is of no use in a WAN. Thus, as Figure 5.2 suggests, the IP packet with its source and destination addresses are the only means available to route traffic from one computer to another. If you aren't assigned an IP address by your ISP (which of course, you are), you're as helpless as a postal patron without a postal address.

However, as explained in Hour 3, the IP address of 32 bits has proven to be cumbersome and inefficient. Because hundreds of thousands of IP addresses are now in use (with a theoretical base of about four billion), it becomes an impossible task for a router to store even a small percentage of these IP addresses in its routing table. Even with classless IP addressing, also explained in Hour 3, routing with IP addresses is too slow and awkward.

Interestingly, ATM addresses the IP addressing problems by not using addresses! Instead, ATM places the IP packet inside the user data field of an ATM protocol data unit (PDU), which is called a *cell* (not to be confused with a mobile phone cell; they have no relationship to each other). Then ATM routes the IP packets though the WAN by using *labels* that have been placed in the ATM cell header. Unlike an IP address, an ATM label has no network association, nor a node associated with a network. In fact, it has no relationship to any location, until the WAN associates it with such. Stay with me; I promise this seemingly strange concept makes good sense.

Let's use the postal address as an example of a label. First, a street address and a city and state have location significance. They're bound to geography. But a ZIP Code is not bound to a locality, *until* the post office so designates. For example, a ZIP number for, say, Los Angeles, can just as easily be associated with another location. Thus, a label is free from an association with a specific physical node until a label-switching node has mapped the label number to this node. Second, with the use of only one label, traffic for all the computers in an office can be reached, because the network has associated a label number (perhaps label 334944) with the gateway router at a specific office complex.

Taking this hypothetical system as an example, even though thousands of IP users may reside on your LANs in your headquarters, each with an IP address, a WAN router may store only one entry in its forwarding table: that of label number 334944. Consequently, instead of a router having to store thousands of IP addresses about your company at the Los Angeles gateway router, it need store only one label. This concept aggregates multiple addresses to one label. It's a powerful technique for improving the operations of relaying traffic through a network.

Here's another beauty of label forwarding versus IP address forwarding: After the traffic reaches the final WAN node, such as a router, the software strips away the ATM header and its label. It has done its job by getting the traffic to the gateway router that's connected to the LANs in your organization. Recall that residing in the ATM data field is the IP packet, with its intact destination and source IP addresses.

Thereafter, IP takes over and Layer 3 (in concert with Layer 2's Ethernet) is now used to route the data to the computer that's attached to one of the LANs in your office. If you have a T1 link or a DSL line going to your office or home, it's likely that ATM is responsible for getting the IP packet all the way to that router sitting in your office— perhaps on your desk. If you take the time to examine the user manuals for your DSL or T1 services, chances are good they will reference ATM labels. They're called by cryptic names (VPI or VCI), but these monikers are nothing more than fancy names for a label.

Creating a Connection in the WAN

ATM sets up a two-way path in the WAN for a user's packets to traverse during the user session. This idea is similar to a telephone network setting up a connection for a phone call. However, the ATM network nodes are quite intelligent and have the capacity to find the most efficient and reliable end-to-end path for the user's specific needs. Although the creation of this connection might entail a short delay before the users can begin their respective transmissions, a "circuit" can be premapped and set up permanently. The idea is similar to a leased line in the T1 world, which is often called a "permanent circuit." In the ATM network, the guaranteed resource is always there. It might not be an established end-to-end such as that of a point-to-point leased line service. But the network provider is obligated to provide the user with the illusion of a permanent circuit. (And the provider had better be sure that it has sufficient capacity to meet unexpected bandwidth requests!) This concept is called a *permanent virtual circuit*.

In earlier discussions, we learned how IP addresses are advertised and then used by routers to forward traffic. For label-switching networks, an additional task correlates a label to an IP address and the location of the node with this address. Thereafter, when a router receives IP packets, it maps the destination IP address to the appropriate label. Then only labels are used for forwarding until the IP packet reaches the final destination.

Critical Network Ingredients: Quality of Service (QoS) and Traffic Engineering (TE)

From its inception, ATM was designed to provide network managers with extensive quality of service (QoS) and traffic engineering (TE) operations. Most WAN label-switching networks have implemented an ATM traffic-engineering feature for controlling the amount of traffic users are allowed to send into the network. For example, my ISP monitors the number of bytes my network sends during a window of time. If my network exceeds a predefined limit, the traffic is "throttled" at my LAN site. This monitoring tool prevents the WAN from becoming congested. The idea is similar to the stoplights installed at the traffic ramps onto freeways. The difference is that the traffic ramp apparatus flow-controls *all* users of the traffic ramp (as a group), whereas ATM traffic engineering controls *each* user. In a manner of speaking, each user's packets are controlled by a specific traffic light and a traffic ramp.

In addition, ATM permits a user to request a certain QoS from the network. For example, if Tommy and I are putting together a fancy video show, with the requirement for low delay and high throughput, I can request my ATM network provider to guarantee Tommy and me a certain level of service to meet the requirements for our program.

Notwithstanding all these fine features, if your network is to interact with a wide area ATM network, and you think you or your users will need QoS features, make certain your network provider has provisioned these capabilities in its product. ATM is quite powerful from the TE and QoS standpoints. But most of the ATM operations are optional, and a network might not have them coded in its software.

The ATM Cell

The ATM PDU (the cell) is quite small—only 53 bytes, with 5 bytes used by the ATM network for the label and other control functions. Consequently, most user traffic must be segmented and placed in more than one ATM cell for transport across a WAN. This small user payload versus overhead is just the tip of the iceberg, because other overhead bytes consume some of the remaining 48 bytes to properly identify the user traffic segments *in each cell*. Consequently, ATM consumes a lot of the network's bandwidth. Additionally, most of the QoS and TE services, although admirably powerful, consume a lot of overhead bytes.

The "small cell" idea made sense when ATM was first being designed (about 15 years ago). The conventional 1,500-byte packet incurred excessive queuing delays at network nodes and adversely affected applications requiring short delays, such as voice transmissions. But now, with improvements in CPU and memory speeds, larger packets can be handled without affecting the quality of the transmission.

Nonetheless, ATM is widely used. In spite of its overhead, it provides the computer network industry with a full set of TE and QoS operations and a fast method for routing traffic between end users.

Frame Relay

Prior to the introduction of ATM into the marketplace, the prevailing Layer 2 protocol for WANs was Frame Relay. For a while (in the early 1990s), it held a prominent position in the WAN marketplace. Even though it is being supplanted by ATM, your wide area carrier might provide attractive frame relay offerings. For example, AT&T offers frame reply products in 22 states. Frame Relay is a sound, efficient technology. Keep it on your list of things to check when you are shopping for WAN services.

MPLS

MPLS is similar to ATM in that it uses labels to make routing decisions. It also supports a variety of QoS operations. In conjunction with other Internet standards, MPLS offers a diverse set of TE tools. Given these characteristics, you might ask why MPLS exists. It appears to be a redundant technology *vis-à-vis* ATM.

If MPLS had been conceived before ATM came along, it is likely that ATM wouldn't be a factor in WANs. But MPLS wasn't published as a standard until ATM had begun its commercial deployments. Thus, as of this writing, ATM has a stronger presence in the marketplace than MPLS. But I think MPLS will eventually replace ATM. Here's why:

▶ MPLS permits a variable-length packet. The MPLS PDU can vary from a few bytes to several thousand bytes. Consequently, it makes better use of precious bandwidth than ATM does.

▶ Like ATM, MPLS requires a connection setup operation (and can use the idea of a permanent virtual circuit). However, MPLS provides additional features beyond that of ATM for this operation.

▶ MPLS has been designed to operate with the Internet architecture and protocols, such as IP. Certainly, ATM also interworks with IP, but not as gracefully as MPLS.

Putting More Pieces Together

Let's put a few more pieces into the networking puzzle. We'll use Figure 6.3 and these abbreviations to help us. Also, notice the legend at the bottom of Figure 6.3, which shows the order of invocation of the layers. The down arrow means transmit; the up arrow means receive.

IP: The Internet Protocol

E: Ethernet

A: ATM

D: DSL

M: MPLS

S: SONET

T: T1

ULP: Upper-layer protocols

As I key in this paragraph and then send it to a backup server somewhere on the Internet, my sterling verse is sent to a local router (*very* local—perhaps in my office, or on my desk) via my local Ethernet and the IP packet. In Figure 6.3, my local computer is executing all layers of the Internet model, but we're only concerned with Layers 1–3. My machine executes IP at L_3, and it executes Ethernet at L_2 and L_1.

At my local router, the Ethernet frame is received through the router's Ethernet link and sent up to its IP module. Hereafter, Ethernet is not executed until the traffic arrives at the remote server. The destination IP address in the IP packet (the IP address of the remote server) is examined, and the local router's forwarding table reveals that the packet is to be sent to a "next node," which is my ISP (shown in the figure as "Local LAN/WAN Gateway"), to eventually reach the remote server.

Notice that my local router and my ISP's router operate with ATM at L_2 and DSL at L_1. Consequently, the IP packet is placed into ATM cells and sent across the DSL link to my ISP. At this node, it may execute L_3 and look at the destination address in the IP packet. For this example, it does not because my local router has already made a correlation of the destination IP address (the remote server at the other end of the figure) to an ATM label. Thus, my ISP router's job is simplified because it doesn't have to deal with IP.

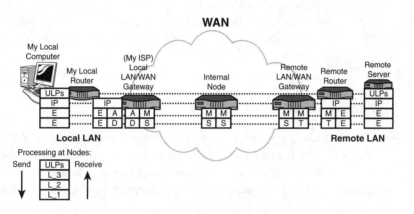

FIGURE 6.3
Communications end-to-end

In this example, my ISP has migrated to MPLS for exchanging traffic between network nodes. As seen on its send side, it correlates the ATM label to an MPLS label (and, of course, it strips away all that ATM overhead).

Notice that L_1 is now SONET and remains so during the operations inside the network. If you now trace the Layer 1 configurations on the right side of the figure, you'll see that the remote LAN/WAN gateway maps the SONET frames into T1 frames for sending to the server's remote router. Then T1 is stripped away, and Ethernet is re-created for use on the LAN between the remote router and the remote server.

Finally (although all these operations likely took place in less than half a second), the remote server processes the IP packet, which contains my source IP address and the remote server's destination IP address. The data has arrived!...and usually quickly and error free.

But now what? Thus far, all these extraordinary systems have transported my traffic (my textual paragraph) to the remote server. But this server hasn't yet executed the upper layers of the model. When it does, my paragraph will indeed be stored on a backup server disk. Notice by the dashed lines that the data, headers, and trailers of the upper-layer protocols (ULPs) are processed only at my local computer and the remote server.

We continue our layered-protocol journey in Hour 15, "Connecting to the Internet: Key Supporting Operations," by an examination of the top layers, especially Layers 4 (TCP) and 7 (DNS). For Hours 7–14, we assemble more building blocks for the network and add more pieces to the networking puzzle.

Summary

This hour explained the major features of a WAN and why it's different from a LAN. The key components of a WAN were examined, as were the three key WAN interfaces. Also explained were the principal WAN L_1 carrier systems and those that make up Layer 2. The pros and cons of address and label switching were highlighted. The hour concluded with a look at how a packet is sent through a WAN between two LANs and how the WAN's carrier systems and protocols contribute to this transport.

Q&A

Q. *Contrast a WAN with a LAN.*

A. The WAN is usually a public network; the LAN is a private network. A WAN spans greater distances than a LAN and employs more expensive and higher-capacity L_1 technologies than a local network. Because of these differences, WANs and LANs typically implement different procedures to manage traffic.

Q. *Name the three interfaces associated with a WAN.*

A. The three WAN interfaces are the user-network interface, or UNI; the inner-network interface, or INI; and the network-network interface, or NNI.

Q. *The prominent so-called residential broadband products come in three offerings. List them.*

A. Digital subscriber line (DSL), cable modem, and satellite services are the three residential broadband products.

Q. *Why was SONET developed to enhance or replace the T-Carrier technology?*

A. The T family of carrier systems don't provide a stable clocking source for the digital images (1s and 0s) traveling across communications links. Thus, proper synchronization of signals is awkward for T technology. In contrast, SONET is a synchronous technology, with highly accurate clocking mechanisms. In addition, SONET has better network management operations and better "grooming" (multiplexing/demultiplexing) capabilities than the T-Carrier technology.

Q. *Why is ATM or MPLS employed for relaying traffic in a WAN instead of IP?*

A. IP forwarding relies on the IP address, which entails more overhead than label switching. ATM and MPLS use label switching. In addition, ATM and MPLS support more traffic engineering and quality of service (QoS) features than IP does.

Q. *Why is Ethernet not employed in a WAN?*

A. From its inception, Ethernet was designed to be distance limited because of how its users share a link. Its L_2 protocol limits how far apart the Ethernet devices can be from each other. In addition, the Ethernet (MAC) address is considered to have local significance only and was not designed to be used in a WAN.

Q. *If the IP packet is not processed in a WAN, how can IP traffic be sent from one LAN to another, but through a WAN?*

A. The IP packet is placed inside another protocol data unit (PDU), such as an ATM cell or an MPLS frame, and sent transparently through the WAN. It is the job of the WAN gateway node or the local sending router to correlate the destination IP address into a label. The WAN then uses this label to transport the IP datagram to the remote user.

Mobile Wireless Networking

What You'll Learn in This Hour:

▶ Basic concepts of mobile wireless networks

▶ The prominent mobile wireless standards

▶ Cellular systems

▶ Wi-Fi (Wireless Fidelity)

▶ Bluetooth

▶ Basics of security issues

▶ Implementation considerations

During the past six hours, we have made frequent yet general comments about wireless networks. Because they are a major component in modern networks and because you will likely deploy them in your own internet, it's appropriate we provide more details about them.

The emphasis in this hour is on *mobile* wireless networking. Fixed networks, such as a nation's microwave systems, are important, but they are not covered here because of their transparency to your networks. For example, you might have leased a DS3 line across the United States, but you will not know if AT&T is placing your DS3 payload over microwave or cable. On the other hand, wireless networks such as Wi-Fi, Bluetooth, and cellular most likely will be quite evident in your operations.

Understanding Wireless Networking

The options for wireless networking have greatly increased over the past few years. As one example, thousands of public wireless networks are now installed in hotels, coffee shops, and airports—"hot spots" available for our use. As another example, longer-distance wireless communications can take place through cellular telephone technology and satellite systems. That's good news for users, especially with the recent explosion of local area network (LAN) wireless standards and products, because most are centered on Wi-Fi and Bluetooth, which are readily available to all of us.

Signal Interference

Radio connectivity provides an easy way to extend a wired or wireless LAN. Wireless LAN (WLAN) equipment operates in part of the frequency range that the FCC has reserved for unregulated use at 2.4 gigahertz (GHz). Be aware that "unregulated" means just that: It is possible to experience interference from others' unregulated signals. Fortunately, the FCC has placed distance limitations on how far these signals can be propagated. Thus, your next-door neighbor might "pick up" your wireless emails from your local network, but your mother-in-law across town won't have access to them. In any case, Hour 20, "Security," will explain how to secure your traffic.

The major difference between a wired network and a wireless network is how computers or other devices, such as personal digital assistants (PDAs), connect to the network at Layer 1 of the Internet/OSI model. Wireless installations use radio or infrared signals to send and receive data. Use of the radio spectrum is more common, so let's center our discussion on radio networks.

A computer must be outfitted with a network interface card (NIC) that can send (and receive) data as a radio wave (rather than as an electrical signal over a wire). To connect to a network, a device must be installed to connect the computers and other machines. In a wired network, the device is a hub, bridge, router, or switch. In a wireless network, the central connecting device is called a wireless access point (WAP). The WAP can also be a hub, bridge, router, or switch with both wireless and wire-based ports. Thus, most access points provide for wireless connectivity as well as port connections to a wired network, such as the Internet.

A network combining wired and wireless connectivity is often referred to as a *hybrid* network. Figure 7.1 shows the layout for a hybrid network.

Typically, wireless routers include a WAP, an Ethernet switch, firmware for IP forwarding, Network Address Translation (NAT), and the Domain Name System (DNS) to interwork with a WAN gateway. The wireless router allows wired and wireless Ethernet devices to connect to a WAN device such as a DSL modem. This modem is often a network card inside the router.

A wireless router can be configured through a central utility. If you are installing a WLAN to attach to the Internet, your ISP will provide this service for you, most likely from an ISP web server.

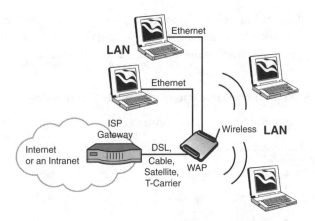

FIGURE 7.1
A typical hybrid network

When you will not be communicating with a WAN, you might opt for a wireless network bridge. This device operates at L_1 and L_2 of the layered model. This configuration can be useful for connecting two Ethernets, say, in two separate homes or offices. A wireless network bridge is simple to use.

Let's make one more general point about the subject. Wireless repeaters can extend the reach of an existing wireless network. Repeaters allow the signal to propagate around barriers and corridors. Be aware that each repeater will add latency for each hop, and the end-to-end throughput will be limited by the lowest-capacity link in the chain.

A Brief History of Mobile Wireless Networks

Mobile wireless networks in America appeared 80 years ago. On April 7, 1928, the first mobile radio system went into operation in Detroit, Michigan. These early systems required enormous bandwidth. A 120-kilohertz (KHz) spectrum was required to transmit a voice signal of only 3KHz. By the 1960s, technology supported a "modest" 30KHz voice channel.

The mobile phone you likely have nearby as you read this sentence is a relatively new technology. In the United States, it was first implemented as a national service in 1983. This first generation (1G) mobile phone (the Advanced Mobile Phone System, or AMPS) used 30KHz of bandwidth. What's more, AMPS was built around analog technologies. The voice signals were sent over analog waveforms—no discrete 0s or 1s in those days. Nor did AMPS have significant capabilities for sending data between computers. A few specialized devices allowed some data applications, but they were limited in their capabilities.

In the early 1990s, the industry began migrating to second-generation systems (2G). The major features introduced then are those we have in our third-generation (3G) cell phones today, as described in the following list. (By the way, 1G is now obsolete, and 2G is rapidly decreasing in use.)

▶ All images are digitized into binary bit streams of 1s and 0s.

▶ It uses less bandwidth than 1G networks.

▶ It supports video and data applications.

▶ It enables use of small phone sets.

▶ It provides higher-quality signals.

▶ It provides better security.

▶ It might provide interfaces to the Internet (and the Web) using the Internet protocols.

▶ It might support email.

▶ It provides text messaging.

In comparison to wire-based broadband, the 2G and 3G bandwidth are more limited. The bit rate varies, depending on network conditions and specific implementations, but a mobile phone user will not obtain the throughput and response time of conventional DSL and cable modem links.

As mentioned, the mobile wireless industry (usually called the mobile phone industry) is entering into 3G technology. One goal of 3G is to provide for a higher transfer rate for each user. The 3G standards stipulate different data rates, depending on the Layer 1 technology. For example, the international standard CDMA2000 defines a maximum data rate of 307 kilobits per second (Kbps).

Is this bad news? Yes, if we are to depend on the conventional mobile phone channel for high-capacity support. Fortunately, other wireless technologies are readily available that offer more bandwidth and are examined later in this hour.

The Cell Concept

Many wireless systems, including those just described, are implemented with the cell concept. A cell is a geographical area using low-power radio frequency transmitters. Low-power devices cannot send signals over long distances, which permit frequencies to be reused in nonadjacent cells. Given the finite frequency spectrum and the continuous jousting for radio bandwidth among the wireless service providers, frequency reuse is an important capability. Without frequency reuse, cell phone markets would be of such a small capacity that the limited customer base could not pay for the cost of building and maintaining the network.

The mobile phone communicates with the cell's base station (a control facility with sending and receiving antenna) on control channels. These channels are predefined frequency bands reserved for call management traffic. Using the control channels, the base station (with guidance from a remote control center) assigns the mobile phone a specific frequency to be used for a call. For 2G and 3G systems, the phone is also assigned a specific slot of time it can use on that frequency. Thus, 2G and 3G permit multiple users to be multiplexed onto one physical radio channel.

Using the control channels, the phone user can dial up a party and then employ the user channel for ongoing communications. During the time the mobile phone is within a cell, the base station is monitoring the phone's signals. If the base station detects that the signal is growing weaker, it requests the control station to determine whether the phone unit is moving out of the base station's cell coverage. If it is, the network sets up procedures for an adjacent cell to take over the call—an operation that is usually transparent to the mobile phone users.

The worldwide mobile phone system is an elegantly simple set of networks. The mobile phone users' locations are maintained (continuously, if the phones are turned on) by the mobile network providers working together to exchange information about the locations of all the mobile phones. In addition to phone numbers, other identifiers and locator information are exchanged between the providers to keep track of the mobile customers.

Therefore, not only can a mobile phone network hand off calls between cells within a network, it can hand off calls between cells across networks. When you first turn on your mobile phone, a service provider in the local cell picks up your phone's signal on a control channel, which carries its phone number, its ID, and the ID of your service provider. In a matter of seconds, this local provider has sent a packet to your provider about your new location. Your location is then continually updated.

When you turn off and then turn on your phone, its location is reupdated. Don't like Big Brother watching? Then don't use a cell phone.

The mobile cellular phone network is an extraordinary technology. As the industry migrates to 3G, cell phones will be increasingly used for higher-quality video, data, and graphics applications. As well, more and more cell phones are being outfitted with native-mode Internet capabilities.

Now let's examine several prominent wireless network standards and products and see how we can use them to enhance your network.

Wi-Fi

The Wi-Fi technology (published in the IEEE 802.11 standards) is used as a low-cost, limited-distance connection. But nothing precludes Wi-Fi use over greater distances with higher power and more expensive components. For this discussion, the emphasis is on the former technology.

Wi-Fi uses a spread spectrum radio technology. Spread spectrum was developed by the military to guard against enemy radio frequency jamming and eavesdropping. Spread spectrum spreads the signal across a range of frequencies in the public bandwidths.

▶ **Frequency hopping spread spectrum (FHSS)**—As this name implies, using a set pattern, the partnering mobile devices simultaneously hop from frequency to frequency. The receiver can receive frequency hopping spread spectrum data only if the sender and the receiver use the same hopping pattern (which is controlled by a hopping-sequence algorithm that is established during an initial session handshake). According to FCC rules, no transmitter can stay on a single band for more than 0.4 seconds within a period of 30 seconds for the 2.4GHz band. Each transmitter must also cycle through 50–75 radio bands before restarting the hopping-sequence algorithm.

▶ **Direct sequence spread spectrum (DSSS)**—In DSSS, the transmitter modifies the data with "chips," or extra data bits inserted into the data stream. Only a receiver that knows the algorithm for the insertion of chips can decipher the code. Because of the effect of the chips, the effective throughput of DSSS is currently limited to 11 megabits per second (Mbps) in the 2.4GHz band.

The Wi-Fi implementations 802.11b and 802.11g use DSSS. Bluetooth (which is discussed in the next section) uses FHSS.

Although the 802.11 standard provides for a number of different specifications for wireless networking, these L_1 specifications are the more prominent:

▶ **802.11a**—This standard provides up to 54Mbps of throughput and operates in the 5GHz band of the radio spectrum. (Because of overhead, a user can reasonably expect a throughput of around 25Mbps.) The 2.4GHz band is more popular; thus, 802.11a might experience less interference. Keep in mind these higher frequencies are more prone to error and cannot as easily penetrate walls and other solid objects. Also, as of this writing, public networks (public "hot spots") use the 2.4GHz band.

▶ **802.11b**—This specification provides a maximum data rate of 11Mbps and operates in the 2.4GHz band, utilizing DSSS. However, 802.11b devices have been known to suffer from other machines operating in this band. For example, your baby monitor might get in the way of this Wi-Fi component. Nonetheless—and this interference is rare—802.11b is extensively deployed throughout the world.

▶ **802.11g**—This specification provides 54Mbps (with about 20–25Mbps of net throughput) in the 2.4GHz band. It's currently the fastest growing implementation of 802.11 wireless specifications for home networks and small LANs.

The 802.11 wireless specifications are collectively referred to as Wi-Fi (Wireless Fidelity). To promote 802.11 as the standard for wireless (there's another possibility that is discussed in a moment), the Wi-Fi Alliance, a nonprofit organization, was formed by a number of the companies that provide 802.11 wireless technology and services.

One more point about 802.11a. This technology does not use FHSS or DSSS. It uses a multiplexing scheme called Orthogonal Frequency Division Multiplexing (OFDM). OFDM splits the radio signal into numerous subsignals that are transmitted simultaneously at different frequencies. This enables a large amount of digital data to be broken into chunks and then transmitted.

Don't Overlook 802.11n

During your evaluation of WLAN options, make certain you examine the latest offerings for 802.11n. As of this writing, 802.11n products are beginning to appear in the marketplace. Make sure you and your team factor in this technology because it offers up to 600Mbps transmission rates—a significant improvement over the other Wi-Fi technologies.

But be careful. For testing and research purposes for this book, I purchased an IEEE 802.11n-compliant router (as advertised in the router vendor's literature). I discovered the machine didn't yet support this Wi-Fi specification. The technical "help desk" informed me the company had experienced some problems with 802.11n. I suggested that it might consider having the technical teams occasionally meet with the marketing department.

Bluetooth

Although not currently a competitor for WLAN implementations, another wireless specification shares the same 2.4GHz bandwidth range as 802.11: Bluetooth. Bluetooth was created in 1998 as a standard for connecting mobile devices (such as

PDAs) by a number of companies (such as IBM, Nokia, and Toshiba) interested in mobile computing strategies. Bluetooth was initially designed as a strategy for implementing a personal area network, or PAN—meaning the Bluetooth specification is intended to be used on devices we use on a daily basis, such as phones and printers; and personal convenience devices, such as PDAs.

The Bluetooth visionaries conceived a wireless environment that would surround us while we went about our daily chores, allowing us (and our tools) to be freed from the constricted wired world. Wireless phones, wireless disks, wireless coffeemakers, skillets, and toasters—all controlled by a wireless "server" that contained loads of breakfast-making software in the OSI application layer. This futuristic automated kitchen is not yet a reality, but in our hurry-up, fast-food world, it's probably in the building contractors' floor plans.

Anyway, Bluetooth is an open standard (as is 802.11) and can provide a transfer rate of 1Mbps. The net data rate depends on which other protocols you use with Bluetooth. Later versions support higher data rates. If this issue is important to you, check for the following: Version 1.2: 1Mbps; Version 2.0: 3Mbps. You might also check out an emerging proposal referred to as the WiMedia Alliance, which is in the process of defining a much higher data rate. As of this writing, the specific bit rate has not been defined.

Bluetooth provides a lot of possibilities for providing communication links between handheld computing devices, mobile phones, and other devices, such as wireless headsets, keyboards, printers, bar code scanners, PlayStations, and graphic pens. There's also talk of developing Bluetooth into a full-blown LAN infrastructure medium (which would make it a competitor to 802.11).

Bluetooth is designed for low-power consumption, which, of course, results in a short-range signal area. Thus, its range is power-class-dependent: Class 3: approximately 1 meter, Class 2: approximately 10 meters, and Class 1: approximately 100 meters.

As long as the received signal is powerful enough for translation, Bluetooth devices can be located in different rooms. During start-up, the nodes execute the Link Manager Protocol (LMP) to set up the wireless link (an L_2 protocol). During this phase, the devices authenticate each other and negotiate the size of the packet to be exchanged. The Service Discovery Protocol (SDP) is also employed to perform handshakes to determine the type of device and the types of services each device supports.

You won't have to be concerned with the details of the Bluetooth protocols. They're mentioned to give you a better appreciation of the power and flexibility of Bluetooth, and to once again show how useful the OSI/Internet layered model is in explaining computer networking technology.

Are Wi-Fi and Bluetooth in Competition?

Wi-Fi and Bluetooth are not competitors. Their "place" in the networking picture—based on their characteristics—has been well thought-out by their developers. Wi-Fi is more expensive, yet it provides for a greater signal area and higher data through-puts. They both use the same frequency spectrum, but, as noted earlier, they use different techniques at L_1 for sending and receiving signals.

Wi-Fi is an attractive alternative to wire-based LANs. Many homes and companies use it to obviate pulling Ethernet cable between rooms. Bluetooth can be used to replace USB-type connections, such as keyboards, flash RAM, printers, and cameras.

Frequency Interference Between Wi-Fi and Bluetooth?

As stated earlier, 802.11 and Bluetooth use the 2.4GHz band as defined under Part 15 of the U.S. Federal Communications Commission Rules and Regulations. Bluetooth devices should not interfere with Wi-Fi devices because Bluetooth uses FHSS and 802.11 uses DSSS.

However, this equipment can be affected by interference from microwave ovens and cordless telephones. The chances are slight, but keep that possibility in mind when you're nuking your coffee in the morning while talking on the Bluetooth phone set.

Security Considerations with Wireless Networks

The common procedure to protect traffic over a wireless channel is to encrypt the user data. Hour 20 provides information on encryption in general. For this discussion, the focus is on wireless channels specifically.

Wireless networking makes many folks squeamish because of security issues. After all, we're sending our data into the air, making it a possible target for eavesdroppers. Data sensitivity has become increasingly important to those in the medical field because of HIPAA (Health Insurance Portability and Accountability Act) regulations related to the protection of patient information. Even a dentist with a small practice might think twice about implementing a wireless network in the dental office because patient data might be at risk.

Because of the vulnerability of "air data," wireless networks have a security strategy. WEP (or Wired Equivalent Privacy) is a protocol executing in the MAC sublayer of the data link layer (L_2) of the Internet/OSI model. WEP encrypts the data sent from point to point on the WLAN using a shared secret key. This means that WEP is in force as data moves from a wireless client to an access point or to another wireless client. Keep in mind: If the data enters a wired LAN, the WEP protection ends.

In the early 2000s, WEP was used in many products, but it was found to be vulnerable to hacking. Thus, Wi-Fi Protected Access (WPA-2) is in many products today and offers better protection. Nonetheless, you should check your system to determine if the data is encrypted, because some products default to a clear mode (encryption free) of operation. If the Wi-Fi product itself doesn't provide this level of security, you can secure your data by other means. In Hour 20, we explore these alternatives.

Implementation Considerations

Implementing a wireless network is not much different from implementing a wired network. You must plan your network layout and then acquire the necessary hardware to get the network up and running. You should plan for growth, security, and all the other issues that you would plan for if you were implementing a wired network. We won't get ahead of ourselves about this subject, as Hours 9–19 contain a lot of information about network implementations. But a few comments specific to wireless networks are in order.

In terms of network size and growth, keep in mind that Wi-Fi implementations such as 802.11b are inexpensive and fairly easy to set up. However, they provide limited bandwidth. Also, the more users on the network, the less the throughput and the longer the response times will be (which, of course, is true with any network). So Wi-Fi shouldn't be considered to support a large base of users. For this community, you should use wired Ethernet.

The number of access points you decide to deploy depends on the number of users. Each access point provides specifications for the number of users who can connect to the access point without suffering drops in performance and reliability.

As you plan your Wi-Fi network, keep in mind the range of the medium. Indoors, you're looking at ranges of 150 to 300 feet (the maximum distance from a client to an access point), unless you install repeaters. Building construction can also affect the range, so consider setting up test equipment before you outfit all your users with Wi-Fi hardware.

You must determine the access point range boundaries in your building and between your buildings, which will help you determine the number of access points you will need to accommodate your users. Also, allow some overlap between the access point range boundaries so that users can roam within the building or between buildings.

Regarding hardware, many products are available for both access points and Wi-Fi network interface cards (NICs). For small networks, companies such as Linksys and D-Link provide access points and wireless NICs. Many of the access points provide firewall capabilities, and some (designed for home use) have parental control capabilities for Internet connections.

For larger networks, companies such as 3Com and Cisco provide high-end access points for enterprise networking. For example, Cisco offers products simultaneously supporting Wi-Fi standards 802.11a, 802.11b, and 802.11g.

Make sure you research and test your Wi-Fi hardware as you would hardware for a wired network. A good starting point for more information about Wi-Fi is the Wi-Fi Alliance at www.wi-fi.org. This organization provides information on Wi-Fi standards and provides information on Wi-Fi-certified products, Wi-Fi network implementation, and other Wi-Fi-related news.

Summary

In this hour, we discussed wireless networking. Starting with a brief history of cellular systems, we covered the elegant efficiency of the wireless cell concept. We examined wireless standards such as the IEEE 802.11 and the Bluetooth specifications. We looked at the different implementations of 802.11 and Bluetooth, and methods for securing a wireless network. We concluded the hour with some recommendations on implementation strategies.

Q&A

Q. *What type of device can you use to interwork a wireless network with a wired network?*

A. The wireless access point (WAP) is the key device for this interface. It often contains an Ethernet switch, firmware for IP forwarding, as well as address translation and domain name services.

Q. *List the major differences between a wireless Ethernet and a wire-based Ethernet.*

A. The differences between the two are as follows:

- ▶ Wireless Ethernets are easier to install.

- ▶ Wireless Ethernets are more subject to security breaches.

- ▶ Wireless Ethernets usually have less throughput capacity.

- ▶ Wireless Ethernets are more apt to suffer from signal degradations.

- ▶ Wireless Ethernets are vulnerable to channel interference.

Q. *How does frequency hopping improve security and reduce channel interference?*

A. Because of the frequent changing of transmit and receive frequencies, it will be highly unlikely that an unauthorized party will be able to monitor another's traffic. As well, it will be unlikely that two senders are sending on the same frequency at the same time.

Q. *Wi-Fi and Bluetooth use the same frequency spectrum. So why does your Wi-Fi PC not interfere with your Bluetooth toaster?*

A. These devices do not interfere with each other because (a) they use different spread spectrum techniques, (b) they employ protocols that allow them to understand they are not allowed to send/receive traffic to/from each other, and (c) a smart Wi-Fi PC would never condescend to communicate with an obtuse Bluetooth toaster.

HOUR 8

Remote Networking

What You'll Learn in This Hour:

- ▶ Reasons for remote networking
- ▶ The history of remote access
- ▶ Remote access requirements
- ▶ Remote access with SLIP, PPP, and L2TP
- ▶ Using VPNs and the Internet for remote access

In today's world of commerce, business is often accomplished on the run as employees travel from location to location to conduct their affairs. People find it advantageous to access their employer's network from home, a branch office, and other locations. Walk through a hotel lobby, an airport lounge, or even a café, and you will encounter network surfers, busy at work communicating with their company's information systems...or perhaps busy playing online Scrabble.

Whatever the network session might be, remote access employs several connectivity strategies to provide users connections from a remote site to corporate, institutional, and home networks. Since the 1970s, dial-up modems have provided one way of accessing a corporate network. For the past decade, higher-speed connections and new remote networking standards have expanded options, including the use of virtual private networks (VPNs) over the Internet. In this hour, we'll explore these strategies for remote connections.

Early "Remote Control"

The first widely used remote access system was Telnet. One example of Telnet was its partnership with UNIX. Users needed to connect to their UNIX host system when they weren't directly connected to the system's central processor unit (CPU). Thus, in 1969

Telnet standards were published to provide guidance on building software for a remote client to communicate with a host computer. To the user, there would be no difference between a Telnet session 1,000 miles away and a session with a terminal sitting next to the UNIX host. (In those days, this host was called the mainframe.)

The first PC remote access solutions were built using Telnet's remote control behavior. It isn't surprising that remote control was the first method of remote access used for personal computers because initially, personal computers weren't considered sufficiently powerful to do very much local processing. Because of its age and lack of security features, Telnet has seen diminished use, and many implementations have been replaced with Secure Shell (SSH), which is examined in Hour 20, "Security."

Remote Control for System Administration

In the early days of PC remote access, when employees needed access to their applications and files while on the road, an information system (IS) person would arrive at their desks with floppy disks in tow. The IS technician would then install remote control software on both the user's desktop and the laptop computer. The IS person would then instruct the user to put the desktop system into a mode in which the computer waited for a call while the user was out of the office. The user would take his trusty eight-pound laptop on the road, and if he needed to read email, check a schedule, or gain access for any other reason, he would dial in to the desktop computer. The screen of the desktop computer would appear on the laptop, and the user could slowly read email or work with other applications. When the session was over, the user would disconnect the laptop's modem, and that would be the end of data access for that session. This mode of communicating seems far-fetched now, but not so long ago it was the prevalent method for remote access.

One area where remote control has increased and, in fact, has become one of the preferred methods for remote access to computers is system administration. Some organizations have elected to avoid phone support for their workers, preferring instead to simply install a system management remote control agent on each end user PC. With the agent in place, a user can report a problem with his computer, and an administrator can use the agent to temporarily take over the user's desktop across a network.

Help desks from Internet service providers (ISPs) or companies such as Microsoft and Dell make extensive use of remote control system administration systems. These technical centers also take control of a remote customer's computer to diagnose and fix problems.

Modems and Remote Access

We've danced around the subject of modems in several parts of Hours 1–7. Now is the time to explain them because they are a vital part of the remote access equation. The term modem stands for modulate-demodulate. A modem accepts digital data in the form of positive or negative voltages from a computer and modulates it into an analog form that can travel over conventional phone lines. At the other end of a connection, another modem translates the analog signal back into a digital format such that the computer on the other end can process it. A general view of the process is depicted in Figure 8.1.

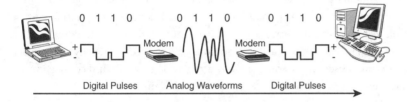

FIGURE 8.1
The modulation/demodulation process

You might ask, "Why are modems necessary at all? Why not just transmit the data digitally?" Modems are necessary for the majority of users who need to access networks because conventional telephone installations are designed to carry analog signals. After all, we humans speak in analog signals, not in binary 1s and 0s.

Unless a user has migrated to digital services, such as digital subscriber line (DSL), the modem remains a vital tool for remote access communications. I have opted for high-speed digital access when possible, but I still use modems when I travel to vast parts of the globe where digital facilities aren't available. As examples, I have used dial-up modems in places such as the Caribbean, Versailles, France, and Beijing, China, because dial-up was the only way I had to connect to my home and office networks and the Internet.

Modem Standards and Universal Connectivity

Fortunately, for the data networking industry, all modem manufacturers have settled on a common set of specifications for building their machines. The standards, commonly called the "V-Series" modems, are published by the International Telecommunications Union (ITU) and range from the "ancient" devices that transmitted data at 300 bits per second (bps) to the modern broadband modems, capable of transmissions speed in the megabit per second (Mbps) range.[1]

For a while, in the 1960s and 1970s, a few hardware firms were building proprietary modems, notably AT&T. As well, Hayes Communications' Smartmodem added a

[1] If you want to know the details (now mostly history), look at my book The V Series Recommendations: Protocols for Data Communications over the Telephone Network.

command set to the AT&T modems to instruct the modem how to dial numbers, answer calls, and go "on-hook" and "off-hook." Because AT&T's products didn't find extensive success in Asia and Europe, the 1970s saw the beginning of a migration to the V Series modems (along with the Hayes command set).

Cellular and Broadband Modems

Cell phones use modems, and so do broadband connections on cable, satellite, and phone systems. All are classified as modems because they modulate and demodulate analog frequencies. However, these modems employ complex coding and compression techniques to allow megabit data rates. In addition, they are "intelligent" enough to correct certain distortions to a transmission and even to adjust their transmission rates based on the current conditions of a connection. Many of these modems are housed in the same shell as a router. The broadband connection sitting next to my PC is supported by a so-called DSL modem/router.

> ### Bit Rate and Baud
>
> You might hear someone refer to a modem's transmission rate with the term "baud," but this usage isn't correct. Baud refers to the rate of change of the state of an analog signal. The original AT&T (Bell) 103 Model transmitted 1 bit for each state change; thus, the bit rate was the same as the baud. Thereafter, clever modulation techniques were used to code multiple bits per baud. For example, a 2,400 baud modem represented 8 bits per baud and had a 19,200bps transmission rate. Today, broadband modems not only employ advanced coding and modulation operations, they also compress the bits into a smaller stream for transport across the media.

Modern Remote Access Protocols and Procedures

Over the past several years, a variety of technologies have become available to enable computers to join networks from remote locations as opposed to remote-controlling a remote computer on a network. These factors include the following:

▶ An increase in the processing power of laptop computers

▶ The huge increase of Internet use and the universal acceptance of the Internet remote access protocols

▶ An increase in the installed base of higher-quality analog phone lines

▶ The increase in high-speed data access provided by cable and DSL modems

▶ The increased numbers of TCP/IP implementations

▶ The introduction of enhanced security features to allow the use of the public Internet as a medium for connecting private local area networks (LANs)

The Point-to-Point Protocol (PPP)

The Point-to-Point Protocol (PPP) was developed to solve several problems that evolved as more people began to use computer networks. Several vendors and standards organizations developed network layer protocols (L_3 of the OSI model), such as IP, IPX, AppleTalk's L_3, and IBM's SNA L_3. Consequently, machines (such as routers and servers) had to support more than one Layer 3 protocol.

It was recognized that the negotiation of various options between two users would be helpful and efficient. For example, compressing parts of a packet would yield better throughput. As another example, an ISP might want to assign an IP address to a dial-up user. Until PPP was developed (as well as its predecessor, the Serial Link Interface Protocol [SLIP]), these operations were performed with proprietary protocols; or worse, they weren't performed at all.

In addition, the networking industry had no standard method for "encapsulating" the various vendors' protocol stacks into a packet. Thus, if a packet arrived at a router, this machine had to somehow figure out if the packet was an Internet Protocol (IP), Internetwork Packet Exchange (IPX), Systems Network Architecture (SNA), Xerox, or AppleTalk packet. Although the router could indeed figure it out, the process was slow and cumbersome.

PPP solves these problems. Although most vendors have migrated to IP, PPP is still widely used for setting up addresses, negotiating a few options, and (especially) authenticating the remote user. Equally important, PPP is also used to ensure the two point-to-point communicating parties have a reliable physical connection with each other before data is sent. Thus, IP cannot send packets until PPP has performed a successful handshake with the other machine, such as an ISP router. Furthermore, PPP will not perform this handshake if the two modems aren't communicating properly. That is, PPP will be enabled to operate only if the physical channel (L_1) and the Link Control Protocol (L_2, or LCP) are operating properly.

Supporting Protocols to PPP

After it has been determined that, say, a client and the client's ISP have an acceptable modem connection (either dial-up or broadband) and an L_2 link protocol is in place, PPP executes its LCP to set to set up a PPP relationship between the two parties. During this procedure, LCP might also send "Configure" packets to negotiate options (such as the size of an IP packet that will be used during data transfer) and any authentication procedures. For the latter feature, older systems use the Password Authentication Protocol (PAP), whereas newer dial-up connections have migrated to the Challenge Handshake Authentication Protocol (CHAP), which is examined in Hour 20.

After LCP has finished these key handshakes, PPP executes its Network Control Protocol (NCP) to negotiate options specific to the specific L_3 protocol. For example, with IP, compression and IP addresses can be negotiated. As another example, with AppleTalk, network zone information can be exchanged.

Finally, after NCP has completed these tasks, user traffic can be exchanged between the two parties. But "finally" might be an unfair characterization of PPP's operations, because these negotiations take place almost instantaneously. Also, even if you don't have a conventional dial-up operation on your network, it is likely your broadband or ISP still use PPP to make certain the link between your network and the provider's network is operating properly.

Other Useful Features of PPP

As you might have noticed, certain features, such as negotiating which L_3 protocol is to be used during a session, are somewhat antiquated because IP has largely taken over this role. Another feature that was put into PPP to deal with the diversity of protocols but is still useful today is called auto-detection, a service provided at the data link layer (L_2) of the OSI model.

Today, the data communications industry has migrated to a more restricted set of procedures and protocols used for L_2 operations. Nonetheless, the data link procedures for Wi-Fi, Ethernet, Cellular, ATM, Bluetooth, dial-up modems, and so on aren't the same. They might vary only slightly, or they might vary significantly. This situation could make our life quite complex. After all, how are we to know the minute details of each bit that makes up the control fields of a data link protocol? Even if we know them, how are we to choose the correct hardware and software to accommodate these protocol data units (PDUs)?

PPP helps in this task. It provides the procedure for detecting and interpreting certain (not all) data link protocols' frame formats. Once again, these operations should remain transparent to you, but knowing this capability might be helpful to you someday.

Following is a list of other services that are part of the PPP platform. Check your network vendors to determine if these options are supported:

▶ **Vendor extensions**—Allows the support of a vendor's proprietary procedures on a PPP link.

▶ **Maximum receive unit**—Allows the two parties to negotiate the size of the packet to be used during the session.

▶ **Quality control**—Provides a means for monitoring the quality of a link, specifically when and how often a link is losing a packet.

▶ **Compression**—Supports the compression of several of the control fields of a PPP packet.

▶ **Loop back**—Allows checking for a signal that is mistakenly looped back to its sender.

The Layer 2 Tunneling Protocol (L2TP)

PPP was designed for two endpoints to communicate with each other, such as in a point-to-point dial-up connection. The Layer 2 Tunneling Protocol (L2TP) extends PPP to operate between separate machines across one or more networks.

A tunneling protocol uses the concept of encapsulation, wherein one protocol's contents (its packet) are placed (encapsulated) inside another protocol's packet; the latter is called the delivery protocol. Tunneling is quite useful if traffic needs to be sent through an incompatible network or it needs to be placed on a secure path (a tunnel) for transport through a nonsecure, perhaps untrusted network.

For this explanation, PPP packets are encapsulated within L2TP (see Figure 8.2). A user dials in (or is connected through a broadband link) to an L2TP Access Concentrator (LAC). This machine, which could be a vendor's network access server, is usually the initiator of the tunnel. The telephone connection isn't carried through the Internet; the physical call is terminated at the LAC.

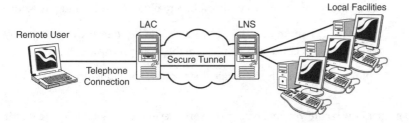

FIGURE 8.2
L2TP configuration

The LAC is responsible for configuring the tunnel; it builds tables for passwords and makes contact with an appropriate machine to form the other end of the tunnel (where the other party is located). This other machine is the L2TP Network Server (LNS). It's the server side of the tunnel; thus, it waits for calls (and new tunnels). After a tunnel is set up, the traffic moves bidirectionally between the two parties. These operations are part of the services of a virtual private network (VPN). Other VPN services are covered later in this hour.

When a network user accesses the ISP access server (the LAC), the ISP uses CHAP to challenge the authenticity of this user, an important part of the overall operations of PPP and L2TP. After the user is authenticated, the LAC undergoes operations to place the user's traffic onto an existing tunnel (using parameters and identifiers the user furnishes), or, if needed, create a tunnel for this session. A tunnel is identified with a tunnel ID, and sessions through the tunnel are identified by a session ID.

Again, security is of the utmost concern when using PPP and L2TP. Thus, CHAP and yet another Internet standard, RADIUS (Remote Authentication Dial-In Service), are instrumental to running a secure network. We leave this subject for now and return to it in Hour 20.

Ideas for Enhancing Dial-In Security

For the subject of remote access, following are several measures you can take to enhance your network's security:

▶ Ensure that the system logs all incoming calls and login attempts. This procedure can help locate users who are trying to guess passwords.

▶ Limit login attempts to three or fewer, and lock out any user who hasn't produced a correct password for a given user ID after repeated unsuccessful attempts to log in.

▶ Use access tokens in addition to user IDs and passwords. Access tokens are particularly difficult to crack because anyone logging in must have access to a known and trusted user token in addition to a valid user ID and password.

▶ Change the PPP settings so that the remote user has a secure login. Security protocols such as CHAP can help secure the login process.

▶ Encourage (force?) users to change their passwords frequently.

No matter how secure you make your network, never cease trying to make it more secure. Security is a process, not a destination.

Using the Internet for Remote Access: The VPN

In the past, dial-up strategies were the only method of establishing a remote connection with a private LAN or WAN. The Internet now provides users the VPN. A VPN is a secure connection established over the Internet between a remote user and, say, a corporate network. The VPN is a conduit (a tunnel) that moves private data across the public Internet, a concept shown in Figure 8.2. To take advantage of VPN for remote access, an organization provides for the appropriate infrastructure:

- ▶ Invests in a contract with a national or international dial-up ISP to provide local dial-up phone numbers.

- ▶ Provides cable modem or DSL service to users who require high-speed remote access. Indeed, migrating away from conventional dial-up service will lead to more productive operations for all concerned.

- ▶ Sets up server/VPN hardware between the organization's network and the Internet to authenticate users using VPN software. Manufacturers in the networking business sell VPN hardware and software and provide extensive training for their customers. If your network is going to have users spread out over a wide part of a country or globe, you'll likely need assistance from specialists, because the configurations of the remote networking machines can be involved and complex. Take advantage of the expertise of your vendors' staffs; before long, you'll be able to take over and run the operation on your own. If you don't want to become involved in this level of detail, talk to your vendors about service contracts to help you manage the network.

Again, networking vendors are well acquainted with interworking their VPN hardware and software. You might discover that using the Internet instead of building your own network is less expensive and less complex.

If your organization is set up to do everything locally, dial-in servers that manage PPP connections and authentication are an effective way to ensure effective security on your network. But if you have users who are far apart—from Boston to San Francisco, for example—you might consider using the Internet as the media to connect your remote offices.

VPN offers more flexibility than users trying to dial in to the company network. Although both dial-in remote access and VPN require a remote access server to authenticate remote users to the corporate network, dial-in requires corporate modem pools to service dial-in customers. In the case of a VPN, the only additional hardware that needs to be deployed is the L2TP LACs and LNSs. (For a large enterprise, you might also want to bring in RADIUS servers, a topic for Hour 20.)

With this setup, any user in the world who can connect to the Internet can access the corporate network. Of course, this user must have a username and password that will allow a connection through the VPN remote access server. Cisco Systems, Microsoft, and a host of others provide VPN software that uses IPSec (IP security) for authentication and security. In the long term, this might prove to be the most efficient method for providing remote users access to secured networks.

In the case of Microsoft's various server products, VPN server capabilities are built into the Network Operating System's (NOS's) Remote Access Service (RAS). Figure 8.3 shows the RAS snap-in that's part of Microsoft Windows Server 2003, which is used to manage and configure VPN access to the LAN.

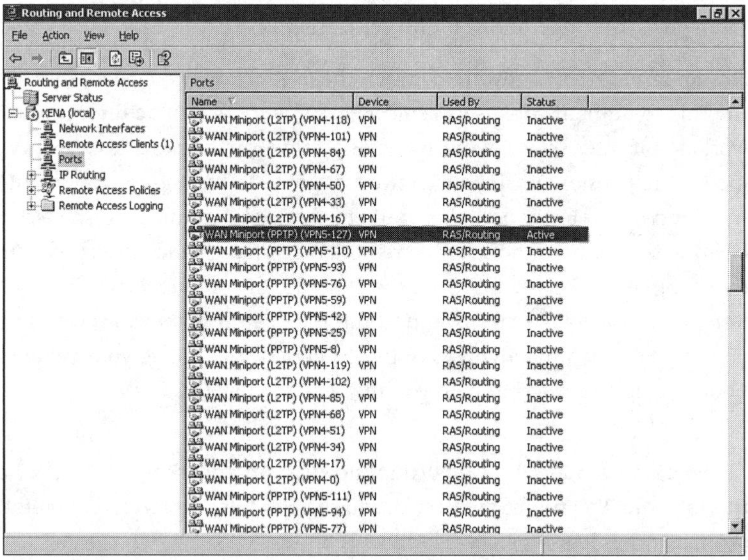

FIGURE 8.3
NOSs, such as Microsoft Windows Server 2003, provide utilities for configuring and managing VPNs.

Remote Access Hardware: Build or Buy?

Even though Internet-based remote access is becoming increasingly common, some organizations will build their own remote access solutions. The following discussion deals with the ramifications of doing so and provides some insight into what's involved in building a robust remote-access architecture.

Remote access hardware comes in various options from numerous manufacturers. It would be pointless to attempt to list them all here. Instead, this section focuses on the build or buy question that faces people who have to purchase and deploy remote access solutions.

Whether to build or buy a remote access solution is a difficult question. The answer depends on a variety of variables, including your company's size, how fast your company is growing, how many people will be using the remote access system, and how easy or difficult it should be to upgrade.

The process of selecting hardware for a user base that is growing by leaps and bounds has been compared to buying clothes for a child. By the time you bring the clothes home and get the child dressed, more often than not, the kid has outgrown them. Alternatively, if the clothes do fit, the child doesn't like them and won't wear them. Over time, a rule of thumb—somewhat of a joke, but not entirely—has emerged for remote access equipment: Figure out how many simultaneous users you'll have, and then at least double that capacity (unless of course, you *aren't* in a growth industry. The current real estate market comes to mind).

Building a Remote Access Solution

If you have only a few users, it's possible to create a remote access solution based on connecting two or more modems to a server computer. Most server operating systems offer solutions for remote node access, including Microsoft's Remote Access Service (RAS) and Novell's NetWare remote connection services. UNIX and Linux distributions also provide remote access services.

These systems offer several positive attributes, including the capability to use an operating system's built-in security and login handling. Typically, home-built remote access systems provide fine performance at a reasonable cost. The downside of building your own remote access server solution is that it can be difficult to support if you have a problem. All too often, the operating system vendor blames a problem on the multiport card vendor and vice versa, which gets you nowhere.

Buying Turnkey Remote Access Solutions

The alternative to building a remote access system from standard hardware and parts is to purchase a dedicated system. Dedicated systems usually don't follow conventions and might or might not interface directly with your operating system. In spite of their proprietary architecture, or nonstandard vendor-dependent designs, many of the dedicated remote access solutions available in the market offer great value for what they do.

In the case of VPN, some companies also provide VPN hardware, including Cisco and Nortel. In the case of Cisco, an entire line of VPN routers is available that provides data encryption and a web-based device manager. Many of the VPN routers available are deployable right out of the box and provide a good alternative to attempting to deploy VPN as a service of a particular NOS.

Summary

In this hour, we discussed what remote access is and why it has become so important over the past several years. PPP was highlighted because of its wide use. L2TP was also examined because of its increasing use. The hour concluded with an analysis of the alternatives for deploying a remote access system.

This is the end of Part II of this book, "The Basics." You should now be familiar with fundamental network concepts. Part III, "Building Networks," provides guidance on building a network, starting at the planning stages, and winding up with the system that will take care of your networking needs.

Q&A

Q. What is a remote node?

A. It's a computer connected to a host system, such as a mail or file server across a communications link or a network.

Q. Which protocol is commonly used for remote node communications?

A. The Point-to-Point Protocol (PPP) is often used for remote node communications.

Q. The PPP was designed for dial-up links. Will it operate over dedicated DSL?

A. Yes, as long as the link is up and running, PPP doesn't care if the link is dial-up or dedicated.

Q. Why use L2TP?

A. PPP was designed to operate over a conventional dial-up link, not through a network or networks. L2TP extends the capabilities of PPP across internets and the Internet.

Q. *What is a virtual private network (VPN)?*

A. The term virtual private network is used in two contexts. In the first, it means the use of a public network whose throughput and response time performances give the user the illusion he's using a highly tuned network—that is, highly tuned to this user's needs but without extensive security or quality of service (QoS) operations. In the second context, it means the use of a public network whose access and egress nodes provide extensive secure communications services (at a minimum) to the user.

HOUR 9

Planning for the Network

What You'll Learn in This Hour:

▶ The concept of best practices

▶ The steps used to create and maintain a network

▶ Best practices for security

By now, I trust we agree that building or upgrading a network, even a small one, requires an understanding of networking concepts. Adding a new condiment to the networking stew, it also requires planning. For even a small enterprise, a computer network cannot be successfully implemented with an ad hoc approach. In addition, the design must factor in immediate needs while considering longer-term issues.

Planning and building an enterprise network is a challenge for even the seasoned professional. Nonetheless, the tasks involved to bring up a network can be facilitated by using the concept of *best practices*. This model provides a framework and an associated checklist for completing these tasks. Best practices help the designer remain focused and organized—essential ingredients for effectively networking computers and other devices, such as servers and routers.

In this hour, we examine the concept of best practices and their role in creating a new network and enhancing an existing system.

Best Practices and Building Computer Networks

We humans have learned there are smart and not-so-smart ways to go about solving a problem. For example, a solution does not always lend itself to reliance on past experiences. In this situation, we need to take ad hoc, off-the-cuff actions.

But for many situations, it comes down to, "Why reinvent the wheel?" In our modern world, we've learned some basic best practices to employ to, say, manage a mortgage firm, conduct counter-insurgency wars, or build a computer network. For the former two, we can only say that the best practices associated with these endeavors are often ignored. But for the last operation, building a computer network, we'll use this hour to make sure these practices are "front and center."

The term best practices was coined by consultants in the 1980s to describe the institutional behaviors that had become ingrained and codified into *effective* standard operating procedures. From these experiences, it was concluded the use of best practices could provide an organization with a sensible, flexible set of rules to aid in decision-making about a complex process.

Best practices have also come to exist for networking. They transcend operating systems, hardware platforms, protocol innovations, and other rapidly changing components of networking. Instead of dealing with specifics, they are a set of concepts that can be applied to various situations.

Because computer and networking technology evolve so quickly, relying on best practices that can be applied to any network operating system or hardware allows you to remain focused on the big picture rather than becoming mired in the minutia. Some of the benefits of using best practices are as follows:

▶ Best practices offer a perspective that enables network planners to step out of the upgrade cycle long enough to take a strategic look at their current operations. Rather than focusing on today's problems, best practices provide a perspective with which to examine the infrastructure and procedures of the underlying pieces and determine whether they are working together productively.

▶ Best practices offer a way to assess and codify policies and procedures and discard those that are not productive or are counterproductive. As you assess your organization in preparation for a network installation or network upgrade, remember there is no one single set of best practices for everyone. What is best for one organization is not necessarily best for another. Every organization is different; as a result, best practices cannot be slavishly copied from a successful organization or the *Harvard Business Review*—your organization must define them for itself. Still, with regard to building a computer network, certain practices are universal.

▶ Codifying and instituting best practices often results in cost savings. Cost savings aren't an automatic corollary of the institution of best practices. However, in many cases, best practices save money by increasing efficiency.

With respect to networking, using best practices shouldn't be an option if the goal is a robust, flexible, functional architecture. No one would ask an architect to build a small house only later to ask that it evolve into a skyscraper— but that's what routinely happens in networking. Nightmare tales of ad hoc networking are legend in the consulting world. A classic example is the company in which several well-meaning department heads independently built their own networks, leaving the internal networking staff the onerous Frankensteinian job of stitching everything together. The complete system never operated very well, and the company expended enormous resources for a subpar solution.

The complexity of data networks at even the small local area network (LAN) level has made it imperative for network managers to review the way they execute their user job requests, desktop configuration management tasks, network management issues, and technology updates. It's not uncommon for a network manager to find his time focused almost entirely on short-time crises, leaving little time to deal with organizational issues. Naturally, this crisis focus does little good. First, constant crises burn out network managers; second, crisis management creates an adversarial relationship between management and users.

Instituting best practices when a network is being planned is the best way to ensure the network will function well and meet the goals set for it.

Planning Best Practices: Plan, Design, Implement, and Tune

An old saying claims, "Change is the only constant." If you've ever doubted this cliché, look at the changes that take place in a computer network from month to month or even week to week. The rate of change is so rapid it's difficult to plan for the future. Consider the evolution of the Internet, particularly the World Wide Web. We've witnessed the dot-com boom. We've seen a seesaw battle from the various network operating system companies as each software giant seeks industry dominance. Throw into the mix open source possibilities, such as Linux, and it's easy to understand why it's difficult for the network professional to keep pace with this ever-changing industry.

Although keeping up with change can be a big challenge, it's a necessity when dealing with the dynamics of computer networks. Being aware of the emerging products and technologies will allow a network manager to make selections leading to lowering networking costs. In the hope that I've convinced you of the values of staying educated, developing plans, and using best practices, let's look at some strategies for dealing with change.

If you were building a house, would you start nailing boards together willy-nilly, or would you work from plans? You'd probably work from plans. If you didn't, you might get a house...or you might not. Even when you do have a plan for a house, you can face spur-of-the-moment issues pertaining to the latest building materials as well as construction techniques you want to place in the plan as building is under way. The desire to make changes is always a temptation and sometimes a necessity.

That's what building or upgrading a computer network can be like. When you're creating or enhancing a network, because of the rapid steps in technology, it's especially important to ensure you follow a logical process. Otherwise, you'll wind up with a technology that no one can make sense of.

The suggested process can be simply stated as plan, design, implement, and tune:

▶ **Plan**—Plan your network from a user perspective. Stating the obvious, know what your network must do to aid its users! It sounds simple, but if you don't know why you're building it, you're not likely to reap much benefit from it. Be careful here. It's not uncommon for highly trained technicians to create a technically elegant network without a lot of input from the user community. More than once, I've heard, "That's not what I wanted!"

▶ **Design**—Design your network. What is design? One definition is that it's taking a beautiful idea and proving why it won't work. Competent engineers don't look for successes during the design process; they look for potential points of failure. That's a good way to look at designing a network. It must be capable of doing what you need it to do without breaking down at every turn.

Network design includes a variety of tasks, which we'll examine in more depth in the next hour. The chief task is capacity planning, or figuring how much your network will grow and trying to ensure you have enough capacity to deal with this growth. But the main trick to successful design (of any type) is to look for what doesn't work and to solve problems before you implement the design. Another word of caution: It's usually quite difficult to redo a network once it's up and running. Therefore, don't hurry the design phase; insofar as possible, take your time.

▶ **Implement**—Implementation is the process of physically realizing the design. Most likely, the design process will miss something. One approach to address this situation is to take a phased, step-by-step approach to implementation. By this, I mean testing individual components first and then piecing them together into a larger whole. This practice allows you to verify the soundness of the hardware and software configurations and to isolate problems for their proper identification.

▶ **Tune**—Implementations always leave some loose ends. Tuning is the part of the process in which you try to rectify the small flaws in your creation. Note that tuning isn't intended to compensate for fundamental design flaws. Don't try to patch a network with a flawed design. If you do, you'll likely end up with an automated mess on your hands.

Applying the Best Practices

To apply the ideal of best practices for your organization, you need a crystal ball. Because crystal balls are in short supply, you have to think hard about your business, your organization, and the available technology. You will need to judge what a network must do to keep your company competitive, serve your users, and not break the bank in the process. If you're going to be responsible for capacity planning for a network (and if you're the person building the network, this is almost certainly the case), answer the following questions. They represent a starting point for your reflections. As you work through these questions, take notes and add questions of your own.

1. How many workstations (computers) does your current network have?

   If your network has 5 or 10 workstations, planning should be relatively simple. If, on the other hand, you have to support 500 workstations, you'll need to structure and plan in more depth. Large networks are a challenge because they require the delivery of high-quality services to a variety of users. Most of these people can't be supported in an ongoing, one-on-one basis.

2. How many workstations will your network have a year from now?

   This question follows on the heels of the first question. The degree of expected growth can help determine what equipment you initially roll out. A 5-workstation network that will have 10 workstations the following year requires less overall power and flexibility than a 5-workstation network that will grow to 25 or 50 workstations during the same time frame. Clearly, if your network is growing at a rate that outstrips the ability of existing staff to service each user and each request manually, there will be a strong need for the services mentioned under question 1.

3. Do you or will you provide file services for your users?

   If you do, you have to make provision for a file server. Discussed in earlier hours, file servers tend to be overbuilt; if you can afford more power than you need now, get it. If you centralize data storage, you need to plan to back up that data adequately—otherwise, your users will lose confidence in the shared network storage and will not use it. They'll resort to building their own set of databases and files, which can easily morph into a situation in which your company has conflicting data.

4. Will you provide Internet email services for your users?

   If you do, you will need a mail gateway. You will need to contract with an Internet service provider (ISP) to handle your bulk mail, and you'll probably need to register a domain name on the Internet.

5. Will you provide other Internet access (the Web, File Transfer Protocol [FTP], Telnet services) to your users?

   If you're going to provide Internet access for your users, you need routers, servers, and firewalls. You can also roll the email server into this system. Chances are, you'll also need to go to the ISP marketplace and select an ISP that can provide you access across a high-speed line (a T1, digital subscriber line [DSL], or other high-speed access).

6. Are there other services you're providing to your user base? And are your users utilizing services "hidden" to the IS staff?

   If you're providing other services to the user community, make sure any changes (additions and deletions of hardware and software) consider these services. Another important question: Are your users employing services you're not aware of? You might respond, "How am I to know?" Some advice: You had better find out! Before making wholesale changes to your computing and networking environment, it's a good idea to canvas the user community to let them know these upcoming changes might affect their "private" (supposedly) standalone packages. The last thing you want is for an important user department to come to you *after* implementation and say, "Look what you've done! I can no longer run my application! What happened to my chat service? Where are my movies?" To forewarn your users is to forearm your position—not to mention your job security.

7. Do you now provide centrally administered remote access for your users? Will you ever have to provide centrally administered remote access for your users?

   Remote access is generally best provided by computers dedicated to the task of providing remote access. In most cases, this means implementing a server computer with virtual private networking (VPN) capabilities. For more about VPN, see Hour 8, "Remote Networking."

Questions Are Often Answered with Questions

As you use the best practices questions listed here to help you develop an approach to building a network, you'll find the answer to a question might actually generate additional questions. Make sure you have all the facts and a solid plan before you begin the process of building or upgrading a network.

By the Way

What you can create by answering these and other questions (questions that arise as you brainstorm the possibilities for your network) is a document specifying what you want the network to be capable of doing. You should end up with a written record that lays out the network requirements and design to meet these requirements.

Even if you're feeling confident about the answers you've formulated from the questions discussed so far, you'll likely come across two issues that can still give you headaches (typically because the issues continue to evolve). They are (a) interoperability by using standards and (b) network security. Let's look at these issues.

Interoperability by Using Standards

Although network and computer technology changes quickly, you don't necessarily have to concede your network becoming an outdated mucilage of hardware and software as soon as new products become available. Ideally, your network will be set up to be "future-proof," or immune to technology shifts as much as possible. Given that computer network technology changes as rapidly as it does, you might be led to think that future-proofing is...well, far into the future.

Although complete immunity from the dynamics of change isn't possible, you can be somewhat shielded from these transformations by deciding to follow the authoritative standards published about computer networks. As you might recall from Hour 3, "Getting Data from Here to There: How Networking Works," the Internet Engineering Task Force (IETF) sets standards for TCP/IP-based networks and publishes those standards in documents called Requests for Comments (RFCs). The specifications set forth in the RFCs are available, free of charge and without copyright restrictions, to anyone who wants to use them.

What does this mean in terms of best practices? First, it means you should be aware of the many IETF standards. (Go to www.isoc.org.) You don't have to know the standards in detail, but you should at least know what's been standardized, what's pending for standardization, and what's not standardized. This approach allows you to select products that are likely to interwork with each other.

The other benefit of using standards-compliant products is its simplification of your purchasing decisions. If a vendor's products are proprietary (that is, they do not conform to open standards), unless they offer a valuable service not covered in the RFCs, they should be out of the running.

> **Don't Accept Nonstandardized Products**
>
> To be fair and to give credit to other standards groups, the RFCs are specific parts of the standards published for computer networks. In previous hours, we've mentioned the fine work done by the International Telecommunications Union (ITU), the American National Standards Institute (ANSI), the International Organization for Standardization (ISO), the Institute of Electronic and Electrical Engineers (IEEE), the Electronic Industries Association (EIA), and others. The point of this discussion is this: Unless you have a specific need that cannot be satisfied by products adhering to standards, don't accept proprietary solutions. In the long run, they will complicate your network and your life.

You should ask yourself whether you want to make your network standards compliant. In most cases, the answer is yes. Now that I've fostered the decision upon you, kindly take note of that decision, because you'll take it into account when we discuss hardware and software selections in the upcoming hours.

Improving Security Using Best Practices

Best practices are quite helpful as a tool to provide security to a computer network. A network might work well enough and provide its users with their needs, but if a user illicitly sends a copy of data out of the building and gives it to a competitor, or if a hacker accesses your company files, then you as the network manager are out of luck.

A company can tolerate occasional network downtime; the enterprise data is not compromised and lies ready in wait to assume its duties. In contrast, rarely can a company tolerate a security breech; its data is often compromised and thus, cannot be trusted.

Security measures and procedures have come a long way in the past decade. Vendors and standards groups have devoted enormous efforts to devise ways to safeguard automated information systems. These efforts came about because of the large number of "cyber-villains" who have made it their life's work to punch holes in our computer network defenses and create viruses and other malware (a collective term for software and procedures designed to harm electronic information systems). Sometimes the intrusions are merely annoying. Other times, they're quite destructive.

Because you can't control the behavior of those who threaten the network from outside (although you *can* develop a strategy for blocking their attacks), you can institute best practices to help secure the network internally. And this relates to user behaviors. Some best practices for security you can institute include the following:

▶ Enunciating usage policies and procedures

▶ Defining secure behaviors

▶ Monitoring what you have defined

Security is an ongoing process. You should never conclude that the network is secure and all the work is done. Good security, as you'll find in Hour 20, "Security," requires monitoring and vigilance.

Enunciating Usage Policies and Procedures

Before you set up your network, you should define how users are and are not allowed to use data. Any violation of these rules, whether it be using flash disks, Zip drives, CDs, DVDs, laptops, PDAs (personal digital assistants), email, web pages, unauthorized Internet access, or other parts of the network, must be punishable by sanctions up to and including dismissal and legal action.

Companies should incorporate these rules into an employee handbook (after all, data is like any other company property) and acknowledge them with a written and signed statement by the employee.

Defining Secure Behaviors

Because each company's business is different, we haven't defined an exact set of rules. However, the following questions can help you figure out where your potential security holes are

1. Do you have your servers physically secured?

2. Is each server's operating system "hardened" against common intrusions?

3. Are controls in place to reduce Internet-based spyware, adware, and unwanted cookies?

4. Does each user have a unique password?

5. Are passwords regularly changed according to a schedule?

6. Is there a clearinghouse for passwords?

7. Are all logins, logouts, and file activity recorded at the server?

8. Are all file-copy actions to removable media logged?

9. Do your users understand their roles in helping secure the network?

10. Do you have a way to monitor and audit security?

These questions represent only the beginning of a list of security questions. Think about how your users work: Do they have read/write access to a corporate database? Do they have physical access to the various servers that make up the network? Just as with capacity planning, security is a subject that gets bigger the deeper into it you get.

The purpose of these questions is to help you determine how you want your network to operate. This material comes in useful in the hours ahead when you design and administer your network. Again, if you want to read more about security, go to Hour 20, which deals with these issues in more depth.

Monitoring What You Have Defined

"You can't monitor what you can't measure." It's as true for networks as it is for anything else. If you're setting policies on your network, whether for access control, intrusion detection, or performance, you'll need to be able to monitor activity to ensure your goals are being reached.

Why Monitor?

You don't need to be a large corporation's Network Operations Center (NOC) to monitor. If you've got a cable modem or DSL modem and your computer is directly connected to the Internet without a personal firewall, chances are good your computer has been scanned for security vulnerabilities by someone who means you no good.

So why monitor? The average time online of a new, not particularly well-secured system prior to being attacked and compromised is three days. Yes, three days. So it's a good idea to find some way of protecting your system and, more importantly, auditing the results.

How Do I Monitor?

We'll discuss monitoring in more depth in Hour 20. For this introduction, you need to be aware of the threats coming from the Internet and take action against them by configuring your existing software to remove vulnerabilities and adding software that monitors remaining vulnerabilities. Attacks can come from anywhere, and you can only defend against attacks you know about.

Collating What You've Learned

At this point, you've answered (or thought about) a lot of questions regarding what your network should do and how you want it to work. Your conclusions can help guide you in the hours ahead, when you design, build, and administer your network. If you can, assemble the information you've gathered into a document so that you have the questions and answers available for later review. You'll find it useful for helping you get back on track as you go forward through the process.

By the Way

Summary

In this hour, we examined the issues related to using best practices to determine the infrastructure and the policies and procedures that define your network. Hours that follow expand on these ideas. As you design or upgrade your network, be aware of the issues we've raised here related to network planning, interoperability, and security.

In the next hour, you'll go through the process of designing your network, step by step. You'll bring all you've learned in the book so far to bear on the process—so reviewing what you've read up to this point would be wise.

Q&A

Q. *How can you plan for growth?*

A. If the enterprise's user base is slated to grow, planning can track this growth. Another important aspect for planning pertains not just to users, but to new applications, such as adding a new product line to a company's market. As well, you should consider the changing of the users' usage profiles. For example, increased use of web-based video will have a pronounced effect on the bandwidth needed to support the video traffic.

Q. *Why is interoperability so important to network planning?*

A. The need for interoperability affects everything else when you're planning a network. Software or hardware that doesn't work with other software or hardware (or that does so only under certain conditions) limits the capability of your network to do its job.

Q. *What are some "best practices" that pertain to network security?*

A. Best practices include defining a set of rules and behaviors for your network users, detailing proper and best practices for their use.

Q. *How do products that adhere to published standards aid a network plan?*

A. They greatly facilitate writing and executing the plan.

HOUR 10

Designing a Network

What You'll Learn in This Hour:

▶ How to determine the user requirements for the network

▶ How to define the major functions of the network

▶ How to determine the type of network needed to satisfy the users' requirements

▶ How to write the specifications for the network's operations

In the previous hour, we examined how an organization and your project team can use best practices to develop the strategies and policies for building or upgrading a computer network. In this hour, we look at more detailed issues related to creating a network, including how to define the network's capabilities, establish the network blueprint, and design the network.

For this discussion, we once again assume you're the lead network designer and head up a group of talented computer network specialists.

These Next Hours Pertain to Creating New Networks and Upgrading Old Ones

Please keep in mind this important point: These next six hours (10–15) are written primarily with the scenario that you, as the lead network designer, and your staff are tasked with creating a network (or networks) from scratch. However, in today's world, most companies already have computer networks up and running. Obviously, these networks won't be created; they'll evolve from "older" networks—perhaps ones that are no longer meeting the requirements of the user community. Thus, many of the ideas in these hours also pertain to altering, upgrading, and enhancing an ongoing system.

By the Way

Advances in network hardware and the progress in using standardized communications protocols have made the overall process of connecting communications devices a much easier task than in the past. In addition, the industry has learned from its mistakes, and sets of best practices of documented experiences have proven to be effective in building and managing computer networks.

Notwithstanding this good news, creating an effective and efficient network entails considerably more than assembling the various hardware and software components. Why? Because the issues of, say, capacity, response time, throughput, ease of use, reliability, and security can't be resolved by simply attaching machines together and loading them up with off-the-shelf software packages.

Networks must also be designed to fulfill the needs of their users. Thus, any network worth its salt is tailored to its user base. With this important idea in mind, let's begin our discussion with an examination of six steps to build a network that will fulfill its job description: *satisfying its users.* The steps follow:

1. Identify the uses of the network.

2. List which tasks execute on which computers.

3. Select the type of network: to centralize or not to centralize.

4. "Draw" the network.

5. Write the specification.

6. Build the network.

Step 1: Identify the Uses of the Network

What do the users do who will use the network? Do they work with networks from home but also have to ensure the rest of the family has access to constrained computer resources? Are your users members of a consulting firm who use computers to handle job requests, client tracking, and billing? Are they members of a department of a large corporation who must use company web pages to interact with their customers? All these users have different requirements from a network.

No matter what your organization does, its network must accomplish one task to be considered successful: Ensure that whatever the requirements are, they can done better, faster, and more efficiently by using a computer network. If the network doesn't do that, it will be a failure, regardless of the quantity and quality of technology deployed.

The first order of business is to determine why your organization requires a network. For the balance of this discussion, we will focus on a mid-scale or large organization.

However, keep in mind that the same ideas apply to a small business, but perhaps not with quite as much formality.

The first task of step 1 leads to the desks of the senior managers of the organization. Make an appointment to meet with them and talk about (a) what the organization's core business is now and (b) how they want to change or improve the operations that support the core business.

These meetings shouldn't involve a broad discussion of what networks can do but a more specific discussion of what a network can do for the company. You need to pin down the core purpose of how a new network or a network upgrade will make the company a more productive place.

Any questions you pose should be open ended; try to see if the managers have a vision related to the company's future, and try to understand what that vision is and what its ramifications are in relation to computer and networking technologies.

Companies Are Much More Than a Mission Statement

By the Way

Interviewing key managers or corporate officers will supply you with much more information on a company's goals and purposes than the corporate mission statement. Mission statements are often designed for the company customers and are particularly tailored for company brochures. The better you understand the company and its reason for being, the better you can plan and implement the network.

After you've interviewed the senior executives, it's time to work with the folks on the production floor and in the cubicles. Sit with them and find out what they do. Be up-front about the purpose of your visit; it will help break down suspicion that you're there to increase their workload! If possible, work alongside employees to see what they do and how they do it. This exercise will provide you with valuable information about the nature of their work and how they use the company's data.

There's no substitute for getting into this level of detail. The network designers can't design a network if they don't know the nature of work the network must perform. On more than one occasion, I've watched highly trained technicians put together a set of networks with almost no input from the user community. Not surprisingly, none of these networks performed satisfactorily to their customers.

During this time, it's helpful to ask the employees what would make their jobs easier. Don't fish for computer-related improvements; instead, fish for concrete answers, such as, "If I could find a way to track all the phone conversations everyone has with Mr. X, I would be better prepared when he calls me." Clearly, whatever gives rise to this kind of response doesn't necessarily require a computer (a public notebook could also work quite well in this example), but it offers insight into another question: What data and information should this conceptual network (or network enhancement) process to satisfy this user's specific need? Such a question can be parlayed into part of the network specification, which is discussed later in this hour.

The goal of these interviews is to understand (a) how the organization functions and (b) what information its employees need to support these functions. The next part of step 1 is optional, but you might find it helpful: distilling these organizational issues into a list of action items that will improve the operations of the enterprise. Following are some of the points that might result from this analysis:

▶ Increased responsiveness to customers

▶ Easier access to customer data

▶ More up-to-date information (and identifying this information)

▶ Better capability to handle an increase in business

▶ Greater flexibility in order handling

These ideas represent typical organizational goals; they're generic descriptions of many companies' objectives. It's likely the responses you receive and the list you create will be more specific than these items and will address the issues that the employees face each day.

After you have completed your interviews and distilled the information in a document that lists the core issues affecting what purposes the network must fulfill, you're ready to quantify the network. By quantification, we mean you can examine specific issues pertaining to the resources that will serve the user base.

For example, your design team should determine how many users the network must support. Don't mistake this number for the number of computers, routers, servers, and so on needed for the network; that's the next question, and the two aren't the same thing. One computer can adequately serve multiple users if they don't have to interact with it on a constant, real-time daily basis. The one-computer-per-desktop model works for many offices—particularly in cases in which users work constantly on productivity software, including word processing, database, and spreadsheet applications, but it doesn't hold true everywhere. For example, in a factory floor shop, one computer used for laser-based barcode inventory control might serve 20 to 30 users. A healthcare practice might have a few public computers so that doctors can key their patient reports, but they probably wouldn't be dedicated systems. Instead, each doctor would log on, briefly enter a report, and then go on to the next patient.

Whatever the situation, determine how many users the network will serve. Nearly every network will grow over time, so keep expandability in mind. However, also keep in mind that initially you need a count of current users and those who will need to access network services when the network is first rolled out.

After you have determined how many people will be using the network, look at who those users are. Are they management who will use the computer primarily for administrative purposes such as memo writing and messaging; will they be office workers; or will they be people on a production floor? This analysis is an important part of the process because it leads to the next question: How many computers will the network have initially? Stated another way: How many computers will have only one user, and how many will be shared by many users?

After you and your team have determined how the users will interact with the network, you can determine how many computers the network will have. It's a relatively simple matter: Look at how the users will interact with the network and determine whether the ratio of computers to users is one-to-one or one-to-many. If it's a one-to-one ratio, the user count equals (or, in client/server networks, is just shy of) the number of computers. If it's a one-to-many ratio, it's likely that computers will be allocated according to job function. In other words, if a group of users access a computer only for checking work in and out with a barcoding system (common in some manufacturing settings) or for checking in parts picked in a warehouse, the network will deploy only as many computers for that group as will concurrently use them.

So, if a single user queues up at a time, one computer will do. If 10 users queue up and their tasks take time (say, more than half-a-minute each), you might recommend several computers for this group. Once again, the number of computers you allocate to user groups will depend on the users' needs. As with anything else, think it through and try to "rightsize" your design (that is, design enough capacity but not too much or too little).

Step 2: List Which Tasks Execute on Which Computers

The second step in the network-design process seems obvious: Know which aplications and tasks have to be performed at each of the computers on your network. Unfortunately, it isn't quite as straightforward as it might appear: This step is less about following the workflow trail than it's about continuing the rightsizing process.

In networking, rightsizing is a process that starts early on and continues after the rollout of the system. It starts with knowing the physical limits of your network (how many users, how many computers), but it doesn't end there. It isn't enough to know how many systems are out there; you also have to know how powerful each computer should be and what each computer should be capable of.

For example, the barcoding computers mentioned at the end of the step 1 section don't have to be very powerful; they're doing one task that doesn't require much processing horsepower or memory. Nor do they need soundcards or high-end video adapters.

On the other hand, some users will need all these things and more. Let's look at a couple of hypothetical cases that illustrate how to determine the quantity of horsepower and the range of features a given network system will require.

The Many-User Computer

Computers used by many users can be built minimally, as in the warehouse barcode example. Conversely, they can be built with all the bells and whistles. As with any other system, the features depend on the application. Here are some of the possibilities related to computer configuration:

▶ **Simple task: Simple computer**—A computer, such as the one that would be involved in the warehouse barcode example, wouldn't need a fast processor, a large amount of memory, or a big hard drive. Because video quality and sound capability aren't an issue, a legacy computer already available at the company would suffice. In case of new hardware, a minimum configuration system will likely provide more than enough power. Because it's difficult to buy a computer with less than a certain CPU speed and memory capacity, you could go with a bargain-basement model in terms of features. Notwithstanding this minimalist approach, you'll still need to configure the computer hardware to run the barcode software and the appropriate OS.

▶ **Complex task: Powerful computer**—Although multiuser computers deployed in a warehouse or manufacturing environment might not require a high-end configuration, you will run into situations in which you have to configure computers that will be accessed by numerous users. Because of the tasks they perform, they will likely require a powerful and feature-rich configuration. For example, you might deploy a kiosk computer that requires sound and multimedia capabilities and is configured with a touch screen.

▶ **Multiple tasks: Single user computer**—Single-user computers generally occur in office environments. No matter the job title, many people have become knowledge workers because their currency is dealing with information, including formatting, managing, and analyzing data. Depending on the nature of their jobs, they tend to require higher-end computers, but they also have widely varying connectivity requirements. For example, some workers might be able to leave their work behind at the end of the day and require no remote access;

others might require access from home; still others might require two or more computers to be able to do their jobs. Again, as in the other scenarios listed here, you must determine the tasks that will be accomplished on the computer and then configure the computer hardware so that it will run the OS and application software allowing the individual to be productive.

Even knowledge workers will require different classes of computers. Some users might be able to do their job with minimal configurations, whereas others—the "power users"—require computers that can run more complex software applications, such as simulation models. Users who travel might require a laptop configuration that gives them power on the road but also supplies them with all the capabilities they would need from a desktop computer when they're in the office.

As you can see from the discussion in this section, you and your team must spend time determining what people will be doing with their computers and how these computers must provide them with the technology to get their jobs done. You can't just configure a generic computer for every user; you must make sure that each computer is configured with the appropriate features and power to meet the users' requirements.

Step 3: Select the Type of Network: To Centralize or Not to Centralize

Another issue is how centralized the network administration and security must be for the network to run effectively. Typically, the centralization issue is related to scale and the nature of business (that is, the nature of the data and its overall importance to the business). Small businesses with only a few users who need to share data and other resources (such as printers) typically do not require a centralized network, nor do they require a separate server or Network Operating System (NOS), which can be a great cost saver for a small office or company. Let's look at peer-to-peer networks, and then we'll discuss centralized server-based networks.

Peer-to-Peer Networks

Peer-to-peer networks, which are supported by most desktop OSs such as Microsoft Windows and the various distributions of Linux, allow users to share directories and folders with each other with little interaction from a network administrator. Each resource is secured by its own password (which can include printers and other devices). In terms of network management, each user becomes the administrator of his own computer. In terms of security, peer-to-peer networks might not be secure because people often supply their passwords to co-workers. However, in an environment in which the data shared by these workers isn't of a highly proprietary or sensitive nature, users can easily communicate and collaborate on the network.

For example, Microsoft Windows (both the Professional and Home versions) provides a Network Setup Wizard that walks a user through the process of configuring a small peer-to-peer network. Figure 10.1 shows the Network Wizard Setup screen where you define the name of your network. In the Windows environment, a small peer network is referred to as a workgroup.

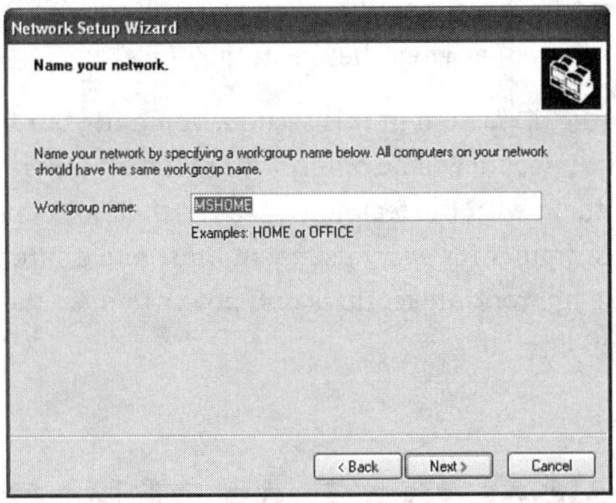

FIGURE 10.1
Microsoft Windows XP provides a Network Setup Wizard for creating a peer network.

Not only does the Network Setup Wizard make it easy to connect to other users who are running Windows, but a disk can be created during the network setup process that allows you to bring other versions of Windows into the network configuration.

The wizard can help you set up the following items:

▶ Connecting to the Internet through a dial-up or broadband connection

▶ Sharing an Internet connection with other computers (on a home network)

▶ Setting up a computer name, computer description, and workgroup name

▶ Setting up file and printer sharing

A Simple Network Does Not Mean a Secure Network

Most desktop OSs support peer networking capabilities. Although these networks are easy to get "up and running," they can be a security problem because users control the various security levels placed on shared files, as well as the procedures for interworking with the Internet.

Server-Based Networks

The alternative to the peer-to-peer network is the centralized network. This arrangement uses a server or servers to centralize the administration of the network. This model also provides for centralized security. Users log on to an authentication server and, once on the network, they can only access resources assigned to them by the network administrator.

In terms of network scale, you will likely find the server-based model is the better solution when you go beyond 10 users. However, it isn't necessarily the number of users who dictate the client/server model, but the level of security required to protect the company's automated information systems.

Client/server networks are more secure than peer networks. Their files are usually stored in a central location and are backed up on a regular basis. As stated, an administrator controls user access to data and software.

Server-based networks often entail the installation of more than one kind of server. Following are some commonly used servers:

▶ **File server**—A file server's job is to provide a central location for the company's data. The network administrator can assign different levels of access to each file contained on the file server. Some users can have full access (meaning that they can even delete files on the file server), whereas other users might only be able to access a file or files in a read-only mode (meaning that they can't edit the file).

▶ **Print server**—A print server hosts a printer or printers on the network. It not only allows the network administrator to control print jobs, but it also provides the memory and hard drive space to spool print jobs in the print queue as each print job waits to be printed.

▶ **Communication server**—A communication server provides a communication platform for the network. For example, Microsoft Exchange supplies an email, calendar, and contacts platform allowing users to communicate and share appointment, address book, and meeting information. Other examples of communication server software include Lotus Notes and Novell GroupWise.

▶ **Application server**—An application server hosts applications, including specialized data associated with an application. Application servers provide the backend processing power to run complex databases and other applications. User computers require a client application to access the services that the application server provides. Microsoft SQL server and Oracle are two examples of client/server database environments.

▶ **Web server**—A web server can host internal and external corporate websites. Even companies that do not deploy a web server on the Internet can use a web server internally, allowing network users to view and share information.

▶ **Mail server**—A mail server provides users with electronic mail boxes, including mail lists, buddy lists, storage for old mail, and storage for pending and received mail.

▶ **Authentication server**—This server allows legitimate users to log on to the network. Each network OS supplies authentication servers.

A number of other specialized server types—for example, DNS and DHCP servers—can also be deployed on a network. We will look at these specialized servers in Hours 16 and 17.

File Servers and Security

Requiring users to log on to the network and use file servers to store and "serve up" data enhances the level of security for a network. As mentioned, file servers allow network administrators to assign access rights down to the file level (meaning below the folder or directory level, which is a limitation for peer networks). Typically, file server security for PC-based OSs follows some simple rules:

▶ **Inheritance**—Security inheritance works similarly to financial inheritance; what a parent has can be inherited by a child unless it's blocked by third parties. In security inheritance, a user gets access to a particular directory (for example, F:\ DIRECTRY). Whatever access a user has to F:\ DIRECTRY is inherited by any and all subdirectories of F:\ DIRECTRY (for example, F:\ DIRECTRY\ ONE, F:\ DIRECTRY\ TWO, and so forth). Inheritance is a useful tool to ensure that a user has as much access as she requires to a given part of the server's disk.

▶ **Access rules**—In general, users are limited to three levels of access to a given file or directory on a file server:

  ▶ **No Access**—Users cannot access the file or directory.

  ▶ **Read-Only Access**—Users can access the contents of a file or directory but cannot modify it.

  ▶ **Read-Write Access**—Users have the rights to access and modify files and directories.

Various NOSs enable additions to these three basic access rights, but it should be possible to ensure reasonably good security using only these three rules.

Easier Backup

One benefit to storing network files on a centralized server is this: You can back up the files simply by duplicating the server's hard drive to tape or some other media. Here's an example of this operation.

Assume that your network has 50 user workstations. If all the users store their files on their workstations, you'll have to back up all or part of their hard drives to ensure that no data is lost if a system crashes. Further, suppose that all users have 100 megabytes (MB) of files on their workstations' hard drives (for many users, a conservative estimate). Backing up this quantity of files across the network for this many users could take 10 or 12 hours and present a formidable coordination challenge.

By contrast, backing up a server's hard drive with an attached tape drive or some other backup device can take as little as an hour or so. Clearly, backing up files from a single server to another storage device takes less time and is more controllable than the scenario of coordinating 50 users' activities.

A tape drive system is an attractive option for backing up an enterprise's database files. Tape media allows for an extended archival of data at a reasonable cost. As mentioned in earlier hours, tape access is sequential in that the read/write heads do not move across the tape (as in a random access hard disk drive). In addition, after the data has been accessed, the tape must be rewound.

However, for disk backup, you're not concerned with reading any particular record, so the issue of sequential versus random access is not an issue. In addition, high-speed can achieve transfer rates of 80 megabytes per second (MBps).

Several varieties of tape drives are available:

- 4 millimeter (mm) digital audio tape (DAT) drives that handle up to 8 gigabytes (GB) of storage

- Digital linear tape (DLT) that handles 20–40GB of storage

- Advanced intelligent tape (AIT) that backs up as much as 60GB per tape

Some tape drives handle only one tape at a time. However, devices called tape changers can handle whole libraries of hundreds or thousands of tapes. The kind of tape drive you select depends on what your needs are today and what you expect them to be in the foreseeable future. Remember that the amount of data that seems huge today could seem a pittance tomorrow.

Easier Configuration Management

Storing files on a server offers compelling advantages. However, there's more to centralized management of a network than simply storing files on a server. As a guideline, if you have more than 10 workstations, it's necessary to find a way to inventory the hardware, audit the software on the hard drive, install new software, and ensure that the workstation adheres to configuration standards.

Configuration management is the art (or science) of using a central console to ensure user workstations have the correct hardware and software installed and the software and hardware is set up according to standards. For large computer facilities, configuration management of software is a complex operation. It's usually supported by a large database with a proprietary front end that allows a network administrator to view and modify the configurations of users' workstations. Most management software requires each system to implement an agent (a piece of software that interacts with the administrative database) on the workstation. Often, agents can be installed automatically as a user logs in to the network.

However, there's a payoff for mastering the intricacies of configuration management software. Network administrators who install and use configuration management software report they have better control over their users' workstations. They can inventory the network quickly and install and upgrade software for many users simultaneously. In addition, they can set up alarms that register unauthorized tampering, which helps keep the theft of hardware and unauthorized employee installed software under control. In the long run, the "hassles" of configuration management will reap dividends for your company.

A variety of manufacturers—including McAfee, Microsoft, Tivoli, IBM, Digital, Hewlett-Packard, and others—make high-quality configuration management tools. Many packages are modular, so you don't have to purchase the whole package to get the services you need.

Choosing a Topology

Regardless of the choice for a client/server or peer setup, you will be required to select a topology. Because peer networks are by practice used to keep the overall cost of the network down, many companies end up using a hub or switch to configure a simple Ethernet star network.

Keep in mind that the network topology is usually determined by the network architecture that is deployed and not the client/server or peer models being used. Most local area networks (LANs) now use some flavor of Ethernet, whereas wide area networks (WANs) employ Asynchronous Transfer Mode (ATM) or Multiprotocol Label

Switching (MPLS). The points are (a) a physical topology is often part-and-parcel of the communications protocols, and (b) the choice of a client/server or peer arrangement has no bearing on the physical network topology.

Step 4: "Draw" the Network

By the time you reach step 4, you should know the following:

▶ The purpose of the network

▶ The specifics of the network's use (which users do which tasks)

▶ The "quantity" of both users and computers

▶ Whether the network will be centralized or decentralized

▶ The network topology

After you know these basics about the "conceptual" network, you're ready to go to the whiteboard. Get a set of markers in at least four or five colors, go to the whiteboard, and then start drawing your network.

Try It Yourself ▼

Drawing the Logical Network Diagram

The first drawing you make is the logical diagram. It details the applications that operate on workstations and the resources that the workstations must access.

1. Start by drawing a workstation for each type of user (for example, one warehouse floor computer, one analyst's computer, one accounting computer, one secretary's computer, and so on). Just make a circle for each computer, drawn in a line across the top of the whiteboard or page (see Figure 10.2).

FIGURE 10.2
The first stage of the logical network diagram

2. Underneath each computer, list the applications the machine has to run (see Figure 10.3). This could include word processing, spreadsheets, email, scheduling, and more for a user's desktop computer, or a single application for a dedicated machine, such as a factory or warehouse inventory computer or an in-office computer dedicated to routing email.

▼

FIGURE 10.3
The second stage of the logical network diagram, showing the applications needed

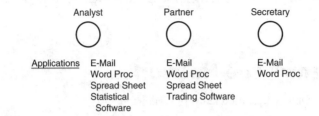

3. Make a list of the resources each workstation computer will share. In general, peer networking has a lot of these shared resources (such as printers, scanners, shared modems, and so on); client/server networks will have fewer shared resources. No matter whether you've elected to use client/server or peer, add these resources to your diagram (see Figure 10.4).

FIGURE 10.4
The third stage of the logical network diagram, showing the shared resources

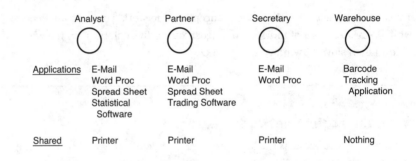

4. If the system will participate in a network-wide security scheme, note which group of users has login access to the various pieces of the system (see Figure 10.5). For example, business desktop users can log in to the file server, warehouse supervisors can log in to the transaction server, and administrators can log in to anything anywhere. This step helps ensure you provide the correct levels of security.

5. Add the workstation OS to the bottom of the list (see Figure 10.6). The OS is usually something like Windows Vista, a Linux flavor, or Mac OSX.

    Although UNIX can be used as a client, outside of academic computing centers and high-end engineering workstations, it is not common as a workstation OS. If you have more than one workstation OS, ensure that you have more than one computer drawn; each workstation OS should be shown on a separate machine.

6. Add the quantity of each type of workstation to the bottom of the list (see Figure 10.7).

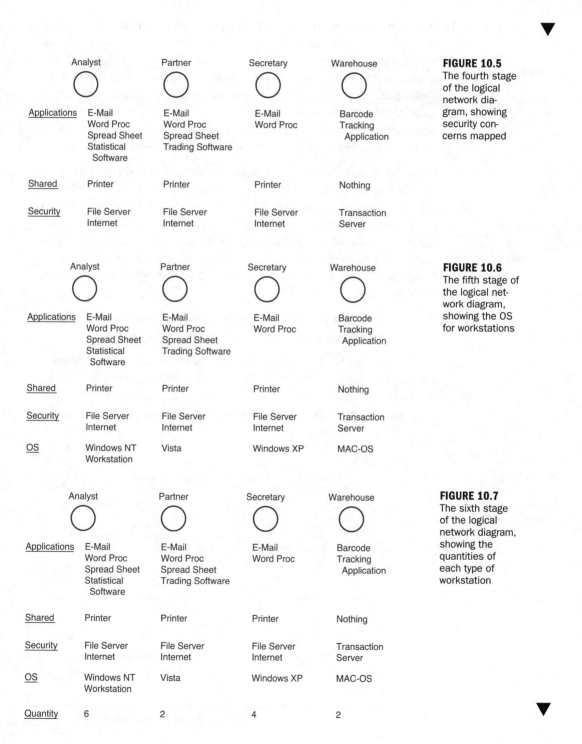

FIGURE 10.5
The fourth stage of the logical network diagram, showing security concerns mapped

	Analyst	Partner	Secretary	Warehouse
Applications	E-Mail Word Proc Spread Sheet Statistical Software	E-Mail Word Proc Spread Sheet Trading Software	E-Mail Word Proc	Barcode Tracking Application
Shared	Printer	Printer	Printer	Nothing
Security	File Server Internet	File Server Internet	File Server Internet	Transaction Server

FIGURE 10.6
The fifth stage of the logical network diagram, showing the OS for workstations

	Analyst	Partner	Secretary	Warehouse
Applications	E-Mail Word Proc Spread Sheet Statistical Software	E-Mail Word Proc Spread Sheet Trading Software	E-Mail Word Proc	Barcode Tracking Application
Shared	Printer	Printer	Printer	Nothing
Security	File Server Internet	File Server Internet	File Server Internet	Transaction Server
OS	Windows NT Workstation	Vista	Windows XP	MAC-OS

FIGURE 10.7
The sixth stage of the logical network diagram, showing the quantities of each type of workstation

	Analyst	Partner	Secretary	Warehouse
Applications	E-Mail Word Proc Spread Sheet Statistical Software	E-Mail Word Proc Spread Sheet Trading Software	E-Mail Word Proc	Barcode Tracking Application
Shared	Printer	Printer	Printer	Nothing
Security	File Server Internet	File Server Internet	File Server Internet	Transaction Server
OS	Windows NT Workstation	Vista	Windows XP	MAC-OS
Quantity	6	2	4	2

▼

7. Next, draw lines from each workstation type to each system that the workstation type requires access to. In other words, if an accounting PC requires file storage resources on a file server, select a colored marker, draw a line between the two systems, and write the name of the resource the workstation client will use. If a workstation has a shared printer, ensure that other systems using it are connected to it by drawing lines of a different color than the first. If a router provides connectivity between the network and the workstations but must first route data through a server, draw that full path as well in yet another color.

Make certain each connection documents the network protocols that will carry the traffic. Today, most networks use a single protocol stack, the Internet Layers 3, 4, and 7 running on top of the Ethernet Layers 1 and 2. But multiple protocols can also run side by side on a network. If you're not certain which protocol a particular service will use, put a question mark next to its connection line and make a note to find out as soon as possible which protocols will work there. Remember: Finding out what you don't know is almost as important as finding out what you do.

For a review of this aspect of the process and the various protocol stacks used in LANs and WANs, you might want to refer back to Hours 3 and 6.

When you have completed this exercise, you've successfully created...abstract string art! Actually, you've created a set of dependencies you can use to determine which computers need access to which resources (see Figure 10.8). Copy what you've done on the whiteboard into your notebook for future reference.

FIGURE 10.8
An example of a finished logical network diagram

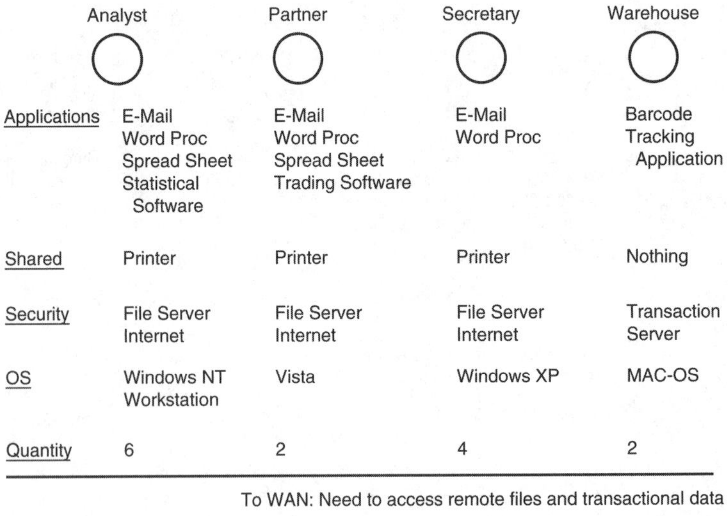

	Analyst	Partner	Secretary	Warehouse
	◯	◯	◯	◯
Applications	E-Mail Word Proc Spread Sheet Statistical Software	E-Mail Word Proc Spread Sheet Trading Software	E-Mail Word Proc	Barcode Tracking Application
Shared	Printer	Printer	Printer	Nothing
Security	File Server Internet	File Server Internet	File Server Internet	Transaction Server
OS	Windows NT Workstation	Vista	Windows XP	MAC-OS
Quantity	6	2	4	2

To WAN: Need to access remote files and transactional data

After you've determined the various resources to be shared (which was probably rendered much simpler by drawing it than by trying to create a comprehensive list), you're ready for the next great task: drawing the physical network.

Try It Yourself

Drawing the Physical Network Diagram

Drawing the physical network really isn't as difficult as it might appear. If you already know which clients have to be connected to specific resources and which topology you'll be using, you're halfway there. Let's assume that we are going to deploy an Ethernet network, because it's the most commonly deployed local network architecture.

1. Start by drawing the physical center of your network, such as a router or a hub. If you're deploying a network of any size, a router would be more practical. Routers are now priced such that it makes sense to take advantage of their greater capability to control bandwidth. Indeed, you might find it difficult to purchase hubs that are configured with a high density of ports.

Routers Allow Segmentation of the Network

By the Way

The use of routers allows the network designer to segment a larger network into smaller subnetworks. I highly recommend subnetting your network, a topic introduced in Hour 3, "Getting Data from Here to There: How Networking Works," in the section "Alternatives to the Conventional Address."

If a large network using Ethernet is not subnetted, traffic can experience excessive delays as the network nodes contend for use of the media. This situation is common on collision detection networks, such as Ethernet. By breaking the network into smaller subnets, routers can be deployed to regulate traffic flow. Also, the physical topology of the network does not prevent a network from being segmented.

The downside to subnetting is its increased complexity, but this situation is outweighed by the benefits. In addition, subnetting can enhance security as well as the management of Internet names and addresses.

▼

2. Draw as many boxes as you need for additional switches or hubs that you will use. Then connect lines between the switch and the segments; each of these lines represents the cable that connects the ancillary switches (or most likely routers) to the central switch.

3. Next, draw the servers and mark them as connected directly to the switch (see Figure 10.9). A server connected to a switch offers compelling advantages in terms of performance at the workstation because the server has a direct connection to the port to which the workstation is connected. This holds true even if a workstation is connected through a secondary switch or hub connected to a switch port; the collision domain of individual switches or hubs is usually fairly small, so there isn't much competition for bandwidth.

FIGURE 10.9
The completed connectivity diagram

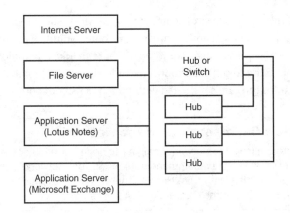

4. Refer to the drawing of the logical network and do some analysis. Look at which workstations require access to which servers, and try to group them.

5. After you analyze the relative bandwidth requirements of your users, you're ready to start figuring out which class of user has to connect to which device. Take the time to think about this issue. If users don't have sufficient bandwidth initially, they will have network problems and consequently lose faith in the network. It's important to roll out systems that work for the users; otherwise, the network has no credibility. Figure 10.10 provides an example of using a centralized switch and hubs providing connections for each segment.

Now that you've drawn your network both logically and physically, you have a body of work you can use to see whether what you've done makes sense. One of the benefits of working graphically is that you can begin to see how your users

▼

are grouped based on common access. If you begin seeing patterns in how users work and you're using a switch, you might elect to extend the pattern and formalize it. For example, all accountants need to have access to the inventory data, so the user group called Accountants is granted that right globally.

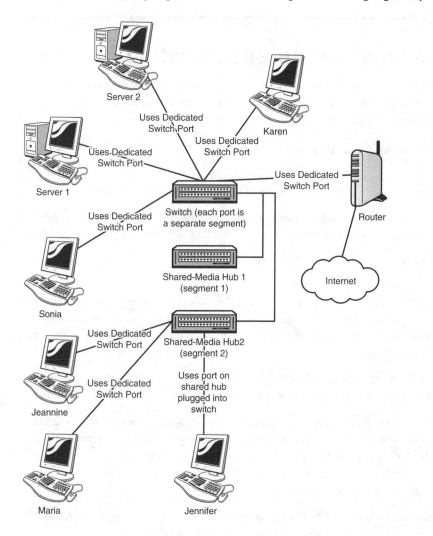

FIGURE 10.10
The physical network drawing (simplified to a small user base for purposes of illustration)

After you've made changes to your network drawings based on patterns you've discovered (such as to segment or not to segment your network), you're ready to start drawing the workstations and connecting them to the appropriate network device (such as a hub or router port). When you do this, note how many of each type of computer are connecting to each port; that way, you can ensure that you connect only as many workstations to each hub as each hub has ports.

▼

When this process is complete, you'll have a set of drawings that provide you with connection-oriented data you might otherwise have missed. These drawings will enable you to quantify the number of hub and switch ports you'll need for your network.

▲

Step 5: Write the Specification

If you've gotten this far, it's fair to say you've come a long way! You now have enough information about your users and the conceptual network to write a document that includes the following:

- ▶ The purpose of the network

- ▶ The specifics of the network's use (which users do which tasks), which now translates into the user community's requirements for the network

- ▶ The overall schemes for a client/server or peer-to-peer model and the use of communications protocols

- ▶ The network topology, which now is quite specific, as suggested in Figure 10.10

You also have a pair of diagrams portraying the logical and physical connections the network requires. Pat yourself on the back—you deserve it. You've created the basis for an initial specification document, which enumerates all the preceding points and includes the diagrams.

After you've created the specification document, you're ready to meet with other users to look over the plans and ensure all the bases are covered.

Now's the time to write the specification for the network. The specification document should take into account all the points in the preceding section and list, quite specifically, the various uses of the network. Specifications don't have to be long, but they must be complete and clear; as English teachers are prone to say, "It should be as long as it needs to be—but no longer."

The purpose of a specification document is twofold: to limit the scope of the network design and to provide a reference document for network administrators.

A sound specification document helps limit the insidious process called scope creep (a process whereby the scope of a job "creeps" bigger and bigger while the job is in progress). This is why it's so important to get buy-in from the overall user community. If users keep demanding new features ("let's just add this one new feature; it's not much, and it won't slow things down"), the network might never be built. However, if the network builder can point to the specification document and ask whether the feature is included, he might be able to build the base network before beginning to add further features.

The other purpose of a specification document is to ensure the network builder and subsequent network administrators have a reference guide to the underlying design of the network. It's surprising how easy it is to forget the basic specs of a network if you're not confronted with them every day. The specification document provides a reference for the details that can easily be forgotten.

The specification document should include, at least, the following information:

▶ Why is the enterprise building the network in the first place?

▶ What will the network be used for; that is, what applications must it support?

▶ How many people and computers will the network support?

▶ Will the network be peer or client/server?

▶ What is the network architecture (such as Ethernet)?

▶ What are the response time and throughput requirements for the network?

▶ What are the security requirements for the network, including information on the access rights of the users?

▶ What are the reliability requirements for the network?

▶ If possible, include a section on growth, including a projected increase in users and/or traffic. The section should map out a general strategy for handling this growth and the implications for the user community if the strategy is not supported (not funded).

Anything that concerns the network user community (and you and your staff!) is fair game for this document. You'll also have something to refer to when the going gets confusing. The more detailed the specification document is, the more useful it will be to your users and to your job security.

Write a specification with care, and take your time. Review the document frequently to ensure it contains the depth of information needed to send out vendor bids. Try to avoid using buzzwords. As much as acronyms can ease discourse for people who are conversant with them, they do very little except increase technophobia in users who don't know what they mean. And that's important, because when you're done writing the specification, it's going to be reviewed by users, among others.

Meeting (Again) with Users

When the specification is complete, set up a meeting with the people whose work will be affected by the network. This group will include users, managers, and senior-level people, as well as a technology consultant or in-house IS (if either of these positions exists).

Meeting with Users to Review the Final Specification Should Be Icing on the Cake

If you've been meeting with the users on a regular basis, which is essential, the specification review should be a rather unexciting affair. The best network designers are not necessarily the most technically gifted. For certain, they must be bright and creative, but they must also have sufficient social skills to foster rapport with the users.

Let's posture here that you're the leader of the team for building the network. From the onset of the project, you should have been meeting on a regular basis with the users—from the top level to the folks on the factory floor or at the desks. If they see you coming through the door, and they don't much bother to look up, you're on the right track. If they say, "What brings you here?," I can say with assurance that your so-called final specification review meeting is not going to be pleasant.

Get to know your users and their work. Get in their back pocket. I promise it will pay enormous dividends to you and to them.

Use the information you've acquired at the meeting to revise your network specifications. Give revised copies of the specification to the attendees, and get them to provide approval of the specification as articulated in that document. Getting concerned parties to sign off on a specification can save you untold hours of grief later in the process. Among other benefits, it helps inhibit scope creep.

Step 6: Build the Network

After you've diagramed the network and written and (perhaps) revised the specifications for the network, you're ready to build the network. An important step in building the network is purchasing the hardware that will make up the network.

Computer hardware is evolving at a rapid pace, so the recommendations you might have collected relating to hardware purchases could be overtaken by marketplace innovations—even if only a short time has passed. You need to spend time researching the hardware you'll deploy: the servers, client computers, and network connectivity devices.

Selecting Network Hardware and Software	By the Way
Selecting the hardware and software for a network entails a lot of research and patience. Keep in mind interoperability and expandability. Check out Hour 11, "Selecting Network Hardware and Software," for more information.	

After you've settled on the hardware and software, you're ready to begin building the network. The next hour describes several strategies for selecting the specific pieces for a computer network (which you can review when you write the specification document described in this hour). Hour 12, "Assembling a Network," will provide guidance for building the network.

Summary

In this hour, we examined the process by which your network is designed. We learned how to determine the user requirements for the network and how to define its major functions. We also learned how to analyze the user needs to determine the type of network that will satisfy those needs. Finally, we learned how to write specifications for the network's operations. In the next several hours, we'll work through some of the specific parts of designing your network, including selecting the network hardware type, the NOS, and the network protocol.

Q&A

Q. *Why is it important to identify the intended use of a network at the outset of the design process?*

A. Doing so ensures the network is built to serve the organization's needs.

Q. *Why is an open, user-oriented examination and discussion of network plans useful?*

A. This examination allows you and your design team to measure the function of the network in relation to users' needs and to ensure that the planned network can accomplish the functions outlined earlier. It also allows you to establish buy-in from network users and corporate officers.

Q. *What are the six steps to build a network?*

A. The six steps are as follows:

1. Identify the uses of your network.

2. List which tasks execute on which computer.

3. Select the type of network: to centralize or not to centralize.

4. "Draw" the network.

5. Write the specification.

6. Build the network.

HOUR 11

Selecting Network Hardware and Software

What You'll Learn in This Hour:

▶ Key factors in selecting network hardware and software

▶ Additional guidance on servers, routers, and NOSs

▶ Ethernet considerations

▶ Pros and cons of client/server and peer-to-peer networks

▶ The network "bottleneck"

As you see from its title, this hour is devoted to the topic of selecting the hardware and software for your up-and-coming network. Of course, in many situations (and emphasized in Hour 10, "Designing a Network"), an enterprise will already have one or more networks in place. Nowadays, it's rare to come across a company meandering along in a nonnetworking environment. So, be aware that this hour pertains to creating new networks as well as upgrading existing networks.

The hour is also designed to tie together many of the general concepts about the subject that were set forth in previous hours. It also includes guidance on dealing with vendors. Specifics on this latter subject, such as creating detailed vendor evaluation guidelines and writing legally binding contracts, are beyond the scope of this book.

We've discussed issues relating to planning and documenting the new or enhanced network. In this hour, we look at making decisions related to the physical structure of the network and the client/server or peer-to-peer operating systems (OSs) that will be deployed on the network. Also in this hour, the pros and cons of these two approaches are discussed in more detail.

Evaluating the Server Hardware

For server hardware, you have many vendors and many vendor models from which to choose. Vendors also offer a variety of additional features to improve the performance of their products. As introduced in Hour 4, "Computer Concepts," the processor, motherboard, memory, hard drives, and interface cards are important components to evaluate during the hardware selection process. Other key factors are the nature of the server backup and the media to connect servers to other machines.

The server (or servers) will likely play a key role in your network. Make sure it's located in a well-ventilated and physically secure room. As a rule, it's recommended you purchase a server with two or more processors. This approach enables the server to handle more simultaneous tasks from clients, resulting in faster response time and increased throughput. Most vendors offer products with two processors. Some support a concept called hyperthreading, which gives the illusion of a single processor appearing as two processors to the server OS.

For some servers, a low-end processor will operate at 300 megahertz (MHz)—not very fast. You and your users will be well served if you do not lowball this part of the hardware selection. My recommendation is to purchase the highest speed and largest number of processors that the company's budget will allow.

A low-end server does not need much RAM memory—only 256 megabytes (MB). However, like the processor decision, it is recommended you configure the server with a lot of memory. How much? As much as you can afford—but with a caveat. Memory is easy to add later. So, perhaps you start with a few gigabytes (GB) and then add more later, if needed. But make sure your OS is capable of addressing the additional memory. For example, Vista 64 is needed to address the 4th GB of memory.

Modern server-based disk drives come in capacities ranging from a modest 40GB to terabyte (TB) capacities. However, servers support multiple hard drives, so you do not need to purchase the biggest drive. You can add more hard drive capacity later.

The issue of power consumption should also be considered when evaluating potential disk systems. Ask the vendor to furnish data on power usage; ask for an explanation of the vendor's design rationale for the efficient use of power for the drives.

Make certain your server selection includes sufficient network interface cards (NICs), associated connectors, and disk drives for proper backup of the company's data. Table 11.1 is a summary with associated considerations and recommendations, courtesy of Microsoft.

TABLE 11.1   Comparison of Drives

Description	Considerations	Recommended For
IDE[1] or ATA[2]	Slower and cheaper than other types. Only one drive can be accessed at a time.	Small network, with little use of hard drives.
SATA[3]	Faster and more expensive than IDE. Only one drive can be accessed at a time.	Small network, with moderate use of hard drives.
SCSI[4]	Faster and more expensive than IDE or SATA.	Larger network, with extensive use of hard drives.

[1] IDE = Integrated Drive Electronics

[2] ATA = Advanced Technology Attachment

[3] SATA = Serial Advanced Technology Attachment

[4] SCSI = small computer system interface

Don't forget the redundant array of inexpensive disks (RAID) discussion from Hour 5, "Network Concepts." With this idea in mind, it is recommended you purchase more than one disk drive and implement at least RAID level 1 or 5.

Evaluating the "Interworking" Hardware

You will need to select one or more devices to tie together the servers and computers to allow the machines to "interwork." In previous hours, we called these machines by various names. For this discussion, we'll be more specific. But before explaining them, bear in mind that the previous discussion about server hardware components generally pertains to interworking hardware as well. That is, processor, memory, and disk capacity are as important for these machines as they are for servers. Here's a summary of these devices:

▶ **Hub**—This device sends data from one computer to all other computers on the network. It's a low-cost, low-function machine that usually operates at Layer 1 of the OSI model and ties together the computers attached to it through multiple (twisted pair or optical) ports. It acts as a repeater for a signal passed from, say, port 1 (through the repeater) to port 2. For Ethernet hubs, it participates in the collision detection operations, which can affect response time and throughput. In addition, the need for hubs to detect collisions restricts the size of the network and the number of hubs that can be installed.

Don't overlook hubs; they're inexpensive and easy to install and maintain. However, they are declining in use.

▶ **Switch**—This term is one of the more confusing buzzwords in the industry. Because of its early use in telephone networks (the famous circuit switch) and packet networks (the famous X.25 packet switch), it has evolved though many years to have more than one meaning. First, it (now) is usually associated with a device that relays traffic by using a Layer 2 address. As examples, an Ethernet MAC address, or an ATM/MPLS label. Second, it usually contains software that supports the building of routing tables—a technique to improve traffic flow in a network, and a substantial improvement over a hub.

▶ **Bridge**—To confuse matters, the bridge performs the same operations as those just described for a switch. However, be careful here. The term bridge is often associated with a LAN device that uses Ethernet MAC addresses for routing. Thus, there's no such thing as an ATM or MPLS bridge. They're called Asynchronous Transfer Mode (ATM) or Multiprotocol Label Switching (MPLS) switches. (On behalf of the data communications industry, I offer apologies for these confusing terms; thanks for bearing with me.)

▶ **Router**—A router, which was introduced in Hour 5, is a more powerful device than a hub, switch, or bridge. Its principal operations are at OSI Layer 3 with IP addresses. High-end routers can also be configured as firewalls and extensive network management features. Some can be configured for their ports to operate as Layer 2 bridges. They are flexible and powerful machines.

▶ **Wireless access point (WAP)**—The WAP (introduced in Hour 7, "Mobile Wireless Networking") interworks the wired and wireless worlds. We learned that most WAPs operate with the IEEE 802.11 specifications. Many routers have the capacity to act as WAPs.

So, which do you choose? The decision depends on the size and geographical range of your user base. That stated, as a general practice, I opt for routers with WAP interfaces. You can purchase them for a modest price for a home network at your local office store or acquire them for a large enterprise network with a variety of capabilities.

Hardware Selection Considerations for Ethernet Networks

It's highly probable that you and your design team will be making decisions about local Ethernets.

Ethernet is the easiest network architecture in terms of shopping around for wiring, network cards, switches, routers, and other equipment. Even the most bare-bones computer equipment store will provide connectivity devices and Ethernet NICs.

As mentioned in Hour 3, "Getting Data from Here to There: How Networking Works," Ethernet provides different flavors such as 10BASE-2, 10BASE-5, and 10BASE-T. The 10BASE-2 and 10BASE-5 implementations are old technologies, and you will have to search around to find one of these Ethernet types that's still up and running. Although 10BASE-T has been the Ethernet standard for several years, nearly all new deployments of Ethernet are 100BASE-T or 1000BASE-T.

100BASE-TX and 1000BASE-T are in many products. These standards use twisted pair cables standard (RJ-45) connectors. They run at 100 megabits per second (Mbps) and 1 gigabit per second (Gbps), respectively. However, each version has become steadily more selective about the cable it runs on, and some installers have avoided 1000BASE-T for everything except short connections to servers.

Given their ubiquity, Ethernet 100BASE-T and 1000BASE-T are the clear choices for the majority of networks. Both are inexpensive and integrated into almost every new network device, and most network equipment manufacturers offer them. They're also standardized, which helps ensure interoperability between equipment made by different vendors. You probably already know that Internet service providers (ISPs) use Ethernet connections and NICs to connect home and small office users to digital subscriber line (DSL) and cable modem networks for Internet access.

Working with Ethernet 100BASE-T

For the sake of discussion, let's say you and your team opt for Ethernet LANs (specifically, 100BASE-T). 100BASE-T is versatile, widely available, and scales easily. It's simple to install and maintain, and it's reliable. Many manufacturers make network cards for everything from Intel-compatible desktop systems to Macintoshes to laptops. You can find a 100BASE-T Ethernet card for almost any system.

Additionally, 100BASE-T cabling offers an upgrade path. If you use the proper type of wire or cabling (called 568A or B), the network can support 100BASE-T networks. This upgrade path is part of what makes 100BASE-T a solid choice for a network topology. And because you can chain 100BASE-T hubs together (if you use hubs), you can increase the size of a network relatively with relative ease.

Using a Crossover Cable

By the Way

Contrary to some claims, it's not true that a network of only two computers running 100BASE-T needs a hub. If there are two computers on a 100BASE-T network, they can connect using a special RJ-45–ended cable called a crossover cable. Crossover cables are designed to enable hubs to connect to one another, but they can join two 100BASE-T computers as well.

However, omitting the hub in a two-computer 100BASE-T network is not advisable. How will you add a third computer without a hub? Never doubt that the third computer will make an appearance eventually. I mention the possibility of cross-connecting computers, but I don't recommend it.

Working with Ethernet 1000BASE-T

If you're concerned a 100Mbps LAN will not meet your capacity needs, don't hesitate to examine 1000BASE-T. In the past few years, the marketplace and product lines for Gigabit Ethernet have matured. Gigabit Ethernet is now widely available in off-the-shelf products.

If your installation already has 100BASE-T hardware and software and you want to begin an upgrade to 1000BASE-T, make sure your evaluations include assessments of the gigabit products being backward compatible with the megabit products. If they are, your network will still be restricted to the lower rate, but you'll be on a path to migrate to a higher-capacity technology.

Implementation Ideas for Megabit Ethernet and Gigabit Ethernet

100BASE-T and 1000BASE-T are used in network peripherals such as printers and file servers. Almost all these devices have a 100BASE-T port, and many of them now support a gigabit port. By the time this book is published, I suspect Gigabit Ethernet will be as common as Megabit Ethernet.

Here's a recipe for the ingredients necessary for a 100BASE-T or 1000BASE-T network:

▶ Two or more computers. Almost all computers can use some form of Ethernet, from laptops to desktop PCs to UNIX systems and Macs.

▶ One Ethernet network card per computer.

▶ One hub/bridge/router with enough ports to connect all your computers, or the use of Wi-Fi if machines are confined to a local area.

▶ Enough patch cords to connect each network card's RJ-45 socket to the router's RJ-45 socket. A patch cord is an eight-conductor cord (meaning four pairs of wires) with an RJ-45 jack at both ends. (It looks like a really fat phone cord.) Patch cords are available at computer stores for a couple dollars per cable.

100BASE-T and 1000BASE-T are star topologies, which mean that everything has to connect to a concentrator—or, more correctly, a hub, bridge, or router.

> **Using Small Network Hubs or Bridges for Small Networks**
>
> Be aware that many small Ethernet hubs and bridges (small in terms of the number of ports they provide) have a special port designed specifically to connect a hub to other hubs (or stack them, in the parlance). If you connect a computer to this port (usually port 1), that computer won't be capable of using the network because the hub doesn't use the stacking port like the rest of the ports. The problem is that stacking ports usually don't look different from regular ports. So read the documentation on your hub to find out whether it has a port dedicated to stacking, and save yourself some frustration.

By the Way

Selecting the Network Type: Client/Server or Peer to Peer

Earlier in this book, we discussed the pros and cons of client/server and peer-to-peer networking strategies. In the next section, you'll have the opportunity to see how you can justify your decision to go with client/server or peer to peer. Earlier, I assumed you and your team had chosen the client/server technology, but it's a good idea to lay out in more detail how these systems operate and offer some points for your consideration in making selection choices.

As discussed, two important issues relating to choosing the type of network are scale and cost. A small office with little or no expansion will not need to deploy an expensive network server and run a Network Operating System (NOS) so that only a few users can share a few files and a printer. With this thought in mind, let's discuss client/server or server-based networking. We then take a look a peer-to-peer networking.

Client/Server Networking

Client/server networking entails two basic operations that are provided by a centralized server: authentication and support services. Workstations on the network don't require services from other workstations on the network. The service architecture of the network resides on one or more redundant, protected, regularly maintained, and backed up servers. These servers are dedicated to specific tasks: file services, Internet/wide area network (WAN) connectivity, remote access, authentication, back-end distributed applications, and so forth.

In other words, workstations connected to a "pure" client/server network see only servers—they never see one another. A client/server network is a one-to-many scheme, with the server being the one and the workstations being the many. This architecture is the model used by large commercial websites, such as Amazon. The client is a small graphical front end that's delivered fresh from the server each time it's opened and a large server architecture at the back end that handles ordering, billing, and authentication. No user of Amazon knows another user is currently online—there's no interaction between users, just between the servers and the client system.

The client/server model is useful for large businesses that have to manage their computer users' computer resources efficiently. In a pure client/server environment, a great deal of the software that clients use at their workstations is stored on a server hard drive rather than on users' own hard drives. In this configuration, if a user's workstation fails, it is relatively easy to get the user back online quickly by simply replacing the computer on the desktop. When the user logs back in to the network, she'll have access to the applications needed to work.

The TCP/IP-based technology of the Internet has changed the accepted definition of client/server somewhat, with the focus being on distributed applications, where a "thin" client (such as a web page application running in a browser) works in tandem with a much larger server. The advantages of this model stem from the application's capability to run in a browser. Because browsers are universal—that is, they can run on Windows machines, Macs, UNIX boxes, and other systems—applications can be distributed quickly and effectively. Only the copy at the server needs to be changed for a web-enabled application, because the changes will be distributed when users open the new page.

A client/server architecture is appropriate if one or more of the following conditions apply to your situation:

▶ Your network user population is large, perhaps more than 20 computers. On a larger network, it might not be wise to leave resources entirely decentralized as you would on a peer-to-peer network, simply because there's no way to control the data and software on the machines. However, the size of the company's user base shouldn't be the only criteria. Indeed, size might be irrelevant, if the users are working on independent projects with little or no data sharing.

▶ Your network requires robust security. Using secure firewalls, gateways, and secured servers ensures that access to network resources is controlled. However, and once again, installing a firewall in the router that connects your LAN to the Internet may be all you need for security. In this situation, your company doesn't need a dedicated security server. Even more, the individual workstations will be running their own security software and performing virus scans periodically.

▶ Your network requires that the company's data be free from the threat of accidental loss. This means taking data stored on a server and backing it up from a central location.

▶ Your network needs users to focus on server-based applications rather than on workstation-based applications and resources. The users access data via client/server-based technologies such as large databases, groupware software, and other applications that run from a server.

Peer-to-Peer Networking

Peer-to-peer networking is based on the idea that a computer that connects to a network should be capable of sharing its resources with any other computer. In contrast to client/server, peer-to-peer networking is a many-to-many scheme.

The decentralized nature of peer-to-peer networking means the system is inherently less organized. Knowing this, also note that the recent computer OS offering from Microsoft (Windows Vista) has powerful peer-to-peer networking functions.

Peer-to-peer networks that grow to more than a few computers tend to interact more by convenience or even chance than by design. As examples, Windows Vista and Windows XP provide a Networking Wizard that automatically sets up basic network configurations; it's a fine service, especially for network neophytes.

Peer-to-peer networking is similar to the Internet: There are no hard-and-fast rules about basic user-to-user interactions. With a client/server model, you can establish rules for user-to-user interactions through the server(s).

Peer-to-peer networking is appropriate for your network if the following conditions apply:

▶ Your network is relatively small (fewer than 10 computers, although depending on the number of users accessing any one computer for resources, you could get by with 15–20).

▶ Your network doesn't require robust security regarding access to resources.

▶ Your network does not require the company data be free from the threat of accidental loss.

▶ Your network needs users to focus on workstation-based applications rather than on server-based applications and resources. This means that users run applications such as productivity software (Microsoft Office, for example) installed on each computer. Each user works in a closed system until she has to access data on another peer-to-peer computer or a shared printer.

Most of the time, home networks can use peer-to-peer networking without a problem. The only piece of the network that you likely need to centralize is Internet access, and you can easily obtain this operation via a combination device that serves as a hub/switch/router, a firewall, and a DSL modem.

> ### Server-Based and Peer-to-Peer Networking on the Same Network
>
> In some situations, you might discover you need a server-based network. However, you might want to make it easy for users to collaborate, so you allow workstations to share resources through peer-to-peer networking. These two environments can coexist. Just keep in mind that allowing peer-to-peer networking degrades your ability to secure the network. Files that would typically reside on a file server might end up on individual workstations, making it more difficult to back up important data.

Now that we've looked at client/server and peer-to-peer networking, let's look at client OSs—specifically those that provide peer-to-peer services—and then we can tackle NOSs. This latter subject is highlighted in this hour, which acts as an introduction to more detailed discussions in Hours 16 and 17.

Peer-to-Peer OSs

In a peer-to-peer network, there's no NOS *per se*. Instead, each user's workstation has desktop OS software that can share resources with other computers as desired. Typically, OSs include the capability to configure a protocol and share resources. Most peer-to-peer OSs provide a relatively limited range of sharable devices, although file sharing (or shared disk space) and networked printing are standard features.

Following is a summary of client OSs that provide peer-to-peer services:

▶ **Microsoft Windows**—Microsoft Windows has provided peer-to-peer networking capabilities since Microsoft Windows for Workgroups 3.11. Each of the subsequent versions of Windows has provided increasingly more powerful peer-to-peer capabilities. Microsoft Windows (both the Home and Professional versions) even provides a Network Setup Wizard that makes it easy to configure a Windows workgroup (a workgroup being a peer-to-peer network). We'll look more closely at Windows peer-to-peer networking in the next section.

▶ **Linux**—Linux has become a flexible and cost-effective OS for both the home and workplace. Numerous Linux distributions are available that vary in their degree of user friendliness. Linux provides several ways to share files and other resources such as printers. It includes the Network File System (NFS), where a Linux computer can act as both a server and a client.

▶ **Macintosh OSX**—Although our discussion has centered around Intel-based computers, we should mention the peer-to-peer networking capabilities of the Apple Macintosh and its various offspring such as the Mac PowerBook. Peer-to-peer networking has been part of the Mac OS since its beginning.

Peer-to-Peer Networking OSs

In Hour 4, you learned about client OSs. If you review the list of OSs presented there, you'll find many of them are capable of working in a peer-to-peer environment. Since the early 1990s, almost every client/single-user OS has been shipped with at least a limited collection of network protocols and tools. This means that you can use almost every client OS to build a peer-to-peer network.

By the Way

Windows is the most dominant desktop OS in terms of installations. Let's take a closer look at peer-to-peer networking with the most widely used version of Windows, Microsoft Windows XP. This discussion includes configuration examples, which should help you in making selection decisions about using them.

Peer-to-Peer Networking with Microsoft Windows

As mentioned, Windows for Workgroups was the original "do-it-yourself" network for Intel-compatible personal computers. It was designed around Microsoft's MS-DOS OS and Windows shell. A number of different versions of Windows have come and gone; we've seen Windows 95, Windows 98, Windows Millennium Edition (Windows Me) for the home user, and Windows NT and Windows 2000 for business network users. The most widely used version of Windows, Windows XP, comes in two versions: Home and Professional.[1]

The Home version is designed for the home or small office user who will work in a Microsoft workgroup (meaning a peer-to-peer network). Windows XP Professional provides additional features and is designed to serve as a client on a server-based network. Don't buy the Home edition if you're going to implement a client/server network.

Microsoft's peer-to-peer networking products are based on the idea of a *workgroup*, or a set of computers that belong to a common group and share resources among themselves. Microsoft peer-to-peer networking is quite versatile and can include computers running any version of Microsoft Windows.

Additionally, on a given physical network, multiple workgroups can coexist. For example, if you have three salespeople, they can all be members of the SALES

---

[1] *Windows Vista is Microsoft's latest OS product that I've mentioned several times thus far. To date, it hasn't cornered the market and has met with increasing skeptics, including me. Thus, we concentrate on Windows XP.*

workgroup; the members of your accounting department can be members of the ACCOUNTS workgroup. Of course, there's a common administrative user with accounts on all machines in all workgroups, so central administration is possible to a limited extent, but it isn't an efficient administrative solution.

Windows peer-to-peer networking is straightforward. Computers running Windows XP (or earlier versions of Windows) are configured so that they're in the same workgroup. You can do this in the Windows XP Computer Name Changes dialog box (shown in Figure 11.1), which is reached via the System's Properties dialog box. (Right-click on My Computer and select Properties.)

FIGURE 11.1
Configure a Windows XP computer to be part of a workgroup

The alternative to configuring the workgroup manually is to use the Network Setup Wizard.

The wizard walks you through the steps of configuring the workgroup and can even generate a file that you can use to add other Windows computers to the workgroup—even computers running earlier versions of Windows. You start the wizard via the Windows Control Panel. Select the Network and Internet Connection icon in the Control Panel, and then select Set Up or Change Your Home or Small Office Network. Figure 11.2 shows the wizard screen that allows you to select a connection method.

After the workgroup is up and running, any user in the workgroup can browse the workgroup for shared folders and printers. You can map folders that users access regularly to a member computer as a network drive. Workgroup members can view workgroup computers and their shared resources using the My Network Places window. Figure 11.3 shows the two members of a workgroup named Habraken.

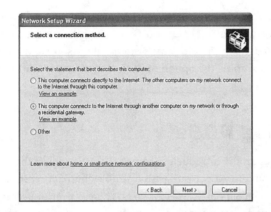

FIGURE 11.2
The Network Setup Wizard walks you through the steps of creating the workgroup.

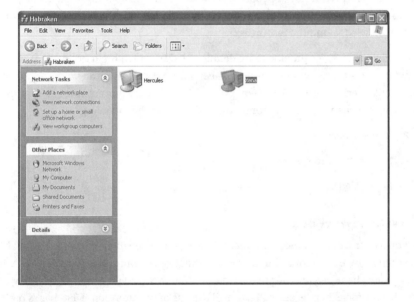

FIGURE 11.3
Workgroup members can browse the workgroup member computers.

Remember That Peer-to-Peer Networks Permit Sharing of Resources

For resources to be available for a workgroup, such as folders and printers, each user must share the folders and the printers of the workgroup. As just described, Windows makes it easy to set up workgroups. In addition, workgroups are easy to administer because each user manages the resources that they offer to the workgroup. However, they do pose problems in terms of protecting the shared resources.

By the Way

Workgroups are fine when users can collaborate in a friendly atmosphere and are computer savvy enough to ensure that important data is used appropriately (and backed up). Because each resource (such as folders) can require a separate password, any more than a few users can create an environment of confusion. If your company has more than 10 users or the company's automated resources are valuable and sensitive, you should examine the option of deploying a server running a NOS, which is our next topic.

Evaluating NOSs

This section continues the introductory material on the subject that was included in Hour 4. If you're building a network with a sizable chunk of centralized services, one of the following client/server NOSs is for you. Whereas peer-to-peer networks are similar to a cooperative group of people with diverse functions but no single leader, a client/server network is similar to a hierarchy—the server is the leader, the one with all the knowledge and the resources.

The following sections provide more details of NOSs, which are used in client/server networks. As we describe each of them, keep in mind that you and your design team must make decision about which one will be installed in your network...assuming you opt for a client/server environment. We'll look at the following:

▶ Novell NetWare

▶ Microsoft Windows Server

▶ Linux/UNIX

Novell NetWare

You and your team will face a problem during your assessment of Novell's NOS. It's a powerful software platform, but its market share is declining. How you react to this reality must be based on your team's view of NetWare and your company's view of Novell. Our focus here is on the technical aspects of the situation. First, here's a bit of history.

In the early days of PC internetworking, Ray Noorda's Novell invented NetWare. It came as a balm to early PC-networking system administrators who were used to dealing with the innumerable networking schemes that appeared in the early to mid-1980s. NetWare provided reliable, secure, and relatively simple networking. In the early years, the business world snapped up as many copies as Novell could turn out.

Over the years, NetWare matured. Its focus broadened beyond the local LAN into WAN configurations. With the advent of NetWare 5 and NetWare Directory Services (NDS), Novell had a product that enabled a global network to provide its users with the same resources, no matter where on the network those users logged in.

But in 1994 and 1995, two things happened that made Novell stumble. The first was the introduction of Microsoft's Windows NT, which Novell failed to view as serious competition. Microsoft's aggressive marketing and the ease of use of Windows NT quickly made inroads into Novell's market share.

Novell's second slip was in failing to realize that the rise in public consciousness of the Internet fundamentally changed the playing field for NOS manufacturers. Novell had used its Internetwork Packet Exchange (IPX) protocol for close to 15 years; it saw no reason to change.

Novell has made up for a number of earlier missteps in relation to NetWare. The NOS now embraces Transmission Control Protocol/Internet Protocol (TCP/IP) as its default network protocol. A recent version of Novell's NOS, NetWare 6.5, also integrates several open source services from the Linux platform, including Apache Web Server, which is one of the most popular web server platforms in use.

Administrative tools for managing NetWare were also rather meager in earlier versions of NetWare. However, NetWare 6.5 provides many new tools, including the NetWare Remote Manager, which you can use to manage network volumes and monitor server settings. Remote Manager is accessed using a web browser, which makes it easy for an administrator to open it from any workstation on the network. Figure 11.4 shows the NetWare Remote Manager in a web browser window.

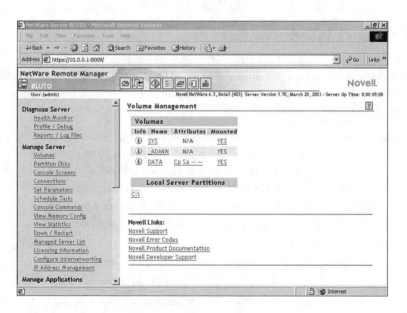

FIGURE 11.4
The NetWare
Remote Manager

In 2003, Novell announced Open Enterprise Server (OES) and released it in March 2005. OES consists of a set of applications (such as the eDirectory) that can run over a

Linux or a NetWare platform. Some network experts state Novell is shifting away from NetWare and toward Linux. As we learned in Hour 5, the company has assured its customers that it will support whatever NOS they want.

NetWare might well be appropriate for your company's network. It's fast, efficient, and easy to install and configure. The Novell Directory Service hierarchy for network objects (such as users and groups) has been upgraded to the Novell eDirectory to provide an easy-to-use hierarchical system for tracking servers and other objects on the network. NetWare can also accommodate situations in which your network spans multiple LANs (across WANs). In addition, it provides the scalability expected from a well-performing NOS platform.

With recent changes to NetWare's software and changes in NetWare licensing structure, it's certainly worth your while to take a serious look at NetWare when you're working through the process of determining the best NOS for your network.

> ### Select the NOS That Makes the Most Sense for Your Network
>
> These sections on specific NOSs are not intended as recommendations, but rather should be considered starting points as you research the different platforms available. Cost, scalability, and ease of administration are just a few of the factors that should be part of your selection process.

Microsoft Windows Server

Windows NT Server, the first edition of Microsoft's popular server software, emerged out of the breakup of IBM and Microsoft's shared OS/2 initiative. Although Windows Server OSs offer a fairly simple graphical user interface (GUI), it's a true multitasking, multithreaded NOS.

Since Windows NT was introduced in 1993–1994, Microsoft has weathered a storm of criticism regarding its reliability, scalability, and robustness. To be fair, some of this criticism has been deserved because some releases of the Windows NOS have had a number of flaws. However, Microsoft has persevered and continued to refine its NOS as it passes through product cycles (NT Server 3.5 to NT Server 4 to Windows 2000 Server to Windows Server 2003), up to and including the current iteration, Windows Server 2008.

The most significant change in the Microsoft server products was the upgrade of the Microsoft NOS from NT Server 4 to Windows 2000 Server. Microsoft's flat domain model was replaced by a hierarchical directory service called Active Directory. Active Directory holds all the objects that exist on the network, including domains, servers, users, and groups. We discuss how the Microsoft domain model works in comparison to Active Directory in Hour 16, "Microsoft Networking." Active Directory allowed Microsoft to compete on a level playing field with NetWare's NDS (now eDirectory) and Sun's Network Information Service.

UNIX and Linux

Unlike NetWare or Windows NT, UNIX is not a monolithic OS owned by a single corporation. Instead, it's represented by a plethora of manufacturers with only a few clear standouts. The most common UNIX systems are Sun Microsystems' Solaris, IBM's AIX, and Hewlett-Packard's HP-UX.

In the PC-hardware world, Linux, a UNIX clone, has trumped various UNIX systems, including commercial variants such as Santa Cruz Operation's SCO UNIX, Novell's UNIXWare, and Sun's Solaris for Intel. Linux has also grabbed greater market share than other community-based OS developments such as BSD (Berkeley Standard Distribution), OpenBSD, and FreeBSD.

UNIX and UNIX-like OSs come in many flavors, and some features and commands vary widely between versions. In the end, though, it remains the most widely used high-end server OS in the world.

However, the UNIX world is fragmented by a host of issues that derive from UNIX's basic design: UNIX is open-ended and is available for almost any hardware platform. UNIX has existed for more than 30 years, and its design has been optimized, revised, and improved to the point at which it's quite reliable.

Unfortunately, the availability of UNIX across many different platforms has led to one significant problem that blocks its widespread adoption: Software written for one version of UNIX usually doesn't run on other versions. This lack of compatibility has led to UNIX receiving a dwindling share of the server market except at the very high end where absolute reliability is a must. Linux and the Open Source/GNU movement have ameliorated a good deal of the incompatibility issues by ensuring that the source code for most Linux-based software is available. This means that with a copy of Linux with a C-language compiler, you can compile—that is, translate from source code to machine instructions—a variety of software.

UNIX has a reputation for being difficult to master. It's complex; there's no doubt about that. But after you assimilate the basics (which can prove daunting), UNIX's raw power and versatility make it an attractive server platform.

Interestingly, Linux, which is essentially a UNIX clone, has begun to make a great deal of headway in the server and workstation market. It's begun to put a dent in Microsoft's market share both in the server and desktop OS categories.

In spite of its complexity, however, any version of UNIX makes for efficient file, print, and application servers. Because of 30 years of refinement, the reliability of a UNIX system is usually a step above that of other platforms. UNIX uses the TCP/IP networking protocol stack natively; TCP/IP was created on and for UNIX systems, and the "port-and-socket" interface that lies under TCP/IP has its fullest expression on UNIX systems.

We will look more closely at the UNIX and Linux platforms in Hour 17, "UNIX and Linux Networking." Most of our discussion will relate to Linux because its open source development makes it an inexpensive and intriguing NOS to explore. Linux has become a cost-effective and viable alternative to some of the standard NOSs, such as NetWare and Microsoft Windows Server.

The Network "Bottleneck"

For this discussion, let's assume you and your team have decided on the following technologies for your LANs:

- ▶ **Gigabit Ethernet**—IEEE 1000BASE-T

- ▶ **Wi-Fi**—IEEE 802.11g

For your connection to the Internet, you've selected the following:

- ▶ DSL from the local phone company

Be aware your connection from the Internet to your users' computers and the network servers is only as fast as the lowest-speed link in the communications chain. Here are the three links to this chain:

- ▶ **DSL**—3Mbps (offerings vary)

- ▶ **Ethernet**—1Gbps

- ▶ **Wi-Fi**—54Mbps

Consequently, for a session with the Internet when, say, high-resolution video images are streaming down to a user computer, they will be "streaming" at roughly 3Mbps, the lowest bit rate in the links' chain. The software involved in this process is quite powerful and can mitigate (to some extent) the differences in the links' capacity. Buffering the data and using time stamps to "play out" the packets in a consistent manner are two examples of this wonderful "soft stuff" in operation. But the software can't create extra bits to fill the Ethernet/Wi-Fi pipes.

I think it's fair to say that most users in small businesses will not notice the DSL bottleneck. If it becomes a problem, and it likely will when scores, hundreds, or thousands of users are using this DSL user-network interface (UNI), you and your team must move to a higher-capacity link to the Internet. We examined the selection options in earlier hours. To review briefly:

- ▶ Leasing a DS3 (T3) link

- ▶ Determining if Wi-Fi is available as a UNI with the ISP

- ▶ Bringing Synchronous Optical Network (SONET) to your premises

Make certain your user community needs these expensive links for real-time processing. Real-time means immediate, perhaps interactive access to the data coming from the Internet or an internet. Perhaps the users can simply download the data onto hard disk and later play it back through the high-capacity LAN links.

On the other hand, for larger companies, it's likely a conventional DSL link will not provide sufficient bandwidth for the entire user community. Advice: Make sure you have budgeted for this contingency.

A Word Regarding Network Protocols

Although selecting the appropriate NOS platform is an important task, selecting the network protocol you will use to move data on your network is just as crucial. Because most corporations, businesses, and home users want to be connected to the Internet, it has become essential for network servers and clients to be configured for TCP/IP.

As you've probably noticed in the discussion of NOSs provided in this hour, all the current versions of the most widely used server platforms execute TCP/IP as their default communications protocol stack. In fact, if you want to use additional network protocols, you'll have to add them yourself. I recommend that you opt for no other protocol stack than TCP/IP.

Our discussions have dealt with ideas about "selecting" network hardware and software. Regarding the selection of so-called network protocols, you really have an easy job: Go with the TCP/IP protocol stack. In the final analysis, it's the last remaining soldier. NetWare's IPX, Xerox's legendary protocol stack, AppleTalk's Layer 3, and IBM's SNA Layer 3 have been left in the networking dust.

Summary

In this hour, we discussed ideas for selecting network hardware and software. We highlighted Ethernet, which is the most widely deployed LAN technology. We also examined peer-to-peer versus server-based networking and discussed Microsoft's peer-to-peer offerings. Our discussions also included an introduction to popular network server platforms. We learned about the potential bottleneck problem that might crop up on the link between your company's network to the Internet. We also learned how to overcome this bottleneck: Pay more money for more bandwidth.

Q&A

Q. *What's the most widely used LAN network architecture?*

A. Ethernet is the most widely used. Most new implementations are based on 1000BASE-T.

Q. *What are typical peer-to-peer OSs?*

A. Peer-to-peer OSs include Microsoft Windows XP (and earlier versions of Windows) and various distributions of Linux.

Q. *What are the most common PC NOSs?*

A. NOSs include NetWare, Windows Server 2003 and 2008 (and Windows 2000 Server), various UNIX platforms, as well as a number of Linux implementations.

Q. *What is the de facto standard for network protocols?*

A. TCP/IP and the TCP/IP-related protocols are the de facto standard.

HOUR 12

Assembling a Network

What You'll Learn in This Hour:

▶ Preparing to assemble the networking hardware

▶ I/O and IRQ concepts

▶ How to install adapter cards

▶ How to set up a wiring closet

By this hour, we've acquired a solid understanding of the operations of computer networks. We've covered the fundamentals of network hardware, software, and protocols. We've focused on how to establish the user requirements for a network, as well as how to design the network.

You've already learned how to identify network hardware, and in this hour, you and your design team will pull it all together and deal with how to plug pieces of the network together.

This hour will familiarize you with installation processes for the hardware you've read about in preceding hours. It is not a comprehensive guide; such a treatise would require an entire book. Rather, it's intended to introduce you to the process of "putting the network together." Armed with the information you'll learn this hour, you'll be able to confidently engage the vendors.

Before Installation

Although computer hardware might look robust and impervious to damage, it's not. Computer and network electronics powered by electricity can, paradoxically, also be damaged by electricity. Although your computer hardware is likely powered by 120-volt wall current, don't assume that the motherboard or hub actually uses that much electricity. Most computers and networking equipment use 5 volts or so at the motherboard. Static electricity can build up to 20,000 volts or so and can wreck computer equipment by burning up the delicate wiring inside a silicon chip.

So that you don't inadvertently burn up some expensive piece of computer equipment while working on it, this section describes a few precautions you should take before installing the network—for your own safety and the integrity of the computer and networking equipment.

First, take measures to prevent electrical damage to yourself and the computer:

▶ Wear a wrist strap when you're working on a computer. A wrist strap is a small device that connects you (usually one of your wrists) to the computer. This simple device ensures you and the computer have the same electrical potential. In layman's terms, it means you won't be transmitting static to the computer and burning up parts while you're installing them. Wrist straps are available at computer stores for a few dollars. Use them.

▶ Always shut the computer's power off before working on it. This idea is common sense, but stories abound about people opening up the case to a computer while its central processing unit (CPU) is busily engaged in adding and subtracting. Installing an adapter card in a computer that's powered up is pretty well guaranteed to burn up the card, the card slot, and (often) the motherboard itself.

▶ Always unplug the computer before you open it to install equipment. Again, this might seem like common sense, but surprisingly few people think of it. It's a corollary to the preceding direction, and it ensures the power is off. In addition to the near certainty that you'll damage computer equipment by working with it while it's on, you're also taking a chance of harming yourself. Electrical shocks are neither pleasant nor particularly good for your health.

By the Way

To Unplug or Not to Unplug

There's a school of thought that not unplugging a computer grounds the computer better. This in theory has merit. But making sure no electricity is flowing to a motherboard on which you are working is more of an issue than grounding. If you use an antistatic wrist strap or, even better, an antistatic mat, you should not have worries related to static electricity. Always touch the metal frame around the motherboard before starting to discharge any static that might have built up.

Next, take precautions while you're opening the computer's case and, say, installing adapter cards:

▶ If you're opening the case and the top doesn't come off easily, don't force it. Forcing a computer case may damage the box and its contents. Granted, the plastic envelopes that encase computer components (and other modern electronic products) challenge the most avid box shredder. Nonetheless, force will merely strengthen the case against you...so to speak.

Don't Just Rip into the Computer Case

Watch Out!

In the early days of computer networking, taking the top off a case was a risky proposition. The number of cables in an IBM XT was daunting. The arrangement of ribbon cables within the case generally ensured that if the case cover was yanked off unceremoniously, you were almost guaranteed to snag a cable and likely damage it.

Since those days, PC manufacturers have improved the cable routing inside computers. Today, most computer vendors no longer require its customers to use tools to open the case. Nonetheless, it pays to be cautious. An acquaintance recently disassembled a computer for which the case cover was part of the cable routing—it had clips into which cables slid to route around the inside of the box. If he had just yanked the top off, he would have torn off at least two cables. Taking the time to figure out how the top should come off saved him a lot of time and aggravation.

▶ If you have to disconnect anything, mark all the cables and their associated connections. This exercise makes reassembling a disassembled computer much simpler. You can use a marker to label the cables, and you can draw some diagrams depicting which cables connect to which devices. The best way to mark connections is the one that helps you reconnect what you disconnected. Masking tape and a Sharpie marker are your friends!

▶ When you're installing adapter cards, make sure the adapter card and the adapter card slot have the same interface. In other words, don't put a PCI card into an ISA slot or vice versa. Doing so can damage the computer, the adapter card, and (more often than not) your company's budget.

▶ Don't use force to fit adapter cards into slots. This is a sure-fire way to damage the card and void the warranty. If a card doesn't fit, pull it out and look at it. Is it the correct slot interface? Is the metal strip on the back of the card (the "slot cover") in the way somehow? Close examination can often enable you to figure out why a card won't fit. Sometimes it's necessary to bend the bottom of the metal strip to fit—other times, the card just has to be rocked in slowly and gently. This process can be tedious, but it prevents cracked motherboards. You'll learn more about the process of installing adapter cards in the next section, but this precaution deserves to be repeated because it has caused more equipment failures than all the static in the world.

▶ Use proper tools. Have a good Phillips screwdriver and a nutdriver set, if possible. Tweezers are useful for picking up small parts. A small pair of needle-nose pliers can come in handy as well. If your tools are magnetized, either demagnetize them (heat works) or replace them—magnetism and computers just don't go together. And of course, to repeat what was said previously, use a wrist strap.

Working on networking equipment need not be difficult if you're careful. It's mostly a matter of developing what writer Robert Pirsig calls a mechanic's feel: a sense of respect for the physical properties of an object and an understanding of how much force is enough. It's common sense; don't force anything. If you do, something is probably wrong to begin with.

Installing Adapter Cards

Adapter cards are inescapable, particularly in the Intel-compatible computer world. Because not all computers come with built-in networking (although that's changing), at some point, you're going to have to take a deep breath, open a computer case, and plunge inside to install a network adapter card.

You should be aware of two things related to network cards and other device cards that you might install in a computer: input/output (I/O) addresses and interrupt requests (IRQs). Because most expansion cards are now plug-and-play (meaning the operating system, or OS, configures them automatically), you don't have to worry about manually setting I/O or IRQ settings. However, if you have to troubleshoot a malfunctioning card or are dealing with older hardware, it doesn't hurt to understand the basics of these settings.

I/O addresses for network cards generally range from about 200h (decimal 512) to about 380h (decimal 896). 200h is a hexadecimal (base 16) number. Again, plug-and-play cards will take care of this for you. Table 12.1 provides a list of common I/O addresses.

TABLE 12.1 Commonly Used I/O Addresses

Device	Memory Address
COM1 (first serial port)	03E8
COM2 (second serial port)	02E8
LPT1 (printer port)	0378
IDE hard drive controllers	170 or 1F0
Sound cards	220 and 330

Most network cards use addresses outside the common list of addresses. But watch out! Some network cards might use memory address 0360. Although this address doesn't seem to conflict with anything, unfortunately, sometimes the software device driver takes up too much space. When this happens, the software device driver can take from 0360 all the way to 0380 in memory, which conflicts with the printer port at 0378.

When a device, such as a network card or a video card, has to get the full attention of the computer system, it uses an IRQ. An IRQ is a request that the system stop whatever else it's doing at the moment and give its attention to the device requesting attention. Table 12.2 provides a listing of common Intel-based IRQ settings.

TABLE 12.2   Common Intel-Compatible IRQ Settings

IRQ #	Function
0	Reserved for use by the OS (system timer).
1	Reserved for use by the OS (keyboard controller).
2	Used to access IRQ 9 and above. Use only as a last resort.
3	Used for COM2 communications serial port (often built into the motherboard).
4	Used for COM1 communications serial port (often built into the motherboard).
5	Usually unused and available.
6	Reserved for use by the OS (floppy drive controller).
7	Used for the printer port (also called LPT1).
8	Reserved for use by the OS (system clock).
9	Usually available, but use as a last resort. Refer to IRQ 2.
10	Usually available.
11	Usually available.
12	Often used for bus mice (as opposed to serial mice, which connect to COM ports).
13	Often unused and available.
14	Usually used for Primary IDE disk drive controllers.
15	Reserved for use by secondary IDE controllers.

The important thing to remember when you install a network card is to try not to use the memory address or IRQ that other cards or the motherboard are using. If you do, the card will not work.

Now that you have a basic understanding of how I/O and IRQs work, let's install a NIC into a computer.

▼   **Try It Yourself**

Install an Adapter Card

This section provides a hands-on view of the process of installing an adapter card in a computer. Remember that these instructions aren't universal, because computers vary in their card architectures. The basic idea is to understand the steps and adapt to what you find when you open the computer.

1. Shut off the computer's power and disconnect the power cord.

2. Identify the card. Put on a ground strap, take the adapter card out of its packaging, and examine it (see Figure 12.1). What is its interface?

FIGURE 12.1
Determine the slot interface by looking at the edge connector (the shiny gold connectors at the base of the card).

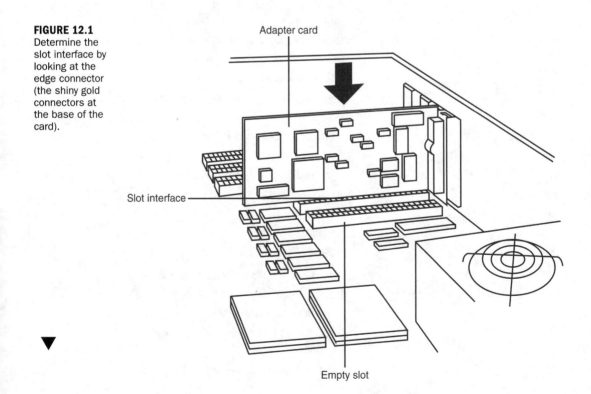

Adapter card

Slot interface

Empty slot

3. Just about every new NIC you buy will be PCI and will also be a plug-and-play card. Most OSs (including Windows, Linux, and UNIX) have no problem recognizing "mainstream" network interface cards (NICs) such as 3Com or Intel and setting the appropriate I/O and IRQ for the card. Some NICs that are considered soft-set cards might require that you install the card and then run software that came with it before the OS can configure them. (In the rare situation in which you're dealing with old NICs, you might have to set switchblocks or jumper blocks, which are normally used to determine one or more of the adapter card's settings [I/O address, IRQ]. Look at the surface of the card. If you see switchblocks or jumper blocks, refer to the manufacturer's documentation to determine what settings they manage.)

Jumps Are Not Jumping Much

Recent trends have eliminated jump blocks by using auto-configuration operations or a software-controlled option (as seen in Figure 12.2). These modes are fast and require little technical knowledge.

By the Way

---

4. After you figure out what card type you're working with (again, in most cases, we are talking plug-and-play), open the computer. While opening the computer case, rest the NIC on its antistatic packaging (usually a bag made of silver mylar plastic). Computer cases vary greatly: Some require that you unscrew the case (usually on the back), whereas others snap together. If the case cover doesn't lift off readily, don't use force; look for flanges and hidden hinges that could be preventing the case cover from coming off.

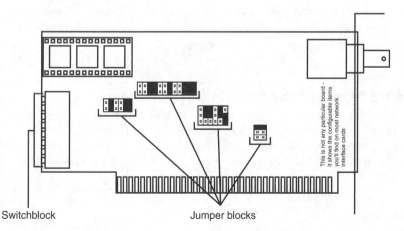

Switchblock   Jumper blocks

FIGURE 12.2
A jumper block and a switch-block. The jumper is a small piece of metal and plastic that makes an electrical connection like a primitive switch.

▼

5. Select the slot where you want to install the card and remove the slot cover—a small piece of sheet metal that covers the slot in the back of the computer when no card is installed (refer to Figure 12.1). The slot cover is usually held in with a 1/4-inch or 5/16-inch screw that often has a Phillips slot as well. Save the screw after you've removed the slot cover—you'll need it to fasten the card when you're done.

6. Install the card. Then take it and line it up with the slot. Ensure that the sheet-metal piece that resembles the slot cover faces the outside of the computer. After the card is lined up in the slot, gently but firmly press it into the slot. You might have to gently rock the card back and forth. When the card is fully seated in the slot, most of the connections on the bottom edge will be hidden inside the connector, and the part of the card that screws in will be level against the back of the computer's chassis. Screw the card in using the slot cover screw you removed earlier.

7. Finish up. Replace the case cover on the computer. Then plug in the power cord and restart the computer. You'll have to install device driver software (used to enable adapter cards and other hardware to interact with the OS; device drivers are discussed in Hour 4, "Computer Concepts") to make it work; read the manufacturer's directions to do so. Again, in the case of plug-and-play NICs, the OS should recognize the new device upon startup and walk you through the process of selecting the best driver for the hardware.

▲

See? Cards aren't so difficult to install after all. If you take a bit of time to do it correctly the first time, you can prevent the majority of headaches from damaged hardware. It's worth your while to look at your computer's manual and determine which slots have the same interface as the adapter card you want to install. If the computer has more than one slot with an interface that matches your adapter card's interface, use whichever slot is open—no slot is preferable to any other.

Installing Other Adapter Cards Is Straightforward

By the way, this procedure isn't limited to network cards. You install all adapter cards in more or less the same way. So after you know how to do it, you can become an installation fiend, putting cards in left and right and wowing all your relatives (who will hail you as a computer expert and have you working on their PCs in short order).

Working with Wiring

After the network cards are installed, the next step is dealing with the wiring (unless you're working with a wireless network setup). The next sections focus on some of the issues related to wiring your network. It's basically a hands-on version of the wiring concepts you learned in Hour 5, "Network Concepts."

Most of the back end of a network (such as servers, hubs, switches, and routers) should be behind locked doors. It isn't because contact with the equipment is hazardous (it's not); it's that you don't want just anyone to have access to your servers and connectivity equipment. Just innocent curiosity could bring your whole network down, and there's always the chance of malicious intent and sabotage.

As a result, it's a good idea to set up a wiring closet if you're building a network to serve an enterprise—whether that enterprise is a business, a town hall, a library, or whatever. And a wiring closet doesn't have to take up a lot of space, it just needs to be secure; it's perfectly acceptable for a wiring closet to simply be a centrally located closet that authorized personnel can access to install electrical power and route cables. A lot of the time, the phone closet can double as a wiring closet without too much difficulty. In some cases, the wiring closet might also double as the server closet, so you might want to secure a space that will also allow only authorized personnel to deploy racks that contain your servers and other connectivity devices.

The basic wiring closet usually contains several items:

▶ **A set of 110 blocks**—A 110 block is a device, usually mounted on a wall, that has a row of RJ-45 jacks on it. Each jack is connected to a wire that runs out to a network wall jack elsewhere in the office. 110 blocks are also called patch panels (see Figure 12.3). You can install and terminate your own patch panels. (It's pretty easy, in fact.) Because the wires that connect to the contacts on the back of the panel are color coded, it's difficult to make a mistake. Nonetheless, specialized tools are involved, and it's wise to learn from someone who already knows how to do it. Be advised that the punch-down block (as the 110 block is also called) is fast being replaced by cable runs that directly connect to switches, hubs, and other devices.

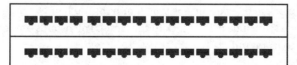

FIGURE 12.3
A patch panel or a 110 block

▶ **One or more switches or hubs**—Switches or hubs (which you might also hear referred to as concentrators) tend to be stored in the wiring closet for two reasons. First, they're generally pretty small—they can fit in a briefcase if an ethically impaired person has the mind to steal one. Second, they make great listening devices; if a network card set up in a special way called promiscuous mode is plugged in to the concentrator, it's possible to read every data packet passing over the network. Because this represents a huge security risk, it's best to lock switches or hubs (see Figure 12.4).

FIGURE 12.4
A typical switch
or hub

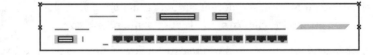

▶ **Wiring bundles**—Because the wiring closet is where all your office network wiring converges, you'll usually have a bundle of cables connected to the 110 block. Wiring bundles represent one end of what can be an arduous task: running cables up hill, down dale, across ceilings, and down walls. If you have a lot of wiring to do, it's often better to let a professional pull and terminate your network wiring. Doing so reduces the aggravation factor quite a bit, and if anything is wrong with the cable, the installer will warrant it. In home networking situations (or a small office), you might be involved in pulling your own wiring though walls or ceilings.

Watch
Out!

Keep Your Cable Runs Away from Power Cables

Do not run network cables any closer than one foot (25 centimeters [cm]) from wall-current electrical cables because the power cable's 50 or 60 hertz (Hz) cycle can interfere with data transmission. Also, keep your cables away from light fixtures in the ceiling if you're pulling cable along a drop ceiling.

▶ **Patch cords**—Patch cords are the cables that connect the 110 block to the switch or hub (see Figure 12.5). You need one patch cord to connect one port on the 110 block to one port on the switch or hub. You'll only need patch cords if you decide to include a 110 block in the closet. Patch cords are sometimes referred to as rat tails.

Wiring closets aren't absolutely necessary, but they do make life easier and more secure. And (for neat freaks) the best part of a wiring closet is that it keeps the messy part of the network behind closed doors.

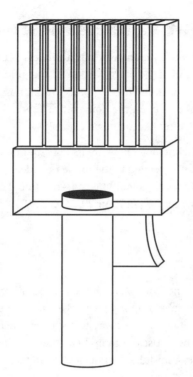

FIGURE 12.5
An RJ-45 connector—a typical patch cord (or network cable end) used for 10BASE-T or 100BASE-T

Connecting a star topology network is easy after the wiring between the 110 block/patch panel and the jacks in offices have been installed. You simply have to plug a patch cord between the computer's 100/1000BASE-T network jack (it's on the network card you installed earlier) and the 100/1000BASE-T outlet in the wall, and then you must ensure that the corresponding port on the patch panel is connected to the concentrator (see Figure 12.6). It's really simple, which is why it's a great design.

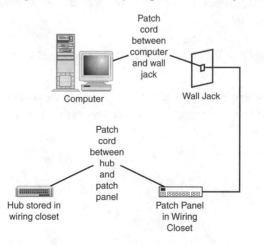

Patch cord between computer and wall jack

Computer

Wall Jack

Patch cord between hub and patch panel

Hub stored in wiring closet

Patch Panel in Wiring Closet

FIGURE 12.6
How computers are connected in a wiring closet/ office jack situation

A Word About Wireless Networking

Obviously, the alternative to wired networks is a wireless network. Wireless networks can provide users a free run of the office because of the radio frequency technology used by wireless network cards and access points to communicate. Wireless networks also provide an excellent option for the home office, especially when trying to pull wire in the home would entail tearing down drywall.

In purchasing wireless technology, there are issues with interoperability between devices. There are also issues related to the range provided by wireless implementations, which can actually relate to building concentration. Finally, there's the issue related to security, a topic covered in Hour 20, "Security."

Summary

The physical hookup of a network is one of the least significant hurdles to successful networking. At the same time, in many people's eyes, it is the most daunting part of the process. In my estimation, the best way to become proficient with hardware installation is simply to do it. Use old computers (they're often pretty inexpensive) and work with them. Make mistakes; you'll learn from them. And in the end, you'll be more successful.

Q&A

Q. *When installing adapter cards in a computer, what do you want to avoid?*

A. You don't want to damage the card either by handling it too roughly or by applying static shock. Both can damage a card badly enough to make it wholly inoperable.

Q. *Why should a wiring closet be close to the center of an office space (if it's possible)?*

A. Keep the wiring closet central to the installation to avoid having to deploy additional switches, repeaters, or other devices to extend the network.

Network Applications

What You'll Learn in This Hour:

- ▶ Location of network applications in OSI model
- ▶ Groupware concepts
- ▶ Client and server aspects of groupware
- ▶ Email and file transfer

In this hour, we move up to Layer 7 of the Internet/OSI (Open Systems Interconnection) model and examine common applications that run on computer networks. The focus is on groupware, email, and file transfer services. Be aware that later hours return to Layer 7. The number of protocols and services offered in the OSI application layer could fill thousands of books, such as the one you're now reading. We concentrate on those software systems that will likely be part of your network. The goal of this hour is to acquaint you with a wide array of fine productivity tools. I suspect you already know about many of them and might be using them. Perhaps I can offer a few more for your consideration.

A network application is usually directly visible to the user, because the user interacts with the application software. For example, email and text messaging require direct input into the application from a user. Indeed, we can view the layered model as consisting of eight layers, with the user or user application setting on top of Layer 7.

Applications that a user runs from a computer network can be installed and run on the user's computer or on a server. Whether run from a server or from individual desktops, the user will notice little difference in performance and services. In terms of administration, running the applications from the server allows for easier updates and more efficient administration.

Introduction to Groupware

Groupware consists of a suite of software modules that allow users to communicate and collaborate with each other. Some people use the terms collaborative software or workgroup support systems to describe this concept. At the desktop, the client side of these applications is collectively referred to as a Personal Information Manager (PIM).

Groupware applications embrace the client/server model of communication. A client runs on each user computer and allows the client computer to communicate with the communication server, which accumulates and holds the application data. Groupware products run on top of a particular network operating system and the lower layers of the OSI model.

For example, Exchange Server from Microsoft is a groupware environment that runs on a Microsoft 2000, 2003, or 2007 server. Three commonly used groupware product suites are Microsoft Exchange Server, Lotus Notes, and Novell GroupWise. Each of these groupware products offers several communication and collaboration features.

Some of the common features of groupware products are these:

▶ **Electronic mail system**—The groupware communication server serves as the mail server for internal email systems or Internet email.

▶ **Group scheduling**—A centralized scheduling system is maintained on the communication server.

▶ **Discussion groups**—Users can read and post messages to a discussion database. They can create discussion groups for the discussion and development of projects. This category of groupware includes electronic conferencing, which consists of message boards, video conferencing, instant messaging, online chats, and shared whiteboards.

▶ **Information databases**—The communication server can host databases such as an employee handbook and a centralized employee address book (including email and phone extension information).

▶ **Task automation**—Forms can be developed that allow users to order office supplies online and invite users to a meeting.

Other sets of software for your consideration are known by the name of collaborative management tools. These systems include the following:

▶ **Project management**—Provides a means to set up, schedule, and track the phases and steps of a project, such as the network you and your team will create.

▶ **Electronic calendars**—Allows its users to schedule events and keep all members informed about events and associated deadlines. (Electronic calendars are also called time management systems.)

▶ **Workflow systems**—Provides a means to track the flow of documents and their associated users. In a large bureaucracy, a workflow system can lead to remarkable insights (not to mention surprises) into the overhead of "doing business."

▶ **Shared slide shows and spreadsheets**—Often used in conjunction with the groupware applications cited previously.

Email

One of the important—perhaps the most important—features provided by groupware is email. The sending and receiving of email, although transparent to the end user, works the same as postal or "snail" mail. You create your correspondence or email, place an "address" on it, and then send it on its way. Your network email system takes care of the return address and routes your email across your local network and the Internet. If it gets there, great; if not, it will provide you a notification that the message was undeliverable.

Email started out as a simple function of the early UNIX operating systems. It was composed of an automated file copying operation in which a text file containing a message was copied from a local UNIX system's hard drive onto a remote UNIX system's hard drive.

To get around the nonstandard and often incompatible email systems that permeated the early UNIX environment, a programmer named Eric Allman wrote a program called sendmail. Sendmail offered a large range of options for sending and receiving mail.

Over the past couple of decades, software developers have improved the software and protocols used to send and receive email. Today, a wide variety of email clients and servers are available. Most of them now center around two Internet standards: POP3 (Post Office Protocol version 3) and IMAP4 (Internet Message Access Protocol version 4). Most email servers support both protocols, but POP3 is more common.

POP3 and IMAP4

POP3 allows users to log on to a network and retrieve email messages. The messages can be stored and viewed later, even if the user is no longer connected to the network. POP3 is used by a client computer to collect its email from the mail server. IMAP4 is another email transport protocol that allows users to check their messages but doesn't remove them from the email server. This feature supports a user who wants to view received email from any device or any location. IMAP4 also allows multiple users to have access to the same mailbox.

SMTP

The Simple Mail Transport Protocol (SMTP) is used to send emails, whereas POP3 and IMAP4 are used to retrieve emails. SMTP can deliver messages to one or many recipients. After a user has entered the email, it's sent to a relaying server. This server uses a special record (called the Mail eXchange or MX record, explained in Hour 15, "Connecting to the Internet: Key Supporting Operations") to determine which STMP server to send the email.

As suggested, SMTP is not designed to retrieve messages (called "pulling" messages). It's a "push" protocol, in that it sends messages. POP3 or IMAP4 are pull protocols. Nonetheless, some implementations have a feature allowing reception of mail, especially for a computer that is continuously connected to the Internet. But for most users, why bother? POP and IMAP do the job just fine.

Proprietary Mail Systems

With the advent of PC-based networking in the early-to-mid 1980s, a raft of vendors began building proprietary mail systems to operate in various PC environments. These obsolete systems, which included Lotus cc:Mail, Microsoft Mail, and various packages built around Novell's MHS (Message Handling System), often attempted to rectify what their designers saw as shortcomings in sendmail.

Proprietary email packages for computer networks are usually easy to install and configure. Three of the more popular email and groupware platforms are Microsoft Exchange, Lotus Notes, and Novell GroupWise. These platforms not only provide for the use of POP3 and SMTP to send company email using Internet standards, but they provide a centralized server for the administration of the mail and communication services.

A downside of proprietary mail systems is that they do not work with each other without the intercession of a mail gateway, a computer that converts mail from one proprietary format to another. Additionally, proprietary mail systems can't route mail directly to the Internet. To do so, they require yet another mail gateway to convert mail to SMTP format, the section of the TCP/IP (Transmission Control Protocol/Internet Protocol) protocol suite that handles mail routing.

Open-Standards Email

An alternative to proprietary mail systems is the use of open standards. As with most things networked, the Internet Engineering Task Force (IETF) has published an extensive set of standards for running email applications over the TCP/IP protocol suite. Internet mail standards are surprisingly simple. As long as your network uses TCP/IP, it's possible to use Internet mail; all you need is a server to run the server-side mail application software and the software to run at the client to retrieve mail from the server.

There are many manufacturers of server and client Internet mail software. The beauty of the standards set forth by the IETF is that any client can work with any server as long as both pieces conform to the standards: SMTP for "push" side operations and POP3 or IMAP for the "pull" side.

Common standards-compliant email includes the following:

▶ Open-source sendmail, usually running on UNIX or Linux

▶ Commercial sendmail from sendmail.com, usually running on UNIX or Linux

▶ Procmail, usually running on UNIX or Linux

▶ Fetchmail, usually running on UNIX or Linux

▶ Microsoft Exchange Server running the Internet Mail Connector

Sendmail, procmail, and fetchmail are (mostly) open source. This means that you can download the code from the appropriate web location (www.sendmail.org for open-source sendmail), configure and compile it on your UNIX or Linux system, and run it. Commercial sendmail and Microsoft Exchange are commercial solutions that offer vendor support.

Configuring Email

Getting an email client up and running requires you to install and configure the client to send and receive email. To configure the client, you must first configure an email account on the server for the client. For example, on a server running

Microsoft Exchange Server, a new Exchange Mailbox is created in the Windows
Active Directory, as shown in Figure 13.1.

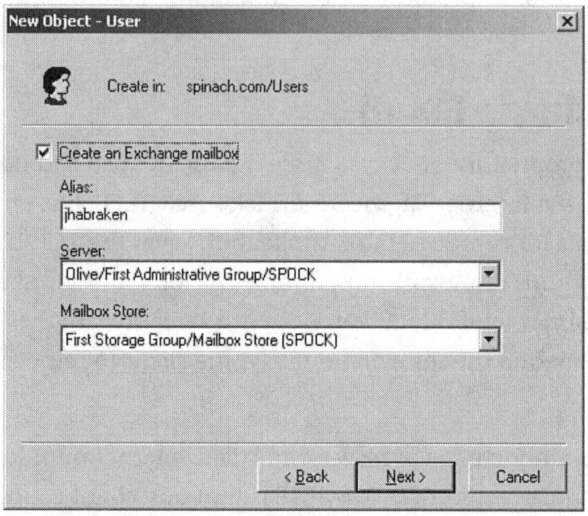

FIGURE 13.1
Users require an
email account on
the mail server.

After you've created the account (whether a proprietary platform account or an
Internet email account), you can configure the client application. For example,
Microsoft Outlook walks the user through the steps of creating a new account, as
depicted in Figure 13.2. It allows different account types to be created—such as
Microsoft Exchange, POP3, IMAP, and HTTP (Hypertext Transfer Protocol)—and can
serve as the client for a number of proprietary mail systems.

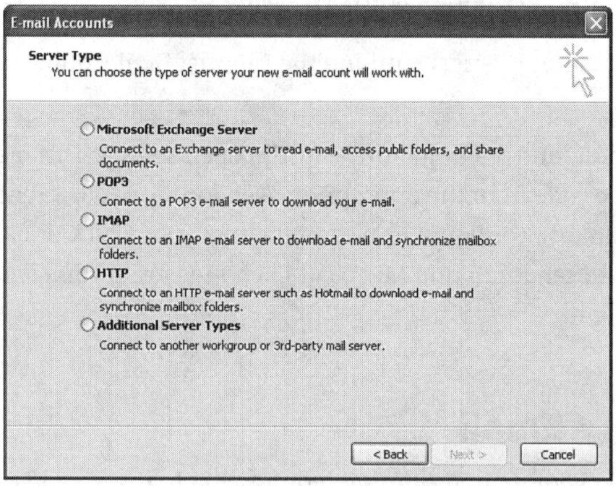

FIGURE 13.2
You must then
configure the
email client to
communicate
with the mail
server.

When configuring the email client, you will need to specify the user account, user password, and name of the mail server. When dealing with Internet email, you typically specify both a POP3 and SMTP server.

Multipurpose Internet Mail Extensions (MIME)

Although being able to send text messages over a network or the Internet is useful, the fact that we can attach files to email messages makes it a great way to send all sorts of personal and professional items. Examples are application files (programs you can run on your computer), picture files, video files, sound files, and so forth.

However, until the advent of MIME (Multipurpose Internet Mail Extensions), these kinds of files could not be carried over regular email channels. The problem was the design of SMTP, which supports only one format for coding text into binary images (strings of 1s and 0s). Equally serious, this format (the famous 7-bit ASCII character set) does not support diacritics (phonetic marks used in many languages).

As a result, the IETF decided to create a set of extensions for the SMTP mail standard that enabled files of many different types to be attached to email. Rather than defining all the file types and creating a new SMTP version each time a new file type came into existence, the IETF decided that it would create a system to which new file types could be added without changing the whole mail system. The IETF's efforts resulted in the MIME standard, which is used to code files of various types across the Internet. Today, SMTP and MIME are so closely related that SMTP/MIME email is now a common term.

To gain sense of the power of MIME, we can now send and receive files containing other languages, audio and visual information, graphic representations, and computer software programs.

As the Internet matures, many new file types will become available. Fortunately, MIME is sufficiently open-ended that it will support new types of files. In this regard, it's extensible, allowing the addition of new content types. MIME is a valuable protocol; without it, the rest of the Internet-compliant email system would lose a significant portion of its utility.

Diagnosing Email Problems

Problems encountered with sending and receiving email usually boil down to problems with the client's mail server. This holds true no matter what mail system your network uses. Oh, and there's always that pesky problem that can shut down any client/server-based system (such as email): connectivity issues. If there's a network problem, even a perfectly working email client and an email server that is up and running can't talk if the network infrastructure doesn't provide the appropriate connectivity. Think of it this way: The lower layers of the Internet/OSI model must be operating correctly for the protocols in Layer 7 to function.

Remember that connectivity issues don't always relate to a faulty router or a problem with cabling; other problems that control the capability of computers to communicate on the network can also be at fault. On occasion, you might notice a network provider (such as Verizon) has experienced a "down" with its email system. These outages are quite rare because an unreliable email product would be the death knell to that vendor.

Accurately diagnosing network communication problems requires a keen understanding of the TCP/IP protocol stack and network troubleshooting. We discuss TCP/IP in Hour 14, "Connecting to the Internet: Initial Operations," and network troubleshooting in Hour 22, "Network Troubleshooting."

Dealing with Spam

Spam = an associated curse of using the Internet.

As I'm sure you know, spam is unwanted email, and it can fill our In box. We don't like it, but let's be more specific. What exactly is spam?

An electronic message is spam if: (1) the recipient's personal identity and context are irrelevant because the message is equally applicable to many other potential recipients; and (2) the recipient has not verifiably granted deliberate, explicit, and still-revocable permission for it to be sent; and (3) the transmission and reception of the message appear to the recipient to give a disproportionate benefit to the sender.[1]

Spam not only is a nuisance, it costs companies and institutions work hours and ultimately money. It's beginning to clog the Internet to the point at which it's become a major problem. Some spam is innocuous, but a lot of it's unsuitable and objectionable.

Higher-end email clients, such as Lotus Notes and Microsoft Outlook, provide filters that you can use to move spam directly to the trash bin, and some email clients can block spam based on email addresses or the domain of the sender. A number of other tools on the market also do a good job fighting spam. The following list provides some of these; consider it a list of possibilities, not necessarily recommendations:

---

[1] *Sourced from http://www.mail-abuse.com/spam_def.html*

▶ CloudMark is an excellent spam fighter; it's an inexpensive subscription, and it works well.

▶ Bayesian filters, which are available from various sources on the Web, block spam based on local algorithms and what you select as spam. They usually require some setup efforts ("training the filter") but can trap more than 99% of unwanted emails.

▶ For people using Linux or UNIX and sendmail, SpamAssassin is another accurate server-based tool to help block spam. Recent enhancements to SpamAssassin also support Windows-based systems.

▶ Subscriptions are available to businesses to filter spam based on black hole lists. They keep a database of known spammers and deny messages coming from those email addresses and domains. In addition, some sites provide tutorials and product announcements on spam.

▶ A good spam fighter that integrates well with Microsoft Outlook (and Outlook Express) is SonicWALL. It provides a home or corporate user with the ability to filter and block spam messages. You can find more information on SonicWALL at www.sonicwall.com.

In corporate environments, it falls on the network administrator to find strategies and set rules to minimize spam on the corporate network.

You might want to devise a set of rules that users must follow on the network. For example, you might have a rule that forbids users to sign up for any Internet services or special websites using their corporate email accounts. This tactic is one way spammers build their long list of email addresses: They capture corporate email names and add them to their spam list. Spammers like to use corporate names because the name is often setup to reach many recipients.

Scheduling and Calendars

Anyone who has worked in an environment that requires the staff to meet periodically knows how difficult it is to schedule a meeting that works for all the potential attendees. I think everyone will agree that just tracking your own personal and business appointments can be problematic. We use every possible kind of system to stay organized: calendars, daily planners, and a lot of little scraps of paper.

Groupware products such as Microsoft Exchange and Lotus Notes also provide scheduling and calendar features that make it easy to schedule appointments, meetings, and other events. Let's look at an example of how this works in the Microsoft Exchange environment.

By the
Way

Groupware Scheduling Features Do Not Embrace a Common Standard

There have been several proposed calendaring standards. None have been embraced as an industry standard, and calendar software packages are still proprietary. Some products include selected sets of the ITU X.400 standards. All interface with POP3 and IMAP4.

Currently, Microsoft Exchange owns a large share of this market, largely because of the lack of a real standard and Microsoft's position.

Rather than working on standards, several vendors are working on open source standards-compliant mail/calendaring clients. Hopefully, implementation will overtake design in this case and provide useful products that a standard can be derived from.

Each user's calendar (meaning her current schedule containing appointments and scheduled meetings) is held in folders on the Exchange server. This means that when any user attempts to schedule a meeting from Microsoft Outlook's Calendar feature, Outlook can check to see if the invitees for the meeting are available or busy. Figure 13.3 shows the Plan a Meeting window in Outlook 2003. The AutoPick button provides a user with the ability to find open time slots for the meeting that will accommodate all the attendees.

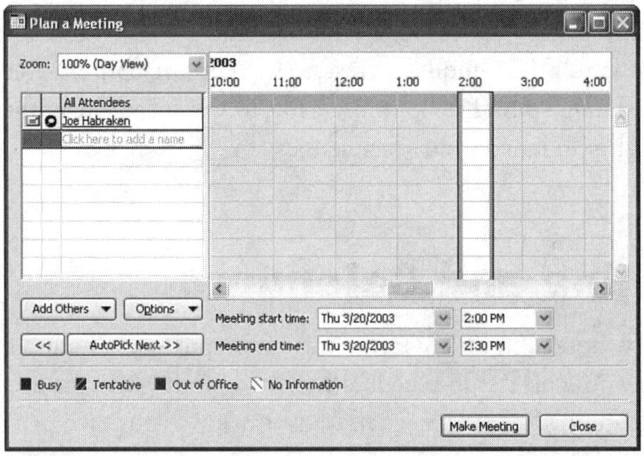

FIGURE 13.3
A user scheduling a new meeting has the calendar resources on the Exchange Server to accommodate the attendees' schedules.

After the user schedules the meeting, the meeting is posted to the Exchange Server. This process also sends out email meeting requests to all the attendees. Figure 13.4 shows a sample of a meeting request email.

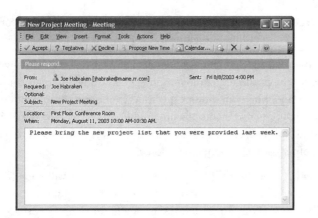

FIGURE 13.4
Meeting requests are sent out to the invitees.

Because the Microsoft Exchange Server environment enables the Outlook client to reconcile all attendees' schedules with the meeting date and time, the system should be foolproof in terms of "Ah! I didn't get the message about the meeting!" However, if users haven't kept their calendars up-to-date, this system won't work any better than a paper calendar or the scraps of paper mentioned earlier.

Groupware products are not limited to just scheduling meetings. You can also assign tasks and appointments to users. For example, when a task is assigned to a user, the user can accept or decline the task. Because messages are sent back to the originator of the task whether the user accepts or declines, groupware, such as Microsoft Exchange, makes it easy to track job assignments and their status.

By the Way

> **Shared Calendars Keep Employees' Schedules Up-to-Date**
> Groupware products also make it easy for users to share calendars. For example, an executive assistant can be given access to the calendar of the corporate officer she serves, allowing her to make and track the executive's appointments and meetings.

Contact Management

Another tool provided by groupware products is contact management. At its most basic, contact management allows a user to store names, addresses, email addresses, and phone numbers in a database. Not only can users create their own contacts list in a groupware client, but they can access group contact and distribution lists that make it easy to send email, phone, or otherwise communicate.

In networked environments, groupware contact software provides a way for a sales force to not only track its clients, but also track the most recent meeting it has had with clients; it can also, in some cases, automatically schedule a time for a next call after a preset amount of time has elapsed.

Like group calendaring, contact management software does not yet have an IETF standard, so for the most part, contact management software interoperates only with itself. Your will find, however, that most contact management software packages— particularly those provided by groupware products such as Lotus Notes, Microsoft Exchange, and Novell GroupWise—do provide the ability to import and export data to and from other contact management software.

Creating a new contact in the different groupware products will vary; however, all the products provide a window that allows you to enter the information related to a particular contact such as name, address, phone number, and so on. Figure 13.5 shows the Outlook Contact window, which is used to enter information related to a new contact.

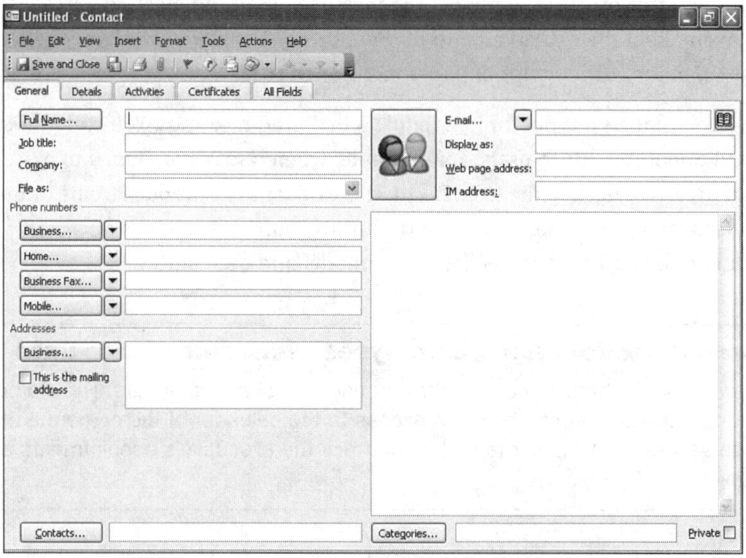

FIGURE 13.5
Contact information is entered in a simple-to-use window.

After you enter the contact, the information is then available to all the users on the network. This not only creates an environment in which client or customer data is readily available to all employees, but it sets up a system in which contact data will more likely be updated because the contact records don't reside on individual computers; they're held on the server.

In the late 1990s, Microsoft integrated contact management features into its Outlook and PIM products. Microsoft also offers Business Contact Manager for Outlook. Even on the Macintosh platform, in 2002, Apple began including PIM and calendar applications with its operating system. The efforts by these companies have led to a decline in native-mode contact management products in the marketplace.

A Sampler of Network-Based Applications

As mentioned, various groupware products are available. Each provides the standard groupware features such as email, scheduling, and contacts.

In the sections that follow, I will briefly discuss Novell GroupWise, Lotus Notes, and Microsoft Exchange/Outlook. You'll find that each is similar at the user level. So, in terms of deciding to use a particular platform, you should look at the server side of each groupware product and see how they'll fit into your current network implementation.

Novell GroupWise

GroupWise is Novell's entry into the groupware software market. It consists of a GroupWise client and server. You can deploy the GroupWise server product on a Novell NetWare server, or you can run it on a Microsoft Windows server such as Microsoft Windows 2000 or Microsoft Server 2003. Alternatively, you can run the GroupWise client on several client platforms such as Windows, Linux, and the Mac operating system. Figure 13.6 shows the GroupWise client window on a Windows XP computer.

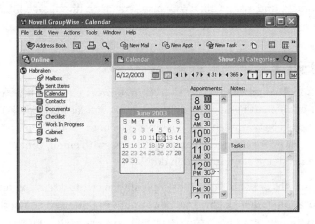

FIGURE 13.6
The GroupWise client window

The GroupWise server product (version 8 as of the writing of this book) is fully integrated with NetWare's eDirectory hierarchical object database, so client accounts are actually created within the eDirectory.

Users are provided access to the GroupWise post office when their NetWare eDirectory user accounts are created. Figure 13.7 shows the eDirectory New User dialog box. To include a user in the GroupWise post office, you must select the Add User to Group-Wise Post Office check box.

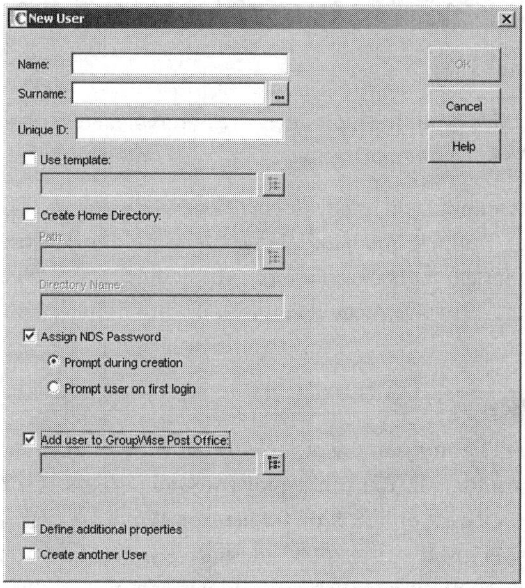

FIGURE 13.7
GroupWise post office access is provided via the user's eDirectory account.

GroupWise provides all the tools that users expect from a GroupWare product: email, calendar, contacts, and tasks. GroupWise also provides a handy web interface tool that allows users on the road to access their GroupWise account via the Internet.

Lotus Notes

Lotus Notes from IBM provides a client/server groupware platform that can be run on a number of different network operating systems such as Microsoft Windows, Sun Solaris, and Novell NetWare servers. The server side of the Lotus Notes platform is called Lotus Domino Server, and it can provide users with email, contacts, tasks, and different discussion and communication databases.

One of the strengths of Lotus Notes is its capability to create discussion databases. These databases are much like Internet newsgroups in that users can post a particular message and then other users can post comments related to that message (or post a new message). This allows users to have an online dialogue without having to clutter their email In boxes. For example, several workers involved in the same project could design a discussion database and then post status information, tips, or even frustrations on the database.

The latest version of Lotus Notes is 8, with three releases:

- **Version 8.0**—Server versions for Windows, Linux, Solarix, AIX, and client versions available for Linux, Windows, and Vista.

- **Version 8.0.1**—Support added for Widgets and Google Gadgets.

- **Version 8.02**—Support for Office 2007 files.

Some industry watchers (*Forbes Magazine*, for example) state that Lotus Notes is losing its customer base. IBM claims otherwise and says its customer base has more than tripled during the past 10 years. Lotus Notes is a fine product that I don't believe is going away.

Microsoft Exchange/Outlook

Microsoft Exchange Server runs on a server class computer that already has the Windows network operating system installed on it. Exchange Server is tightly wrapped with Microsoft's Active Directory (the hierarchical database used to store objects on a Windows network). Users in the Active Directory gain access to the Exchange Server resources by clicking the Create an Exchange Mailbox check box on their User Properties dialog box.

Exchange Server is managed using the Exchange System Manager, which allows the network administrator to manage mailboxes and public folders (such as those holding distribution lists and other public contacts). Figure 13.8 shows the Exchange System Manager window.

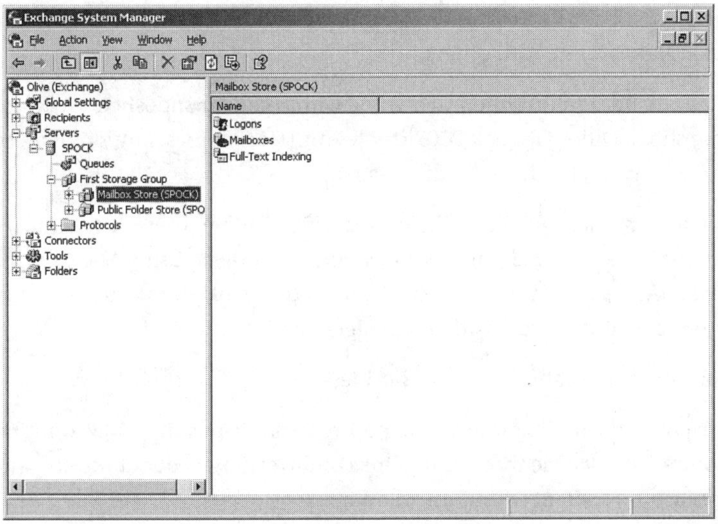

FIGURE 13.8
The Exchange
System Manager

The latest release of Exchange Server is 2007. Here are some of its features:

▶ Supports both IPv4 and IPv6

▶ Enhancements for operating with POP3 and IMAP4, including port settings (see Hour 14) and authentication operations

▶ Additional features for MIME support

▶ Quality of service (QoS) features

▶ Support for Secure Realtime Transport Protocol (SRTP)

Outlook is closely linked with Microsoft's Office desktop productivity suite (products such as Microsoft Word, Excel, and so on). In a special folder called the Journal, Outlook can log all documents generated in Office for future reference. This allows a user to track her activity in relation to her use of other Office applications. Not only does the Journal track Office application use, but it can be set up to track activities within Outlook itself, providing a user with an even higher degree of organization.

The most current versions of Outlook (2003 and 2007) support the mail protocols (POP3, IMAP4, HTTP) as well as Microsoft's proprietary Exchange-based mail systems. The products also offer groupware applications that you can download from the Microsoft website.

Since its introduction, Outlook has become a powerful mail client, and its groupware features have steadily become stronger. Here are a few examples for the features of Outlook 2007:

▶ Create and subscribe to Internet calendars. Users can add a static Internet calendar, subscribe to a dynamic Internet calendar, or create their own Internet calendars to share with others.

▶ Send calendar information to anyone with calendar snapshots. With calendar snapshots, Office Outlook 2007 creates an HTML representation of a user's calendar so it can be shared with others.

▶ Publish Internet calendar to Microsoft Office Online. Users can create a new Internet calendar and publish it to share with others. Using Microsoft Passport credentials, you or your team can invite a group of coworkers, customers, and so on to view and work with your calendar.

▶ Customize and share electronic business cards.

▶ Prevent junk email and reduce exposure to malicious sites. New antiphishing features can disable threatening links and warn users about possibly malicious or phishing content within an email message.

▶ Improvement of graphical user interfaces (GUIs).The GUI screens are easier to view. The options presented on the screens are concise and unambiguous.

File Transfer and FTP

The Internet standards include a widely used file transfer system, called the File Transfer Protocol (FTP). As its name implies, FTP defines the procedures for the transfer of files between two machines. FTP also supports data transfer between a device other than the original server (and client). The operation is known as a third-party transfer.

If you have used FTP, the chances are good that some of its operations were displayed on your computer screen, usually in status indicators called FTP reply codes. For example, a code of "1yz" indicates a file transfer command is being acted upon. Of course, most users don't care about such details, and many products, while capturing these codes, do not make them available on the GUIs.

FTP provides a file-sharing environment that can control access to the file server by requiring a login name and password. This means that the FTP server must validate a user and his password before he can access files on the server.

On the Internet, many public FTP sites allow an anonymous logon. Anyone can log on to the FTP site using a username of "anonymous." The password for an anonymous logon is often your email address. A site allowing anonymous logons is referred to as an anonymous FTP site. Figure 13.9 shows Apple's anonymous FTP site that has been accessed using the Internet Explorer web browser. Note that the command FTP replaces the HTTP in the address window because you're accessing an FTP site rather than a website (HTTP).

Please note that on a Windows-based computer, the directories on the FTP site appear in the Internet Explorer window the same as local directories would. You are potentially accessing files that reside on a computer clear across the world, but the computer's connection to the Internet makes the directories and files appear as if they are local.

Because we use web browsers to access anonymous FTP sites, most of us have never had to use an FTP client. Several FTP clients are available and can be used to access FTP sites without using a web browser. If you're accessing FTP sites that require a username and password, you'll need an FTP client. You can find a number of freeware FTP clients (and some demos for commercial software) on the web. Just key in File Transfer Protocol (FTP), and you'll be presented a wide range of sites to visit.

So, what are the flaws of FTP? And if there are many, why is it so popular? First, FTP is an old Internet protocol that was designed during the days when most Internet users weren't concerned with security breaches. (How times have changed!) Thus, FTP isn't set up to easily deny hackers access. That stated, additions have been added to FTP to ameliorate these problems. Second, FTP software logic, although well struc- tured, consumes bandwidth during the exchange of several packets to set up the association between the two FTP users. Third, FTP employs two separate connections: one for control and the other for data transfer. In hindsight, this technique isn't nec- essary and adds yet more overhead to the process.

So, why use FTP? Because it's the accepted standard for transferring files between computers. Some other standards for file transfer made a go of it but were never suc- cessful. As long as you and your design team have addressed the security faults of FTP, you shouldn't worry about using it.

I've used FTP for the submittal of manuscripts to book publishers, articles to maga- zines, and essays to a reader community. An FTP server is identified with a uniform resource locator (URL). The server contains a folder whose name I share with anyone who wants access to it. With an FTP server password, a party can open the folder and, at his leisure, access my material.

Summary

In this hour, we've explored network applications, with a special highlight on email and file transfer systems. We examined groupware concepts and some of the commu- nication features provided by groupware products. We discussed scheduling, contact

management, and file transfer. We also looked at some of the most popular groupware platforms.

Q&A

Q. *What network model do groupware products embrace?*

A. Most groupware products embrace a client/server model, where a desktop
client is used to access information stored on a network server.

Q. *Why are Internet/TCP/IP standard applications more desirable than applications that use proprietary communications protocols?*

A. TCP/IP is a vendor-independent standard; applications that adhere to it can
work with other TCP/IP applications. By contrast, proprietary systems require
gateway protocol converters to communicate with other systems.

Q. *What are some of the services that groupware products provide to users?*

A. Groupware products provide email, scheduling, calendars, contacts, and other
collaboration features.

HOUR 14

Connecting to the Internet: Initial Operations

What You'll Learn in This Hour:

▶ How and why the Internet was created

▶ ISPs and IXPs

▶ How traffic is sent across networks using peering arrangements

▶ The BGP

▶ More details on IP

▶ Operations of the TCP and the UDP

In this hour, we look at the Internet in more detail. Using the general concepts outlined in previous hours, we examine how traffic is transported across the Internet through Internet service providers (ISPs) and Internet Exchange Points (IXPs). We examine ideas on how to select an ISP and how we might exploit the features of the Internet Protocol (IP), the Transmission Control Protocol (TCP), and the User Datagram Protocol (UDP) to provide better performance.

Origins of the Internet

In the late 1960s and early 1970s, networks were not designed to allow resource sharing among users in different locations. Network administrators were also reluctant to allow users to tap into their systems due to concerns about security as well as excessive use of their network resources. As a result, it was difficult for a user to share software or data with someone else or, for that matter, to exchange electronic messages. Most existing networks, which unto themselves were few and far between, were "closed." They were not compatible with others.

During this time, a small group of bright men came up with the common-sense notion to share resources among user applications. (This idea is believed to have been espoused in 1962 by J.C.R. Licklider of MIT.) But to do so, it was recognized network administrators would have to agree on a set of common technologies and standards to allow the networks to communicate with each other. It also followed that applications, such as electronic mail and file transfer, should be standardized to permit interworking end user applications (not just the networks).

Licklider was in charge of computer research at a U.S. Department of Defense establishment named ARPA (the Advanced Research Projects Agency). He and others at ARPA began to think about the usefulness of "computer networks." Around this time, research was being conducted on packet switching (see Hour 2, "The Benefits of Networking") to get around the problems of using conventional telephone circuit switches. These packet switches were eventually called Interface Message Processors (IMPs).

By the late 1960s, ARPA and some organizations in the UK had well-conceived visions of packet-switched computer networks. In 1968, a specification (and request for comments) was published for just such a network. It was to be called ARPAnet. By the end of 1969, the ARPAnet was up and running, connecting four sites in California and Utah. With only four sites, it was a modest undertaking, but it was monumental at the time; and it had monumental import for the future.

Thereafter, ARPAnet grew rapidly. In 1972, email was created as an application to run on the network. At about this time, TCP/IP came into existence and was adopted by the Department of Defense in 1980 as the way to do networking. Coupled with DOD's clout, the decision to use UNIX with these (noncopyrighted) ARPAnet protocols, TCP/IP did indeed become the way to do networking.

During the next three decades, the Internet evolved from the original ARPAnet. It changed from a government network to the public network in existence today. For these next two hours, we will fill in some gaps about the history of the Internet as it relates to our task of learning about computer networks. If you want to know the details of the Internet's history, go to www.isoc.org/internet/history/brief.shtml.

Perquisites for an Internet Connection

In previous hours, we introduced subjects dealing with how to connect to the Internet. For this hour, we delve into more of the details. For review, the list that follows summarizes previous material. It doesn't contain all the subjects covered earlier, but the most important perquisites for obtaining an Internet connection. If you're hazy about their functions, it's a good idea to return to the appropriate hour and review them:

▶ **IP and MAC addresses**—Hour 3, "Getting Data from Here to There: How Networking Works"

▶ **Routers, hubs, bridges, and switches**—Hour 5, "Network Concepts"

▶ **Routing and forwarding**—Hour 5

▶ **Physical media**—Hour 5

▶ **DSL and "T1"**—Hour 6, "Extending LANs with Wide Area Networks (WANs)"

▶ **Modems**—Hour 8, "Remote Networking"

ISPs

Now that we have a handle on those subjects, let's focus on how an email message is transported from, say, your computer to mine. Figure 14.1 is used for this discussion. First, we assume that both of us are connected via DSL, dial-up, cable, or some other link to an ISP. Let's assume that yours is Verizon and mine is AOL. As depicted in Figure 14.1, Verizon is identified as network 1 (NW 1), and AOL is identified as network 3 (NW 3).

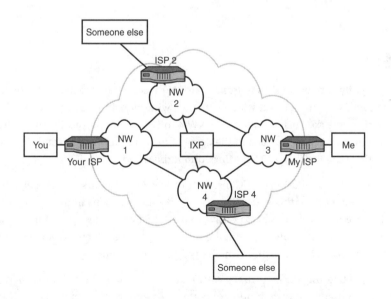

FIGURE 14.1
ISPs and IXPs

Second, these companies offer access to the Internet and numerous other services, such as

▶ Firewalls for security and privacy services

▶ Assignment of IP addresses

▶ Assignment of domain names (not yet explained; see Hour 15, "Connecting to the Internet: Key Supporting Operations")

▶ Email service

▶ Spam filters

▶ Help desk

▶ Text messaging

▶ An array of websites for shopping, news, weather, and so on

▶ Connections to other networks for end-to-end delivery

With the exception of the last item, it's likely you're familiar with these services. Notwithstanding, if this last service isn't provided, the others are worthless. Consequently, the next part of this hour explains how ISPs connect with each other to provide customers with end-to-end service.

IXPs

ISPs frequently connect to IXPs to transfer traffic. In so doing, two networks, such as Verizon and AOL, can connect with each other, without going through so-called third-party networks, such as NW 2 and NW 4 in Figure 14.1. Typically, this more-direct connection reduces costs and the delay of moving traffic end to end. As of this writing, there are roughly 230 IXPs throughout the world.

Another advantage of using an IXP pertains to speed (throughput in bits per second [bps]). In some parts of the world, the physical communications infrastructure (the long-distance link) is poor and expensive to use. The ISPs in these places might only have low-speed, poor-quality links to the Internet. If they can obtain a direct connection to a nearby IXP, they avail themselves of better technology.

The costs of operating an IXP are typically charged back to its participating networks. The fees are based on a combination of port speeds and traffic volume. Some IXPs charge a setup fee and a monthly or annual fee.

For ISPs to use each other's facilities to transport traffic back and forth between you and me, they first enter into an agreement about this matter. This agreement becomes a *peering* relationship and entails the discovery and announcement of routes (IP addresses). These advertisements can also contain IP addresses of other ISPs that can be reached by the network that is doing the advertising. (A simplified view of address advertising is provided in Hour 5 [Figure 5.1]). Upon receiving this information, the peer party executes a *route filtering* operation: It accepts or ignores routes, perhaps deciding to use other routes to reach the IP addresses.

Thus far in this analysis, traffic between NW 1 and NW 3 has been passing through the IXP. In many situations, ISPs forward their traffic between ISPs and not IXPs. A network provider might declare the route between, say, NW 1 and NW 4 to be the primary route. After all, it makes no sense to relay traffic through an IXP if the two ISPs have direct connections. In many situations, the IXP acts as a backup route for directly connected ISPs.

The IXP contains at least one router. Bigger IXPs contain many, usually connected through Gigabit Ethernet at one site. Some IXPs have multiple sites, spread across a geographical region and interconnected with high-speed SONET links.

All ISPs and IXPs use an Internet route discovery protocol to establish associations with other ISPs and IXPs, to advertise IP addresses, and to perform route filtering. This protocol is called the Border Gateway Protocol (BGP).

BGP

BGP establishes and maintains routes between networks in the Internet. For administrative and management purposes, these networks are collectively called and identified by an autonomous system (AS) number. BGP is different from other (older) Internet routing protocols in that it does not make routing decisions (and build routing tables) only on the most efficient route. Equally important, it selects routes between networks based on peering agreements. Thus, BGP allows each network administrator to define a "policy" that directs BPG how to set up logical associations between ASs and advertise IP addresses (prefixes) to construct the routing tables.

Unless you and your team are employed by a large company with substantial networking capabilities, it's unlikely you'll be tasked with configuring BGP. Be thankful! It's a powerful routing protocol, but it has a steep learning curve.

By the Way

> **A Typical IXP**
>
> An example of an IXP is MAE-East. It has sites in Vienna, Virginia; Reston, Virginia; Ashburn, Virginia; New York, New York; and Miami, Florida. It provides several connection services to its members, such as Asynchronous Transfer Mode (ATM) and IP over SONET (Synchronous Optical Network). It connects its five sites with high-speed SONET links.

Peering

Unless you're a network manager of a large company, you need not know the details of Internet peering. That stated, peering is key to understanding how the thousands of ISPs and IXPs set up their connections so you and I can exchange emails. For the curious reader and for the reader who manages a large set of networks, read on; it's a fascinating subject whose "modest" goal is moving user data—error-free—around the earth (through multiple networks) in less than one second.

Peering is an association and connection between different Internet networks for the sole purpose of exchanging user traffic. The term has usually been associated with the idea that there are no fees for peering; the networks provide free pass-through service to each other. However, some literature and implementations use the term to connote some kind of settlement (exchange of money) for the arrangement. To clear up this confusion, the term "settlement-free peering" is used to describe nonmonetary arrangements.

Regardless of how peering is defined, the arrangement boils down to one of two scenarios: (a) A network pays another network for access (which is called a settlement); or (b) networks exchange traffic without settlement.

If an IXP is involved in the peering of two networks, the process is called public peering. If the networks arrange for their own interconnections (such as private, leased SONET links), the process is called private peering. Most of the large U.S. networks in the Internet use private peering. Smaller networks opt for public peering.

Peering is a great concept, and its use has been a key factor in the Internet having near-instant global connectivity for any user. It also provides the means to load-level traffic across multiple networks and reduce dependence on only one transit ISP or IXP.

However, human nature and the nature of business might lead a network to decide to resort to depeering—that is, terminating the association and related connection to another network. Reasons for depeering vary. Here are some examples:

▶ One network is "hogging" the bandwidth of another network and not paying (enough) for it.

▶ One network isn't as reliable as the other network.

▶ One network isn't as secure as the other network.

▶ One network has become a direct competitor with the other network for customers.

Notwithstanding these potential problems, Internet peering has evolved to fulfill the surfer's dream: excluding security and privacy considerations, near-instant access to any Internet-connected computer on earth.

Considerations for Choosing an ISP

Choosing an ISP that meets your needs requires doing some homework, especially if your company's livelihood depends on the reliable and efficient interworking with the Internet. Here are some ideas to keep in mind during your analysis:

▶ Is the ISP redundantly connected to upstream links? Redundant connections assure your company of more consistent connections. In case of a failed path to a destination, a redundant link allows a router to reroute traffic.

▶ Does your ISP have public or private peering relationships? Can it provide you with statistics on throughput, reliability, and delay for all the peering relationships that will affect your company's traffic?

▶ Who will supply the equipment for the ISP connection to your network? You need to find out whether the ISP provides and configures necessary equipment, such as routers, as part of the connection cost or whether you will have to purchase and maintain your own connectivity devices.

▶ Can the ISP provide you with a pool of IP addresses for your network and obtain your domain name for you? Having your own pool of IP addresses provides you with flexibility in bringing new clients onto the network and configuring web servers or DNS servers that require fixed IP addresses. Having a pool of IP addresses is certainly not a requirement to connect to the Internet because there are alternatives, such as Network Address Translation (NAT).

▶ How will the ISP help you secure your IP network? What is the ISP willing to do to help protect your LAN from both frivolous and malicious attacks over the Internet connection? Find out whether the ISP offers firewalls and NAT.

▶ What kind and quality of technical support does the ISP offer? Find out whether the ISP offers 24/7 availability for this support.

How and Why TCP/IP Was Created

Throughout this book, frequent references have been made to TCP and IP. We now examine them and discover why they are widely used and how you can use them in your network. To begin our analysis, Figure 14.2 depicts the layered protocol model in relation to TCP/IP.

FIGURE 14.2
TCP/IP and the
IP stack

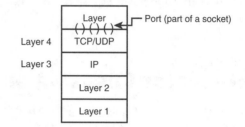

TCP operates in Layer 4 and IP operates in Layer 3 of the Internet/OSI model. This arrangement has significant and positive consequences for transporting traffic across computer networks. To understand why, let's again look back in time. In December 1970, the Network Control Protocol (NCP) was implemented to transport data in the ARPAnet. The protocol was narrow in its functions: It had limited addressing capabilities, a lack of robustness, and no end-to-end host (user computer) error control. These deficiencies led to the development of TCP.

TCP was designed with these key ideas in mind:

▶ The ARPAnet would attempt to deliver packets on a best-effort basis. If a packet did not reach its destination, it was not the responsibility of ARPAnet to resend. It was the responsibility of the sending host.

▶ The "black boxes" that relayed packets (later called routers) would not be aware of the nature of the data in the packets, nor would the boxes retain information about them. Simplicity was the key word.

▶ The network and attached networks would not be involved with the internal operations of each other.

▶ No centralized, global control center would exist. Each network was responsible for itself.

TCP initially supported only end-to-end connections where the following occurred:

1. A logical connection (a handshake) was performed between the two hosts.

2. Data was exchanged in an orderly, sequenced fashion. (Retransmissions occurred in the event of problems.)

3. Another handshake took place to release the logical connection.

Soon after TCP was developed, the designers recognized the flaws of this approach. First, some applications did not need end-to-end acknowledgments and the resending of packets. For example, they knew some traffic would not suffer significant quality problems if an occasional packet was lost. Even more, applications with the need for fast response times could not tolerate the delay of waiting for the retransmitted packet.

The result was the division of TCP into two protocols: TCP and IP. TCP would be responsible for end-to-end flow control, sequencing, and packet recovery. IP would be responsible for addressing and routing of the packet. Therefore, TCP did not have to execute in the routers, only at the hosts. This idea might seem rather insignificant, but it translates into a simple, yet elegant and robust model. Figure 14.3 helps explain why. (As before, the solid arrows symbolize the sending and receiving of traffic down and up the layers; the dashed lines symbolize the logical exchange of traffic between peer layers; and the dashed/dotted lines symbolize the physical transfer of traffic across communications links.)

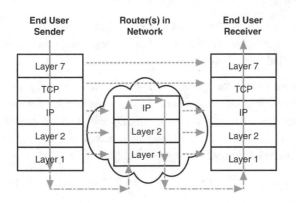

FIGURE 14.3
Transporting traffic with TCP/IP

▶ TCP's significant overhead of handshaking to set up a logical connection, sequence traffic, and perhaps resend packets does not reside in the network. It resides in the end user machines.

▶ The network black boxes (again, called routers today) use the destination address in the IP header to make forwarding decisions. These routers are not tasked with examining data in the packet that deals with Layer 4 or Layer 7.

These two factors lead to (a) a highly efficient and simple network that typically relays traffic with low latency (low delays), and (b) a highly robust service, because the users' computers are executing TCP. The old adage, "Hindsight is 20-20," is altered to describe the amazing foresight of the Internet pioneers, "Foresight was 20-20."

Furthermore, for those applications that still wanted some of the features of TCP (sockets, explained shortly) but did not want handshakes, packet resending, and such, another (simple) protocol was created. It's called UDP and is widely used today for applications such as Voice over IP (VoIP).

Ports

One of the most important functions of TCP and UDP pertains to the Internet port numbers that are placed in fields of their headers; one field for a source port number; another field for a destination port number. As depicted in Figure 14.2, the sending and receiving hosts (computers) use these port numbers to identify the specific type of Layer 7 traffic that resides in the packet. For example, if the data is a BGP message, the port number for passing this data to the BGP software is 179. As another example, if the data pertains to email's POP3, the port number is 110.

Port numbers are managed by the Internet Assigned Numbers Authority (IANA) and are allocated by dividing them into these ranges:

▶ **Well-known ports: Range of 0–1023**—Typically set aside for widely used L_7 applications, but these types of applications might have a port number in the registered port range.

▶ **Registered ports: Range of 1024–49151**—Specific assignments to less widely used applications or vendor-specific applications. For example, port 1270 identifies Microsoft Systems Center Operations Manager. However, this range also includes widely used Internet protocols; for example, port 1293 is reserved for the Internet Security Protocol (IPSec).

▶ **Dynamic or private ports: Range of 49152–65535**—No ports can be registered in this range.

As a general rule, the assigned ports identify a server port and the server software. The client port is selected by the client software (the client's operating system) for each connection by simply starting at number 1024 and wrapping at number 4096. You might ask: Does the client's use of so-called registered numbers create confusion? The answer is no. The operating system keeps track of the source port numbers it chooses and assigns a special ID number to each one.

Table 14.1 lists some of TCP/UDP ports and their assigned numbers.

TABLE 14.1   Examples of TCP/UDP Ports

Number	Name	Description
20	FTP-Data	File Transfer Protocol (Data)
21	FTP	File Transfer Protocol (Control)
23	TELNET	Telnet
25	SMTP	Simple Mail Transfer Protocol
42	NAMESERV	Host Name Server
53	DOMAIN	Domain Name Server
69	TFTP	Trivial File Transfer Protocol
80	HTTP	Hypertext Transfer Protocol
103	X400	ITU X.400 (Electronic Mail)
111	RPC	SUN Remote Procedure Call
110	POP3	Post Office Protocol, version 3
115	SMTP	Simple Mail Transfer Protocol
143	IMAP	Internet Message Access Protocol
179	BGP	Border Gateway Protocol

Sockets

A port makes up part of a socket, which is the complete identifier for the end-to-end connection between two hosts. Thus far, we've been using the term "application" to designate the software that's identified by ports (and now sockets). You might also come across the terms "process" or "thread," depending on the literature or operating system involved. Whatever the term used, an Internet socket is (a) the interface between the L_7 process and TCP or UDP, and (b) the end-to-end connection between two hosts.

The complete bidirectional connection is identified by a socket pair: a send socket and a receive socket. Each socket consists of (1) an IP address, (2) a port number, and (3) the "protocol" field in the IP header that indentifies if the packet contains a TCP or UDP header (and perhaps others, which are not pertinent to our discussion).

Therefore, for an Internet session to take place, the two communicating parties are uniquely identified (throughout the entire Internet) by the following:

▶ **Send socket**—(1) Source IP address, (2) Source socket, (3) Protocol ID

▶ **Receive socket**—(1) Destination IP address, (2) Destination port, (3) Protocol ID

One of the main functions of a TCP handshake is to set up the connection so it is thereafter identified by the socket pair. The appropriate L_7 application can then process the incoming packet by the use of the receive socket identifier.

In a client/server network, the operating systems might set a TCP server socket to be in a listening state, which means it's waiting for clients to send in a TCP handshake packet. If a remote client has not yet sent a connection request, this listening socket simply sets the remote IP address to 0.0.0.0 and the remote port number to 0. The operating system is responsible for keeping track of all Internet sessions by storing information about each socket pair.

You and your team might have to become familiar with socket operations. They vary, depending on the operating system. But they're all consistent with regard to the rules documented in the TCP standards. You might want to use the UNIX netsat-an command, which will provide you a list of all sockets that the OS currently defines; as well as netstat-b, which will provide information on which application program created which socket. If you do use these commands, you won't see the state of a UDP socket, because UDP is a connectionless protocol.

IP Features

Hour 3 explained the major features of IP. This section provides more details. Don't forget that specific IP implementations might not perform these services:

▶ **Type of Service (TOS)**—Requests various levels of (a) precedence, (b) delay, (c) throughput, and (d) reliability of packet delivery. Some implementations use the precedence and reliability fields to identify packets for network control operations, such as a packet containing route advertisements. For your private internets, consider using the delay and throughput fields to establish enhanced quality of service support for time-sensitive traffic, such as voice and video.

▶ **Time to Live (TTL)**—Time the packet can remain active as it finds its way to the destination. Often implemented with a maximum permissible hop count (number of nodes that can be traversed). This option ensures that IP packets don't "thrash around" in the network indefinitely—a problem called endless loops. If you become concerned that significant volumes of your traffic are not arriving at the proper destinations, consider checking how this field has been set. It could be that the hop count value is too low.

▶ **Protocol**—Identifies the next protocol that's to receive the packet at the destination. Protocol 6 is reserved for TCP; protocol 17 is reserved for UDP. For private networks, some companies use their own protocol numbers to pass IP packets to tailored Layer 4 processes.

▶ **Fragmentation**—Allows an IP packet larger than the permitted L_2 frame size to be reduced to fit into the frame and then reassembled at the receiving IP node.

▶ **Options**—Provides for other optional services but isn't used much in current networks. Here are two examples of IP options: (1) route recording: stores the IP address of each node that processes the packet; (2) source routing: contains IP addresses of the nodes that participate in an end-to-end route. These useful services have now been "taken over" by other protocols, such as TraceRoute and ATM.

TCP Features

Like IP, TCP offers a range of services to the user. Like IP, the services vary, depending on the software vendor's product. Also like IP, the services might be transparent to the user, as well as nonconfigurable. Here is a summary of TCP services:

▶ **Connection services**—TCP is a connection-oriented protocol that maintains status and state information about each socket pair. This ongoing connection awareness, and its associated connection setup and closing, provides a network administrator with a lot of information about user sessions.

▶ **Reliable data transfer**—Ensures all data arrives error free at the receiving TCP module. Using an error-check field in the header, the receiving TCP module will discard damaged packets. The sending TCP will not receive proper acknowledgments from the receiver and will resend lost or damaged data. If data arrives correctly, the sending module will receive an acknowledgment packet from the receiver. This end-to-end integrity operation is quite important to users.

▶ **Proper sequencing**—TCP ensures all user packets are assembled in the proper sequential order at the receiving host. This operation allows network components (say, IP at L_3, ATM at L_2, or SONET at L_1) to mix up a user's original payload (for example, sending packets through different routers in the Internet). TCP will not present a packet across the receiving socket until all packets have arrived in order.

- ▶ **Flow control**—TCP can flow-control the sending socket, which can be a useful tool to prevent buffer overrun and saturation of the receiving machine.

- ▶ **Graceful close**—Before the socket pair and the associated end-to-end connection are closed, TCP makes certain all packets associated with this connection have been received at the destination host.

UDP Features

Many applications do not require the connection-oriented and data integrity features of TCP. Indeed, not only do they not need them, but they can't tolerate them. Because of its behavior, TCP introduces delay (latency) in ongoing packet delivery between two parties. As an alternative, UDP is widely employed for the following scenarios:

- ▶ **Voice or video applications**—This traffic cannot tolerate the delay in waiting for the arrival of a retransmitted packet. Fortunately, a few missing packets in a voice conversation or a video show cannot be detected by the receiving audience. UDP is ideal for these applications.

- ▶ **The L_7 module performs TCP services**—If a Layer 7 application is programmed to perform retransmission, resequencing, flow control, and other TCP-like services, it makes no sense to duplicate them.

Summary

"TCP/IP." The term is so common we hear it spoken in movies. We see it written in mass-market books.

We watch examples of Internet socket management on TV. Jack Bauer and his *24* companions are constantly opening "sockets" to thwart the bad guys: "Let me open a socket, Jack. That's all I need to tap into 10 FBI databases, 20 GPS connections, 30 AT&T mobile phone calls, and 40 CIA terrorist-simulation models to solve this problem!"

In today's society, fiction is often stranger than facts. But for this hour, we've stuck with facts and learned about the basic tools for connecting into the Internet. In so doing, we also learned how the Internet architecture and protocols came into existence. We now know how our data "moves" from ISPs and IXPs to our remote email partner. We leaned a bit more about IP and a lot more about ports, sockets, TCP, and UDP.

In the next hour, we stay with the subject of "connecting to the Internet" and examine several other important protocols to achieve this connectivity and to provide yet more (and essential) services.

Q&A

Q. *Fill in likely implementations for an Internet LAN link:*

L_1: _____

L_2: _____

L_3: _____

L_4: _____

A. L_1: Ethernet

L_2: Ethernet

L_3: IP

L_4: TCP or UDP

Q. *Fill in likely implementations for an Internet UNI link:*

L_1: _____

L_2: _____

L_3: _____

L_4: _____

A. L_1: DSL, cable modem, T-carrier family, or satellite

L_2: ATM or MPLS

L_3: IP

L_4: TCP or UDP

Q. *What is peering?*

A. Peering is an agreement between ISPs to use each other's facilities to transport traffic back and forth between their respective customers through each other's networks.

Q. *What is the purpose of the Border Gateway Protocol (BGP)?*

A. BGP sets up routes and peering arrangements between networks.

Q. *What is an Internet port?*

A. It's a unique number assigned to an application process, which usually operates in L_7 of the OSI model.

Q. *What is the difference between a port and a socket?*

A. A port number is one part of a socket. A socket consists of a port number, an IP address, and a protocol ID.

Q. *Does the Internet provide for end-to-end data integrity? Why or why not?*

A. The Internet doe not provide end-to-end integrity. That task rests with TCP, which operates in the users' machines (host computers). If the Internet provided end-to-end data integrity, significant delay and overhead would result. Besides, some user applications do not need or want end-to-end data integrity services.

Q. *What are the differences between TCP and UDP?*

A. TCP is a rich protocol providing connection management, socket services (with the OS), flow control, resequencing, and end-to-end integrity. UDP is a bare-bones protocol that provides socket services (with the OS).

HOUR 15

Connecting to the Internet: Key Supporting Operations

What You'll Learn in This Hour:

- ▶ Operations of the DNS
- ▶ How to obtain and manage domain names
- ▶ Private and public name servers
- ▶ How to obtain and manage IP addresses
- ▶ How to use DHCP
- ▶ How to build a website

In this hour, we examine several key (read: required) supporting operations to those described in Hour 14, "Connecting to the Internet: Initial Operations." The first subject deals with the Internet Domain Name System (DNS). Next, the subject of Internet Protocol (IP) addressing (introduced in Hour 3, "Getting Data from Here to There: How Networking Works") is examined in the context of providing guidance on obtaining addresses and using them to perform subnetting. As part of this subject, the Dynamic Host Configuration Protocol (DHCP) is examined. This hour closes with a discussion of the World Wide Web (Web), with some ideas on cost-effective ways to create your own website.

The DNS

The purpose of the DNS is to provide name server operations, which entails mapping (correlating) a user-friendly name to a routable address. This service is quite helpful because a user is not tasked with remembering the abstract address of a host computer with whom he wishes to communicate. Rather, the sending user need only know an easy-to-remember text-oriented value (a name) of the recipient. The name is keyed in during a session or "clicked" in a web or email window; then it's relayed to a name server, which looks up and returns an associated address to the requester.

A Name Is Not an Address

Now is the time to clear up a common error associated with names and addresses. If you were to ask me, "What's your email address?" I would respond by giving you an email name, but not an email address. For example, one of the email names I use is Uyless@UylessBlack.com. This identifier is not an address. Consequently, the correct way to ask the question is, "What's your email name?" Or, to be picky, "What's your email domain name?"

On the other hand, my address, which in this situation is managed by GoDaddy.com (and changes with each logon) is an IP address (discussed in Hour 3). It's much easier to deal with domain names than it is with IP addresses. Thus, the job of a name server is to store names, the associated addresses, and provide this information to the user community.

DNS is an extraordinary service. It allows the assignment of domain names to groups of users in the Internet community without regard to physical locations or addresses. One of my companies, IEI-Press.com, is located in Hayden, Idaho. Later, it might move to Santa Fe, New Mexico. All web names and associated websites use DNS names, so changes aren't necessary for any of the names. Of course, I might change routing arrangements with IP addresses, but this aspect of the operations remains transparent to the general Internet user community. They don't need to know my IP address to get traffic to me. They only need my domain name.

The DNS stores other information as well, such as a list of mail or file servers that are set up to service a specific Internet domain. In addition, authoritative name servers are established for each domain. These servers are responsible for keeping accurate information about names, addresses, other servers, and so on for their respective domains. With this approach, there's no need for a central, Internet-wide server to keep track of these changes.

Domain Name Space

DNS is organized into a naming hierarchy; a general example is shown in Figure 15.1. The domain name space is the scheme used to identify domains that are at different levels in the DNS domain hierarchical tree. The domain name space also defines how the down-level names of *hosts* (meaning individual computers and other devices on a network) are determined. Each host on a network (such as the Internet) is identified with a fully qualified domain name (FQDN).

The domain namespace is divided into different levels, or domains. (Domain names can be up to 63 characters in length and must begin with a letter of the alphabet.

Numerical entries and hyphens are also legal characters for domain names.) The domain namespace resembles an inverted tree. At the base of the DNS tree is the root domain. The Internet root domain is represented by a period.

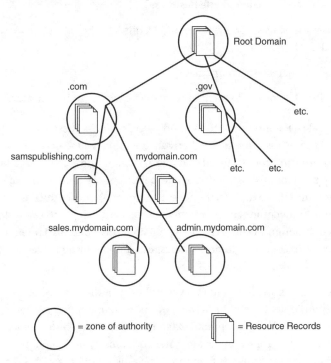

FIGURE 15.1
DNS hierarchy

The highest levels of DNS are the top-level domains (TLDs). These consist of suffixes such as .com and .edu. Two broad categories of TLDs exist. One category is the country code two-letter label, such as jp for Japan, and it's designated as ccTLD. The other category is collectively called generic TLD (or gTLD). Following are some of the top-level domain names available. (You can go to www.icann.org/ for a complete list.)

▶ **.com**—Used by commercial organizations. For example, informit.com is the domain name for InformIT. One of my sites is UylessBlack.com.

▶ **.edu**—Reserved for educational institutions. For example, une.edu is the domain name of the University of New England.

▶ **.org**—Used by noncommercial organizations and institutions. For example, gsusa.org is the domain name of the Girl Scouts of America.

▶ **.gov**—Reserved by the United States for governmental entities. For example, senate.gov is the domain for the U.S. Senate.

▶ **.net**—To be used by companies involved in the Internet infrastructure, such as Internet service providers (ISPs).

▶ **Country names**—To be used by countries. Examples include bs for the Bahamas, ga for Gabon, and uk for the United Kingdom.

▶ **.biz**—Added to accommodate businesses.

▶ **.info**—Can be used for informational websites (or just about anybody looking for a domain name).

▶ **.aero**—For aerospace companies.

▶ **.pro**—Used by professional groups, such as lawyers and accountants.

Below the top-level domains are the second-level domains. These secondary domains consist of company, institutional, and private domains used to access a site on the Web, such as informit.com (InformIT's domain name). Under the second-level domains are subdomains, which divide a larger secondary domain into geographical or functional units. For example, if I have a company that uses the secondary domain name of mydomain.com, and my business is divided into two distinct divisions (sales and admin), I could create two subdomains: sales.mydomain.com and admin.mydomain.com. The domain namespace and the second-level domains mentioned here are shown in Figure 15.1.

This example also shows how a high-level authority in the tree can assign to a lower level the responsibility for administering part of the name space. My zone of authority might start at mydomain.com and extend downward. My name server has responsibility for part of this zone. But, as the system administrator, I might want the sales and administrative departments to manage their own part of our DNS. These two departments receive a zone delegation from me; they then form delegated subzones.

Within each zone of authority, name servers are placed to manage the data. This data is organized into resource records (RRs), and contains specific information, such as domain name = IP address.

DNS Root Name Servers

Currently, 13 well-known root name servers reside in the Internet (see Table 15.1). The job of a root name server is to answer a DNS request and redirect the request to a specific TLD and its name server(s). The root name servers are configured to know the TLD servers, such as .com and .gov. In turn, each TLD has its own servers that know the next level down in the naming hierarchy.

Does this mean that each time we send an email, a query is sent to a root name server to obtain an associated IP address? Not at all. With rare exceptions, a local name server has already cached (stored) this information.

TABLE 15.1 DNS Root Name Servers

Letter	Old Name	Operator	Location
A	ns.internic.net	VeriSign	Dulles, Virginia, United States
B	ns1.isi.edu	USC-ISI	Marina Del Rey, California, United States
C	c.psi.net	Cogent Communications	Distributed using anycast
D	terp.umd.edu	University of Maryland	College Park, Maryland, United States
E	ns.nasa.gov	NASA	Mountain View, California, United States
F	ns.isc.org	ISC	Distributed using anycast
G	ns.nic.ddn.mil	Defense Information Systems Agency	Columbus, Ohio, United States
H	aos.arl.army.mil	U.S. Army Research Lab	Aberdeen Proving Ground, Maryland, United States
I	nic.nordu.net	Autonomica	Distributed
J		VeriSign	Distributed
K		RIPE NCC	Distributed
L		ICANN	Distributed
M		WIDE Project	Distributed

How DNS Works

Now that you have a feel for the DNS namespace, let's look at how DNS resolves IP addresses to FQDNs and vice versa. First, there are two types of DNS servers: master and slave. (Be aware that not all vendors use these terms.) The master server, or the first DNS server you bring up on your network, stores the local name server database: records for each host that provides the hosts FQDN and the accompanying IP address. So as far as creating records and fine-tuning the database are concerned, this is done on the master DNS server. Because a master is responsible for a certain part of the DNS database, it's referred to as the authoritative name server of its zone of authority.

A slave DNS stores a copy of the master DNS database. This operation not only provides two options for computers attempting to resolve FQDNs, but it adds some redundancy to the network. DNS service will continue even if the master DNS server goes down.

So, the DNS server will attempt to resolve FQDNs when requested by a network client (meaning a client in the DNS server's zone of authority). The client computers are capable of making requests of the DNS server because of an entity called the resolver. The resolver is built into applications such as web browsers that execute FQDN to IP address resolution services.

When a client computer attempts to resolve an FQDN to an IP address, the resolver checks a local cache and determines if the FQDN-to-IP address resolution information is available. If the information is in the cache, the process is over and client computer resolves the FQDN to an IP address.

If the information isn't available in the cache, the resolver software uses the IP address of the local DNS server, which is found in the client computer's IP settings, and sends a request to this server.

When the name to be resolved is for a host that is on the local network, the DNS server looks up the name in the DNS database and returns the appropriate IP address to the requesting computer. If the name is for a computer not on the local domain, two things can happen: The name can be resolved using the cache that the local DNS server maintains, or the server caches or remembers hostnames that it has previously resolved with the help of other DNS servers (such as those on the Internet). If the information is in this cache, the DNS server provides it to the requesting client.

When the information isn't cached on the DNS server, the DNS server contacts the server for the hostname's top-level domain. The root server uses the hostname to determine the IP address of the authoritative DNS server for the domain that the particular host belongs. After this DNS server has the IP address of the other domain's DNS server, it can query that server, which then supplies the FQDN-to-IP address resolution information. The local DNS server can then pass this information on to the original requesting host.

As mentioned, the client side of the operation is called a DNS resolver. It's responsible for starting the query that leads to a translation of a domain name into an IP address. The name-to-address mapping might entail the checking of several name servers to find the needed information. However, because resolvers store most recently used information, the hit is usually local.

Getting a Domain Name

Before you can configure a DNS server, you need a domain name. Also, if your company is going to have a presence on the Internet (particularly the World Wide Web), you need a domain name.

You can apply for domain names that end in .com, .org, or .net by contacting a domain name registration provider. (Sites ending in two-letter country codes are handled by other providers.) Whether you choose to be a .com, .org, or .net depends on the type of business you're conducting. Nonprofits use .org, whereas .com is best for most businesses. If the domain name you want to use isn't available in the .com realm, you can take advantage of the new suffix .biz for your business domain name.

Several registration providers are available on the Web. Some vendors not only provide DNS registration and maintenance services, but also email, file storage, and website support. One of my providers is GoDaddy.com, which provides good service.

When you apply for your domain name, you also need to know how your domain will handle DNS services. Your options include deploying your own DNS servers; using the DNS servers provided by the ISP that's connecting you to the Internet; using the servers at your web host provider; or simply using the servers provided by the company that sold you your domain name.

The cost of a domain name is quite nominal when you consider it can help increase the visibility of your company if used to establish your presence with a website. The fees for registering and maintaining your domain name vary among domain name registration providers. You should do a little research before you select a provider.

Also be advised that Internet Corporation for Assigned Names and Numbers (ICANN) limits the leasing of a particular domain name to 10 years. To find a list of ICANN-approved domain name providers, check out the ICANN site at www.internic.net.

Resource Records (RRs)

At the heart of a DNS name server are the resource records (RRs). The DNS standards define a variety of RRs. You and your team should check a vendor's offerings to determine if the server software supports the RRs you need. Table 15.2 summarizes common RRs and their functions.

TABLE 15.2 Commonly Used RRs

Type	Functions
A	Domain name and associated IPv4 address.
AAA	Domain name and associated IPv6 address.
SOA	Start of zone authority. Contains the high-level domain name of this zone and parameters controlling frequency of updates, Time to Live (TTL) values, and so on.

TABLE 15.2   Continued

Type	Functions
CNAME	Allows a host domain name to be given an alias name, usually to provide an easier-to-read name.
MX	The mail server for the domain.
NS	Authoritative name server(s) for the domain.
PTR	Allows a reverse lookup. Given an IP address, what is its associated domain name?

Deploying DNS on the Network

All Network Operating Systems (NOSs) offer DNS support. You can add the DNS service to an existing network server (if it can handle the additional workload), or you can deploy a new server and add the DNS service as you initially load the NOS.

For a DNS server to operate correctly, you must configure it with at least one zone. The zone you create is called a forward lookup zone. A forward lookup zone allows for forward lookup queries, which allow a host to find the IP address using the hostname of a particular computer or device. (It finds the address because the DNS answers the host computer's query.)

When you create the forward lookup zone, you must name it. The name of the zone will be the same as the DNS domain name for the portion of your network that this DNS server is authoritative. For example, if your DNS domain name for your portion of the network was marketing.mydomain.com, the zone name would be marketing.mydomain.com. If you have a network that operates at a higher level in the domain name space (no subdomain as in the marketing.mydomain.com example, where marketing is a subdomain), the forward lookup zone would be your domain name, such as mydomain.com.

When you deploy your DNS servers, you can set up a server that provides the DNS server and maintains the master copy of the DNS database. The forward lookup zone on that server is called the primary zone.

You can also deploy DNS servers that use a read-only replica of the primary zone database and are set up on the network to help the authoritative server for the zone. The replica zone used by these "helper" DNS servers is called the secondary zone.

You can also configure the authoritative DNS server with what's called a reverse lookup. This type of zone resolves IP addresses to FQDNs (meaning that it does the reverse of a forward lookup zone). Reverse lookup zones are configured by entering the network ID of the network (which would be the network IP address provided by your ISP or another company that you acquired your IP address from). The resource record of PTR in Table 15.2 provides the information for reverse lookup.

IP Addresses

As discussed in Hour 3, IPv4 addresses consist of 32 bits of information and are written in dotted decimal notation consisting of four octets in the format x.x.x.x. We learned that the usable pool of these addresses has been divided into classes. For this hour, we expand on these topics.

How Computers See IP Addresses

Computers see IP addresses as a bit stream, meaning a stream of 1s and 0s. For example, the IP address 130.1.32.1 would be represented in binary notation as

10000010 00000001 00100000 00000001

Notice the bits have been divided into four groups of eight, or octets, just as the dotted decimal version of the address.

This is how you convert dotted decimal numbers to binary (bits). Each octet has 8 bits. The decimal value of the bits in an octet from left to right is

128 64 32 16 8 4 2 1

(As you see, the convention uses the base 2 numbering system.)

So, the decimal number 130 (the first octet in our address) is 128 + 2. This means that both the first bit (the 128 bit) and the seventh bit (the 2 bit) are turned on. (They're represented by 1s in the binary format.) To convert the decimal to the binary, you mark the bits that are on with 1s and the rest with 0s. The result is 10000010.

Subnetting

If you and your design team are associated with a medium to large enterprise, it's likely you'll need to become familiar with subnetting. This term refers to the partitioning of a network into smaller parts. One reason for subnetting is to divide the traffic such that Ethernet packet collisions don't create throughput and bottleneck problems. Routers are employed to manage the traffic and act as boundaries between the subnets, an idea shown in Figure 15.2. In this regard, subnetting limits an Ethernet collision domain to only part of a network.

FIGURE 15.2
Creating subnets
with addresses

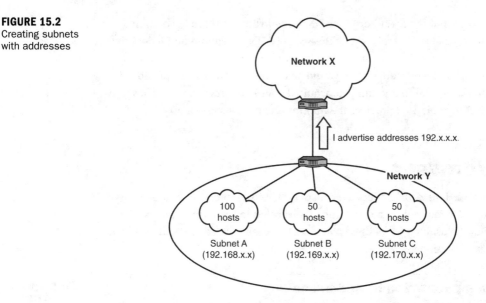

Subnetting also provides a means to use fewer IP addresses. A subnet, such as Subnet A in Figure 15.2, might have all its attached computers, servers, and so on (for example, 100 host machines) use a common set of high-order bits in the 32-bit IP address. This address prefix is sufficient to get all packets routed to these 100 machines. After all, they share the same prefix.

Thus, the router for Network Y could advertise to Network X, "You can reach—through me—any node whose IP address begins with 192.168. These first 16 bits are my network prefix length. You need not check the last 16 bits of the destination IP address in the packet header, because they're private to me; they're my host bits and are only meaningful to the subnets on which my hosts reside. You just forward all packets beginning with 192.168 to me. I'll take care of those remaining 16 bits in my own routing tables."

Thus, Network X doesn't have to store 100 routing table entries for all those nodes sitting behind the router at Subnet A. It needs to store only one entry.

Subnetting is even more attractive than this simple example. Let's assume that the 50 hosts in Subnet B share a common prefix, that of 192.169. Also, the 50 hosts in Subnet C share 192.170. Therefore, the router could advertise to Network X that all nodes with a prefix of 192 can be reached at this router, which is the actual example shown in Figure 15.2. In this admittedly simple illustration, by using the high-order digits in an address space, you can aggregate more and more addresses to one prefix. In this example, all 200 nodes have a prefix of 192. When the router at Network X receives a packet destined for 192, it doesn't care about the remaining 24 bits in the address. That's the concern of the router for Network Y.

Subnet Masks

How does the router at Network X know how long the prefix is, and therefore, how many bits it's to examine in the destination address of an incoming packet? The answer is through the use of a subnet mask.

IP addresses don't mean anything without an accompanying subnet mask. Devices on a network need to be capable of telling what part of the IP address is providing information related to which network the computer with a particular address is on. (Don't forget the example and explanation for Figure 15.2.) The subnet mask determines this information. Devices on the network use the subnet mask to "mask" out the portion of the IP address that refers to the network (actually, the subnet) that the computer (or other device such as a router) is connected to.

Each class has a default subnet mask (with 1s defining the mask):

▶ **Class A**—255.0.0.0 or 11111111.00000000.00000000.00000000

▶ **Class B**—255.255.0.0 or 11111111.11111111.00000000.00000000

▶ **Class C**—255.255.255.0 or 11111111.11111111.11111111.00000000

If classful addresses are used, such as here, the mask can also identify both the network ID and the subnet ID. The network ID, such as 192 in Figure 15.2, represents the high-order (leading) bits that are common to all subnets associated with the network, such as your company's entire routing domain and address space allocation.

Here's an example of subnet mask operations, again using Figure 15.2 as a reference point with a slight alteration. The comparison of the mask to the IP address is performed with a bitwise AND process as follows:

	Decimal Notation	Binary Notation
IP address	192.168.1.194	11000000.10101000.0000001.11000010
Subnet mask	255.255.255.0	11111111.11111111.1111111.00000000
Results in:		
Network	192.168.1.0	11000000.10101000.0000001.00000000
With inference:		
Host	0.0.0.194	00000000.00000000.0000000.11000010

This mask is aligned on an even octet boundary. It needn't be, and it shouldn't be if we're attempting to exploit the flexibility of masking. Here, we alter the mask slightly:

Adding three bits to the mask extends the network/subnet space into the fourth octet of the IP address. Thus, the three high-order bits (base 10) values of 128, 64, and 32 equal 224. The host address has been constricted to the last five bits of the address space: in this case, a decimal value of 2.

	Decimal Notation	Binary Notation
IP address	192.168.1.194	11000000.10101000.0000001.11000010
Subnet mask	255.255.255.224	11111111.11111111.1111111.11100000
Results in:		
Network	192.168.1.192	11000000.10101000.0000001.11000000
With inference:		
Host	0.0.0.2	00000000.00000000.0000000.00000010

I hope this level of detail about IP addresses and prefixes has done you more good than harm! At first glance, it's not a simple subject, and it does require practice and experience to use subnetting effectively. The good news is that vendors' equipment today contains a lot of software to help you with the task of setting up and managing IP addresses. Cisco and Microsoft, as examples, have done a fine job in providing the software and user manuals for the task at hand.

To that end, the next part of this hour discusses some more ideas about network addressing in the context of configuring them in your network.

Getting Your IP Addresses

The Internet Assigned Numbers Authority (IANA), which ICANN operates, is responsible for managing the allocation of IP addresses. IANA designates five regional Internet registries (RIRs) to oversee the management of IP addresses (address blocks) in specific regions of the world. If you want to obtain one or more IP addresses for public use, the typical approach is to work with your ISP or (in the United States) to contact the RIR known as the American Registry for Internet Numbers (ARIN). With either approach, you'll then have other options, as described in the next section.

Many organizations choose to use private addresses, which the information technology (IT) staff typically manages. From Hour 3, we learned about the three classes of addresses:

- ▶ **Class A**—10.0.0.0 through 10.255.255.255
- ▶ **Class B**—172.16.0.0 through 172.31.255.255
- ▶ **Class C**—192.168.0.0 through 192.168.255.255

Configuring Network Devices with IP Addresses

One of the more important tasks for a network administrator is setting up an IP addressing plan. Part of this plan is to determine how many public IP addresses you need. As a general rule, you should "hide" your network and its machines from the public Internet. This means that your LAN will sit behind a firewall and a router (maybe in the same box). These devices (or device) require public addresses. The router performs address translation using NAT. If the firewall sits in front of the router, it also needs a public address. I strongly recommended you consult with your router or firewall vendor for guidance on your addressing plan.

One option for supplying hosts on the network with IP addresses is to configure each host with a static IP address and subnet mask. An alternative to static IP addressing is dynamically assigning IP addresses (and other Transmission Control Protocol/ Internet Protocol [TCP/IP] configuration information) using the DHCP, which requires a network server to provide the service. DHCP clients on the network receive their IP addresses and subnet masks dynamically. We examine DHCP in more detail later in this hour.

Static IP Settings on Servers

Network servers that provide services such as DNS and DHCP (and other special servers such as web servers, mail servers, and in some cases print or file servers) are usually assigned a static IP address. It's recommended you assign permanent IP addresses to machines providing critical services for the network, such as servers. For some nodes, such as DNS and DHCP servers, you must use static addresses.

Each NOS (and client OS platform for that matter) provides its own mechanism for configuring a computer with a static IP address and subnet mask. In most cases, the IP address and subnet mask can be configured during the installation of NOS on the server or can be configured after the installation has been completed.

Let's look at configuring a server running Windows Server 2003. The TCP/IP settings are configured in the Internet Protocol (TCP/IP) Properties dialog box (which you access via the Local Area Connection Properties dialog box for the server). Figure 15.3 shows the Internet Protocol (TCP/IP) Properties dialog box.

The IP address and subnet mask aren't the only information you must provide when configuring a computer, such as a server for IP. You must also supply the default gateway for the server, which is the router interface connected to the segment where the server resides.

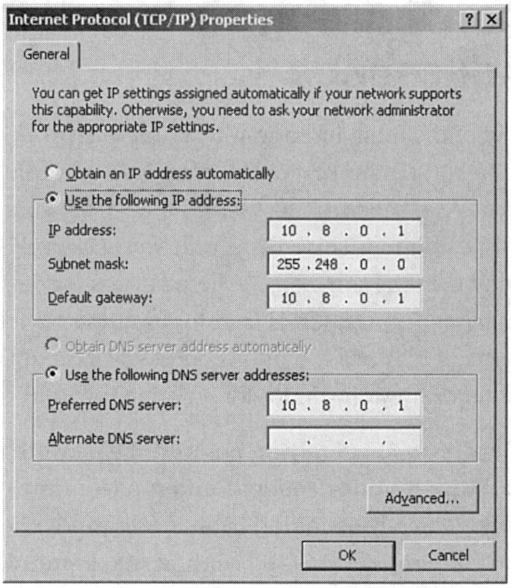

FIGURE 15.3
Entering an IP
address and sub-
net mask on a
Windows server

Internet Protocol (TCP/IP) Properties   ? X

General

You can get IP settings assigned automatically if your network supports
this capability. Otherwise, you need to ask your network administrator
for the appropriate IP settings.

○ Obtain an IP address automatically
● Use the following IP address:
IP address: 10 . 8 . 0 . 1
Subnet mask: 255 . 248 . 0 . 0
Default gateway: 10 . 8 . 0 . 1

○ Obtain DNS server address automatically
● Use the following DNS server addresses:
Preferred DNS server: 10 . 8 . 0 . 1
Alternate DNS server: .   .   .

                                          Advanced...

                              OK   Cancel

Another piece of information you must include in the configuration is the IP address
of the primary DNS server used for name resolution by the server. Large networks
might deploy multiple DNS servers, so there's also the option of providing alternative
DNS server IP addresses. In the case of Windows networks, you might also be deploying WINS servers, so the IP address of the WINS server would need to be included as
well in the TCP/IP configuration of the server.

By the Way

What Is WINS?

On a Windows network that's running pre-Windows 2000 clients, you might need
to deploy a Windows Internet Naming Service (WINS) server. Legacy Windows
desktop operating systems still use NetBIOS names as the "friendly" naming system for the computers (as opposed to DNS on newer versions of the Windows
OS). This means that clients on the network can eat up a lot of bandwidth sending out broadcasts that resolve NetBIOS names to IP addresses. A WINS server
takes care of the NetBIOS name-to-IP address resolution and vice versa, which
cuts down on client broadcasts and frees up valuable network bandwidth. As discussed in previous hours, NetBIOS is rarely used today. It's mentioned here for
those who are using old systems.

For more about networking in the Windows environment, see *Sams Teach Yourself
Microsoft Windows Server 2003 in 24 Hours* and *Sams Teach Yourself Microsoft
Windows Server 2008 in 24 Hours*.

You can see that the TCP/IP configuration for a server requires more information
than just the IP address and subnet mask. Configuring a server with an incomplete
TCP/IP configuration is asking for communication problems between the server and
the rest of your network.

DHCP

DHCP evolved from a protocol called BOOTP. BOOTP was used to assign IP addresses to diskless workstations. It did not assign IP addresses dynamically, however, but pulled them from a static BOOTP file that the network administrator created and maintained.

DHCP allows you to dynamically assign IP addresses to your network computers and other devices. IP addresses are taken from a pool of addresses and assigned to computers either permanently or for a fixed time. Considering that you must configure every client computer on an IP network with such things as an IP address, a subnet mask, a default gateway address, and a DNS server address, there's a significant margin for error.

DHCP simplifies much of the drudgery that would be involved in manual assignments of IP addresses. Most Network Operating Systems (NOSs)—including Sun Solaris, the various Linux distributions, Novell NetWare, and Microsoft Windows Server 2003 and 2008—provide the DHCP service.

So, how does DCHP work? Let's look at how a DCHP client (which is what you call a computer that is configured to receive its IP address dynamically) requests an IP address from a DHCP server.

When a DHCP client boots up for the first time, it must look for an IP address to use for its sessions. The client broadcasts a DHCPDISCOVER message, which is a request for an IP lease that is sent to all DHCP servers (addressed to 255.255.255.255, meaning all nodes on the network). This broadcast message contains the hostname of the client and the MAC hardware address (the address burned into the computer's NIC) of the client.

In the next step, a DCHP server (or servers, if more than one is available) on the subnet responds with a DHCPOFFER message that includes an offered IP address, an accompanying subnet mask, and the length of the lease (that is, the length of time the address can be used). The message also contains the IP address of the DHCP server, identifying the server. The DHCPOFFER message is also in the form of a broadcast because the client doesn't have an IP address at this point.

When the client receives the first DHCPOFFER message (it might receive multiple offers, but it goes with the first appropriate offer it receives), it broadcast a DHCPREQUEST message to all DHCP servers on the network, showing that it's accepting an offer. This broadcast message contains the IP address of the DHCP server whose offer the client accepted. Knowing which DHCP server was selected enables the other DHCP servers on the network to retract their offers and save their IP addresses for the next requesting client.

Finally, the DHCP server that supplied the accepted offer broadcasts an acknowledgment message to the client, a DHCPPACK message. This message contains a valid IP address and other TCP/IP configuration information, which the client stores. For example, a client running a Windows operating system stores the TCP/IP configuration information in its Windows registry.

The DHCP server can also send to the client (a) addresses of DNS servers (preferred and alternate), (b) the IP address of the default gateway to the Internet, and (c) preferred and alternate WINS servers.

Configuring a Network Client for DHCP

Configuring a network client or server as a DHCP server is straightforward. A client (or server for that matter) provides a dialog box that allows you to configure settings related to the computer's network connection.

For example, Figure 15.4 illustrates that the server being configured in the figure can be made a DHCP client by clicking on the Obtain an IP Address Automatically option button. That's all there is to it. The computer then becomes a DHCP client.

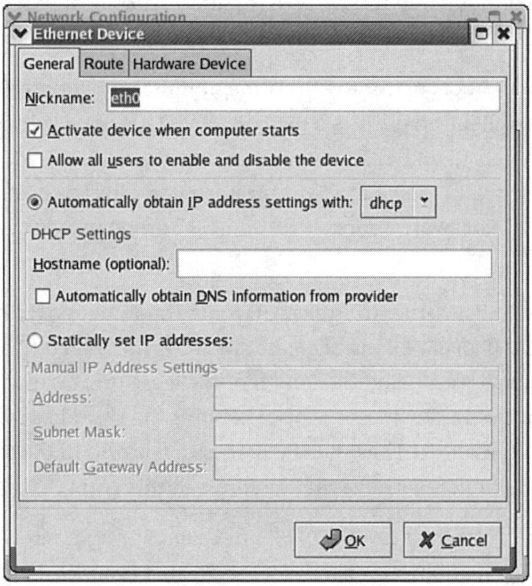

FIGURE 15.4
Operating systems provide various GUIs that make it easy to configure the TCP/IP properties for the computer.

Other client and NOS platforms also typically provide a GUI that allows you to configure the computer as a DHCP client. Figure 15.4 shows the Ethernet Device dialog box on a computer running Linux Red Hat. Note that this dialog box gives you the option of configuring the computer as a DHCP client or as a static IP address.

A real time-saver related to deploying DHCP on your network is that most network clients are configured as DHCP clients by default. So you usually don't have to configure TCP/IP on the clients. This allows you to spend your time setting up the pool of addresses and the other configuration settings that the DHCP server requires.

Deploying DHCP on the Network

The most practical (and time-effective) way to assign IP addresses, subnet masks, and other TCP/IP configuration information to network clients is via the DHCP. This means you have to configure a DHCP server on your network. Networks of any size—particularly those that are divided into subnets—might require multiple DHCP servers.

DHCP Relay Agent

On routed networks, you can configure a server as a DHCP Relay Agent, which relays DHCP broadcasts to DHCP clients on other subnets. This allows you to forgo placing a DHCP server on every subnet. You might also have to configure the routers to pass the DHCP requests from the relay agents.

Did you Know?

Most network platforms, including Windows Server 2003 and 2008, UNIX/Linux, and Novell NetWare, provide the DHCP service as part of their NOS. So you can configure DHCP in any NOS environment.

DHCP servers provide the IP address range (and the subnet mask to be used) to their clients based on the scope that the administrator configures on the DHCP server. The scope is the range of addresses to be assigned to the DHCP clients on the network. Figure 15.5 shows the New Scope Wizard on a server running Windows Server 2003. Notice that this screen allows you to enter the start and end IP address of the scope and the subnet mask to be used.

You can also configure exclusions from the scope, which allows you to configure a scope that contains your entire IP address pool. You can then exclude the addresses that you've assigned statically to the DHCP server and other servers or devices on the network, such as routers. Not only can you configure exclusions, but you can configure reservations—a reservation meaning that a particular device on the network, such as a print server, will always be assigned the same IP address. This is particularly helpful when users are employing the IP address of printer. (The IP address is dynamically assigned but it doesn't change.)

When a server gives an IP address, subnet mask, and other TCP/IP configuration information to a DHCP client, it's referred to as a lease. When you configure the DHCP server's scope, you must also determine how long the IP addresses will be leased to the clients.

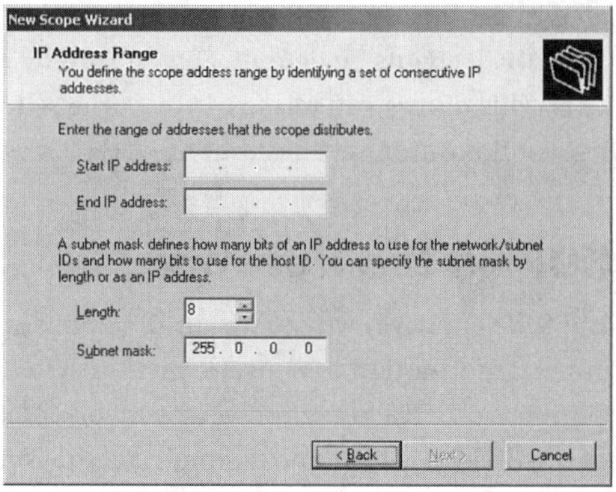

FIGURE 15.5
You must config-
ure a scope on
the DHCP server.

Lease time is up to you. Long leases can be a security liability because the IP addresses are static and might be discerned by a hacker monitoring network traffic. On the other hand, short leases cause a great deal of network traffic because of the broadcast messages and eat up network bandwidth. You'll have to balance the use of your bandwidth with security considerations when setting the lease time.

Another consideration is related to the number of DHCP servers you deploy on the network. As mentioned, routed networks require DHCP servers on each subnet or the use of DCHP relay agents. Larger networks might also require that you use multiple DHCP servers to break up the total pool of addresses available. This also builds some redundancy into your network in case a DHCP server goes down. The other DHCP server on the network can pick up the slack and ensure that all the network DHCP clients have IP addresses.

The Web

The Web is considered by some people to be one of the most significant inventions of the past few centuries. I would not rank it ahead of the light bulb or the transistor, but it clearly has changed the way we do business, as well as how we play.

The term "Web" in the title has led to some confusion. Newcomers to the Web some-times think it's a network unto itself. It's not. It runs over the Internet, and most of its activities take place in L_7 of the Internet/OSI model.

The architecture of the Web is based on a system that allows a user to access hyper-text documents via the conventional TCP/IP protocol stack. Hypertext is text, but unlike conventional text, hypertext interlinks documents, images, videos, and so on.

The term is meant to convey "more than just text." This is evident when you place your mouse over a hyperlink. It might produce a bubble, a blowup with text; it might invoke the running of a video clip; or it might do nothing until you click on it.

We navigate through and around all this information using hyperlinks. A hyperlink, embedded in a document, is a reference to another part of the document—perhaps a different document, perhaps in a different computer, or even in a different network. The term "link" doesn't refer to the L_2 links we've examined in this book, such as a DSL link or an Ethernet link. Rather, it refers to a logical navigational link. For example, when you click on a hyperlink, a web browser (software in L_7) "navigates" you to a different part of a document, a different part of a website, a different computer, or perhaps a different domain.

Yes, domain. The DNS is key to the proper functioning of the Web. And the Web uses a uniform resource locator (URL) to correlate a hyperlink to a domain name. For example, let's assume that a hyperlink of uylessblack exists in a document on your computer screen. If you were to click on this name, it would use a uniform resource identifier (URI) to find where this resource is available and the L_7 protocol needed to retrieve it. Strictly speaking, uylessblack isn't a complete URL. It's a shorthand notation for say, UylessBlack.com. The reason for this notation is to simplify the text on the screen.

Let's take another example. Maybe you key in "Uyless Black" in your search window. This isn't a URL, but your browser (depending on the vendor) will examine the search window's contents and translate it to a full URL. Currently, I am logged onto AOL. I just keyed in "Uyless Black." The AOL software created this URL:

http://search.aol.com/aol/search?query=uyless+Black&s_it=spelling

The URL also includes a number of pages with links to websites about my work.

What does all this jargon have to do with making your computer network more effective? In the final analysis, it's the DNS and TCP/IP that make the Web so effective. In fairness, we should also mention two other Internet specifications: HTML and HTTP.

HTML

The Hypertext Markup Language (HTML) is the code used to define the content and look of web documents. HTML code is stored in a text file that contains markup tags. These tags direct a web browser about how to display a page. This file can be created by using a conventional notepad or a word processing package. Here is an example of HTML code:

```
<html>
<head>
<title>Company XYZ Welcomes You!</title>
</head>
<body>
This website will allow you to get rich quickly.
</body>
</html>
```

The first tag in the HTML document is <html>. This tag informs the browser about the start of an HTML document. The last tag in the document is </html>, which informs the browser of the end of the HTML document. The text between the <head> tag and the </head> tag is header information, which isn't displayed by the browser. The text between the <title> tags is the title of the document, which *is* displayed by the browser. The text between the <body> tags is the text that will be displayed onscreen.

A lot of HTML tags must be written to translate into an attractive and effective website. I am, by heart and soul, a software programmer. But I know that writing code isn't an effective or monetarily productive way for me to spend my waking hours. I no longer write code, and I don't write HTML for my websites.

You can create a website even if you don't know HTML. The tools for this task are called what you see is what you get (WYSIWYG) editors. You can use, say, Microsoft's FrontPage or Macromedia's Dreamweaver instead of writing a lot of HTML code.

HTTP

The Hypertext Transfer Protocol (HTTP) is used to retrieve hypertext documents that have been linked. HTTP relies on URLs to identify which resources it accesses and transports. It operates on a client/server model, with the client as the user (using a web browser) and the server as the website. The server stores HTML files.

HTTP operates in L_7 of the OSI model and uses TCP (not User Datagram Protocol [UDP]). The HTTP client initiates a request for, say, an HTML file. This request is usually a "Get" message, which asks the server to return a copy of the identified resource. In turn, the HTTP server is listening on port 80 for the request. Upon receiving the request, it responds with status information and the file. If a problem occurs, it returns an error message.

These operations appear simple and straightforward. But client/server architectures must account for users doing the following: (a) canceling a request; (b) clicking on a different request; (c) double- (triple-, quadruple-) clicking a hyperlink to initiate multiple requests. The HTTP standards describe why and how some of the HTTP commands (verbs) should be idempotent: multiple identical requests should have the same effect as only one request. The Internet Requests for Comment (RFCs) define the rules for achieving idempotent services.

Ideas for Establishing a Website

If you are well versed in and enjoy software programming, you might consider putting up your own site. By writing all the HTML tags, you'll surely become an expert on the intricacies of web architecture. That stated, I recommend you avail yourself of the many packages and offerings from vendors. Let other companies do the coding for you.

This part of Hour 15 walks you through the tasks involved in setting up a website through shared hosting: contracting with a vendor to host your website. These explanations use Windows as examples. Linux and other systems have similar procedures.

To begin, we assume that you and your team have chosen a company to provide this service. Your first task is administrative: setting up an account. Typically, an end user license agreement is signed, followed by creating a username and password.

Next, if you've not already done so, your vendor asks for a domain name to be associated with your website. You must choose at least one name—ideally, one that reflects your company or your product. Also, it's a small matter to associate more than one domain name with the same website, as long as the domain names have been registered with the Internet authorities. Usually, your web host vendor can help you with obtaining your domain names.

As part of the process, your domain name(s) are assigned to a name server. "Buying" domain names through various vendors is a highly competitive business, and the company through which you buy your domain name will most likely be the company that provides you with name servers. But that need not be the case. At any time, you can change the vendor who manages your domain name and charges you for the service.

Did you Know?

Find Out About Your Name Servers

You can check on your name servers by navigating to www.internic.net/whois.html and executing a Whois query on your domain name. My query on BlacksStreets.com revealed the following:

```
Domain Name: BLACKSSTREETS.COM
   Registrar: GODADDY.COM, INC.
   Whois Server: whois.godaddy.com
```

```
Referral URL: http://registrar.godaddy.com
Name Server: NS41.DOMAINCONTROL.COM
Name Server: NS42.DOMAINCONTROL.COM

Server Name: NS41.DOMAINCONTROL.COM
   IP Address: 216.69.185.21
   Registrar: WILD WEST DOMAINS, INC.
   Whois Server: whois.wildwestdomains.com
   Referral URL: http://www.wildwestdomains.com
```

As part of the setup process, you'll likely be asked if you have an SSL certificate that you want to apply to your site. This certificate (described in Hour 20, "Security," in more detail) authenticates your website to visiting browsers. It's a tool for building trust with your web users.

The hosting company maintains information on your account, which includes a variety of items, including IP addresses, domain names, security profiles, and of course, data on what services your web pages provide your users and how they appear on computer screens. These aspects of web hosting are known by names such as the hosting control center, or simply, "The Store." Whatever they're called, and depending on how well they're designed, they can give you extensive, yet user-friendly control mechanisms for your website.

Rolling Your Own, Rolling with Templates, or Rolling with Your Vendor

A web host account comes in many colors. At one end of the spectrum is (a) your writing of HTML code and your uploading it to your web server. In the middle is (b) your using of vendor-provided templates or macros that translate to HTML code. At the other end of the spectrum is (c) your explaining to the vendor what you want with the vendor creating the HTML code from scratch.

I don't recommend that you use a web provider and opt for (a). If you choose to roll your own, don't bring in a third party to add to your expense. Besides, if the web provider has an ounce of sense, your code won't be trusted in the first place!

But you can certainly write the HTML code and (depending on the web vendor) upload to the web server. If you so choose, open Windows Notepad and key in the HTML code. Then save your file as index.html. If you're not using Windows

Notepad, most software packages allow you to key in text and save it in an appropriate format to be acceptable to HTML. For example, Microsoft Word allows you to key in the code and then save it as an HTML file.

Whatever or whomever creates the HTML files must move them to your hosting account. If your vendor has done the coding, the files will be placed in the proper locations transparently to you. If you have the code, you'll likely use FTP to move the files to your vendor's servers. The vendor will provide you with this information.

After all this work, you should be in business. For testing, you can key in your web domain name, and your web home page should appear on your screen. If it doesn't appear, or the images aren't displayed correctly, take these actions. If you opted for (c), your hosting provider is at fault. Call and complain. If you opted for (a) or (b), chances are good that your HTML tags are faulty or the domain path isn't correct. In either situation, you still need to work with your hosting vendor.

All the web hosting vendors with whom I've had experience furnish extensive statistics about visits to a website. If the site is selling online, the statistics include what and how much was sold. In addition, it's relatively easy to set up hyperlinks to credit card companies or middlemen, such as PayPal. As well, most of these companies offer your "hosting account" email services. Some of them provide you tools to alter your web pages with simple screen entries. If you're selling online, some allow you to dynamically change the products and prices from your computer.

Summary

This hour was devoted to Internet domain names, URLs, IP addresses, and the Web. To conclude this hour, we have good news and bad news. First, the good news: The vendor choices for hosting your website are many, with each offering an array of services. Second, the bad news: The vendor choices for hosting your website are many, with each offering a wide array of services.

Whom do you choose? In spite of the marketing and sales pitches of the web hosting vendor, the effectiveness of your website will rest on the ingenuity and creativity of the HTML programmer(s). How can you access this acumen before code is put to paper? You can't. But you can gain a sense of the competency of the company by how it has interacted with you during your initial contacts. If alarm bells ring during this time, make sure you've not yet signed a contract.

Q&A

Q. *What is an email address?*

A. Strictly speaking, no such thing exists. It's correctly called an email name (perhaps a screen name), which DNS then translates into an IP address. However, don't look down on your friends if they use the term "email address." It's a commonly accepted term.

Q. *Why might a computer configured with a static IP address not be communicating on the network?*

A. A simple typo, such as an incorrect subnet mask or default DNS server IP address, can prevent a computer from communicating on a network. Always check your TCP/IP configuration for your device. When you've inadvertently used the same IP address on more than one device, neither device will be able to communicate on the network.

Q. *How does the deployment of DHCP reduce TCP/IP configuration errors?*

A. Because the DHCP server dynamically assigns IP addresses, subnet masks, and other TCP/IP-related information such as default gateways to nodes on the network, the possibility of errors related to statically entering this data on each computer is diminished.

Q. *How should I determine the domain name that I want to register for my company?*

A. Make the domain name descriptive of your organization. It can be the company name or a term that describes what the company does. The domain name should be easy to remember (long or complex domain names aren't effective marketing strategies) and should be as unique as possible. Spend some time on the Web using a site that allows you to search for whether your domain name is available. You might also want to check out what types of companies have names similar to the one you want to use.

HOUR 16

Microsoft Networking

What You'll Learn in This Hour:

▶ The Microsoft logical network structure

▶ Installing and configuring a Microsoft server

▶ Configuring clients and network protocols

▶ How resources are shared on a Microsoft network

▶ Managing a Microsoft server

▶ The future of Windows Server 2003

▶ Introduction to Windows Server 2008

Although not one of the first big players in the Network Operating System (NOS) market, Microsoft has been in the networking business since the early 1980s. Early networking efforts, such as the development of NetBEUI and OS/2, were collaborative efforts with IBM. LAN Manager was an early effort at Microsoft to develop an NOS.

In 1992, Microsoft launched Microsoft Windows NT (New Technology) Server. The most widely used version in this line is Microsoft Windows Server 2003, which we examine in this hour. We will also look at how Microsoft's directory service provides the logical networking structure and how a server running Microsoft Windows Server 2003 shares resources and is managed.

In this hour, we examine the major steps in setting up a server using Windows Server 2003. We learn how to install and configure the server, how to set up the procedures to allow users to share resources, and how to protect users from each other's potential intrusions. We complete the hour with an introduction to Windows Server 2008. Our emphasis is on Windows Server 2003 because it is still the prevalent Microsoft server produced in the marketplace.

Microsoft's Logical Network Structure

When Microsoft Windows NT Server 4.0 became available in the marketplace, Microsoft had a hit on its hands. The Microsoft NOS made huge inroads into the worldwide server market.

Despite the fact that Windows NT Server 4.0 gained a large market share, it supplied a "flat" directory services model for managing users and resources. The basic administrative unit for the Microsoft network was the *domain* (and still is, but in a slightly different context, so read on). A domain can be defined as a collection of servers (although a domain only needs one server), client machines, users, and other network resources that a domain controller manages. The domain controller is a server running the Windows NOS, and it's responsible for user authentication and maintaining the database of user accounts and resources.

> ### Large Domains Required Backup Domain Controllers
> When a Windows NT domain grew a great deal or an administrator wanted to add some redundancy to the domain user database, backup domain controllers (BDCs) could be deployed on the network. These servers, also running the NT 4.0 NOS, could authenticate users and replicate the user database with the main domain controller.

In the case of Windows NT, the domain model did not provide a branching hierarchy such as was provided by Novell's NetWare Directory Service (NDS). So, the domain model provided a "bucket" or container, in which an organization stored information about its network computers, users, and resources. This model worked just fine. According to Microsoft, a single domain could handle more than 10,000 users.

However, the domain model did prove to be unwieldy on large networks (from a management perspective) because the network had to be divided into different domains or separate containers that shared resources using trusts. A trust (which is still used in the Windows networking environment) is a relationship between two domains that enable the domains to share resources.

With each domain having its own domain controller (and backup domain controllers), not to mention trusts with other domains, network administrators had a lot of issues to deal with in managing a network using this domain structure. Imagine a number of containers connected by garden hoses. Your job is to keep the water level equal in all the containers. Now, perhaps you can understand what it was like (and still is like on NT networks) to try to balance bandwidth, user access, and resource availability on a domain-based network.

By the Way

The Master Domain Model Deploys a User Domain and Resource Domains

In large Windows NT implementations, Microsoft urged network administrators to use the Master domain model. This consisted of a domain that contained the users and groups, which then had trust relationships with domains that contained network resources; these domains were referred to as resource domains.

With the release of Microsoft Windows 2000 Server, Microsoft abandoned the flat domain model and made the Active Directory the new logical hierarchy for Microsoft networks. Active Directory provides a tree structure that allows you to create a branching logical structure for your network that can contain multiple domains. The domain still serves as the basic unit of the Microsoft network structure, and a domain controller still manages each domain. (With Active Directory, multiple domain controllers can be deployed in a domain.)

The next largest unit in the Active Directory structure is a tree. A tree consists of a root domain, which is the first domain that you bring online. Trees can contain multiple domains, including the root domain. Domains that are added to the tree are considered child domains, as shown in Figure 16.1). All domains in the tree have implicit transitive trusts with the other domains in the tree. Transitive trusts create a two-way street between domains, meaning that they share each other's resources equally.

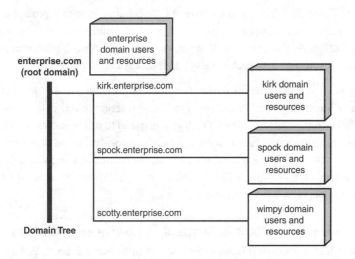

FIGURE 16.1
The Active Directory structure provides for a tree that contains a root domain and child domains.

To create a Microsoft network, you need to bring a domain controller online and create the root domain for the Active Directory tree. Large networks can deploy multiple trees. And, of course, multiple trees can exist, which constitutes a forest. (Yes, it's called a forest.) Let's look at issues related to installing and configuring a Microsoft server running Windows Server 2003, which is the most widely used version of Microsoft's powerful NOS. (Its eventual successor, Windows server 2008, is examined later in this hour.)

Installing and Configuring a Microsoft Server

Microsoft Windows Server 2003 requires a minimum hardware configuration to run (as does any software). The minimum hardware requirements and recommendations from Microsoft are listed here for the standard version of Windows Server 2003:

- ▶ **CPU speed**—133MHz (at least 550MHz is recommended)

- ▶ **RAM**—128MB (256MB recommended as a minimum, which isn't very much)

- ▶ **Disk space for setup**—1.5GB

- ▶ **CD-ROM drive**—12X

- ▶ **Monitor**—Super VGA capable of providing 800×600 resolution

The minimum hardware won't get you very far, particularly when you're going to add a lot of users and services to the network. You should go with a processor in excess of 4GHz and load your machine with the maximum RAM. You also want to have SCSI drives on your server so that you can take advantage of different RAID implementations that help protect server data and system files.

Not only must you meet the minimum hardware requirements to successfully install and run Windows Server 2003, but you must have a server that provides hardware proven to be compatible with the NOS. If you're going to use the server in a true production environment in which you must supply mission-critical services to network users, your server hardware must come right off the Microsoft Windows Server 2003 Hardware Compatibility List (HCL). A copy of that list is available at www.microsoft.com/windowsserver2003/default.mspx.

By the Way

Windows Server 2003 Is Available in Different Versions

Windows Server 2003 (R2) is available in different editions: Express Edition, Workgroup Edition, Standard Edition, Datacenter Edition, and Enterprise Edition. However, be careful about these names and selections, because they might change after this book's publication. Previous releases also include the Web

Edition. Standard is considered the entry-level edition of the NOS. The Enterprise Edition supports more processors and server clustering and is considered the workhorse for large networks. The Datacenter Edition provides advanced clustering features and is only available through Microsoft's Datacenter program. The Web Edition is actually a scaled-down version of the NOS and is designed to serve as a web server only. Another edition of Server 2003, Windows Small Business Server 2003 Standard Edition, includes Windows Server 2003 and a number of Exchange Server 2003 services. All editions now support 32- or 64-bit architectures.

When you have a server with the appropriate hardware in place, you're ready to install the Windows Server 2003 software. The server software offers the ability to perform a clean install or upgrade earlier versions of the operating system. It's best to start with a clean system if possible. Although time-consuming, this allows you to configure all server settings from scratch, particularly security settings as they relate to this particular version of the OS.

Existing domains and forests (in the case of Windows 2000 Server upgrades) must be prepared for upgrade using a utility called addprep that is contained on the Windows Server 2003 CD-ROM. If you're going to upgrade, you should spend some time researching the upgrade process. The subject is beyond the scope of this book. I recommend you study Microsoft's Security Configuration Wizard (SCW), a tool for reducing the attack surface of computers running Windows Server 2003 with Service Pack 2 (SP2). The package provides system requirements, installation instructions, and instructions for troubleshooting simple problems. If you're interested, check out http://technet.microsoft.com/en-us/library/cc757109.aspx.

Let's take a quick look at the installation process. We can then learn how to configure a server as a domain controller and other roles such as a file server.

Create a Network Diagram Before Creating the First Domain

Watch Out!

The installation and configuration process for Microsoft Windows Server 2003 is straightforward and can probably be categorized as "easy." But this doesn't mean that you should bring your server online before you plan your network. Create a network diagram and think about how you want to grow the network and the domains over time. For more about writing network specifications, see Hour 10, "Designing a Network."

The Installation Process

A clean installation of Windows Server 2003 on a server-class computer is straightforward and allows booting from the CD-ROM drive. Once the server has booted to the Windows Server CD-ROM, you're walked through a text phase that allows you to specify (and create if necessary) the drive partition that will contain the operating system. You're also provided with an opportunity to format the partition.

Windows Server 2003 supports three file systems: FAT, FAT32, and NTFS. FAT is a legacy from DOS, and FAT32 was first available with the Windows 95 OS. NTFS is the newest version of the NT file system that provides greater security for files with support for file system recovery. You need to go with NTFS as the file system for your server because the Active Directory requires it.

After you've taken care of the target partition for the NOS, the server boots into a Windows-like environment that walks you through the remainder of the installation. You can set additional networking settings during the process, such as adding network protocols; the default is TCP/IP. By default, the server is also assigned to a workgroup named WORKGROUP.

It's a good idea to go with all the defaults during the installation process. It's easier to change settings after the NOS is fully installed on the server. After the installation is complete, the system reboots, and you're allowed to log in to the server using the administrative password that you set during the installation process. When you have the server up and running, you can configure it for particular roles and services. Let's look at some of the configuration options.

Configuring a Windows 2003 Server

Configuring a Windows 2003 server as a domain controller, file server, or to provide other services, such as remote access, Domain Name System (DNS), or Dynamic Host Configuration Protocol (DHCP) is straightforward. In fact, Windows Server 2003 provides the Manage Your Server window (it opens the first time you run the NOS), which can help you add, remove, and manage all the server's different roles. Figure 16.2 shows the Manage Your Server window, which lists the current roles filled by the server. This window also makes it easy to add new roles.

For example, if you want to make the server a domain controller (which would be necessary to create a new root domain for the network), you can select the Add or Remove a Role link in the Manage Your Server window. This starts the Configure Your Server Wizard, which lists all the possible roles for a server, such as file server, print server, domain controller, and DNS server.

To add a role, all you have to do is select the role in the Configure Your Server Wizard window and click Next. In the case of making a server a domain controller, the Configure Your Server Wizard walks you through the steps of making the server a domain controller in a new forest and tree. During the process, you'll have to supply a full DNS domain name for the root domain you're creating. Figure 16.3 shows the wizard screen that asks for the Active Directory Domain Name.

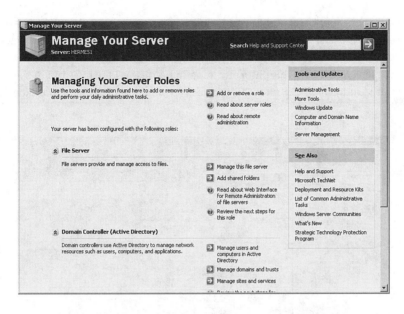

FIGURE 16.2
The Manage Your Server window makes it easy to configure your Windows 2003 server.

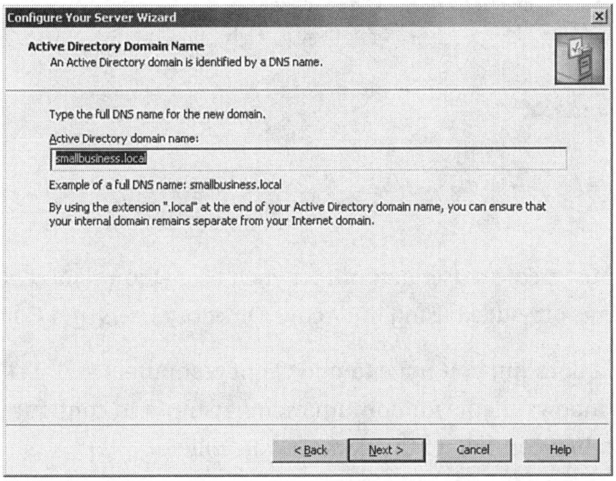

FIGURE 16.3
The Configure Your Server Wizard makes it easy to add roles to the server.

If a service, such as DNS or DHCP, is not currently available on the network, the wizard can configure the server to provide that type of service. After the process is complete, the new role (in this case, domain controller) is added to the Manage Your Server window, making it easy to manage a particular role. For example, after you add the domain controller role, you can quickly start the different Active Directory tools, such as the Active Directory Users and Computers snap-in, directly from the Manage Your Server window.

The Active Directory Users and Computer snap-in is used to manage Active Directory objects such as users, groups, and computers. Figure 16.4 shows the Active Directory Users and Computers snap-in. You'll find that all the Windows server utilities have the same look and feel as this particular snap-in because all the tools run in the Microsoft Management Console. This provides a common interface for managing the server.

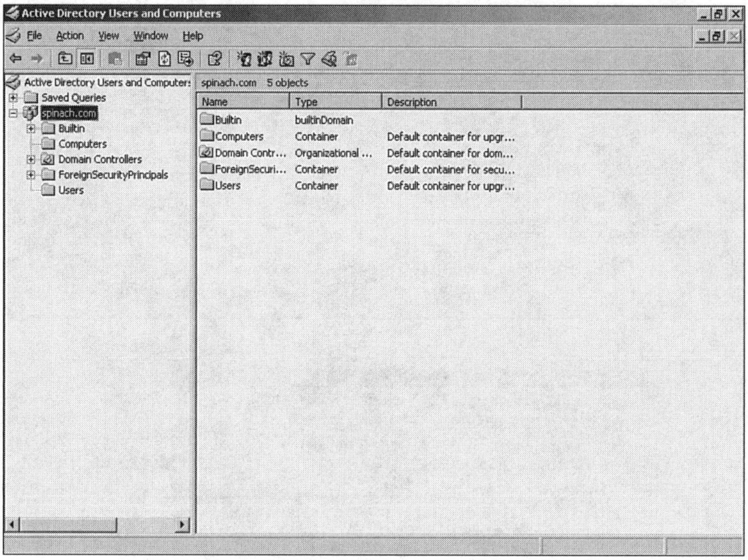

FIGURE 16.4
The Active Directory Users and Computers snap-in is used to manage users, groups, and computers in the domain.

Obviously, you must create a user account for each user who will access resources on the network. Clients are added using the Active Directory Users and Computers snap-in.

After you set up a domain, you have to add client computers to it. Let's look at how you configure Windows clients for domain membership and configure their network protocols so that they can talk to the domain controller.

By the Way

Microsoft Windows Server 2003 Is a Rich and Complex NOS

You can configure Windows Server 2003 for many network services, such as DNS and DHCP. It can provide terminal and remote services to client computers both on the network and over remote connection. All the details related to configuring and managing a Windows server are beyond the scope of this book. For more information, see *Sams Teach Yourself Microsoft Windows Server 2003 in 24 Hours* by Joe Habraken.

Configuring Windows Clients for Domain Membership

Configuring Windows clients to participate in a domain requires you to make them domain members. You also have to make sure that the client is configured with at least one of the network protocols configured on the server. This shouldn't be an issue because Windows Server 2003 is configured with TCP/IP by default, as is Microsoft Windows XP Professional.

Adding Client Computers to the Domain

A domain client can be running any of the different versions of Windows, from the current Vista to Windows XP Professional; to Windows 98; and all the way back to Windows for Workgroups 3.11 (even MS-DOS). However, let's focus on adding a more recent computer to the network because, in terms of implementations, this would be a prevalent operating system of choice for your clients.

For users who already have a valid user account in the Active Directory to log on to the network using one of your network client computers (those that are running Windows NT 4, Windows 2000, or Windows XP Professional), the computer itself must also be added to the domain. You can add the computer to the Active Directory in two ways. First, you can add it on the server using the Active Directory Users and Computers snap-in. Second, you can add the client by changing the computer's current membership on the Computer Name tab on the System Properties dialog box. The second method requires you to run around to each of the client computers or provide users with the administrative rights to add their computers to the domain (which probably isn't that great of an idea in terms of network security).

Try It Yourself ▼

Adding a Computer to the Domain

In this section, we will look at how you add a computer to a Windows domain using the Active Directory Users and Computers snap-in.

1. Click the Start menu, point at Administrative Tools, and then select Active Directory Users and Computers.

2. In the snap-in tree, click the Computer node.

3. Right-click in the snap-in Details pane on the right side of the snap-in. On the shortcut menu that appears, point at New and then select Computer. This opens the New Object-Computer dialog box, as shown in Figure 16.5.

▼

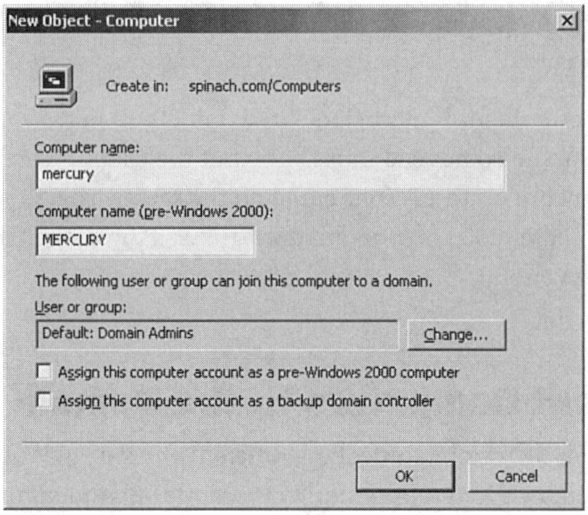

▼

FIGURE 16.5
Enter the name
of the computer
that's being
added to the
domain.

New Object - Computer

Create in: spinach.com/Computers

Computer name:

mercury

Computer name (pre-Windows 2000):

MERCURY

The following user or group can join this computer to a domain.

User or group:

Default: Domain Admins   Change...

☐ Assign this computer account as a pre-Windows 2000 computer

☐ Assign this computer account as a backup domain controller

OK   Cancel

4. Enter the computer's name in the Computer Name box.

5. Click OK to add the computer to the domain.

The computer is now part of the domain. Users can log on to the domain via the
computer.

▲

Adding a Client to the Domain from the Client Computer

To add a client to the domain from the client computer, log in as the administrator
and then right-click the My Computer icon on the Start menu or the Desktop.
Select Properties from the shortcut menu that appears. On the Computer Name
tab of the Properties dialog box, click the Network ID button. The Network Identification Wizard opens, walking you through the steps of adding the computer to the
Active Directory. If you aren't logged in as a domain administrator, you have to provide the name and password for an account that has the rights to add a computer
to the domain to complete the process.

Configuring Network Protocols in Windows

You already know from earlier discussions in this book (such as Hour 5, "Network
Concepts") that if two computers are required to communicate over your network,
they must be configured with the same network protocol. TCP/IP is the de facto standard in terms of networking protocols. The latest versions of the Microsoft NOS (Windows Server 2003 and 2008) and the Microsoft client (Windows XP Professional) are
configured for TCP/IP by default. They are, however, configured to receive their IP
addresses and subnet masks (as well as the primary DNS server IP address and other

IP-related settings) from a DHCP server. (DHCP is discussed in more detail in Hour 15, "Connecting to the Internet: Key Supporting Operations.")

You can access your network connection in both Windows XP and Windows Server 2003 via the Network Connections icon in the Control Panel. Right-clicking any local area connection (typically, clients have only one NIC; servers can have multiple NICs, particularly if they're acting as routers, firewalls, or supplying the Internet connection to a small network) allows you to open the Properties dialog box for that connection. Figure 16.6 shows the Local Area Connection Properties dialog box for a Windows XP network client.

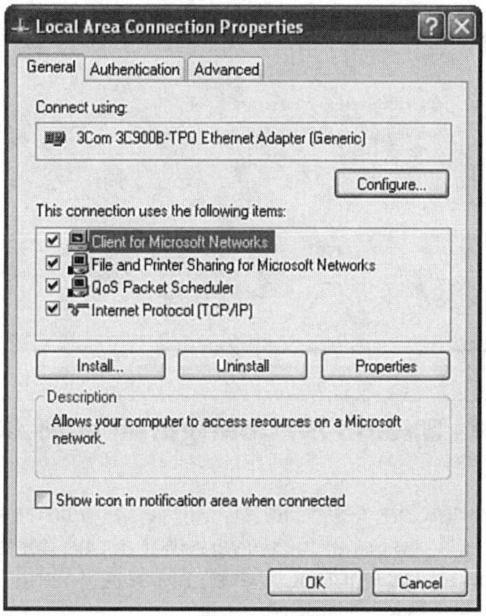

FIGURE 16.6
The Local Area Connection Properties dialog box shows the installed protocols and allows you to configure protocols such as TCP/IP.

You can add protocols to the connection's properties by clicking the Insert button and then selecting a new protocol. Because Windows no longer supports NetBEUI, your only real alternative to TCP/IP is NWlink, which is the Microsoft implementation of Novell's IPX/SPX.

Configuring a network protocol, such as the Internet Protocol (TCP/IP), is just a matter of selecting the protocol in the Properties dialog box and then clicking the Properties button. Figure 16.7 shows the default settings for TCP/IP on a Windows XP network client.

Notice that the client is configured to get its IP address and subnet mask dynamically, meaning from a DHCP server. To assign the client a static IP address, select the Use the Following IP Address option button. You must then supply the IP address, subnet mask, and default gateway (which is a router interface). You also need to provide information, such as the primary DNS server.

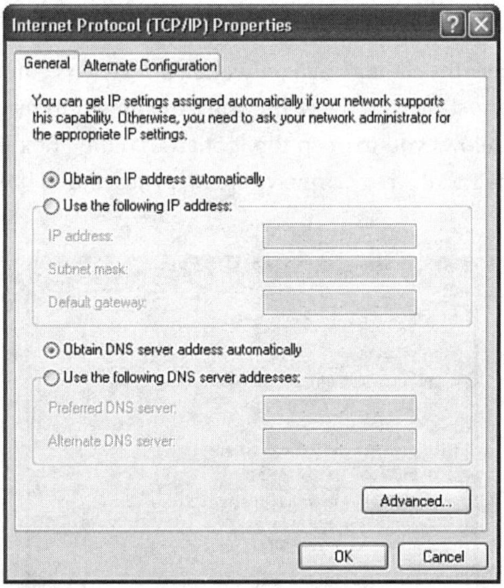

FIGURE 16.7
By default, Windows XP clients are configured to get their IP address dynamically from a DHCP server.

Watch Out!

Windows Servers Should Be Configured with Static IP Addresses

When you configure a network server for TCP/IP, you should assign the server a static IP address. This is essential for servers that act as domain controllers or provide services, such as DNS or DHCP; even file servers should typically be assigned static IP addresses.

After you've set the static IP address for the client or set up the client to receive its IP information dynamically from a DHCP server, you can click OK to return to the Local Area Connection Properties dialog box. Then, click OK to close it.

Sharing Folders and Printers on the Network

After you've configured your server, created user accounts, and connected clients to the domain, the next step is to set up procedures to share files and other resources such as printers. On a small network, you can also configure a domain controller as a file server or print server or to offer services such as DNS or DHCP. On larger networks, you'll deploy specialized servers to take care of one or more services.

On a Microsoft network, file or printer servers don't have to be configured as domain controllers. They're merely member servers and are configured much the same way as a network client. You must add them to the domain using the Active Directory Users and Computers snap-in and configure them for the appropriate network protocol (which, again, in most cases will be TCP/IP).

Adding a role to a member server running Windows Server 2003 was discussed earlier in this hour. You can use the Configure Your Server Wizard to configure a member server as a file server or a print server. In both cases, the wizard allows you to specify the files or the printer that will be shared on the network.

You can also share folders and drives on a server using Windows Explorer. A shared resource such as a particular folder or a drive partition is referred to as a share. You can secure a share using share permissions. On a Microsoft network, you can also secure shares (down to the file level) using NTFS permissions. NTFS permissions are available on drives that have been formatted with the NTFS file format. NTFS permissions allow you to secure a resource down to the file level.

To add a share to a file server using Windows Explorer, locate the folder (or create a new one). Right-click the folder in the Windows Explorer window and select Sharing and Security on the shortcut menu that appears. This opens the folder's Properties dialog box with the Sharing tab selected, as shown in Figure 16.8.

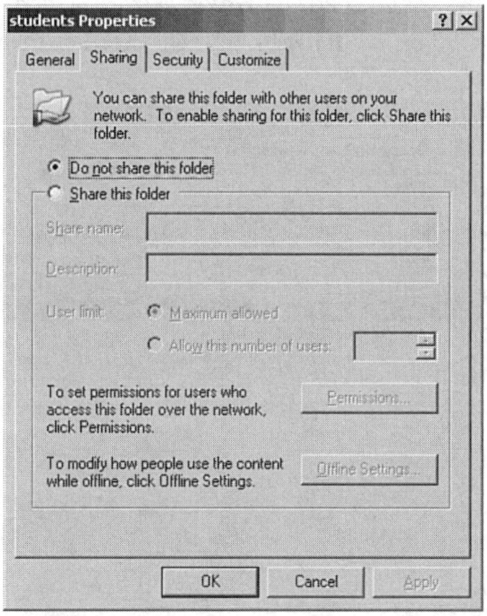

FIGURE 16.8
Share a folder via the folder's Properties dialog box.

All you have to do is select the Share This Folder option button and then supply a share name for the folder. When you have pre-Windows 2000 Professional clients on the network, make sure that the share name is 15 characters or less, or these legacy clients won't be capable of seeing the share when they browse the network. The Sharing tab also allows you to set permissions related to the folder, such as read/write permissions.

After you've set the share properties, you can close the dialog box (just click OK). The share will now be on the network.

You Can Create Hidden Shares

Administrators can set up hidden shares that network users can't view using My Computer or Windows Explorer. When you create the share, follow the share name with a $ sign. Only administrators can see these "hidden" shares on the network.

Sharing a printer on a Windows network is as simple as creating a share. After the printer has been installed on the server (both directly attached printers and network printers can be managed by a Windows print server), it can be shared by adding the print server role to the server using the Configure Your Server Wizard.

Although you can also share a printer via the printer's Properties dialog box, the Configure Your Server Wizard helps you locate the printer, such as a remote printer. It also runs an Add Printer Driver Wizard ensuring that the print drivers needed by network clients can be downloaded from the print server when the client attaches to the printer. Figure 16.9 shows the Add Printer Driver Wizard screen where you select the operating systems running on the network that will need a driver for the printer.

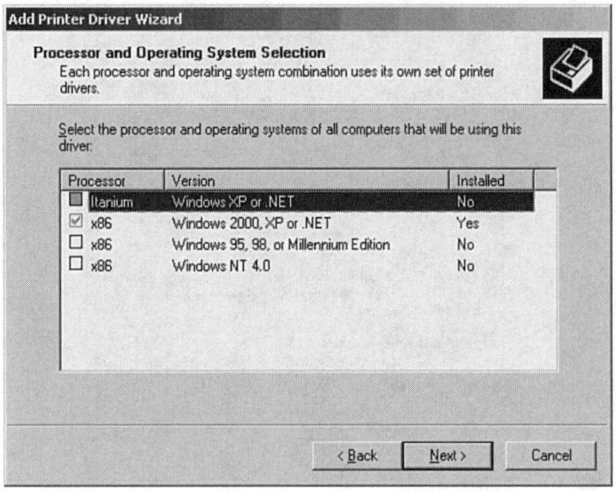

FIGURE 16.9
When you share a printer, you can specify the print drivers that should be available for network clients.

You can use a particular print server to manage printers that are directly connected to the network. (Most laser printers have their own NICs for directly connecting to the network infrastructure.) Keep in mind that the print server must spool the print jobs, so the server needs to have ample RAM and hard drive space. You don't want a print server to be a potential bottleneck on your network.

Managing a Microsoft Server

You've already seen the Active Directory Users and Computers snap-in, which is a good example of one of the Microsoft management utilities that runs in the Microsoft Management Module window. There are snap-ins for managing domain trusts, subnets, and specific services, such as DNS, DHCP, and Routing and Remote Access.

Because we've already discussed creating shares and deploying a file server, let's look at the File Server Management snap-in. This tool allows you to see a list of users attached to the file server and lists which files are being accessed. You can also use the snap-in to quickly create new shares and even back up the file server. Figure 16.10 shows the File Server Management snap-in.

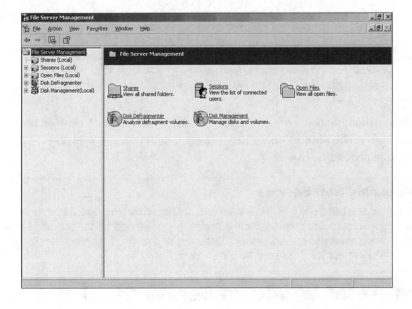

FIGURE 16.10
The File Server Management snap-in

Various other tools and utilities are required to manage a Windows server. For example, you can monitor server and system performance using the System Monitor. The System Monitor allows you to add objects to its window that supply you with counters related to specific hardware performance on the server.

For instance, you could monitor such things as virtual memory or paging use on the computer (when this graph spikes, it's time to add more RAM to the server) or monitor the processor by looking at the % Processor Time. Figure 16.11 shows the System Monitor snap-in window. It can provide statistics in a graph, histogram (similar to a bar chart), or report view. Figure 16.11 shows the graph view.

FIGURE 16.11
The System Monitor allows you to monitor server hardware usage.

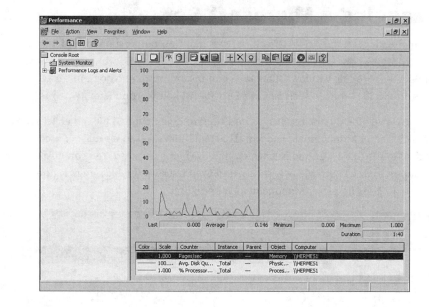

You'll find that managing a server not only requires that you keep a tab on the various services you're running on the network, but entails that you keep an eye on how servers are performing as well.

> **Baselining New Servers**
>
> Whenever you bring any type of new servers online, you should use a performance and monitoring tool to record baseline performance settings for the server's hard drive, memory usage, and processor. Baselining and performance monitoring are discussed in Hour 22, "Network Troubleshooting."

Future of Windows Server 2003

In March 2007, Microsoft released Service Pack 2 (SP2) for Windows Server 2003. It includes previously released patches for security, reliability, and performance improvements. SP2 also offers Microsoft Management Console 3.0 and support for WPA2. In addition, it boasts improvements to its earlier IPSec and MSConfig software. Finally, SP2 adds features allowing for faster processing of packets. However, as of June 2008, no additional service packs are offered for Windows Server 2003.

Windows Server 2008

Windows Server 2008, which was released on February 27, 2008, is the most recent offering from Microsoft for NOSs. Because of its recent deployment, it doesn't yet have a large user base.

Windows Server 2008 is founded on the same platform as the new Microsoft operating system Vista. It builds on the features of Windows Server 2003 and provides an assortment of enhancements to each of the Windows Server 2003 operations discussed in this hour. If you're familiar with the 2003 release, you'll be comfortable with the 2008 offering. The Sams series offers a detailed tutorial on this software: *Sams Teach Yourself Microsoft Windows Server 2008 in 24 Hours* by Joe Habraken.

Summary

Although you might not think that setting up and configuring a Windows server is easy, don't be deceived by the fact that the tools appear to be easy to use. You may find it easy to just key-in a value into a window, but keying-in the correct value might not be quite as easy. The overall level of understanding and experience to appropriately configure a Microsoft network and keep it up and running is quite high. We've only scratched the surface in terms of server management and Microsoft networking in this hour. Many information resources are available at www.microsoft.com. Also, check out www.informit.com for both hands-on and reference books related to Windows Server 2003.

Q&A

Q. *In a domain that has multiple domain controllers, is it possible to "decommission" a domain controller and use it for another purpose without reinstalling the Windows NOS?*

A. Windows Server 2003 makes it easy to promote and demote servers as far as the domain controller role is concerned. If you have more than one domain controller and want to repurpose a server, you can remove the Active Directory from the computer without reinstalling the server NOS.

Q. *How should I approach protecting network shares in terms of assigning permission levels?*

A. Although you can assign permissions for a share to each user, the best way to assign permissions is to create groups in the Active Directory (such as accountants or sales), where the members of the group need the same type of permission level for the share. You can then assign the permission level to the group, saving you a lot of time and keeping your assigned permissions better organized.

Q. *As far as a quick look at how a server has been configured, where's the best place to get this information?*

A. The Manage Your Server window provides a quick view of the roles that have been assigned to a server, such as domain controller, file server, and DNS server. The Manage Your Server window also offers quick access to the Configure Your Server Wizard, which allows you to modify the server's configuration.

UNIX and Linux Networking

What You'll Learn in This Hour:

▶ A short history of UNIX
▶ UNIX and networking
▶ Linux and networking

Numerous software vendors vigorously compete for market share in the Network Operating System (NOS) business. These software companies spend substantial money just on advertising. Each NOS offers a common set of services. Yet, each also has its own flavor. These services and their flavors will be explained in this hour.

One of the first "networked" operating systems (OSs) was UNIX. In this hour, we look at a short history of UNIX and examine the basics of how it works. We also explore Linux, a UNIX derivative. Linux is open source (code that is not copyrighted) and offers some interesting alternatives to other NOS platforms.

How UNIX Got Its Start

In the late 1960s, AT&T Bell Laboratories started work on a multiuser OS, one that could support more than one user session at a time. It was called Multics. Programmers made fun of it; it was large, slow, unwieldy, and built by rules generated by management committees. Multics wasn't extensible either; the resources that came with the system represented the total sum of resources available to the system.

In an attempt to show up the Multics programming team, several AT&T Bell Labs programmers set out to build a small, fast, multiuser OS that would be extensible and would encourage users to modify the system to suit their needs. When the dust settled, the programmers had created exactly what they had set out to create, and in a poke at the Multics crew, they named their OS UNIX. (UNIX implies one, and Multics implies many.)

Initially, UNIX was considered an OS for the computer geek and wasn't taken seriously as an enterprise NOS platform. After all, it wasn't a typical OS monolith of code and was highly modular, allowing for the addition of OS patches and enhancements on-the-fly—and it hadn't been written in the typical plan-it-to-death corporate fashion. A number of people found the small and modular design of UNIX (coupled with the fact that it was inexpensive) a compelling reason to use it. Educational institutions and engineering businesses got on the bandwagon because UNIX could run on computers with less power than the high-end systems that ran OSs such as IBM's VM or Digital's VMS. UNIX made sense for people without deep pockets; they could get mainframe power for microcomputer prices. Although it was an inexpensive NOS, the original AT&T version of UNIX ran on few hardware platforms.

In the mid-1970s, UNIX was rewritten in the C programming language. (Code written in C can be modified and recompiled to run on different types of computer hardware.) The result of this approach was that UNIX became available for multiple machine types. Every distribution of UNIX included the source code or the C language code, which could be recompiled or translated into computer code that could run on almost any platform.

In 1978, Bill Joy, a graduate student at the University of California at Berkeley (he was mentored by Ken Thompson, one of the original UNIX programmers who was on sabbatical at Berkeley), developed an alternative to the AT&T version of UNIX named the Berkeley Software Distribution, or BSD.[1] All the recent versions of UNIX originate from either the AT&T version or the Berkeley Software Distribution (including Linux).

Various types of UNIX installations are being used today. On the low end, Linux—an open source version of UNIX—is used by many organizations as a powerful and relatively inexpensive web and mail server. NOSs such as Novell have integrated Linux code and compatibility into their server platforms. At the next level, UNIX is used to run workstation computers. Some of these machines aren't used as servers; instead, they're used as programming or engineering workstations running complex and high-end graphic-intensive software.

Now that you have a bit of the UNIX history under your belt, let's look at UNIX concepts. We can then examine Linux, the UNIX clone.

---

[1] In Outliers, Malcolm Gladwell devotes a good part of a chapter to Bill Joy, his exploits at school, and later at Sun Microsystems. Gladwell says, "He is sometimes called the Edison of the Internet." Perhaps Gladwell should read up a bit more on the history of the Internet, as Joy came along some 15 years after the brilliant men at ARPA had already put on and taken off their Edison hats regarding the Internet. What Joy did was write another version of UNIX. He didn't invent the Internet. I make this footnote to acknowledge the ARPA engineers about the matter.

Basic UNIX Concepts

One important concept to grasp when working on a UNIX platform is that every-thing is considered a file. Hard drives and other hardware devices, as well as pro-gram and data files, are all seen in UNIX as files. What this means is that you can read and write to them. For example, in the case of writing to the computer hard drive, UNIX sees it as writing to a special kind of file called a block device.

A second important concept is that UNIX has standard input and output, which is also called redirection. Standard input and output, from a UNIX perspective, means that you can chain programs together and stream the output from one file into the input of the next program in the chain. For instance, there's a ps command in UNIX that lists all the programs (called processes in UNIX). If you type ps at a UNIX command-line terminal, it tells you which processes are running. But if you're at a command-line screen, you're often limited to the 25 lines that the screen has, so the output of the ps command scrolls across your screen too fast for you to read.

You can redirect the output of the ps command to a command called more, which dis-plays only one screen of data at a time, by typing ps ¦ more. This gives you the output of the ps command, but it only displays it one screen at a time, while you use the space-bar to scroll through all the pages of output. The ¦ symbol is called a pipe because, in this case, it "pipes" data from the output of one command into the input of the next.

In most OSs, you must perform significant programming to be able to filter or mod-ify the contents of a file. In UNIX, however, this isn't the case. UNIX is basically a ker-nel, the center of the OS; a series of small, modular programs with focused purposes can be run on-the-fly. Using standard input (the keyboard or a file), standard output (the screen), and pipes (represented by the ¦ character), you can pass data between programs and accomplish complex tasks right from the command line.

Pipes are effective tools, but they don't do everything that you need for redirection. Let's say you want to take the output of a particular ps command and put it into a file so that you can read it in a text editor and print it. You could, at that point, type ps > /tmp/ps-output. This action would take the output of the ps command and redirect it into a file in the /tmp directory called ps-output. (This filename is ad hoc; you can name a file whatever you want.) This command would be read as, "Run a ps command, and redirect the output of it to the file /tmp/ps-output."

What happens if you want to create a log file that just keeps having new informa-tion tacked onto the end of the file? Instead of using >, you would use >> to make the command ps >> /tmp/ps-output. If you read this command literally, you would get the following: "Run a ps command and put the output into the /tmp/ps-output file. If there is an existing /tmp/ps-output file, don't overwrite it; instead, append the new output to the end of the existing /tmp/ps-output file."

The third UNIX concept is that every file on a UNIX system is mounted in a hierarchical file system. The file system starts with a slash (/) and is called the root file system. This logically includes the whole world (of the system). Disk drives are resources mounted within subdirectories of the root file system; consequently, all the disk space available within a system is theoretically available to any file system. Figure 17.1 shows the root of the file system on a computer running Sun Solaris UNIX and the subdirectories contained. (Linux uses a similar hierarchy.) The ls or list command was used to view the contents of the root directory.

FIGURE 17.1
The file hierarchy
of UNIX/Linux

UNIX enables file systems to use available disk space, whether there's 1 disk or 50 in the system. This makes UNIX file systems extensible. Because more than 1 file system can span more than 1 disk, the concept of file system becomes independent of the concept of a physical disk. In this way, UNIX makes efficient and flexible use of disk space.

Finally, before closing out this section of the hour, we should visit one more concept related to UNIX: interoperability and adherence to Open Systems standards.

If UNIX systems adhere to the open standards published by the Internet Engineering Task Force (IETF), they can interact with one another without significant problems. An IETF-compliant UNIX from one vendor can interoperate with a UNIX from another vendor without fear that one vendor's interface won't work with another's. This capability is why things such as web services and Internet email are so often entrusted to UNIX or Linux systems; they adhere to the standards that have been agreed upon by committee and can interwork easily. This reduces cost and makes UNIX a more predictable system than proprietary OSs.

UNIX/LINUX as a Network Platform

UNIX/LINUX servers can offer file and print services as well as more complex services, such as Domain Name System (DNS) and web hosting. In earlier versions, deploying UNIX servers for the first time required a network administrator to deal with a fairly steep learning curve because the environment was administered from the command line. With the advent of Windows and the Mac graphical user interface (GUI), even UNIX aficionados could see the usefulness of a GUI interface. UNIX and Linux distributions now provide GUI interfaces, which makes it easy to become familiar with the services and features that the UNIX and Linux platforms provide.

When a UNIX or Linux installation is made on a server (or on a workstation, in the case of Solaris and many Linux distributions), a root account must be established. This root account is equivalent to the administrator or admin account found on other platforms, such as Microsoft Windows or NetWare respectively.

The root account is used to administer, manage, and monitor the system. Network administrators who deploy UNIX and Linux servers don't run the servers as root because leaving the system up and running with root logged in can create security holes. When the system administrator wants to configure or manage the server, all he has to do is quickly log in as the root, which can be done from the command line using the su command. After the administrator invokes the su command, he need only provide the root password as shown in Figure 17.2 (which displays a server running Red Hat Linux).

Notice that the command-line prompt in Figure 17.2 changed to # when the administrator logged in as root. After he has finished working as root, he can log off of root (and back to the other user account that was entered during the system bootup). It's just a matter of typing exit and then pressing Enter.

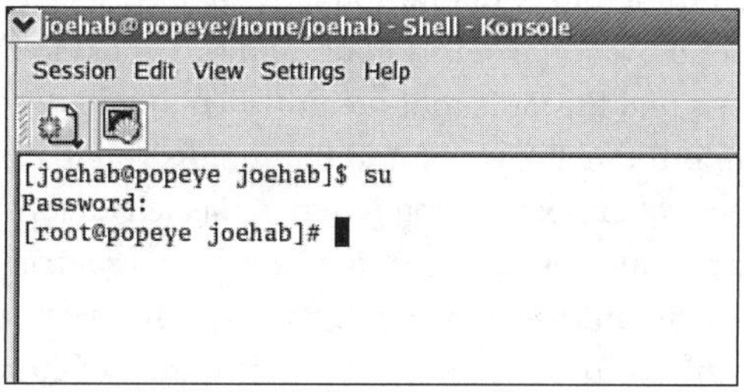

FIGURE 17.2
The administrator can quickly log in as the root at the command line.

An effective way to explore the possibilities of UNIX is to look at the open source Linux platform. Numerous distributions of Linux are available, many of which you can download free. When you would like support and easier access to system upgrades, you might want to purchase a particular Linux distribution. Red Hat Linux, SUSE Linux, and Mandrake Linux are some of the more popular distributions. Because the Linux kernel software operates under a free software licensing called the General Public License (GNU), companies such as Red Hat are able to take the Linux kernel and add their own proprietary software code to create their own particular flavor of Linux.

Network Services and Settings on a Linux Server

Servers running Linux distributions, such as Red Hat, can offer network services such as DNS, Dynamic Host Configuration Protocol (DHCP), and web server. As far as server installations worldwide, Linux comes in second to the Microsoft server platform (which is making Microsoft increasingly nervous). Configuring (and adding) network services to a Linux server requires the administrator to be logged in as root.

You can configure network services from the command line or by using various GUI utilities. A common service deployed on Linux servers is that of web server. Apache Web Server, which runs on Linux (and has been adapted to the latest version of Novell NetWare), is a popular web server platform that provides a reliable and secure web environment.

You can also configure network settings for the server via a GUI utility. The network configuration tool (or "neat" as it is referred to) allows you to view and configure network hardware devices. It also provides you with the ability to configure Transmission Control Protocol/Internet Protocol (TCP/IP) settings for a network interface. You can create hostname-to-IP address mappings using the tool and enter information related to the DNS settings for your computer, such as the hostname and DNS server settings.

The Network Configuration utility allows you to set parameters related to network connectivity. It's beyond the scope of this hour (and this book) to cover all the various command-line utilities and the GUIs that are provided to manage a Linux server. Interestingly (and unfortunately), you'll find that unless you're using a proprietary customized distribution of Linux that you purchased (such as some of the enterprise networking versions provided by Red Hat), the "free" open source versions of Linux change frequently. Useful utilities come and go with each version of a particular distribution. This is mainly because of the open source nature of Linux; programmers build new utilities and then lose interest over time so that some useful utilities never get upgraded and become unavailable.

The fact that the various GUI tools seem to come and go in the Linux environment is one reason to learn how to use the command line in Linux if you're seriously considering deploying Linux as a network server platform. Although any command line has somewhat of a steep learning curve, Linux commands (and the UNIX commands that they are based on) are fairly intuitive. For example, to add a user in Linux, you use the adduser command. Figure 17.3 shows the adding of a user kimrich with a password of password.

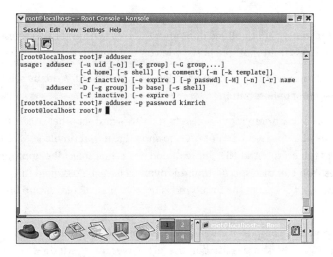

FIGURE 17.3
You can use the adduser command and its various switches to add users to a Linux system.

Options for Sharing Files

There's more than one option for sharing files on a Linux network. The Network File System is also available in the Linux environment, enabling Linux computers to share files using a Virtual File System interface that runs on top of the TCP/IP protocol. (NFS was developed by Sun Microsystems for UNIX and has long been a mainstay of the UNIX world.) Users can manipulate shared files on a remote server as if the resources were stored locally on their computers.

NFS is a good example of a client/server environment in which a Linux computer can be configured as both an NFS client and a server. To configure the NFS server, you can use the NFS Server Configuration tool in a GUI environment or configure the NFS settings via the command line. Directories that you share using NFS are referred to as shares.

Try It Yourself   ▼

Create an NFS Share

In this section, we examine how you add an NFS share to a Red Hat server using the NFS Server Configuration tool.

1. Click the Add button in the NFS Server Configuration tool. The New Share dialog box opens.

2. Supply the directory name that you want to share. (You can use the Browse button to locate it.)

▼

▼

3. Specify the hosts that you're allowing to access the share. You can specify hosts by hostnames (full qualified domain names, or FQDNs) or IP addresses. To allow access from multiple hosts, you can use the asterisk (*) as a wildcard.

4. You can also set the permissions to Read-Only or Read/Write by selecting the appropriate option button.

5. You can allow anonymous access to the share and set other access parameters, such as allowing remote root users to share local root privileges. Select the User Access tab on the Add NFS Share dialog box. Then select the appropriate check boxes. You can also specify that anonymous users be assigned the privileges of a local user or assign the anonymous users to a particular group on the Linux computer.

6. When you've completed entering the information for the new share, click the OK button. The share is listed in the NFS Server utility window.

▲

After the share is configured, you must start the NFS service to make the share available. Click the Apply button in the NFS Server utility window. A message box appears asking you if you want to start the NFS service. Click Yes. You now have an NFS share that users can access on the network.

Upgrading a Linux Server

Upgrading a Linux server can be a little more complicated than upgrading a Windows or NetWare server—particularly when you're using a freeware version of a Linux distribution and haven't purchased support for your version of Linux. You can find individual Linux software packages (such as a management utility, word processor, email package, or desktop utility) in different file formats.

For Red Hat, you can easily install new software using RPM (Red Hat Package Manager) files. These files have .rpm as their extension. The files have been specially prepared so that you can install them quickly on your system using the Red Hat Package Manager utility. All you have to do is download the file (typically from www.redhat.com) and then locate it on your system using the Conqueror browser (a combination file and web browser used on Linux systems where KDE has been installed). Selecting the file in Conqueror starts the Red Hat Package Manager and allows you to install the software.

Summary of Network Servers

It's common for a server on a network to supply multiple services, particularly on smaller networks. The degree of server specialization (meaning the number of servers on the network that supply only one or two services) depends on the size of your network. A large network with heavy network traffic requires more servers (running specific services) than a small network that might be capable of deriving all of its services from one or two server boxes. The following list summarizes the different servers and the services they provide:

- **File server**—A file server's job is to serve as a home for the files that users on the network need. This can include files that many users share. These files are typically held in what is called a public folder, which can include private folders that are specific for a particular user.

- **Print server**—A print server hosts a network printer and serves as the control conduit for the printer. Because print jobs need to be spooled (placed on the computer before they are sent to the printer) before they're printed, the print server supplies the hard drive space needed. The print server also queues up all the print jobs being directed to the printer.

- **Communication server**—A communication server runs specialized software that allows users on the network to communicate. It provides services such as electronic mail and discussion groups to allow users to share information.

- **Application server**—Application servers host various applications, such as specialized databases. Even typical desktop applications, such as word processors and spreadsheet software, can be stored on an application server. This makes updating software applications much easier because the software doesn't reside on every client workstation.

- **Web server**—Web servers enable you to create a website that can be accessed internally by your employees or by folks surfing the Internet. Web servers aren't for everyone, and many companies still use web hosting companies to get their websites up and running on the Internet.

- **DHCP server**—This server uses DHCP to provide DHCP clients with IP addresses, subnet masks, and other TCP/IP configuration information, such as a default gateway and preferred DNS server.

- **DNS server**—The DNS server takes care of the IP address-to-FQDN resolution (and vice versa) on the local network (or local zone of authority, as it is referred to). Some NOS platforms require that a DNS server be available on the network even if the network isn't connected to the Internet.

▶ **Authentication server**—The authentication server provides the logical hierarchy for tracking objects such as users on the network. Typically, the first server that you bring online handles user authentication and stores the object database for the network.

All the NOSs that we've discussed in the book—such as Microsoft Windows Server 2003 and 2008, Red Hat Linux, Novell NetWare, and UNIX platforms such as Sun Solaris—provide these network services as either part of the "basic" NOS or as an add-on service. Although planning and configuring a network homogenously— meaning using just one NOS for all services—makes the learning curve a little more reasonable for the network administrator, many networks are in fact heterogeneous.

These networks deploy different NOS platforms for different services. For example, a network might be running the Microsoft NOS to authenticate users and provide other services yet still take advantage of legacy NetWare file and print servers. The network might even be more heterogeneous in that the web server might run a version of Linux or UNIX to take advantage of the Apache web server platform.

Whether you have the luxury of deploying one NOS or work on a network that deploys more than one NOS, it's the network administrator's job to supply the appropriate services to the network clients.

Summary

In this hour, we examined UNIX and Linux. UNIX is one of the oldest and most reliable of the network platforms. Linux, a clone of UNIX, provides inexpensive tools to implement a UNIX-like server environment. Linux provides all the features you would expect from an NOS. You can configure and manage a Linux server or client from a GUI or work with commands at the command line.

Q&A

Q. *What distribution of Linux is best to implement?*

A. The distribution of Linux that you should select for your network depends on your implementation. If you're using older (legacy) hardware and want to use Linux as a client OS, pick the distribution that requires the least amount of hard drive space and the most basic hardware configuration. In term of server implementations, go with distributions that provide both support and updates. Two popular Linux powerhouses are Red Hat Linux and SUSE Linux.

Q. *What type of network services can UNIX/Linux servers offer?*

A. UNIX/Linux servers can offer network services such as DNS, DHCP, and web services (and pretty much any service you expect from a network server platform). UNIX/Linux servers are particularly popular for web server implementations.

Q. *I want to keep my Windows clients but add a file server to the network. Can I use Linux?*

A. Yes, a Linux server running (for example) Samba can act as a file server on a Windows network. It's basically equivalent to a Windows NT Server. So, if you're running a Windows 2003 Server domain, you have to run the domain in mixed mode to accommodate the Linux/Samba server. (Samba is a free software networking protocol. Check it out at http://us3.samba.org/samba/.)

HOUR 18

Putting the Pieces Together

What You'll Learn in This Hour:

▶ The Internet layered model

▶ Key interfaces and protocols explained in Hours 1 through 17

▶ How interfaces and protocols fit into the model

▶ How interfaces and protocols correspond with each other

We've covered a lot of material in only 17 hours. Perhaps you're thinking, "It's taken me longer than 17 hours to read the 17 chapters!" If you've only read the material, you can succeed in making it to this page in about 17 hours. However, if you've studied the material, I suspect (and hope) the journey took a bit longer.

Nonetheless, because of the scope of the material covered in this book, this is a good time to summarize and review the key network components we've studied thus far. We also examine how these components correspond to each other. First, we review the functions of the layers of the Internet layered model that were introduced in Hour 3, "Getting Data from Here to There: How Networking Works." Next, we identify the layers in which the network components reside. We also show the layers in which the Internet protocols reside. Finally, we review Ethernet and Internet names and addresses and explain how these identifiers fit into packets and frames. Thus armed, we can tackle the remaining hours with more confidence.

Review of Internet Layered Model

Figure 18.1 provides a general schema of the Internet layered model. We learned that the conventional OSI model contains seven layers. In contrast, the Internet model contains five layers, with Layers 5 and 6 folded into other layers, usually Layer 7. The layers perform these services:

▶ **Layer 7 (application)** contains the applications most familiar to users, such as email, text messaging, and file transfer. Most of the software used by network servers resides in this layer.

▶ **Layer 4 (transport)** is concerned with ensuring user data arrives safely at its destination. If a packet fails to reach the end user, the sending Layer 4 resends the packet. This layer is also responsible (in cooperation with the operating system, or OS) for ports and sockets.

▶ **Layer 3 (network)** provides network addressing, (maybe) route discovery, and routing services.

▶ **Layer 2 (data link)** defines a set of rules for transporting traffic on one communications link from one node to another node.

▶ **Layer 1 (physical)** is concerned with physical images, such as electrical, electromagnetic, and optical signals; the network interface cards (NICs); the wire; and cable. The modem is an example of a Layer 1 device.

FIGURE 18.1
Functions of
Internet layers

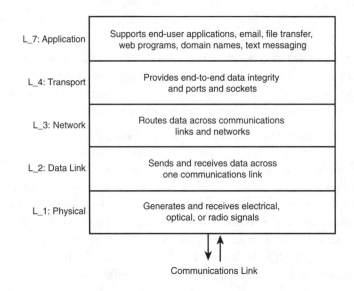

Key Network Components' Position in the Layers

In Hours 1 through 17, we learned about key components (principally software and protocols) used to operate a communications network. Figure 18.2 shows the placement of these components in the Internet layered model. We won't rehash each of them, but we'll offer amplifying comments to add to previous information. By the way, if some of these names don't ring a bell, consult the index at the back of the book to review discussions about them.

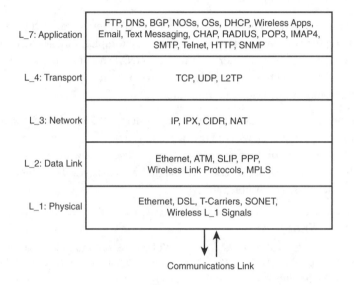

L_7: Application	FTP, DNS, BGP, NOSs, OSs, DHCP, Wireless Apps, Email, Text Messaging, CHAP, RADIUS, POP3, IMAP4, SMTP, Telnet, HTTP, SNMP
L_4: Transport	TCP, UDP, L2TP
L_3: Network	IP, IPX, CIDR, NAT
L_2: Data Link	Ethernet, ATM, SLIP, PPP, Wireless Link Protocols, MPLS
L_1: Physical	Ethernet, DSL, T-Carriers, SONET, Wireless L_1 Signals

Communications Link

FIGURE 18.2
Position of components in the layers

Just because a network component is shown to reside in one layer doesn't mean it can operate correctly with only that layer. All network components at a higher layer *must* use one or more components at the layer(s) below to function properly—for that matter, to function at all. For example, IP can't operate at Layer 3 if Layers 1 and 2 aren't in place.

Most of the network components and their associated standards published by the Internet Engineering Task Force (IETF), Institute of Electronic and Electrical Engineers (IEEE), International Telecommunication Union (ITU), and other groups operate in one layer. Exceptions are Ethernet, whose IEEE standards define L_1 and L_2 procedures, and the various wireless technologies (Cellular, Wi-Fi, and Bluetooth) that reside in two or more of the layers.

With rare exceptions, Internet Protocol (IP) is the L_3 protocol that the applications and protocols in Layers 4 and 7 use. Internetwork Packet Exchange (IPX) is a counterpart to IP but is sinking into the sunset. Some forms of text messaging and other wireless applications haven't yet migrated to IP, but they will.

The same holds true for the use of Transmission Control Protocol (TCP) or User Datagram Protocol (UDP) at Layer 4. Recall from Hour 14, "Connecting to the Internet: Initial Operations," that TCP is used for traffic that requires end-to-end acknowledgments and overall data integrity. UDP is used for applications such as voice and video that don't need, and can't tolerate, the overhead of TCP.

We dealt briefly with L2TP in Hour 8, "Remote Networking." It's an enhancing protocol to PPP that uses IP to get its traffic to other nodes. It doesn't use TCP or UDP; thus, it's placed in L_4 of the model.

Several of the components in this model don't concern themselves with the sending and receiving of traffic between network nodes. As examples, Classless Inter-Domain Routing (CIDR) and Network Address Translation (NAT) don't unto themselves generate packets. I've placed them alongside IP in Layer 3 because they deal with IP address mapping, subnetting, and translation.

The operations of OSs and Network Operating Systems (NOSs) reside in Layer 7. These critical software packages are the heart and soul of computers, servers, and routers. They generate and receive a lot of traffic between network nodes and, of course, they initiate a lot of processing at the nodes themselves. Thus, they use the lower layers for these communications.

> ### A Layered Exception
>
> Placing an OS or an NOS in Layer 7 shouldn't be construed to mean that this software depends on the lower layers. It's quite the opposite, because Oss and NOSs control the operations of all these layers.

Many of the TCP and UDP port numbers have been reserved by the OS and NOS vendors. As examples, Microsoft's Windows Internet Naming Service (WINS) package is identified with Internet port number 1512; the Windows File System is identified with number 5009.

In the past, OS and NOS messages were transported between nodes with vendor-specific protocols, such as NetWare's IPX, Apple's L_3 AppleTalk, and IBM's L_3 Systems Network Architecture (SNA). With a few minor exceptions, vendors have migrated to the Internet protocols at Layers 3 and 4, and the IEEE, ITU-T, and IETF protocols at Layers 1 and 2. As cautioned in previous discussions, beware of the vendor who offers you proprietary network protocols. These vendors are becoming increasingly rare and are destined to become extinct.

Names, Addresses, and Sockets: The Cogs of Communications

In several of the past hours, we emphasized the value of the Internet's standardization of names and addresses and software identifiers. Without these conventions, it's fair to state that you and I would not be able to surf the Web or even send an email to each other.

We won't rehash these services, but if they still seem a bit vague to you, look at these hours for information on the following names, addresses, and sockets:

> Mac addresses: Hour 3
>
> EtherType: Hour 3
>
> IP addresses: Hour 3
>
> IP Protocol Number:Hour 14
>
> Ports and sockets: Hour 14
>
> Domain Names: Hour 15

Relationships of Names, Addresses, and Sockets

Again, let's tie together more pieces of the network puzzle. Figure 18.3 is used in conjunction with Figure 3.2 in Hour 3 and Figure 14.2 in Hour 14. Assume that data is forwarded out of Layer 7 from the sender to the receiver (Figure 3.2). At Layer 4, TCP or UDP creates a header containing the destination and receiving port numbers. The receiving Layer 7 software is Microsoft's WINS, so the destination port number must be 1512. The sending port number is taken from a pool of numbers.

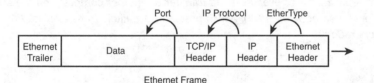

FIGURE 18.3
The Ethernet frame and layer process IDs

Next, the data is passed to IP at L_3. Here, IP (in conjunction with the OS) adds the source and destination IP addresses and places in its Protocol ID field a 6 for TCP, or 17 for UDP. Then, the data is passed to Ethernet at L_2, which adds the source and destination MAC addresses and fills in the value 0800 in the EtherType field to identify the IP packet.

At the receiver, the process is reversed, as seen in Figure 3.2. The MAC and IP addresses are used to route the data to the correct node on the network. The EtherType, IP Protocol ID, and destination port number are used to pass the data to the correct process in L_3, L_4, and L_7, respectively.

Common Locations of Components at Network Interfaces

In Hour 6, "Extending LANs with Wide Area Networks (WANs)," we introduced the three interfaces of a computer network. Recall that these interfaces represent the physical communications links between computers, servers, and routers. They aren't operations within a machine. They represent the "pedal to the metal" traffic that flows between nodes. In Hour 6, Table 6.1, "Prominent WAN Interfaces," explained the interfaces and set the groundwork for more explanations in Hour 7, "Mobile Wireless Networking." Look at Table 6.1 in Hour 6. Granted, its contents are not a simple set of rows and columns, but I trust the table will make sense to you.

Summary

This hour has reviewed several key concepts discussed in previous hours, including the Internet layered model and the positions of major processes and protocols in the layers. In addition to this review, we've learned how the layers, protocols, and interfaces interwork with each other.

Q&A

Q. *Your system is to execute a file transfer to another computer on the same local area network (LAN). Which protocols are likely to be executed for this operation?*

    L_7: _____

    L_4: _____

    L_3: _____

    L_2: _____

    L_1: _____

A.   L_7: FTP

      L_4: TCP

      L_3: IP

      L_2: Ethernet

      L_1: Ethernet

Q. *Your system is to execute an email transfer to another computer across your DSL. Which protocols are likely to be executed for this operation?*

L_7: _____

L_4: _____

L_3: _____

L_2: _____

L_1: _____

A. L_7: POP3

L_4: TCP

L_3: IP

L_2: ATM

L_1: DSL

Q. *Your system is to execute an email transfer to another computer across your cable modem. Which protocols are likely to be executed for this operation?*

L_7: _____

L_4: _____

L_3: _____

L_2: _____

L_1: _____

A. L_7: POP3

L_4: TCP

L_3: IP

L_2: ATM

L_1: Cable modem digital signal

Q. *You aren't interested in end-to-end data integrity for these two operations. What changes are made to the protocol stack?*

A. UDP is executed instead of TCP.

HOUR 19

Role of the Network Administrator

What You'll Learn in This Hour:

▶ Review of network management jobs and tasks

▶ Computer networking education and certification

▶ Key concepts in administrating a computer network

▶ Ideas on effective project management

A network administrator is the person responsible for ensuring the health and well-being of a network. We've examined much of the information that a network administrator must know, such as computer hardware, network protocols, and Network Operating Systems (NOSs). An understanding of this information, coupled with experience and a healthy dose of common sense, enables an administrator to keep the network up and running.

A network administrator may be called by another title. For example, a network engineer at a large company could, in practice, also be a network administrator, although the scope and responsibilities related to a network engineer's job would probably be greater than those of a network administrator at a small company. A small company that employs only a network support specialist to handle day-to-day problems and support (and uses consultants for major network installations or roll-outs) has in effect made the network support specialist the de facto network administrator—at least in relation to basic network and client computer issues.

In this hour, we'll explore the jobs associated with network administration. We'll also examine issues related to different paths of education and certification for the network administrator. Finally, we'll discuss planning and installing a network and look at some of the nontechnical issues related to network administration, such as budgeting and network project management.

Information Technology Jobs

Although we've concentrated on network design, management, and administration in this book, numerous other jobs and career paths relate to network administration. In the mid to late 1990s, there was a boom in the information technology (IT) field, with resultant job opportunities. Although hi-tech communications have cooled down somewhat, IT is still a sound career choice.

Computer networking professionals operate at many levels in a corporate structure. As examples, the chief information officer (CIO) operates at the top of the corporate ladder, IT managers and administrators operate somewhere in the middle, and technicians and support personnel operate near the bottom rungs. IT itself has a "pecking order." Let's look at a range of IT positions and their relative standing in the IT field, from bottom to top. Note that the job titles are generic monikers.

▶ **Help desk analyst**—Help desk personnel serve as the first line of support for many companies and institutions. They help users diagnose computer or networking problems and provide necessary remedies either over the phone or online. Working the help desk requires a broad knowledge of the company systems and networks and typical end user problems, an ability to provide quick fixes, and the social dexterity to deal with irate users. The help desk analyst is an entry-level position.

▶ **User support advisor**—User support personnel are responsible for working with users and for setting up new computers, connecting them to the network, and making sure the appropriate software is installed. Support advisors are also involved in diagnosing user problems and repairing them (similar to the help desk personnel). Support advisors are typically more hands-on than their help desk counterparts. The advisor positions are often entry level or one step up from the help desk.

▶ **Support specialist**—Support specialists are responsible for a particular aspect of the network infrastructure, such as server maintenance, network expansion and setup (including pulling wires), or the maintenance of a particular set of services, such as routers and DNS servers. Support specialists might also be responsible for network backups.

▶ **Network administrator**—Network administrators are responsible for planning, implementing, and maintaining the network infrastructure. This position requires an in-depth knowledge of NOSs and networking hardware. The person must manage the strategies for making network resources available to users and anticipate potential bottlenecks and security flaws in the network. The network administrator position usually resides in the middle of the company's IT pecking order or at the senior level.

▶ **IT director**—The IT director is responsible for the overall planning and implementation of the network infrastructure. The responsibility includes managing the personnel who are specialists in different areas, such as LAN, databases, WAN, and web services. The IT director is also the conduit to upper management and is responsible for the budgets, inventories, licensing, and reporting (to upper management).

As mentioned, this list of personnel represents a generic set of job descriptions. Obviously, not all these positions are at the network administrator level, but they can serve as stepping stones for employees to work toward becoming a network administrator.

The job title for a position varies from company to company. One organization might call the LAN administrator a network administrator, whereas another might define the position as a systems manager. The salaries of these positions depend on the size of the business and the actual responsibilities listed for the position. As well, the responsibilities of the job dictate the level of knowledge and experience required.

Computer Networking Education and Certification

In many cases, the first wave of computer gurus, programmers, and networking professionals who found their way onto a company's organization chart were self-taught. Many worked their way through the ranks by moving up the corporate pecking order through hands-on experience or, unfortunately, from transferring from another department that had nothing to do with computers or networks. During one of the times when I was writing code, my boss had no experience whatsoever with software, hardware, or data networks. His area of expertise was budgeting. But we programmers were happy about that. He gave us support, did all the number crunching, and wrote the long-range plans. He left us to our coding sheets, which was fine by us.

Today, it's not uncommon to find network administrators who have business degrees or web designers who have majored in political science. It's also not uncommon to encounter computer professionals who have had productive careers and either didn't finish or didn't attend college. (Bill Gates was a dropout.) Some of the most talented network people I've come across gained their college degrees in "soft" subjects, such as languages and music.

Times have changed. Today, many technical schools, community colleges, and universities offer information science and IT degrees.

Another way that IT professionals gain their knowledge base and meet the requirements for a job is by acquiring professional IT certifications. These certifications can be vendor specific or generic.

For example, Microsoft, Novell, Cisco Systems, and Sun Microsystems offer different certifications and designations related to their products. In terms of generic (meaning nonvendor-specific) certifications, the Computing Technology Industry Association (CompTIA) offers several certifications related to different skill sets. For example, the CompTIA Network+ certification is designed for professionals with nine months of experience (or more) in network administration and support.

To attain a particular certification, the candidate must take an exam or set of exams. Some certifications require only one exam; others require a number of exams. Here are examples of programs from major vendors:

▶ Microsoft Certified Professional (MCP) is a broad certification program offered by Microsoft. The program offers multiple certifications, based on different areas and levels of technical expertise. To be awarded certifications, a candidate must pass a series of exams. The current certifications are Microsoft Certified Technology Specialist (MCTS), Microsoft Certified Professional Developer (MCPD), Microsoft Certified IT Professional (MCITP) and Microsoft Certified Architect (MCA). (Previous generation certifications include Microsoft Certified System Engineer (MCSE), Microsoft Certified Solution Developer (MCSD), and Microsoft Certified Database Administrator (MCDBA).

▶ Sun Certified Professional (SCP) is a certification program offered by Sun Microsystems. It's meant to test and verify skills in Sun products, such as the Java programming language and the Solaris operating system (OS). The Sun Certified Java Associate (or SCJA) tests a person's knowledge of object-oriented programming, Unified Modeling Language (UML), and the Java programming language. The Sun Certified Java Programmer (SCJP) exam is the entry-level Java exam and a prerequisite to several other Java-related certifications.

▶ Cisco Career Certifications are tests and certifications for Cisco products. There are five levels of certification: Entry, Associate, Professional, Expert, and Specialist. With the exception of Entry, each level requires a selected set of skills, although there's necessary overlap of information in the programs.

▶ Red Hat offers the Red Hat Certification Program. All its tests are hands-on and include installation, administration, and troubleshooting tasks. No paper tests are conducted; all is done live.

▶ Numerous educational institutions and IT training centers across the United States and worldwide offer courses that allow you to prepare for specific exams. There are even boot camps to help you prepare for an entire certification track for a protracted period of time (in some cases, a week).

▶ You can take these exams at testing centers in your area. Pearson VUE offers many IT certification exams. For information on locations and exams offered, see Pearson VUE's website at www.vue.com. You can also take exams at Thomson Prometric testing centers. Check out its website at www.2test.com.

Additional Thoughts on Managing the Planning and Installation Processes

As you've seen throughout much of this book, two important tasks a network administrator must face are the planning of a network and its subsequent installation. Hours 10, 11, and 12 discuss issues related to planning and installing a network. The main tasks involved in network administration are planning, designing, implementing, and tuning.

When viewed in this light, network administration appears to be pretty simple: four straightforward steps that lead to network nirvana. Perhaps, but perhaps not. Building and managing networks is easier than in the past because of the Internet standards, the acceptability of NOS platforms, and the plug-and-play features for many components. Nonetheless, a lot can go wrong in a computer network. Pay attention to the details. When in doubt, read the user manuals. And for larger enterprises, make certain you or your personnel have taken (and passed) the NOS and router certification programs. If this isn't the situation, I recommend you contract with a firm to take over the running of your systems.

A Few Thoughts on Budgets

After you've worked through the issues related to planning and running a network, another aspect of a network administrator's job is dealing with budgets. Many people have had a basic accounting or personal finance class at some time in their educational experience. Therefore, the arithmetic involved and the structuring of a budget is no mystery. Most companies also have a form or template that can be used to create a department's yearly budget. Getting the budget down on paper is relatively straightforward. The difficult aspect of working with IT budgets relates more to justifying the expenses than listing them accurately.

In most companies, the network infrastructure serves as a communication and productivity tool for the employees. The problem with justifying a network budget is quantifying how the computers and the network make the employees more productive and therefore generate more income for the company. I'm not talking about companies with websites that generate measurable sales or software companies in which programmers need computing tools to generate product. For the run-of-the-mill business that uses computer technology as just another tool, it's often difficult to measure the cost effectiveness of the network infrastructure. In many situations, computer networks don't generate measurable income.

This means that when you create your network budget, you also need to accumulate any information that will help you justify the budget when you meet with upper-level managers. Here are a few ideas for justifying your IT implementation:

▶ Do research on other companies that use a particular technology. Most hardware and software vendors provide white papers and case studies that allow you to see how a particular aspect of the network infrastructure improved a particular company's capability to do business. Having some facts available—especially those related to a competitor—can help justify proposed expenses.

▶ Talk to salespeople in the field and find out how certain aspects of your network infrastructure (such as dial-in or VPN connections for remote users) have made them more effective.

▶ Look at the average employee's workload and determine the time savings and increased productivity that new hardware tools and software will provide.

▶ Compute the travel costs required for employees involved in a company project that includes branches of the company at different locations. Providing a groupware product to employees that offers an environment for communication and collaboration, such as Microsoft Exchange or Lotus Notes, might negate the need for much of the travel. You must prove that the cost of servers, software, and training to roll out the groupware environment will be less over time than the cost of travel and lodging.

▶ Determine if older equipment, such as PCs, can be donated to a nonprofit organization and create a tax savings for your company that helps sweeten a proposal for upgrading workstations and servers.

The bottom line, so to speak, is that you need to not only create a budget that provides accurate funding for your network plan but be able to sell the budget to the people at your company who control the purse strings.

Managing Network Projects

As a network administrator, you'll likely become involved in many projects critical to the mission of your enterprise. Managing a project requires that you exercise control over two things: resources (including technical tools and personnel) and time. Managing people and equipment seems straightforward enough, but how do you control time? Time control relates to creating and then sticking to a schedule for the project.

Although a schedule is only a best guess, accurately assessing the human and technical resources for a project can go a long way toward helping you meet the schedule. Identifying milestones in the schedule also can help you assess where you are in relation to the completion of the project. If you are off schedule at a particular milestone, you can judge whether you need to increase the number of resources (such as technical staff) that are needed to complete the project on time.

Remember that your project has a budget. Throwing a lot of overtime and other technical costs at the schedule might allow you to complete the project in time, but it might also run your project over budget. In addition, it might result in a completed project whose final implementation produces incomplete results...or worse, inaccurate results.

Although project management is a subject that can fill an entire book (and has), here are some general pointers related to network project management:

▶ Define the project in a short abstract (known as an Executive Summary). An abstract is a quick overview of the project. Supply the purpose and perhaps even the level of project difficulty so that you can determine the staff and resources required to complete the project.

▶ Organize the project around goals and outcomes rather than tasks so that each interim goal or outcome can be quantified in terms of individual tasks. This approach makes it easier to create a schedule. Identifying the interim outcomes for the project allows you to break the overall project down into various phases (creating milestone dates for the completion of each phase). Breaking down the project into a series of interim goals makes it easier to schedule personnel and resources and take stock of the project as it's in process.

▶ After the project has been given the go-ahead, assign specific dates to your different interim outcomes or milestones. I've seen far too many badly planned projects in which the schedule is broken down into week one, week two, and so on with no specific dates other than a best-guess completion date. You need to have a specific schedule and a plan to meet each milestone date.

▶ Provide local authority to keep the process moving. If you're working on an implementation project at several sites, you need to designate a site manager who can make critical decisions related to keeping the project moving on a day-to-day basis. If every decision related to the project requires your authorization, and you're unavailable, you're going to have a lot of team members sitting on their hands waiting for you to make a decision as to their next step. Delegating authority requires you to stay in frequent contact with those who you've empowered. Give them the responsibility and the authority to carry out the responsibility.

▶ Closely monitor the progress of the project (in terms of interim goals). This allows you to track the differences between your plan and what's unfolding. Monitoring requires regular meetings with project personnel. You should also build some type of reporting instrument (a weekly report, for example) that allows you to keep your finger on the pulse of the project.

▶ Build some sort of testing into the process. This allows you to test whether each interim goal or outcome has been met.

Project Management Skills Are as Important as Technical Skills

No matter how much you know about the bits and bytes of computer networking, managing a computer network center and associated projects is a different ball game. This hour should be of help, and hundreds of books are available in the local book store that espouse different approaches. There's no one "best" way to be an able network administrator and an effective project manager. I've found success with this approach: Hire the best people you can find. Train them with the best teachers you know. Pay them well. Give them guidance and support. But make sure all this investment is not wasted by your micro-managing them; that is, let them off the leash. That's why you spent all the up-front money in the first place!

Your proposed budget can reflect the possibility of special projects that might pop up in the coming year. I'm not suggesting you pad your budget, but you do have to communicate effectively with upper management so that you have a clear understanding of where they expect computer technology to take them in the future. If there's a chance that management wants a new tool made available, it should be reflected in the budget even if it's only in some dollars that are earmarked for exploring a particular technology on a limited, test basis. The actual rollout of the technology can then be incorporated into the budget for a subsequent year.

You can keep track of your projects—including the resources and personnel required and the timeline for the project milestones—in different ways. One way is to maintain a hard copy notebook or calendar that tracks the project. Another is to use Microsoft Excel to track resources, personnel, and timelines in a worksheet.

When you're managing a large, complex project, consider taking advantage of project management software. Numerous project management software packages are available, including Primavera SureTrak, Journyx Timesheet, Niku Projects, Vertabase Pro, and Microsoft Project, to name a few.

A real benefit of using project management software, such as Microsoft Project, is that you can configure each task in the project so that it's dependent on tasks that must be completed before the particular task can be started. This type of project tracking also keeps you honest in that you have to stay on track and approach each task in the proper order as you move from the start of the project toward completion. Being able to assign resources and predecessors (tasks that must be completed before the current task) and log notes related to a particular task really helps you keep a project organized. Project management software also makes it easy to generate reports related to a project.

Using project management software allows you to centralize the information related to a project. It obviates the mess of separate sheets of paper, Post-It notes, and other unorganized errata that can become the downfall of many ill-fated projects. Staying organized and using a timeline to accurately track the project is a necessity of managing even the smallest of IT projects.

However, don't succumb to the lure of the CRT screen's Gantt Charts. Project management software won't manage the project. That's your job. Don't become so engaged with the tools to track project progress that you aren't engaged with your staff and your users.

Summary

In this hour, we examined IT jobs related to network administration and network support. We also discussed the certifications that computer networking professionals can pursue and viewed the big picture of planning and implementing a network. Finally, the discussion included information related to budgeting and network administration, with tips about managing network projects.

Q&A

Q. *What are some ways to learn networking skills and upgrade your network administration skill set?*

A. Many colleges, universities, and private training schools provide courses in network administration and related topics. There are also many vendor-specific and nonvendor certifications, such as those offered by Microsoft and Sun Microsystems.

Q. *What are some ways that you can help explain a network implementation's return on investment to your corporate officers when dealing with budgets?*

A. Conduct research on how other companies have improved their business by implementing the network technologies you plan to implement. Talk to company employees—particularly salespeople—and learn how new network tools can improve their ability to do their job. Compare the costs of network communication tools in relation to the travel required if the network infrastructure didn't provide various communication possibilities.

Q. *Cite some good practices related to managing network-related projects.*

A. Some good practices include organizing projects around goals and outcomes, determining the individual tasks required to meet a particular goal, creating a definitive schedule for the project using real dates, and empowering the people who work for you to do their work.

Security

What You'll Learn in This Hour:

▶ Definition of key security terms
▶ Computer network vulnerabilities
▶ Defending against vulnerabilities
▶ Tools for defenses

We begin this hour with an explanation of several basic but important terms pertaining to security. We then survey the security dangers faced by computer networks. Next, we explain several effective defenses employed to thwart these dangers. We conclude the hour with a look at specific tools to implement these defenses.

Network security is surely the most important job for the manager of a computer network. An efficient and fast network—one providing wonderful email, file transfer, and web page services—is all for naught if it's not secure. And if the network you manage isn't secure, your job isn't secure.

How important is security to the industry? Very. For example, in the eight months I have been using the Vista operating system (OS) on one of my PCs, roughly 85% of the Microsoft Vista patches have pertained to security.

Network security issues have changed significantly over the past two decades. Network security once focused on protecting network resources from accidental erasure or unauthorized use of resources. Although remote access dial-in schemes for network access posed a potential risk for the network (and still do), the administrator was required to secure what was essentially a closed system. This meant the major security issues pertained to users' passwords and the rights assigned to these users.

When a company's internal network was attached to the Internet, the situation changed. Many security issues now relate to outside attacks. These attacks can be direct, such as an attacker accessing an internal network by spoofing a legitimate user, or indirect, such as by attaching malicious payload to an email message that is sent out as spam.

If you assume responsibilities for network security in your organization, keep these happy thoughts in mind:

▶ He that is too secure is not safe.[1]

▶ Distrust and caution are the parents of security.[2]

Basic Terms

Before we proceed into the security dangers and defenses against these dangers, a few definitions are in order. First, the term encryption means the changing of the syntax of a message (cleartext), making it unintelligible to the casual observer. This altered data is called ciphertext. Decryption is the opposite of encryption. It means changing the ciphertext back to the original intelligible format—that is, changing it to cleartext.

Encryption and decryption are performed using one of two methods. The first method is known by three names: private, symmetrical, or conventional. Whatever name is used, this method uses the same key (a value) for encryption and decryption. This is a secret key that the sender and receiver of the message share. The sender uses the key to encrypt the cleartext into ciphertext; the receiver uses the key to decrypt the ciphertext into cleartext.

The second method is known by two names: public or asymmetric. Public key security has become the dominant method of both encryption and authentication in computer networks. This method uses two keys (actually key sets): one for encryption and the other for decryption. They correlate with each other because their values are created using complementary values and algorithms. Thus, text that is encrypted by one key can be decrypted by the other. The idea is to allow one key to be disseminated to the pubic (the public key) while the other key is held in secret (the secret key). Therefore:

▶ **For encryption**—A sender's cleartext is encrypted by the receiver's public key. It can only be decrypted by its complementary private key, which is known only to the receiver who holds it in a secure place. The sender knows only the public key.

▶ **For authentication**—A cleartext value (a known value—say, a password) is encrypted into ciphertext by the sender's private key. This data can only be

---

[1] *Thomas Fuller, Adages and Proverbs. Secondary source: Leonard Roy Frank, Quotationary, Random House, New York, 2001, p. 760.*

[2] *Benjamin Franklin, Poor Richard's Almanac, July 1733. Secondary source: Ibid.*

decrypted into a cleartext value (the known password) if the receiver possesses the complementary public key.

A *digital signature* validates the authenticity of the sender by using asymmetric keys. Assuming a sender has sent or otherwise made available to the receiver the sender's public key, this key is applied to a "digital signature," which is a known value. If the resulting decryption operations result in the computation of this known value that the sender encrypted, the sender is considered legitimate. (That is, the sender is authentic.)

A *security certificate* establishes a secure communication connection between two parties. Each certificate contains a public key and a private key. When a web browser communicates with a secured server, a handshake authenticates the server and the browser client. A security certificate is issued by a trusted source, known as the *certificate authority* (CA), which usually verifies the domain name and issues the certificate. For example, VeriSign is a well-known CA.

Security Threats

What is an effective strategy for protecting the resources attached to a network? You must understand the various types of security threats, most of which result in the denial of service (DoS) to the users of the network. They are as follows:

▶ **Virus**—A virus is a piece of code that "infects" a software program. It attaches itself to the program and executes when the program is run. It might or might not infect other programs. The result might be only irritating, such as the execution of a lot of superfluous code or funny icons appearing on a computer screen. But it might also be dangerous; for example, it might be able to access the files on a computer and destroy them.

▶ **Worm**—A worm runs as an independent program that replicates itself over and over again until it saturates a computer system or a network. A worm can result in clogging or flooding, resulting in the DoS to the user community.

▶ **Trojan horse**—A Trojan horse is a piece of code that comes in the form of a virus or a worm. It's so named because it hides itself, perhaps in a user's login, and then exploits the user's profile to do damage. It's possible that a Trojan horse might not be found because, after doing its deeds, it exits the system without leaving a trace of itself.

▶ **Bomb**—Many Trojan horses (with their viruses or worms) don't do harm immediately. Some are triggered by a time threshold; after a date has passed, the bomb "explodes."

▶ **Replay**—This violation is an attack on a resource by capturing data, perhaps modifying it, and resending it. An example of a replay attack is applying a transaction to a database more than once: say, one's payroll record.

Security Defenses

Different defenses are employed to combat these threats. They are as follows:

▶ **Privacy/secrecy/confidentiality**—The assurance that a user's traffic is not examined by nonauthorized parties. It a nutshell, it's an assurance that no one "reads your mail."

▶ **Authentication**—The assurance that a legitimate party (or parties) has sent the traffic a user receives. For example, if a user receives a legal document from an attorney through the Internet, this user is confident that his attorney sent it, not someone else. This idea is also called data origin authentication.

▶ **Integrity**—The assurance that the traffic a user receives wasn't modified after the proper party sent it. This service includes antireplay defenses—that is, operations that prevent someone from reinjecting previously authenticated packets into a traffic stream. Because of its anti-injecting operations, this service offers sequence integrity, which means "rogue" packets might be rejected if they don't meet certain rules. For Internet Protocol (IP) networks, this idea is called connectionless integrity.

▶ **Access control**—The prevention of unauthorized use of a resource. This service might prevent someone from monopolizing resources or deny the user of the resource entirely. Resource monopolization is a common security attack that leads to the DoS to legitimate users.

▶ **Nonrepudiation**—The inability to deny or disavow a transaction. This service is part of the authentication service described in the second bullet point. An example of this feature is an option in the X.400 personal message service. An email recipient isn't allowed to examine the contents of the message body of the email until she has acknowledged that the email was indeed received. The feature is akin to a postal certified letter. The recipient can examine the envelope, but she can't look inside until she signs the receipt.

Securing the Internal Network

The first line of defense for a private network (one in which a user accesses the network directly, without going through the Internet) revolves around user logon issues and the different levels of access provided to network resources. Without question, users should have a valid username and password to log on to the network. Furthermore, the network administrator must control the assignment of usernames and passwords to all users. A set of rules should be devised to assign usernames and passwords so that someone who attempts to access the network by hijacking a particular user account can't guess them.

Resources on the network can also be secured by assigning the appropriate level of access to the resource for each user on the network. For example, most users only need to be able to read a particular database file on the network. So, it would make sense to give those users only the read permission for rights to that file.

Both user authentication and resource permissions are important to basic network security. Let's take a closer look at how a network administrator can use authentication and permissions to secure the internal network.

User Access

The network administrator is responsible for creating user accounts. Every Network Operating System (NOS) provides a built-in administrator's account that can create and modify network user accounts and manage the resources on the network. This administrator's account is given various names in different OSs, such as root, admin, or administrator.

Not only does the network administrator determine the naming conventions for user accounts, but he also controls the rules for user passwords and the logon hours, as well as days that a particular user can log on to the network.

Assigning complex usernames to your users doesn't enhance network security. It only enhances the possibility of users forgetting their usernames. Let's face it—most network administrators assign usernames based on the first initial and last name of the user. It's a fairly consistent and convenient way to assign usernames.

Creating Usernames

Although the number of characters that can be used to create a username varies per NOS, every OS has naming conventions that you should be aware of before you create your user accounts. For example, Windows provides you with 20 characters for a username. NetWare eDirectory usernames can be up to 64 characters. Certain characters can't be used in usernames. Typically, characters such as the slash (/), backslash (\), and other special characters can't be used in usernames. Some OSs allow spaces to be used in the usernames, and others don't. Again, you need to know your NOS's naming conventions before you create usernames.

Password Protection

The password provides security for the network authentication process. The network administrator (you and your staff) must develop a set of rules for the type of passwords that are allowed on the network. Although you can assign passwords to your users, it's a better use of your time to create the rules for passwords on the network and allow your users to create (and update) their own passwords based on your rules. NOSs allow you to set the conditions that must be met for a password, such as the number of characters, the inclusion of both alphanumeric and numeric characters, and whether the password can contain the user's name.

The best practice for passwords is to use what are called strong passwords. What constitutes a strong password varies slightly from NOS to NOS, but in general terms, a strong password is one that wouldn't be easy to guess by someone who has hijacked a user's account and is attempting to access the network. Microsoft defines a strong password as follows:

▶ It contains at least seven characters.

▶ It doesn't contain user, real, or company names.

▶ It doesn't contain complete dictionary words.

▶ It's a combination of numeric, alphanumeric, and nonalphanumeric characters.

On Microsoft Server 2003 and 2008, network password rules and other policies related to passwords (such as enforcing a password history) are handled using Group Policy, which provides a framework for controlling the user and computer environment in a Windows domain. Figure 20.1 shows the password policy settings for 2003. The 2008 window is quite similar. Note that the policies haven't been enabled for strong password protection.

By the Way

Microsoft Group Policy

Group Policy sets rules in a Windows network environment using Group Policy objects. These objects can contain settings for both computers and users. A Windows server is configured with a number of default Group Policy objects; a network administrator can also create additional objects as needed. For a primer on Group Policy, see *Sams Teach Yourself Microsoft Windows Server 2003 in 24 Hours* and *Sams Teach Yourself Microsoft Windows Server 2008 in 24 Hours*.

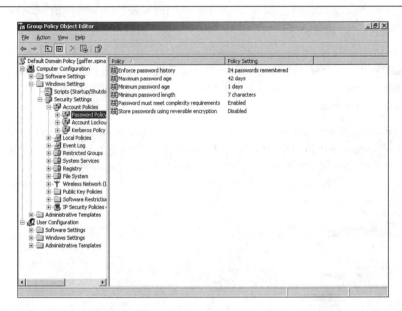

FIGURE 20.1
Microsoft Windows Server 2003 provides Group Policy to control settings related to user password requirements.

Another element related to keeping user passwords secure is requiring your network users to change their passwords after a specific interval. Again, the various NOSs provide you with the administrative tools to create password rules and control the interval for password expiration. Be advised that forcing users to change their passwords on occasion is a good way to protect user accounts, but it can also lead to a lot of headaches in that users either forget their new passwords or start writing down the passwords to remember them. Choose an interval that balances security issues with the short-term memory of your users.

Other Ways to Control User Logons

You can also protect the network from a hacker using a hijacked user account by limiting the logon hours for your users. (If users don't work on the weekend, don't allow weekend logons.) In addition, you can specify the computers that a user can log on to—again, limiting the chance of someone co-opting a username and using it maliciously.

Auditing Logons

After you've done your best to make sure that password protection on the network is strong, you can employ auditing to keep an eye on user logons. Auditing allows you to track both successful and unsuccessful logons. This means if you see numerous unsuccessful logon attempts for a particular user, the user account might have been hijacked and is being used by a hacker attempting to gain access to the network.

Most NOSs have some form of audit mechanism. For example, Windows Server 2003 and 2008 offer their Security log, and UNIX has /var/adm/wtmp, /var/adm/syslog, and other logs. But none of the tools that NOSs provide for auditing do you any good if you don't use them.

Each NOS approaches the enabling of auditing in a different way. Because we've briefly discussed Windows Group Policy, let's look at the enabling of the Auditing Policy on a Windows Server 2003 computer. (Once again, 2008 is similar.) You can access Group Policies for a domain by using the Group Policy Management snap-in, as shown in Figure 20.2.

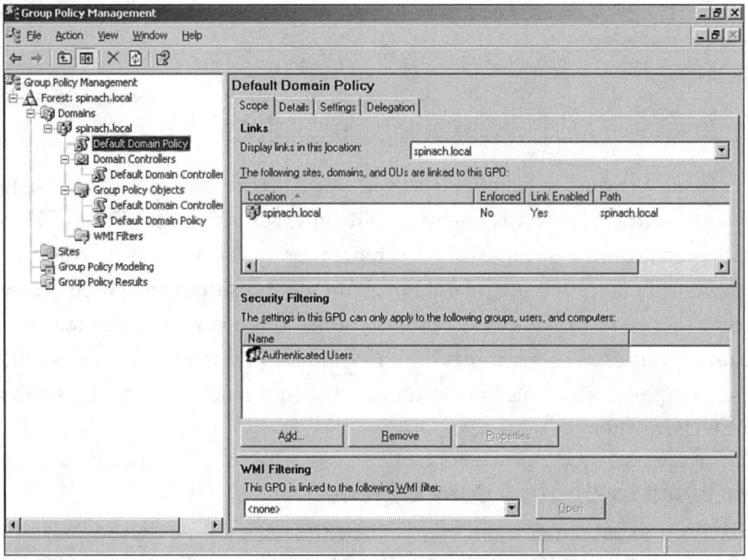

FIGURE 20.2
The Windows Server Group Policy Management snap-in allows you to view the different levels of policies for the domain.

After you've located the particular Group Policy in the management snap-in, you can edit the policy. It's just a matter of right-clicking on a particular policy and then selecting Edit on the shortcut menu that appears. In terms of auditing, the Audit Policy allows you to audit logon events and a number of other events, such as object access and system events.

Figure 20.3 shows the Group Policy Object Editor and the Audit Policy objects available on a server running Microsoft Windows Server 2003. After these various audit objects are enabled, the events are tracked using the Windows Security log. (We'll talk about logs and network monitoring in more detail in Hour 21, "Managing a Network.")

As you can see from our Microsoft example, you can audit logon events and other events that allow you to keep tabs on your network. For example, attempts to access certain items on the network can be audited, allowing you to not only track potential hackers by logon attempts but also attempt to access certain data files or other resources on the network.

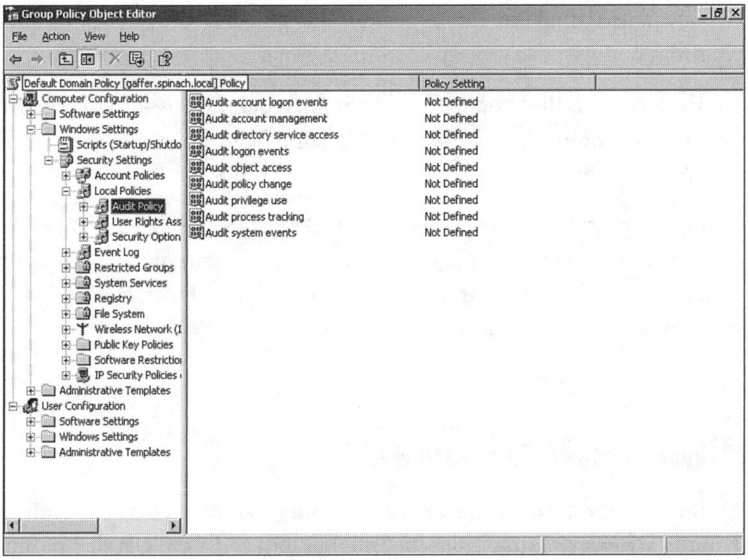

FIGURE 20.3
Auditing is enabled using the Windows Group Policy Object Editor.

Disabling Accounts After Unsuccessful Logon Attempts

When you're setting the different configuration parameters for user accounts, you can set the number of unsuccessful logons that you'll allow before an account is disabled. The settings vary from NOS to NOS, but you should use this feature as another way to secure user accounts. If someone has obtained a username, you don't want to give him the opportunity to guess passwords and then access the network.

Resource Permissions

Securing the network using strategies related to user accounts and passwords is just one way of securing the internal network. Another method of securing important data and resources on the network relates to user rights or permissions to those resources. After a user has logged on to the network, she typically needs to access resources on a file or print server. The level of access that each user has to a share or the volume on a file server is up to the network administrator.

Each NOS has a method of assigning permission (or rights) to folders or directories on network servers. Although it's convenient to give all your users the same access to a resource, you should take into account that each user requires a different level of access to a particular resource; not everyone on the network needs to modify data. For example, an accountant needs to be able to edit spreadsheets on a server, whereas an administrative assistant only needs to be able to view or read the data contained in the file. However, assigning individual permissions for each user to each resource is time-consuming and a hassle to keep organized (in terms of documentation).

A fine feature of NOSs is that you can create groups and then assign access permissions or rights to the group. Then group membership determines the level of access that a user has to particular resources.

Although access rights don't necessarily keep hackers off your internal network, they do allow you to minimize the damage that a careless user can make to important data files or the level of access that a hacker has to a particular resource when they commandeer a particular user account.

Dealing with Viruses

Another threat to your network's security is the virus, explained earlier in this hour. Granted, many viruses emanate from the Internet, but some are generated internally; thus, they're explained in more detail in this section. For this discussion, we concentrate on viruses, but keep in mind that so-called antivirus software typically guards against related attacks, such as worms, Trojan horses, and bombs.

Viruses come in several varieties. Numerous virus types have evolved over the years, and are summarized here, classified based on how they infect a computer. For all, the best defense is antivirus software.

▶ **Boot sector viruses**—Some of the first viruses were boot sector viruses. They're so named because they infect the first sector (the boot sector) of a disk or hard drive. A boot sector virus typically spreads through infected external disks or other removable storage media. Boot sector virus infections are helped along by user forgetfulness. If I place a boot sector virus–infected disk in my computer, nothing happens unless I reboot the system (turn it off for the day and then turn it back on the next morning) and have forgotten to remove the infected disk from the drive. On bootup, the boot sector virus is loaded into the computer's memory (because the computer tries to boot from the external disk). The virus can then infect the hard drive or any disks you place in the external drive after the computer is up and running.

▶ **File viruses**—File viruses infect an executable program, such as an EXE or COM file. When the infected file is run, the file virus is loaded into the computer's RAM. It can then infect other executable files as they're run on the computer. A form of the file virus is the overwriting virus, which overwrites the executable file that it infects.

▶ **Macro viruses**—The macro virus is a fairly recent virus type. Macro viruses are written in a macro language, such as Visual Basic code or the language built into, say, a word processor package. It can infect documents and spreadsheet data files rather than executables. When an infected document is loaded into an application, such as Microsoft Word, the virus code runs as any other macro would in that particular application. Another scary thing about macro viruses is that they aren't OS specific. Because Microsoft Excel can run on a Macintosh and a Windows-based PC, the macro virus can be spread between the two platforms if the infected Excel worksheet is shared. Also, macro viruses aren't confined to Microsoft applications and have popped up in other office suites, such as Lotus SmartSuite. An example of a macro virus is the famous Melissa virus, a Word macro virus that automatically spreads itself via email. When in doubt, don't open those loving attachments.

▶ **Multipartite viruses**—A multipartite virus has the characteristics of both a boot sector virus and a file virus. It can spread from the boot sector of a drive to another drive, and it can attack executable files on the computer. Some multipartite viruses can even infect device drivers (such as the drivers for your network interface card, or NIC).

The only way to keep network computers free of viruses is to invest in antivirus software and run the software frequently. Antivirus software is available in various configurations ranging from desktop file scanning to server-based file scanning to firewall-based file scanning. It's wise to have as many file scanners as possible between the user and his files (whether the files come from the Internet or the local network). Although slight performance degradation is involved with virus scanning, time spent cleaning out virus-infected systems is time well spent. Typically, virus software vendors have a method in which the software that is installed on each computer can be automated and maintained successfully with minimal user input.

Protecting the Internal Network from External Attacks

The discussions thus far in this hour have emphasized measures to secure networks that have no gateways to external networks, such as the Internet. As mentioned earlier, you must address internal threats, but the major dangers come from outside. In this section, we expand our analysis to include the big, bad Internet.

Keep in mind that the earlier discussions on security problems and preventions apply to the interfaces with external networks as well. What's the difference between internal and external network security? For external interfaces, we must add more ingredients to the security soup.

For Internet connectivity, Transmission Control Protocol/Internet Protocol (TCP/IP) is now the standard L_4/L_3 protocol stack. However, TCP/IP and the User Datagram Protocol (UDP) were not designed with security in mind. As discussed in Hour 14, "Connecting to the Internet: Initial Operations," each server protocol in the TCP/IP stack communicates with a well-known port number. As examples, Hypertext Transfer Protocol (HTTP) operates on port 80, and FTP operates on ports 20 and 21. Hundreds of well-known port numbers are registered though the Internet authorities. Each of these ports is a potential path for an attack on a network. Hackers employ a variety of technical tricks to penetrate network security walls. The TCP/IP protocol stack and both client and NOSs provide holes that hackers can exploit. Fortunately, firewalls offer a strategy for blocking these ports.

Firewalls

Even though firewalls are covered in this hour under the subject of securing internal networks from external attacks, these devices are also common in internal local area networks (LANs).

In addition, most OSs and NOSs come with firewall software. The PC I'm using as I type this paragraph is loaded with Vista firewall software, as well as Verizon firewall software. In addition, for some of my Internet connections, I use AOL, which executes its own firewall software for the connection. The router I use to connect to the Internet also executes firewall software. Wow. That's four firewalls, not including the firewall software in the servers.

I recognize a portion of my response time delays are attributable to multiple executions of code, some of which engage in redundant scans and checks. I could opt for configuring the packages to make them more efficient or simply turn one or more of them off. In my Windows XP PC, I have done just that. For my Vista PC, I've decided to let Microsoft, Verizon, and AOL perform their security operations without my inter-ference. Thus far, I've yet to encounter a can of worms—or viruses.

In its simplest terms, a firewall is a system that protects trusted networks from untrusted networks. The concept of trusted and untrusted networks depends on the organization. In some situations, there are both trusted and untrusted networks within a company, depending on the need to know and the need to protect certain resources. In one of my former jobs, the organization installed a firewall on its LAN for the sole purpose of preventing all people—except six employees—from accessing sensitive financial and economic data.

Packet Filtering

One of the key operations that a firewall performs is packet filtering. This term describes an operation in which certain packets are allowed to pass through the fire-wall and others aren't. The filtering operations are based on a set of rules encoded in the software running the firewall. The most common type of packet filtering from the standpoint of a conventional router is done on IP packets. The router examines the IP addresses to make sure the source and destination addresses are legitimate—that is, whether they're trusted addresses.

Filtering on IP addresses can create a tricky situation because many users send and receive traffic in a dynamic fashion. Surfing the Web results in IP addresses at the websites being placed in the packets.

Another common filtering process is on Internet port numbers. This filtering usually takes place in servers and user machines and not routers, because the operation con-sumes overhead. One approach is to filter on certain IP addresses in the router and filter on port numbers in the server or user machine.

It's a good idea to carefully check your vendor's router and server filtering fea-tures to determine if their firewall capabilities meet your needs. Nothing pre-cludes you from creating and configuring the details of the firewall. For example, several inexpensive, effective Linux firewall distributions are available from the Internet. I recommend that you check out www.coyotelinux.com.

Did you Know?

Windows Firewall Settings

If you're using Windows on your computer, you have some control over the firewall software. Using the General tab in Windows Firewall, you can do the following:

▶ Set the firewall to On, which is recommended. With this setting, most programs are blocked with the firewall. You can unblock a program by adding it to the Exceptions list (with the Exceptions tab).

▶ Block all incoming connections, which block all unsolicited attempts to connect to your computer. This might be useful when you want protection when online at an airport or other public venue with a public wireless network. You can still view most web pages and send and receive email and instant messages.

▶ Setting the firewall to Off isn't recommended, unless you have another firewall running on your computer.

Other Key Security Protocols

In this part of the hour we examine several important security systems and protocols. By no means do they represent all the offerings available. But they're found in most vendors' PC OSs, server NOSs, and router OSs.

Password Authentication Protocol (PAP)

The Password Authentication Protocol (PAP) is an older authentication protocol used to authenticate a user to a network server. Most NOS remote servers support PAP. As well, PAP is still used by Point-to-Point Protocol (PPP) in some products, but many offerings have replaced it with CHAP.

Challenge-Handshake Authentication Protocol (CHAP)

As the name implies, the Challenge Handshake Authentication Protocol (CHAP) authenticates a user to an authentication entity, such as a server. CHAP has been used for many years in conjunction with PPP to validate remote login users. Verification takes place with the use of a shared secret, such as a user's password. CHAP also protects against a playback attack.

Remote Authentication Dial In User Service (RADIUS)

RADIUS is yet another Internet protocol and is based on a client/server model. It is used to authenticate remote users with user names and passwords. It also supports the negotiation of configuration services between a user (client) and a server, such as the use of PPP, Telnet, and rlogin.

Transactions between the client and RADIUS server are authenticated through the use secret keys. In addition, user passwords are encrypted between the client and

RADIUS server. RADIUS supports several authentication schemes. For example, a user supplies authentication data to the server either by directly answering the server's login/password prompts or by using PAP or CHAP protocols.

Secure Sockets Layer (SSL)

Secure Sockets Layer (SSL) is used for authentication. Examples are protecting a website and securing credit card information that is sent to the web merchant. An SSL certificate enables encryption of sensitive information during online transactions. When a web browser communicates with a server, an SSL handshake authenticates the server and the client. Encryption takes place with a unique session key.

Each SSL certificate contains authenticated information about the certificate owner. A CA, such as VeriSign, verifies the identity of the certificate owner when it's issued.

Software, such as Linux, supports SSL and allows users to create their own SSL certificate for secure HTTP communications with SSL-capable web servers. For example, an Apache web server is SSL-capable. Also, a number of trusted third-party certificate signers are available. I've mentioned VeriSign. You might want to check out others as well, such as GlobalSign, EnTrust, RapidSSL, and GlobalTrust.

Point-to-Point Tunneling Protocol (PPTP)

PPTP is an extension to PPP that tunnels IP packets inside encrypted PPP packets. It's available in Windows Server 2008 and uses Microsoft Point-to-Point Encryption (MPPE) for the encryption operations.

Secure Socket Tunneling Protocol (SSTP)

Secure Socket Tunneling Protocol (SSTP), a recent addition to the suite of security protocols, is available on Windows Vista and Windows Server 2008. SSTP is an extension to PPP allowing remote access data to pass through a firewall that would normally block PPP and Layer 2 Tunneling Protocol (L2TP) traffic. SSTP encapsulates PPTP data over an SSL channel by using the HTTP Security (HTTPS) protocol.

Secure Shell (SSH)

Secure Shell (SSH) is a common set of software found on UNIX and Linux OSs. You should consider using it if you need secure communications between two devices on your network. It provides better security than older packages, such as rlogin.

DNS Security Protocol (DNSSEC)

DNS Security Protocol (DNSSEC), another authentication protocol, is used to guard against receiving invalid DNS information from servers. Although this possibility isn't common, it's indeed possible that a hacker might want to get "in the middle" of a DNS server and client to intercept their communications.

DNSSEC is available on Windows Server 2008 and can be used to configure DNS zones so they can be authenticated. DNSSEC uses asymmetric keys for its operations.

Internet Security Protocol (IPSec)

The more recent implementations of security products now support the IP Security Protocol (IPSec). IPSec is an Internet standard providing the following security features: (a) access control, (b) origin authenticity, (c) replay protection, (d) privacy, and (e) integrity. With a Windows server, you can provide these end-to-end services from client-to-client, server-to-server, and client-to-server by using a feature in IPSec called the transport mode. Let's review the transport mode and compare it to another IPSec option: the tunnel mode.

With the transport mode, IPSec protects traffic (upper layer data carried in the IP packet) between hosts—that is, end to end. Depending on the installation, it might also protect parts of the IP header. The tunnel mode encapsulates the original IP packet with yet another IP header and operates between hosts or routers (gateways). It protects completely the inner IP header (thus, the user's IP header) and parts of the outer IP header.

What to Choose?

As you can see, you have a wide choice of security tools. I suggest you study all the security features offered in your OS, NOS, and router software packages and then decide which combinations are best for your organization. You'll find some of the operations redundant, so you might want to disable them. But be careful about turning off these settings. I've found that their duplications to do no harm, and by turning them off, you might end up deactivating a specific, unique service that isn't running in the other packages. On the other hand, it's a good idea to experiment with the packages to evaluate the delay and overhead of running them versus their benefit.

Wireless Networks

In Hour 7, "Mobile Wireless Networking," we discussed the basics of wireless networking. In terms of security, wireless networking provides several challenges. These have been made obvious by a new hacker exploit termed *wardriving*. Wardriving entails driving around with a wireless-enabled laptop computer, which is used to find and connect to unsecured wireless networks. This maneuver might provide free access to the Internet and allow hackers to crack the wireless network. Wardrivers often outfit their vehicles with an external wireless antenna, which makes it easier to find wireless "hotspots." A handheld Global Positioning System (GPS) might help map the borders of the hotspot.

How do you protect your network against wardriving? First, you need to learn how your wireless network access point is configured. (An access point is the device that allows wireless clients to connect to a wired network, which is discussed in more detail in Hour 7.) Regardless of the vendor of your access point, the access point has a default configuration, which includes settings such as the administrative password, the default subnet (the range of IP addresses for the device), and security settings related to the 802.11 security protocols Wired Equivalent Privacy (WEP) and Wi-Fi Protected Access (WPA).

Wardrivers know that the default configuration for an access point makes it easy to promiscuously connect to a wireless network. Be aware that you can't run a wireless network out of the box; you must custom configure access points with the highest security possible.

However, even changing default settings for access points doesn't necessarily protect the network. For example, wireless networks use a network name or service set identifier (SSID) that identifies the wireless network. The SSID is used by mobile devices to connect to access points on the wireless network. Each access point vendor configures its access points with a default SSID. For example, access points from Linksys (a company providing wireless access points and NICs) use the default SSID "linksys."

It makes sense to change the default SSID for added protection because wardrivers know what the default SSIDs are for most network access points. However, even changing the SSID doesn't protect the wireless network all that much. SSIDs can be determined using a packet sniffer because they appear in packets as plain text.

Even being conscientious in terms of configuring wireless access points and other wireless devices isn't going to protect a wireless network from wardrivers with too much time on their hands. You need to configure the currently available security protocols (WEP and especially WPA) on access points and take advantage of the security that these protocols provide.

Beyond access point configuration (including security protocols), you can take advantage of other strategies such as virtual private networking. For a higher level of security, you have to go beyond what the 802.11 standards currently provide and take advantage of third-party products. For example, Air Defense provides such products as RogueWatch, a monitoring device, which allows you to monitor your wireless environment for rogue access points and neighboring wireless networks protecting your network from unauthorized connections.

Although wireless networking provides efficient and inexpensive access to internal and external networks, security issues might preclude its use when network devices exchange highly sensitive data. If you do deploy wireless strategies on your network, remember that wardrivers are probably driving around right outside your building. Part of your defense is to configure your machines with protocols such as DNSSEC, SSL, SSH, SSTP, and IPSec. As well, installing a package, such as RogueWatch, allows you to monitor your wireless connections.

WEP and WPA

In Hour 7, we mentioned the WEP and the WPA protocols. Because of some security weaknesses in WEP, it has been deprecated by the Institute of Electronic and Electrical Engineers (IEEE). WPA is now the recommended wireless security protocol. It uses a higher level of encryption than WEP and employs a dynamic key exchange, which doesn't exist in WEP.

As of this writing, WPA is still new and undergoing shakedown. If you're using Wi-Fi in your network, I recommend that you do some research before making decisions on your wireless security configuration. Check out the latest certification of WPA by the Wi-Fi Alliance at www.wi-fi.org.

Best Practices for Securing a Network

We've explained that you need to require strong passwords on user accounts. Also, you should make sure your users change their passwords periodically. These procedures are important first steps for securing user access to the network. Controlling other user behaviors—such as the hours they can log on and the number of concurrent connections that a particular user account can have on the network—are also effective ways to build a sound security system.

Here's a general checklist of best practices related to network security:

- ▶ Make passwords secret.
- ▶ Ensure users log out of the network at the end of their workday.

▶ Maintain security audit logs on your systems. Look for odd patterns of access: Should the junior accounting clerk be logged in to the network at 2:00 a.m.? Question the entries in this log just as you would question phone calls on your business long-distance service. Keep records of questionable access.

▶ Add virus-checking software to your system. Ideally, you'll have one kind of antivirus software on your firewall, others on your servers, and still others on your workstations. Although this might appear to be overkill, you don't want to have to deal with a network-wide virus infection.

▶ Build your network model in a way that fosters security. Adding firewalls to secure the network's connection to the Internet is a must.

▶ Make certain your systems are patched against TCP/IP DoS attacks and different types of email-related attacks. Install the most recent updates provided by your software vendors on both your server and client computers. Make certain you've set software to allow your vendors (OS, NOS, wireless, router, and so on) to keep their security packages up-to-date by automatically downloading their changes.

▶ Instruct your users and system administrators that they aren't to give out passwords, user IDs, or other computer security–related material over the phone unless they're confident the information will be secure.

▶ Physically secure your server computers. Allow only password access to server's consoles, and log all attempts to gain entry to those systems.

▶ Secure backup media in a locked area. (Backup strategies are discussed in Hour 21.

Create a network security plan that includes user education. Security awareness in the user community can go a long way toward securing an organization's network. Keep in mind that no matter how small your company, you always run the risk of attack. The person in charge of network security must never forget to close the gate *before* the cows get out.

Summary

In this hour, we examined the issues related to securing computer networks. We discussed how to use password policies and resource rights to help secure the network. We also discussed the external attacks that hackers can visit upon your network. Solutions such as firewalls and the Internet security protocols were covered in relation to different hacker attacks. We also examined a checklist of actions you can take to keep your network secure.

Q&A

Q. *Can using password expiration as a security measure be counterproductive?*

A. It depends on the effectiveness of your user security education program. The security administrator needs to balance the use of password expiration with the fact that too many password changes (over time) confuse users. They forget their passwords or continue to attempt to reuse their dog's name. In addition, the sudden loss of access to the network can generate resentment from the recent but now former users of the network. So, use common sense when setting up password expiration intervals.

Q. *What security procedures must a security administrator make certain are operational in the network?*

A. 1. The assurance that the user's data isn't examined by unauthorized parties.

2. The assurance that a legitimate party has sent the data that the user received.

3. The assurance that a user's transmitted data isn't altered before it reaches the end recipient. Additionally, the assurance that the data the user receives hasn't been changed.

4. The assurance that a user's resource (files, data, software, etc.) won't experience unauthorized access.

5. The assurance that the receiver of a user's transmission won't be able to deny or disavow the legitimate reception of the transaction.

Q. *Where can you obtain the procedures and services described in the previous question/answer?*

A. All computer OSs and NOSs now provide some or all of these services. In addition, many of them are also available with the Internet security protoocols.

Managing a Network

What You'll Learn in This Hour:

- ▶ Ideas for maintaining and upgrading a network
- ▶ Server and client licensing
- ▶ More details on backing up files
- ▶ Disaster recovery planning

In this hour, we examine key issues a network administrator faces while managing a network. We discuss upgrading network hardware and delve into more detail on redundant array of inexpensive disks (RAID, introduced in Hour 5, "Network Concepts"), with an analysis of how to configure RAID arrays and establish a backup schedule. We also look at some of the issues related to client and Network Operating System (NOS) licensing. We complete the hour with an examination of one of the most important jobs of a network manager: planning and executing a disaster recovery plan for the network.

Upgrading the Network

After your network is built, a natural response is to sit back, relax, and enjoy the fruits of your labor. If the network is operating properly and is stable, it's tempting to put your feet up on the desk and kick back. However, given that hardware and software versions change often, it's pretty much a given that you're going to get caught in upgrade cycles. Obviously, it's in your best interests and the best interests of your users to keep changes transparent. It's also in your best interests to temper management enthusiasm for a new technology they happen to have seen advertised on TV. By advising moderation and testing, you help maintain network functionality and cut down on unnecessary upgrades.

Although it's difficult to serve in the role of naysayer, an important aspect of your job is to maintain and upgrade the network so that your company is getting the most bang for its buck and using the appropriate technology for its business. For various reasons, return on investment (ROI) is difficult to calculate for computer equipment and software. The use of computer hardware or software can't be calculated in an absolute fashion; it's pointless to try to calculate the value of a memo written on a user's PC. But it's your job to keep the network in the best shape possible and substantiate any budgetary needs in as logical a fashion as possible.

Network upgrades should be based on the needs of the company in terms of the business tools that employees need to get their jobs done effectively (both in terms of cost and the users' time). So, it's obvious that as computer hardware and software evolves, you'll need to replace servers, client machines, NOSs, and client applications.

Let's look at some basic strategies for managing hardware growth and upgrades. We can then examine issues related to software upgrades and growth. Before delving into the details, keep this idea in mind: The three most important factors for making the management of a network a successful affair are (1) a satisfied user community; (2) a satisfied user community; and (3) a satisfied user community.

> **Monitoring Network Health**
>
> I don't think any network administrator thinks he can sit back and relax after a network is up and running. Maintaining the network and developing strategies for detecting network problems is a set of tasks that will keep any network team busy. For more about monitoring and logging server performance and events, see Hour 22, "Network Troubleshooting."

Managing Hardware Upgrades and Growth

Not only will network hardware (including client PCs) need to be upgraded over time, but you'll add systems and other supporting hardware because of network growth. Any successful company will grow. This means you won't only have to keep existing employees up and running effectively on the network, but you'll need to plan for and act on network growth. Some strategies for managing upgrades and growth follow:

▶ **Set flexible standards for hardware**—Every year or so, create a standard computer configuration based on the current most powerful computers. Try to stick to it for as long as possible, but not for too long. The benefits of this approach are twofold. The first benefit is that the computers are a known quantity. (If you spec a computer and discover a hardware bug, quirk, or incompatibility, you know that the remainder of the computers of that type will likely share that trait.) The second benefit is cost; over one year, the cost of most computers will decline significantly, making your bottom-line staff very happy.

▶ **Determine whether a complete computer upgrade is required or whether an incremental upgrade is acceptable**—Given the impressive pace at which computers are becoming faster and more powerful, many OEM computer manufacturers and a host of third-party companies are building upgrades that range from faster processors that plug in to the original processor socket to memory upgrades. It's possible that a processor upgrade and an extra shot of memory can extend the life of many an old PC by providing adequate performance at a bargain price (at least in comparison to the cost of a new computer).

▶ **Maintain a complete inventory of what's in your computers, not just the CPU serial number**—If you know what's inside the computer, you can more readily make a call about whether it's wiser to upgrade or replace it. This inventory list also helps when a part fails; rather than taking the case apart, you can simply look up the failed part in your database and order another.

▶ **Perform regular hardware audits with network management software**—If you have to do your inventory by going from computer to computer, it will never get done. However, most network management software has a hardware audit feature; used properly, this feature can help you diagnose a system on-the-fly.

The bottom line is that no matter how big your network and client base, you have to know the different hardware and software configurations that are running on the network. New employees will likely receive newer equipment when they come on board (if they're an addition to the staff rather than replacing a staff member). But you must be sure that veteran employees aren't left in the lurch with older systems that make them less effective (than a newer employee).

Managing Software Upgrades and Growth

In many ways, software is easier to manage than hardware. First, companies tend to standardize on certain software; not using that software puts a user outside the loop. Second, use of software has legal ramifications that force a company to treat software usage more rigorously than hardware. After all, hardware is a capital asset and can be depreciated out of existence; software—even expensive software—is often expensed. It's simply written off as a cost of doing business.

Unlike with hardware, with software, you can do a tremendous amount of management, ranging from setting corporate standards to auditing the versions used. The strategies you can follow for managing software are as follows:

▶ **Use site licensing or volume licensing on your network**—Most software vendors sell volume licenses. Even if only a few workers are using the application, you might still qualify for some kind of volume or site licensing. If you can't use volume or site licensing, it's important that you have enough individual licenses to cover all your products. We examine another aspect of licensing—server and client licensing—in the next section.

▶ **Work with senior management to come up with company standards for software**—This thought should be self-evident, but it's worth discussing. Suppose your company has standardized on Microsoft Word for word processing, but you have a user who insists on using another product. It's much easier to support and license a single word processing product. So having a mandate from senior management that all users will use a particular product will provide you with better control of client behavior and software use.

▶ **Unauthorized software is unsupported software**—On any network, no matter how few users, you must lay down this rule related to software installation: No user-installed software is allowed on the network. If a user installs her own software in defiance of such an edict, and the installation creates a problem, the only support you'll provide is to reset the user's PC back to the original, approved configuration. Allowing unauthorized software is problematic, not just because it's wrong (users do have a proclivity for installing unlicensed copies of software in a work environment), but because it raises the bar on the management hurdle to an unacceptable level.

▶ **Create a standard installation, and stick to it if possible**—If you can install a fixed set of applications on each hard disk so that all disks match, that's good. Most NOSs let you install standard installations on network clients. (For example, Microsoft Server 2003 provides the Remote Installation Service.) Also, products, such as Norton Ghost and Symantec Drive Image, allow you to create a standard client configuration (including applications) that can be quickly installed on any client system using the same standard hardware.

▶ **Use a license management utility**—License management utilities ensure you're never in violation of the terms of your software agreements. License management utilities can be a pain for users who can't get an application because it's at its license limits, but they ensure that you're in compliance. Thanks to the efforts of the Business Software Alliance (BSA) and the Software Publishers Association (PSA), noncompliance is becoming increasingly expensive. It's not uncommon to see extremely large fines for gross and willful license violators.

In terms of managing software upgrades, it's important you make new software tools and more up-to-date versions of software products available to as many users as possible. In most cases, your software upgrade cycle is linked to your hardware upgrade cycle. This approach stems from most new software packages requiring a more robust hardware configuration to operate efficiently.

Using Network Management Software

If you have a medium to large network, you might want to invest in network management software. These enterprise tools allow you to keep track of software installations, hardware configurations, and even supply software distribution and client behavior tracking mechanisms. Different network management software packages are available, such as HP's OpenView, Sun's SunNet Manager, and Microsoft's Systems Center Configuration Server (formerly Systems Management Server).

By the Way

Dealing with NOS and Client Licensing

It's not only essential that you ensure that all applications running on the network and individual client computers are properly licensed, but you must also ensure that you have the appropriate number of client licenses to access the various servers and their NOS. Application licensing is fairly straightforward; you need a license for every occurrence of that application running on the network clients, including remote users. This can take the form of individual licenses or some sort of volume or site licensing (or a combination of these licensing strategies). Client licensing in relation to NOSs, however, can be a little more complicated because more than one licensing scenario can be available for a particular NOS.

A NOS requires that you have a server license for your server (a separate license for each server) and client licenses for your network clients. This doesn't just mean that you have a license for the client operating system (OS) but a license that makes it legal for you to connect to the server as a client.

For example, you can buy a Novell NetWare base package that licenses the server and five client connections. To license more clients, you buy what's called a connection additive license. These additive client licenses range from the addition of 5 to 500 users.

Each NOS platform has its own licensing scheme. When you work with open source Linux products, you might not have to deal with licensing, but no matter what platform you're using, you should take the time to research the type of licensing required for each client on the network. Be sure to examine the discounts offered for multiple users of a package. They vary widely among the vendors.

Microsoft Windows Server 2003 Licensing

Microsoft Windows servers put an interesting spin on client licensing. Windows Server 2003 provides you with three possibilities for licensing network clients: Per User, Per Device, or Per Server.

Per User means you'll purchase a license for each network user on the network. Each of these users can connect to any and all the servers on the network. Per Device means you can license each computer or device, such as a Windows-based PDA. Because of the device license, the device can then legally connect to any and all servers on the network. Per Server means you're licensed for a certain number of concurrent connections to the server. If you have 50 licenses, 50 clients can connect to the server.

Per Server licenses can save you money if you have a network situation in which your employees actually work in shifts. Because only a subset of the employees is connected to the network servers, you can go with the Per Server connection model. When employees put in the same hours, you're probably better off going with the Per User or Per Device models.

All NOSs supply you with some type of utility that you use to add server or client licenses to the network. Microsoft Windows Server 2003, for example, provides the Licensing snap-in, which allows you to add licenses to the network. Figure 21.1 shows the Windows Server 2003 Licensing snap-in.

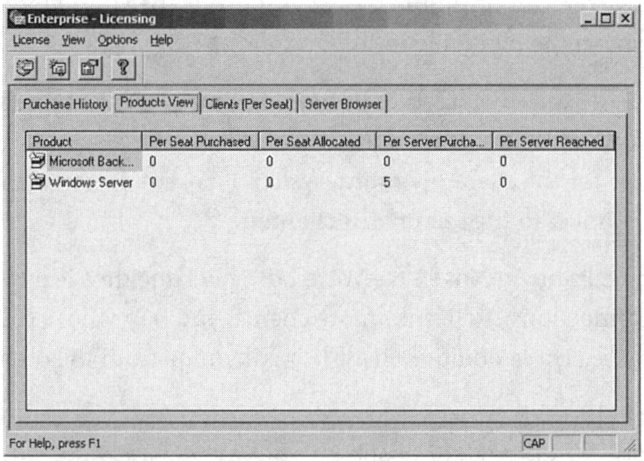

FIGURE 21.1
NOSs, such as Windows Server 2003, include a utility for recording server and client licenses.

Microsoft Windows Server 2008 Licensing

Windows Server 2008 offers Per Server licensing. It also offers Per Seat mode, in which you can purchase a license of each network user. Each of these users can connect to any and all the servers on the network. It's akin to 2003's Per User license, but with a different name.

2008 also offers the User Access license, which allows a user to connect to network services using any device, such as a computer or a PDA. In addition, customers can use the External Connector license to connect to licensed network services. For more information on Microsoft licensing, go to www.microsoft.com/licensing.

It's quite important that you keep track of all your server and client licenses. The same goes for application licenses. You should have a well-organized filing system that allows you to access any hard copy licenses you have; also make sure you use software utilities that allow you to keep track of your licenses. Being caught without the appropriate number of licenses is a good way to lose your job because it could result in fines and bad publicity for your company.

Backing Up Network Data

Hour 5 introduced RAID implementations. RAID provides a method of creating redundancy on network servers, which can help protect valuable network data. The best way to protect network data, however, is backing up that data. Creating a backup plan and implementing that plan is an important aspect of managing an existing network.

When your network is operating smoothly and you aren't detecting problems in your server logs and performance monitoring tables, it might be difficult to accept that you could have a sudden meltdown, resulting in the loss of data. But it *does* happen. It's much wiser to assume that you'll have a crash at some point and to prepare adequately for it.

The Basics of Backup

On first inspection, it might seem a little confusing when you're trying to put together a backup plan for your network. You want to back up all the important data, but you want to do it as effectively (in terms of time and effort) as possible. Although you might throw up your hands and determine that you'll just do a time-consuming and arduous complete backup periodically, there are ways to plan a backup strategy that will protect all the network data (with minimal loss) yet not require you to spend every evening backing up your servers.

Creating an effective backup strategy begins with a consideration of the following:

- ▶ How much data you have to back up
- ▶ How often you want to back up

▶ Whether or not backing up your data requires dealing with open files and ensuring consistent data sets

▶ On what kind of media you want to store your backed up data

▶ What kind of backup scheme you want to use

The first three items determine the choice of the fourth. We discuss backup schemes in more detail later in this hour.

You can use various types of backup media. Some of the popular tape backup types are as follows:

▶ **Digital audio tape (DAT)**—Developed for sound recording, this small high-density tape format can store up to 80GB of data, depending on the specific tape and compression methods. In 2005, Sony announced its intention to move away from this technology, but DAT is still widely used.

▶ **DLTtape (or just DLT)**—This is a half-inch tape format that's quite popular in the industry. Many Fortune 500 companies use DLT for their backup operations. Some DLT units can store 1,600GB of data.

▶ **8mm**—Similar to the 8mm video format, these 8mm cartridges (also known as 8mm Backup Format) can hold up to 40GB of data and can transfer data at speeds up to 3MB per second.

You can also back up data to removable media drives, such as the Zip and Jaz drives made by Iomega. In addition, you can copy files to CD or DVD if you have access to an appropriate burner. Again, the media type you choose is dictated by the amount of data you need to back up. The media type, obviously, dictates the tape backup drives you use.

Many hardware manufacturers produce tape backup drives, including Seagate, Hewlett-Packard, and Iomega. Some of these products come with decent backup software, and some don't. (You might have to buy the backup software separately.) Most NOSs also supply some type of backup utility. Some are better than others, and you'll have to assess whether you can get by with the NOS backup software or you need something more sophisticated.

After you've chosen and deployed the backup hardware you'll use, you need to establish a backup scheme (as mentioned in our list), which needs to include a backup schedule. Let's look at the different types of backups you can make, and then we'll look at a simple scheme called the "Grandfather-Father-Son scheme."

Types of Backups

Three backup methods are available: full, differential, and incremental. These different types of backups are possible because of file markers, which are attributes placed on a file. (In other words, the file is tagged.) Typically, any OS you work with marks or tags a file after that file has been backed up. A file that has changed since its last backup is also tagged. The use of these tags or markers to denote which files have been backed up and which files have not enables backup software to perform various types of backups. Here's a breakdown of how these backup methods work:

- **Full backup**—This type of backup is also called a normal backup or a daily backup (depending on the backup software you're using). A full backup takes all the files you select for backup and backs them up (no matter how the files are currently marked). The files' attributes are then changed to mark the fact that they have been backed up. (If you change the file after the backup, the marker changes and indicates that the file hasn't been backed up since the last changes were made.)

- **Differential backup**—This type of backup only backs up the files that have changed since their last backup. The differential backup doesn't, however, change the marker attribute indicating that the file has been backed up. It leaves the marker alone, meaning the file still reads that it hasn't been backed up since it was last changed.

- **Incremental backup**—This type of backup backs up only the files that have been changed since the last backup (just as a differential backup does). However, an incremental backup changes the archive marker on the files that are backed up to identify those files as having been backed up (which differs from the differential backup method).

The type of backup you should use depends on the backup scheme that you devise. You should determine a particular time of week when you do a full backup (perhaps on the weekend). You can then use differential and incremental backups (which don't take as long as a full backup) to make sure you have the most recent copies of files that have changed since the full backup. A simple use of a single full backup and then sequential differential backups is discussed in the next section.

The Grandfather-Father-Son Scheme

A simple backup scheme is Grandfather-Father-Son. It sets up a sequence of tapes ensuring proper tape rotation so that you don't lose data.

How do you do it? First, label four tapes (or tape sets, if you're employing a tape changer that uses more than one tape per day) Monday, Tuesday, Wednesday, and Thursday. Then, take four more tapes or tape sets and label them Friday 1, Friday 2, Friday 3, and Friday 4. After you've done this, you've created all your repeating tapes. The remainder of the tapes is labeled Friday 5. The Friday 5 tapes are your archive tapes; you use each one only once (at the end of the cycle) and then archive it. This approach ensures that every five weeks, you have an archive tape.

Next, you have to configure your backup software. Typically, the easiest way to back up is via a differential backup. In differential backups, the Friday tape is a full backup, and each successive tape (Monday through Thursday) captures all the changes since the last Friday full backup tape. With differential backups, you only need two tapes to restore a crashed server: the last Friday full backup and the most recent weekday tape. Most commercial backup software can be configured to do differential backups and often have a Grandfather-Father-Son backup scheme or wizard to set it up.

After your software is configured for differential backup (it's seldom hard to configure), you have to start rotating the tapes. Table 21.1 shows how that works.

TABLE 21.1   The Grandfather-Father-Son Backup Scheme

	Monday	**Tuesday**	**Wednesday**	**Thursday**	**Friday**
First week:					
Tape name	Monday	Tuesday	Wednesday	Thursday	Friday 1
Second week:					
Tape name	Monday	Tuesday	Wednesday	Thursday	Friday 2
Third week:					
Tape name	Monday	Tuesday	Wednesday	Thursday	Friday 3
Fourth week:					
Tape name	Monday	Tuesday	Wednesday	Thursday	Friday 4
Fifth week:					
Tape name	Monday	Tuesday	Wednesday	Thursday	Friday 5

Each fifth Friday tape is the Grandfather; Friday tapes 1 through 4 are the Father tapes; and the Monday through Thursday tapes are the Sons. Every Friday tape except the `Friday 5` tape is reused in each five-week period; Monday through Thursday tapes are reused each week.

The operation is simple. It requires some time to set it up and understand it, but then it usually runs smoothly. One caveat: Make sure you change tapes according to the schedule. If you don't, you'll have incomplete backups and you'll be asking for trouble. Also, store all your `Friday 5` (archive) tapes offsite as part of disaster recovery. We examine disaster recovery issues in the next section.

One more thing: Make sure that you periodically inspect your tapes. Magnetic media have a limited life span and become more likely to fail over time. Just think about how scratched up a home videotape gets when you constantly reuse it to tape shows on your VCR. It makes sense to periodically work new tapes into the process so that you're not working with old and possibly unreliable media.

Network and Disaster Recovery Planning

Having a backup strategy for your network is only one part of what should be a complete disaster recovery plan. No one can predict when disaster will strike. Unfortunately, it often takes a disaster to make people consider disaster recovery planning. In the wake of the September 11, 2001 World Trade Center disaster, disaster recovery has become a hot corporate topic. Companies and institutions have spent more time and resources related to planning what they would do in the event of a disaster.

As the network administrator, your responsibilities related to disaster recovery are making plans that allow you to get important data back into the hands of people who need it, and getting it back quickly. This means your disaster recovery plan needs to be multifaceted and anticipate different levels of disaster. Your plan should not center around one type of disaster, such as an earthquake or fire.

For example, in the case of a major snowstorm, employees might not be able to get to the physical locations of the company offices. Yet your business needs them to be online and working. In this case, your disaster recovery plan might dictate that you activate VPN or dial-in access that allows employees to work from home. On the other hand, in the case of a disaster such as a fire that destroys the corporate offices, you will need to use your backup information to rebuild the network data servers at a new location and provide network access to that data.

You can see from the previous paragraph that different disruptions of business continuity (a fancy way of saying recovering from a disaster) require different solutions.

Any recovery plan you implement needs to address different disaster scenarios. Let's look at some of the basics of fashioning a disaster recovery plan.

Creating a disaster recovery plan requires several stages. Those creating the plan need to know several things, such as the current computing infrastructure, the business impact when the infrastructure is damaged, and suspected vulnerabilities in the infrastructure. Let's examine some of the stages required to assemble the information needed to create the disaster recovery plan.

Defining the Computing Infrastructure

Before planning can take place, you must inventory and define the company's computing environment. This means you need to know how many workstations, servers, and other devices are present on the network.

You can create an inventory of network devices in any spreadsheet program, such as Excel. This information is vital to the recovery plan and should be kept in a safe but easily accessible place (such as offsite) in case you need it. (Inventories are also important when dealing with insurance companies.)

Create a detailed network map (you should have created one when you planned the network), as well as other documentation that offers an understanding of what's on the network. Before you can create a recovery plan for the IT infrastructure, the project team creating the plan must understand the IT infrastructure.

You can create network maps using a variety of software programs. Microsoft Visio and SmartDraw are easy-to-use tools for creating network diagrams (and were used to create many of the network diagrams in this book). Another aspect of defining the network infrastructure is a listing of network support positions. It's important that management be aware of the personnel required to keep the network functioning on a daily basis. This means that a listing of positions and functions should be created to use in the disaster recovery planning process.

Not only do you need to assess the current state of the network infrastructure, including personnel, but you should assess future needs of the computing environment. This provides information on how the disaster recovery plan needs to be amended over time to remain effective.

Assessing Business Impact

The next phase of the disaster recovery planning process requires you to assess business impact. This involves identifying critical functions and systems in the computing environment and how their disruption would affect the core business of the company.

For example, let's assume you work at a university. If there were a lightning strike that destroyed switches providing Internet connectivity to dormitories, you would end up with disgruntled students who wanted to surf the Web. However, the impact on the overall business of the institution isn't affected as dramatically as the meltdown of a database system that holds student records and accounts receivables.

You can see that Internet access in the dorms isn't as critical as access to an important database. Part of the process of identifying critical functions and systems on the network is assessing how long the institution can function with the key system unavailable.

Assessing Computing Environment Vulnerabilities

Another aspect of pooling the information for the disaster recovery plan is assessing the various vulnerabilities in your computing environment. For example, to use the university example again, one vulnerability is the large amount of data traffic that can be caused by students downloading programs, MP3s, and other treasures we don't even want to know about. Let's say that there's a snowstorm and students don't have classes. To bide their time, they sit in their dorm rooms downloading videos and other images. This clogs the network, and employees working from home are affected.

You've identified a potential infrastructure problem. Obviously, this scenario wouldn't constitute a major disaster, but a good thing about doing the network vulnerability assessment is that you can fix some of the things that could create problems before disaster actually strikes.

Another vulnerability is your company's connection to an important resource (such as a financial institution) through a single wide area network (WAN) connection. You can minimize this vulnerability by having a redundant connection made to the resource. Identifying vulnerabilities is really troubleshooting the network before trouble happens (which we discuss in Hour 22).

Other vulnerabilities that you'll find during the assessment might lend themselves to being fixed immediately, removing the vulnerability, or being detailed in the disaster recovery plan. Going through the assessment can be an eye-opening experience in relation to how well your network infrastructure was initially planned and laid out.

Developing the Plan

After the corporate computing environment, disaster business impact, and vulnerabilities have been assessed, your project team can begin to develop the disaster recovery plan. This means that vulnerabilities, contingency plans, and how the plan will be implemented in light of a certain type of disaster must be documented, along with other information such as the inventory and other items discussed previously in this hour.

Although a disaster recovery plan is specific to each type of business or organization, there's information that's common to most disaster plans. These items are as follows:

▶ **Employee contact information**—The plan should include information on contacting key employees in case of a disaster.

▶ **Vendor and customer contact information**—Depending on your business, the plan should include contact information for key vendors and contact information for key customers.

▶ **Location of backup information**—The location of offsite storage facilities for data backup tapes and other network information should be identified.

▶ **A listing of security information**—The plan should provide a way for obtaining user IDs and passwords—particularly those for administrative tasks. If the disaster is the loss of network administrators, this type of information must be available. However, because it's so important to the security of the system, you must consider the disaster recovery plan a highly sensitive document.

▶ **Disaster regrouping location**—The plan should provide information on where employees should go if a disaster strikes and the corporate facilities are no longer usable. This location can be a branch office or another designated space (such as conference space provided by a local hotel). It's a good idea to have a place for all employees to meet; think about the World Trade Center disaster and the fact that it was very difficult to determine whether employees had made it out of the buildings.

▶ **Declaring a disaster**—Although this might seem to go without saying, it's important that the plan detail who is in charge of declaring a disaster. Detailed staff information should also be included in the plan so that employees offsite (or on vacation) can be notified that a disaster has occurred.

▶ **Succession planning**—This is another one of those grim subjects; there needs to be information in the plan designating who is in charge if circumstances change. In other words, if the CEO or president of the company is a victim of the disaster, who should lead the company in the aftermath of the disaster? When John Hinckley shot President Ronald Reagan, Alexander Haig, then secretary of state, declared in a press conference that he was in charge. However, the order of presidential succession places the secretary of state below the vice president, the speaker of the House, and the president pro tempore of the Senate. It's a good idea to specify who will be in charge. Why add more confusion to a bad situation?

This list contains just some of the information that should be part of the recovery plan. Creating a disaster recovery plan is a major undertaking requiring a lot of research and input from people within and outside your organization. Because IT disaster recovery plans mandate the assessment of tangibles (computers, software, and data) and intangibles (user behavior), you should do some research before you begin the planning process. Check out www.sans.org. It's the website of the SANS (SysAdmin, Audit, Network, Security) Institute. You'll find numerous papers and articles on different aspects of disaster planning in the IT environment.

Remember that the purpose of a disaster recovery plan is to allow your company to survive a disaster and then continue with its normal day-to-day business. Although your customers will certainly be sympathetic to your plight, they'll quickly begin to look elsewhere for the services that you provide if it begins to affect their bottom line.

Archives

We mentioned archives several times in this hour. I recommend that you and your team establish a plan for long-range archival of data. The plan must include the user community's directions, because users are the proxy owners of the company's data. Archiving can become expensive, and users might not be aware of the costs of storing data and periodically moving it to fresh physical media. On more than one occasion, I've heard users say, "Save everything, forever! Never know when we'll need it." Compromises are likely in order, and you can make valuable contributions to this important operation by making sure users are aware of the complexity and costs of archiving.

Summary

In this hour, we discussed issues related to managing a network, including upgrading and growing a network. We examined data backup and data backup strategies and issues related to server and client licensing. We also discussed some of the basics of creating a disaster recovery plan for your network.

Q&A

Q. *Do small companies need to worry about making sure they have the appropriate software licensing?*

A. Even a company with one employee needs to adhere to the licensing agreements for software products that are used on its computers. It's illegal to run software without the appropriate licenses. Just because a company is small doesn't mean that a software vendor wouldn't consider action if a license violation was brought to its attention.

Q. *What's the best way to sort through the many choices relating to different types of software licensing programs?*

A. Talk to a knowledgeable software reseller or with the software vendor. Don't be afraid to ask questions and get the facts. Selecting the best licensing scenario for your company can often result in substantial savings.

Q. *Is it necessary to have a formal disaster recovery plan for a small company?*

A. Yes! Even if you're a one-person company, you should have a plan (even if it's stored in your gray matter) to back up your files. It won't be a happy situation to learn your photo disk file of your pet dog is lost forever. Not to mention photos of your mate. Jokes aside, all businesses, regardless of size, should have some sort of disaster recovery plan for their network. There must be a set of steps that have been recorded (and tested) that allow you to get users back on to the network with minimal downtime.

HOUR 22

Network Troubleshooting

What You'll Learn in This Hour:

▶ How to monitor router performance

▶ How to monitor server performance

▶ How to use Internet software tools to diagnose TCP/IP problems

Even the best designed network can experience problems. There can be connectivity issues on the network because of problems such as a faulty network interface card (NIC) or a malfunctioning router. Problems accessing important network services can also crop up because of hardware issues on a server. In this hour, we look at some of the tools and procedures for troubleshooting a network. We examine strategies that allow you to analyze problems before they become unmanageable.

Before going into these details, we introduce two more subjects that are keys to the management of computer networks: Management Information Bases (MIBs) and the Simple Network Management Protocol (SNMP).

MIBs and SNMP

An MIB is a database containing information about key software and hardware components in a network. It's used to monitor and manage these components. An MIB identifies each management component as a managed object with a registered Internet identifier. For example, the official identifier for an Ethernet interface is 1.3.6.1.2.1.2.1.2.3. An MIB also defines the values that you can associate with a managed object, such as a MAC address for a PC attached to an Ethernet LAN and the traffic that this node has processed.

Examples of permissible values that can describe an Ethernet interface are "up," "down," "testing, "time of change in operational status," "number of packets sent and received during a measured time," "number of packets discarded and the reasons," and scores of other important pieces of network management information. In addition, each of these values is identified with a unique Internet ID.

The result of using standardized MIBs is the transparent transmittal and reception of network management information between different machines, perhaps containing vendor-specific hardware and software components. For example, if a Windows server sends an alarm message to say, a Cisco router, it doesn't matter if the two nodes are vendor specific. The message is standardized down to the bit level. It's the responsibility of Windows and Cisco software to make whatever translations are needed to allow this transparency. But then, that's the idea of standardized protocols in the first place.

The Internet publishes hundreds of MIBs and defines thousands of objects. Most software and hardware vendors support them. After all, why reinvent the wheel, especially a wheel that won't work on another chassis? For a look at the prevalence of MIBs, go to www.cisco.com/public/sw-center/netmgmt/cmtk/mibs.shtml.

SNMP is the second major Internet network management tool you should know and use. In fact, SNMP and MIBs are inseparable partners. The MIB defines the information about managed resources, and SNMP is the L_7 protocol that carries this information between nodes. SNMP operates over Transmission Control Protocol (TCP) or User Datagram Protocol (UDP) with Internet port numbers 160, 161, and 162.

SNMP defines the type, structure, and format of the network management messages. For example, one type of SNMP message is an alarm (reporting on an unusual condition); another is a get, which asks another node for some network management information.

Troubleshooting Routers

If your organization has installed its own routers, it's likely they're Cisco routers. If your network is small (perhaps a small business or a home network), it's probable that your broadband Internet service provider (ISP) shipped a router (or routers) to you. In the former situation, you'll be tasked with troubleshooting. In the latter situation, your ISP will handle this chore.

As we've learned in previous hours, most of the router's operations take place at the lower three layers of the Open Systems Interconnection (OSI) model. These operations are rich in function, and some are complex in their implementations. For example, subnetting must be done carefully; otherwise, incorrect IP addresses can cause routing and forwarding errors.

You can use the Cisco Discovery Protocol (CDP)[1] to obtain protocol addresses of neighboring devices and discover the platform of those devices. You can also use CDP to show information about the interfaces that your router uses. CDP is media- and protocol-independent and runs on all Cisco-manufactured equipment, including routers, bridges, access servers, and switches.

Use of SNMP with the CDP MIB allows network management applications to learn the device type and the SNMP information of neighboring devices and to send SNMP queries to those devices.

Each device configured for CDP sends periodic messages, known as advertisements, to a multicast address. Each device advertises at least one address where it can receive SNMP messages. The advertisements also contain Time to Live (TTL) information, which indicates the length of time a receiving device should hold CDP information before discarding it. Each device also listens to the periodic CDP messages sent by others to learn about neighboring devices and determine when their interfaces to the media go up or down.

Cisco offers its CDP to help you in your troubleshooting endeavors. It can transmit network management messages on all active interfaces to confirm the correct operations of network devices, the operating system (OS) version, and associated Internet Protocol (IP) addresses. It can operate alongside various Network Operating Systems (NOSs) and OSs. You can determine if your Windows software has CDP loaded by clicking Control Panel, Device Manager, View, Devices by Connection, Show Hidden Devices.

A recent addition to CDP is on-demand routing (ODR). You can use it to discover other Cisco devices, the device type, and the IP address. ODR allows routing information to be contained in its messages. This feature simplifies your job of running and managing routing protocols, such as the Internet's Open Shortest Path First (OSPF), which is a widely used route discovery protocol.

Monitoring Server Hardware

There's an old sport adage that the best defense is a good offense. In terms of networking, it means a network administrator must be proactive and attempt to anticipate potential problems on the network before they affect network services. Because network servers are by definition mission critical, it's important to monitor server performance.

You can use tools to track a server's performance over time and determine if a computer component, such as a hard drive or server memory, will become a possible

---

[1] Sourced from www.cisco.com/en/US/docs/ios/12_1/configfun/configuration/guide/fcd301c.html.

bottleneck under high network traffic (a bottleneck being an impedance to server performance, which can slow a service and user access to that service).

Before we look at some of the different tools that the various NOSs discussed in this book provide, a few words should be said about baselines. When you first deploy your network or a new server on the network, you should record a set of baseline readings for the server's hardware (using the performance monitoring tools the NOS supplies). This allows you to then monitor the server's performance over time as it relates to specific server hardware, such as the drive array, and allows you to tweak server software settings, such as the amount of virtual memory configured on a server (which can be an issue with a server running Windows Server 2003).

As mentioned, the different NOS platforms offer various types of monitoring tools. However, no matter what tools are available, you should monitor certain hardware components on a server over time (using your baseline as a starting point) to avoid bottlenecks. We'll look at these components and at specific tools from some selected NOSs that allow you to monitor server performance.

Processor Performance

Servers are outfitted with fast processors. For example, many server vendors provide high-end servers that take advantage of Intel's Xeon 7460 processor that runs at 2.66GHz. Many servers also offer a motherboard that can take more than one processor. As well, upper-end NOSs are set up to run on multiple processors. For example, Microsoft's Enterprise Edition supports up to 8 processors.

By the Way

Network Servers Come in Many Configurations

When you put together the specifications for a new server, the processor you select is as important as the number and size of the disk drives and the amount of RAM. Intel-based servers are available with Celeron, Pentium, and Xeon processors. A small office situation might only require a basic server running a Celeron processor (but be careful about choosing low-end processors). Larger companies might require Pentium IV and might require a server that allows for multiple processors.

In terms of processor performance, a bottleneck can arise when the processor (or processors) can no longer keep up with the system calls it gets from the different software processes running on the server. You can monitor processor performance by reviewing various performance parameters, such as the number of events that are waiting in line to be acted upon by the processor or the time spent on a particular thread (a thread being a particular part of a program that can execute independently).

Each NOS allows you to view counters (often in a chart format) that relate to processor (CPU) performance. For example, Novell NetWare (eDirectroy 8.8) provides the Server Health table that you can access using the web-based NetWare Remote Manager (meaning that you can monitor server health from any client on the network). Figure 22.1 shows the Server Health table for a NetWare server. Not only does this table allow you a quick view of server status issues such as CPU utilization and failed logon, but any problems (if they exist) are flagged with a red icon in the Status column.

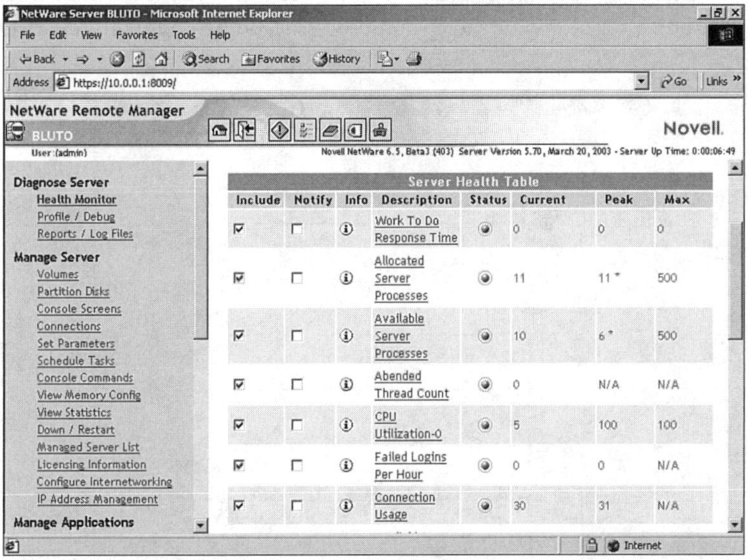

FIGURE 22.1
The NetWare Health table allows you to view CPU utilization and other server performance parameters.

In terms of CPU utilization, it's also helpful to be able to see a graph of CPU utilization over time. By clicking the CPU Utilization link on the Server Health table, you can view a chart as shown in Figure 22.2.

Windows Server 2003 also provides counters that you can view to monitor processor performance (and set up your initial baselines for the server). You can view these counters using the Windows Performance Monitor:

▶ **%Processor Time**—This counter, found under the Processor object, is a measure of the time that the processor is executing a nonidle thread. If it's consistently around 75–80%, you might need to upgrade the processor on the server or add another processor if the motherboard allows for dual processing.

▶ **Interrupts/sec**—This counter, found under the Processor object, is the average number of interrupt calls that the processor is receiving from hardware devices, such as a network card or modem. If it increases beyond 3,500 and the %Processor Time counter doesn't increase, the problem might not be the processor but a device that's sending spurious interrupts to the processor, such as a bad network or small computer system interface (SCSI) card. This can be caused by the device itself or the driver you're using for the device.

▶ **Processor Queue Length**—This counter, found under the System object, measures the number of threads waiting to be processed. If it reaches a value of 10 or more, the processor might be a bottleneck. This means you should go to a faster processor or upgrade to a multiprocessor motherboard on the server.

FIGURE 22.2
You can view server performance in a chart format.

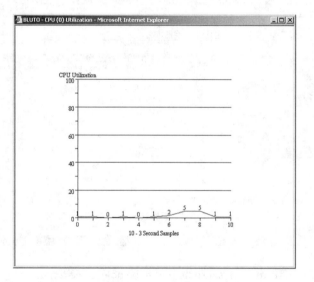

Figure 22.3 shows the Windows Performance Monitor in the graph view. You can configure multiple counters in the monitor window, allowing you to track multiple hardware performance issues with one quick view.

Did you Know?

Out-of-Control Processes and Hardware

In some situations, a faulty line of code or corrupted software can monopolize a server's processing, resulting in poor server performance. In addition, a bad hardware device, such as a malfunctioning NIC, could be sending interrupts to the processor. Most of the tools used for monitoring CPU performance also allow you to view the CPU's interaction with individual threads, which can help in diagnosing whether the problem is bad software (or hardware) rather than the CPU itself.

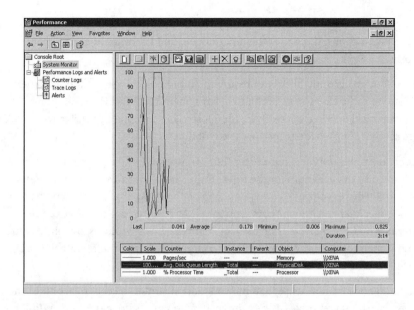

FIGURE 22.3
You can view
CPU and server
performance in a
chart format.

If you determine a server is slowing network services because of a processor issue, you're faced with the possibility of replacing the processor (or adding another processor if possible), adding an additional server, or upgrading the entire server. If one server is providing multiple services (such as a server that is providing DNS, DHCP, and perhaps other services), you can cut down on the number of services that the server is required to supply and deploy another server to pick up the service that was removed.

The bottom line pertaining to server hardware performance boils down to planning. If you planned well up front and determined the potential growth of the network, you probably purchased servers that will provide services effectively even when you have growth spurts (in terms of users) on the network.

Hard Drive Performance and Space

Another area related to server performance that you should monitor is related to the server's hard drive (or drives). Not only is drive performance important, but the amount of available space is an issue, particularly on mail and file servers.

Server drives come in many sizes and speeds. You want to outfit your servers with high-performance drives. Servers that experience traffic of any consequence need to be configured with multiple SCSI drives that can be configured in a RAID array. (RAID is discussed in Hour 5, "Network Concepts.")

The types of events important to monitor are the time that the drive is occupied with read/write functions, the size of the disk's queue, and the amount of free space on the drive.

A drive that's constantly busy with read/write functions is experiencing some type of problem. In some cases, it might help to defragment the drive. However, in most cases, you need to replace the drive with a faster one or replace the drive with a RAID stripe set that supplies faster read/write capabilities.

Another drive performance parameter that can tip you off to a potential drive problem is the disk queue length for the drive. If the queue contains numerous requests for access to the drive, your users are going to experience lag time in accessing and saving their files to the volume. Again, you might have to replace the drive or take advantage of a RAID array. Look back at Figure 22.3, which shows how disk queue length is monitored on a Windows Server using the Performance Monitor. (The Disk Queue Length counter is shown in the monitor window.)

It's a matter of common sense for a network administrator to keep track of the amount of free space on server drives. For example, if a file server's drive is filling up fast, you need to take action. You might add a drive to extend the size of a particular volume or set restrictions of the amount of drive space that you allocate to network users.

By the Way

Hot Swappable Drives

Many network servers are now available (at reasonable prices) with hot swappable drives. The drives are accessed through the front of the server box, and you can add or replace drives while the server continues to run. These servers make an administrator's life much easier.

Figure 22.4 shows a simple Linux utility called Kdiskfree. This GUI tool presents statistics on disk usage and the percent of free disk space.

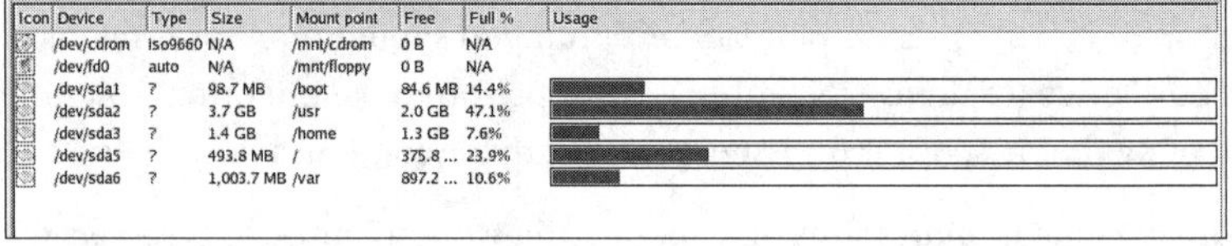

FIGURE 22.4
Utilities, such as Kdiskfree, allow you to keep track of drive utilization.

Memory Utilization

Another key resource on a network server is the server's memory. Although NOS vendors supply customers with specifications related to the amount of memory needed to run the operating system (OS), you should configure the server with enough memory to do its job. In most cases, this is going to be much more memory than the specifications recommend.

When a server uses its available memory, it resorts to a paging file that enables the server to temporarily dump some processes to the server hard drive. (In the Windows environment, the paging file is often referred to as virtual memory.) If you have a server that too often relies on the paging file (because of low available memory), the server is going to slow down and become a potential bottleneck on the network. In most cases, you can remedy this problem by adding more RAM to the server.

Performance counters you can use to track memory usage and health on a server are the number of bytes available to running processes and the number of times the computer must rely on the paging file. Each NOS includes different methods of tracking memory usage statistics. For example, Windows Server 2003 and 2008 provide the following memory counters:

- ▶ **Available Bytes**—If this counter (a measure of the physical memory available to running processes) consistently falls to less than 4MB, you need more memory on the server.

- ▶ **Pages/Sec**—This counter measures the number of times the computer must rely on the paging file (dumping items in RAM to the hard drive temporarily). This event is known as a page fault. If this counter consistently reads 20 on the System Monitor, you should add more RAM. Excessive page faults can cause system-wide delays in terms of server access.

- ▶ **Committed Bytes**—This counter shows the amount of RAM being used and the amount of space needed for the paging file if the data has to be moved to the disk. You should see a value on this counter that is less than the RAM installed on the server. If the value is more than the RAM, you're using the paging file too often; add more memory.

If you look back at Figure 22.3, you can see the that Performance Monitor has been configured to track the Pages/Sec counter. On a UNIX or a Linux system, you can use the command line tool vmstat. Vmstat can provide such information as the amount of free memory and statistics related to the swap file (page file).

The Linux environment also has a system monitor that allows you to view memory and swap usage in a GUI format. Figure 22.5 shows the System Monitor and the counters that it provides.

FIGURE 22.5
Utilities such as
the Linux System
Monitor allow
you to track
memory usage.

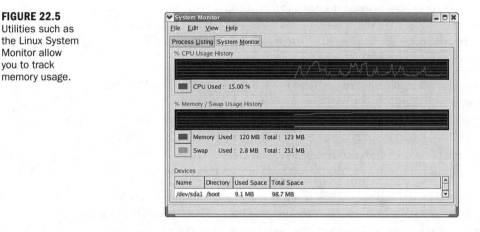

Taking Advantage of Event Alerts

Most NOSs allow the network administrator to configure performance or event alerts. For example, you can set a particular threshold value for a particular parameter such as CPU utilization or hard drive free space. When the threshold that you have set is exceeded, the server's performance utility alerts you to the fact.

Using Event Logs to Track Problems

Another useful tool for tracking server problems is the system log. Each NOS provides tools to record logs on the server. Periodically viewing these logs (even when a problem hasn't been reported or become obvious on the network) can help you nip a problem in the bud and keep important services running on the network.

These logs also show when a process has failed, and, in most cases, the logs can be configured to accumulate specific information related to the server. NOSs provide different types of event logs. System logs track events related to system services and resources. Application logs record events related to the applications running on a server. Security logs record events related to user behaviors such as failed logons or events that you configure, such as the auditing of user access to a particular volume or resource on the server.

You can access event logs via the command line or by using a GUI utility (depending on the NOS). For example, on a server running Red Hat Linux, you can access system logs using the System Logs GUI utility shown in Figure 22.6.

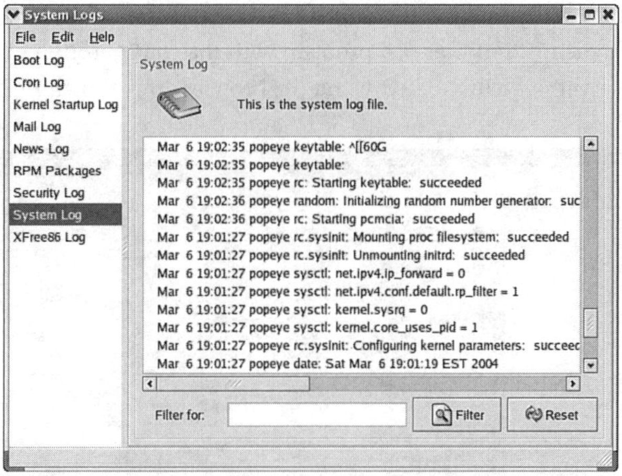

FIGURE 22.6
You can view system logs on a Red Hat server using the System Logs utility.

The System Logs utility allows you to view the system log, security log, and other logs configured on the system. You can filter and reset logs in the utility window.

When you view a system log, you're looking for red flags. You want to know if a particular process has failed or if a particular service on a server is having a problem. Examining Figure 22.6 again, notice that a kernel module failed when the server was booted.

Understanding System Logs

For you to use system logs effectively as a diagnosis tool related to server performance, you need to understand what you're looking at. Each NOS has a unique way of recording and specifying log events. It's a good idea to spend time with your NOS documentation to gain an understanding of what a particular event entails and how you might remedy it.

The Windows Server 2003 NOS (as well as Vista) includes the Event Viewer, which allows you to track events contained in an application log, a security log, and a system log. The Event Viewer employs a system of icons that helps you determine whether there has been a critical event on the server:

▶ **The Information icon**—Denotes the logging of successful system events and other processes

▶ **The Warning icon**—Shows a noncritical error on the system

▶ **The Error icon**—Indicates the failure of a major function (such as a driver failure)

Figure 22.7 shows the system log in the Windows Event Viewer. Note that NETBT has error icons. This means that there's a problem with the configuration of NetBIOS over TCP/IP on the server (which is also causing the browser error shown in Figure 22.7).

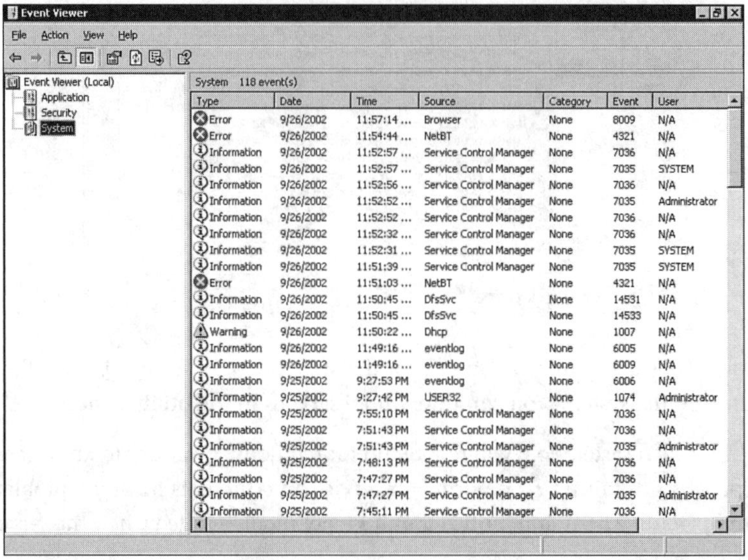

FIGURE 22.7
The Windows Event Viewer uses a system of icons to categorize events shown in the various system logs.

Event logs grant a method of tracking system issues and problems after they've happened. It's important to take the information you find in system logs and use it to fine-tune your server's configuration before you face a major problem. Using event logs in conjunction with performance monitoring (as discussed in the previous section) should aid you in keeping up with server issues before you experience a major network meltdown.

TCP/IP Connectivity Command-Line Tools

So far, we've examined tools that allow you to monitor router and server hardware and software performance and pinpoint real-time hardware and software errors using system logs. Another potential problem area that you'll have to deal with is the realm of connectivity issues. Connectivity problems can occur because of physical cabling or device malfunctions on the network. They may also be attributable to incorrect software configurations. Because practically every data network uses TCP/IP, it makes sense to look at some of the command-line tools you can use to help diagnose connectivity problems on a TCP/IP network.

The great thing about these command-line tools, such as FTP, ping, and traceroute, is that they're available no matter what NOS you're using. Each NOS platform also offers command-line diagnostic tools particular to that platform. Understanding the use of some of the basic TCP/IP-related commands discussed here will help you as you begin to develop your own strategy for diagnosing connectivity issues.

Ping

The ping command is useful for checking the connection between a computer and a remote host or server. Ping uses Internet Control Message Protocol (ICMP), a companion protocol of IP, to determine whether another computer is on the network and whether you can reach it.

To use the ping command, simply type the following:

```
ping the.remote.ip.address
```

such as

```
ping 172.16.0.12
```

This returns one of several types of values. First, if your computer is capable of connecting to the computer it's pinging, it looks like the following:

```
C:\ >ping 172.16.0.12
```

Pinging 172.16.0.12 with 32 bytes of data:

```
Reply from 172.16.0.12: bytes=32 time<10ms TTL=255
Reply from 172.16.0.12: bytes=32 time<10ms TTL=255
Reply from 172.16.0.12: bytes=32 time<10ms TTL=255
Reply from 172.16.0.12: bytes=32 time<10ms TTL=255
```

Ping statistics for 172.16.0.12:

```
    Packets: Sent = 4, Received = 4, Lost = 0 (0% loss),
```

Approximate round-trip times in milliseconds:

```
    Minimum = 0ms, Maximum =  0ms, Average =  0ms
```

This means your computer is capable of sending 32-character packets to the remote computer. The time it takes to send and receive a packet is 255 milliseconds. The stats on the bottom tell you whether you had errors or packet loss.

Now, if you can't connect to a particular computer, you get a different message:

```
C:\ >ping 172.16.0.13
```

Pinging 172.16.0.13 with 32 bytes of data:

```
Request timed out.
Request timed out.
Request timed out.
Request timed out.
```

Ping statistics for 172.16.0.13:

```
    Packets: Sent = 4, Received = 0, Lost = 4 (100% loss),
```

Approximate round-trip times in milliseconds:

```
    Minimum = 0ms, Maximum =  0ms, Average =  0ms
```

In this case, you're sending packets, but no one's replying. Consequently, four packets it sent were lost. This means that the computer you want to connect to isn't on the network—or the computer you're using to ping isn't on the network.

You can also use the ping command to determine whether you can get to a particular network:

```
C:\ >ping 156.234.84.95
```

Pinging 156.234.84.95 with 32 bytes of data:

```
Reply from 12.126.207.17: Destination host unreachable.
Reply from 12.126.207.17: Destination host unreachable.
Reply from 12.126.207.17: Destination host unreachable.
Reply from 12.126.207.17: Destination host unreachable.
```

Ping statistics for 156.234.84.95:

```
    Packets: Sent = 4, Received = 4, Lost = 0 (0% loss),
```

Approximate round-trip times in milliseconds:

```
    Minimum = 0ms, Maximum =  0ms, Average =  0ms
```

The Destination host unreachable message means your computer's default gateway doesn't know how to get to the address at the other end. This message might mean that your router needs some attention.

You can also use ping commands to see whether a particular computer has a functioning NIC or TCP/IP configuration. This is done by pinging the loopback address 127.0.0.1. Figure 22.8 shows the results of pinging the loopback address on a Windows XP computer.

FIGURE 22.8
You can also use ping to check an NIC on a computer.

Using `ipconfig`

On Windows-based servers and clients, the `ipconfig` command is useful. You can use it to check the TCP/IP configuration of a computer and to release (`ipconfig/release`) and renew (`ipconfig/renew`) the TCP/IP configuration for the computer as supplied by the network DHCP server.

Did you Know?

FTP

File Transfer Protocol (FTP) is a widely adopted Internet tool for moving files around on a TCP/IP network. That's what it's intended for, and it's what FTP is usually used for.

But FTP has an odd characteristic that makes it useful for system administrators. While it's transferring files across the network, it measures the throughput of the network, so you can learn how efficiently the network is operating. If you can ping another computer but everything is running slowly, use FTP to send a file to it.

Start with a file that's about 1 megabyte (MB) in size. That's big enough to measure throughput, but it's small enough not to cause the network problems. Send or receive the file from another machine. (You'll need to have an FTP server on at least one of the machines to do this.)

To use FTP, you need to get to the FTP prompt. Type FTP at the command line of your OS, press Enter, and you'll have access to the FTP prompt, as shown in the example that follows. You can then use the FTP command get to download a file.

```
ftp> get telnet
200 PORT command successful.
150 Opening data connection for telnet (512338 bytes).
226 Transfer complete.
ftp: 512338 bytes received in 0.57Seconds 897.26Kbytes/sec.
```

Note that this file shows that I received a 512 kilobyte (KB) file (half a megabyte) in about half a second, and then the system showed how fast the file transferred. There's a catch—the transfer speed is in bytes, which are equivalent to 8 bits each. So, you have to multiply the speed by 8 to get the correct measure.

```
897.26 x 8 = a network speed of 7178.08 bits per second,
or about the best usage you'll see on a 10BASE-T network.
```

This is another use for FTP that isn't usually mentioned in teaching texts, but it's a great tool. If the network is slow, this can help quantify how slow.

Traceroute

Networks can become congested with excessive traffic or with faulty components. Sometimes packets seem to be taking 10 times as long as they should to get from point A to point B.

Traceroute (or tracert on Microsoft systems) is a utility that enables you to learn how packets are being routed across the network. This is helpful if you want to determine specifically which route your packets take. It's also useful if you want to see whether your packets are timing out on the network because they've gone through too many routers.

To use this utility, type the following:

```
Tracert (or traceroute) remote-ip-address or hostname
```

Here's an example:C:\ >tracert sams.com

```
Tracing route to mcp.com [63.69.110.193]
over a maximum of 30 hops:

  1   <10 ms   <10 ms   <10 ms  routerfrelan.anonymouscom [172.16.0.1]
  2   <10 ms   <10 ms    10 ms  12.126.207.17
  3   <10 ms   <10 ms    11 ms  gbr2-a31s1.sffca.ip.att.net [12.127.1.146]
  4   <10 ms   <10 ms    10 ms  gbr4-p70.sffca.ip.att.net [12.122.1.189]
  5    10 ms    11 ms    10 ms  gbr3-p20.la2ca.ip.att.net [12.122.2.70]
  6    10 ms    10 ms    10 ms  ggr1-p360.la2ca.ip.att.net [12.123.28.129]
  7    20 ms    20 ms    30 ms  att-gw.la.uu.net [192.205.32.126]
  8    20 ms    20 ms    30 ms  503.at-6-0-0.XR2.SAC1.ALTER.NET [152.63.53.6]
  9    20 ms    20 ms    30 ms  184.at-1-1-0.TR2.SAC1.ALTER.NET [152.63.50.142]
 10    71 ms    80 ms    80 ms  127.at-6-1-0.TR2.NYC8.ALTER.NET [152.63.6.13]
 11    70 ms    80 ms    81 ms  184.ATM7-0.XR2.EWR1.ALTER.NET [152.63.20.241]
 12    70 ms    80 ms    80 ms  192.ATM7-0.GW7.EWR1.ALTER.NET [152.63.24.209]
 13   290 ms   231 ms   230 ms  headland-media-gw.customer.ALTER.NET
[157.130.19.94]
 14    71 ms    80 ms    80 ms  63.69.110.193

Trace complete.
```

In this case, `traceroute/traceert` completed the trace, and I can see all the routers (14 of them) between my network and sams.com. If you're timed out, or if you get starts in place of the times, that node is usually where your problem is occurring. Consequently, `traceroute/tracert` is useful for settling disputes with ISPs and network providers over the quality of your service.

Nslookup

Sometimes, you need to use an IP address instead of a name (the DNS hostname). Other times, you don't know the IP address for the name. `Nslookup` (short for name server lookup) is a utility that can help you figure out what IP address is associated with a particular name. Here's an example:

```
/$ nslookup www.microsoft.com
Server:  rayban.tibinc.com
Address:  172.16.0.10

Non-authoritative answer:
Name:    microsoft.com
Addresses:  207.46.230.219, 207.46.130.45, 207.46.230.218
Aliases: www.microsoft.com
```

Clearly, these four tools don't compose a whole suite of diagnostic tools, but they come with your OS and can give you a place to start when you're having network problems. It's important that not only do you know how to use ping, FTP, and these other commands effectively, but you become familiar with the other command-line tools that your NOS offers. You'll find them to be of great assistance to you and your staff.

Summary

In this hour, we examined key tools that can help you identify and possibly diagnose problems with server hardware, software, and general network connectivity problems. We learned how to use performance monitor data to establish baselines and monitor potential bottlenecks. We learned that event logs allow the network administrator to pinpoint problems. In addition, we learned that command-line tools, such as ping and `traceroute`, can be used to identify connectivity problems on a TCP/IP network.

Q&A

Q. *What action should you take when a server hardware bottleneck is identified on your network?*

A. You should address the bottleneck by upgrading the server's hardware configuration (such as more memory or an additional processor) or by replacing the server. In some situations, you might be able to deploy a "helper" server—as in the case of services such as DNS, in which a second server can take some of the workload off the server with the bottleneck problem.

Q. *How should baseline information for your servers be stored?*

A. You can capture and store baseline information for servers in numerous ways. For example, in the Windows environment, you can create log files using the Performance Monitor. You can also print hard copies of initial logs, but make sure that you date the printouts. Finally, you can store baseline data and subsequent readings in a simple spreadsheet format in any spreadsheet software.

Q. *If you're having problems with an Internet connection, how can you diagnose the issue?*

A. The first thing you can do is use the ping command to check your default gateway. If there's a problem with the router, ping can help you quickly determine whether the computer can even communicate with the router. If the router is okay and the Internet problem relates to the World Wide Web, you might be dealing with a DNS server issue. Again, you can use ping to see whether the computer with the problem can communicate with the DNS server.

A Day in the Life of a Network Administrator

What You'll Learn in This Hour:

▶ Management of your time as a network administrator
▶ Use of calendars
▶ Hints on working with the user community

The person who serves as the caretaker of the network is the network administrator. The administrator controls the network servers and other machines, such as routers and bridges. It is this person's job to exploit the tools provided by the servers' Network Operating Systems (NOSs) and the routers' operating systems (OSs) to keep the network secure and efficient.

In this hour, we look at the tasks required of the network administrator for supporting the user's needs. In so doing, we gain an insight into an administrator's typical day, a day in which we once again assume you are this person.

Your Job as an Administrator

Although on good days, a network administrator's morning doesn't deviate that much from a typical employee getting ready to show up at work, bad days can mean a quick roll out of bed because of a noisy pager or cell phone alerting that there's a problem on the network. The fix might require breaking out a laptop and dialing in to the network to see whether the problem can be fixed remotely. In other cases, it might mean throwing on some clothes and speeding off to work.

Whatever the case, because the network often is required for employees to do their jobs and execute the core business of the company, you are responsible for resolving the problem as soon as possible.

In some cases, the problem might be easy to handle; for example, you cruise into the user's office and discover that the correct printer wasn't selected on the client computer, and that's why the print job never showed up as a hard copy at the printer. In other cases, you might find that the print server had gone down, and you have to quickly replace a hard drive on the server and rebuild the server from backup media.

After you resolve the problem and get back to your desk, the chances are good that you have a message or messages waiting for you on your phone. You listen to your messages and create a to-do list of users who need assistance right out of the gate, triaging them by order of seriousness, and then you head out on your rounds. You're a computer doctor who makes office calls.

One user is complaining that his copy of the corporate database is locked up. You get to his desk and discover that he's caught in a transitional screen; there's a menu onscreen that he has to deal with before he can get control of the database again. You instruct him how to get through the screen and back into his application; he's happy but complains about the complexity. Oh, well. At least he's working again.

Another user is complaining that his OS keeps locking up, and you find that he has downloaded a software program from the Web that is wreaking havoc with the OS. So you uninstall the offending application and make sure that any file associations are back to their default settings. You also have to let the user know that downloading unauthorized software from the Web and changing major OS settings is not something that network users should be doing. You need to impart this information in a professional, yet firm, manner so that the situation doesn't happen again.

Starting to get the picture? Your day, which can start at the crack of dawn, often begins with troubleshooting problems that have popped up with your user base. After you take care of user issues, you can start your daily tasks. First, you head into the computer room (which is actually the server room; everyone has a computer on his desk, so computer room is sort of a misnomer) and change the media that you use for your server backups. You make the change according to the backup scheme that you're employing; more about backups is covered in Hour 21, "Managing a Network."

You also need to take the time to check your various server logs. (Logging is also discussed in Hour 21.) For example, you might find that someone was trying to get through the firewall last evening, using an executive's user ID but the wrong password; you call the executive whose ID was being used and ask whether he was trying to get in. No, he answers, but his kid was on the computer all night; maybe *he* was trying to get in. You respectfully request that the executive ask his kid to quit trying to crack the firewall; having asked that, you move on to the next task. You might find that a log alert that you set for a file server has been tripped and the file server drive array needs more capacity, so you send an email to all users that the file server will be going down at 5 p.m., and you adjust your personal calendar so that you can stay late and add a drive or swap out the array.

Your day will certainly be busy and varied; other tasks that you might have to tackle are these:

▶ Get a senior executive's personal digital assistant (PDA) synchronized with his desktop computer

▶ Install a router to segment a network

▶ Call several vendors regarding products you're considering for your network

▶ Write a programming script to allow users to connect to a database over the corporate intranet (or coordinating this activity with the programming staff)

▶ Figure out which laptops offer the best value, and submit a report to the CFO

Clearly, you need to prioritize these different tasks. Making the best use of your time and keeping your users (particularly your boss!) up and running require some clever juggling of tasks.

Probably halfway through the task list, you'll take the time to look at your watch and find that the morning hours have passed; it's noon, and you're hungry. Often, you'll eat lunch on the run. Even before digestion sets in, chances are good that more trouble reports will come in from users that force you to change the priorities on your task list and add additional tasks.

On a good day, you might make it through most of the list and even have a little time to look at trade journals; on a bad day, you will still be troubleshooting problems well after most of the other employees have called it a day. Obviously, you can't really end your day until you deal with "major" network problems and take care of daily tasks related to the network, such as checking security logs and making sure that the backup media is ready to go when the daily backup automatically kicks in on the network.

I don't want to paint a picture that a network administrator's day is completely hectic and stressful, but it's a field that requires patience and high energy. If you work with a group of administrators, the team approach to problem solving provides a way to keep any one administrator's task list manageable. If you're the only computer guru at a small company, you'll have to learn to deploy hardware and software that helps cut down on major snafus; good planning and implementation can save a lot of headaches in terms of the same problems cropping up day after day. Let's look at some of the common daily tasks that are necessary to keep a network up and running.

Daily Tasks

As you can see from the previous section, it's essential that you stay organized and keep your task list up-to-date. This also means integrating important daily tasks into the chaos of the moment as users report problems and you detect issues on the network. As you make your list and complete tasks, keep old records of what you've done by date. The benefits of doing so are twofold: First, you have a record of what you did and when you did it (invaluable when you're trying to remember how to fix something you worked on six months before). Second, keeping dated records provides a list you can use during yearly evaluations. It also creates a linear timeline that can help identify patterns and avoid burnout.

Different calendar and scheduling programs allow you to keep track of appointments, tasks, and project timelines. For example, groupware products, such as Lotus Notes and Microsoft Outlook, can give you all the tools you need to stay organized. Figure 23.1 shows just the beginnings of a network administrator's typical daily task list in Microsoft Outlook. You can arrange tasks by due date, and you can assign tasks to other members of your network team.

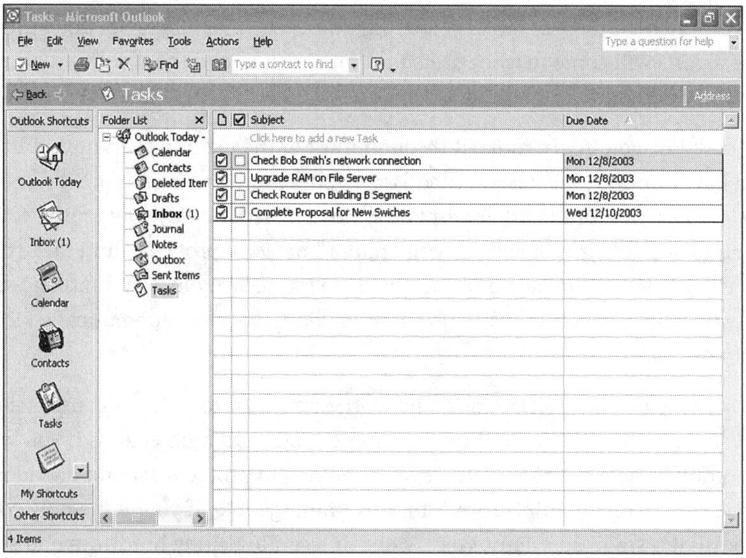

FIGURE 23.1
You can use groupware applications such as Outlook to stay organized.

Because you typically deploy these types of applications on the network, it makes sense for you to use them. I've seen cases in which the information technology staff had no problem deploying a particular groupware product but couldn't answer even basic end user questions related to using the software. You have to be both expert and generalist. You need to know networking inside and out, and you need to know how to tell an end user how to create a new task or send an email attachment in Outlook.

Because you aren't always at your computer, it's important to make the case that the company provide you with a PDA, which you can synch with the groupware calendar you're using. The PDA attached to your belt is assurance that you always have your schedule and task list readily available.

One of the most important things you can do, however, is to make time for yourself inasmuch as that is possible. Your effectiveness as a network or system administrator is directly related to how much you know, so even if your company doesn't pay for education, educate yourself. Read everything you can on networking, and take note of things you think apply to you. If you have access to a more experienced networking professional, be shameless about learning as much as you can from her. Network professionals are usually quite willing to answer questions and assist in problem solving.

If you can, take a half hour every day and dedicate it to learning a tiny bit of programming. Even if you don't intend to program, understanding the process of coding and being familiar with the data structures that full-time programmers use is a major advantage when you're talking to tech support. In addition, being able to put together a 10–15 line program to hotfix something in an emergency is a useful skill—and one that your employer will certainly appreciate.

Of course, if you're an administrator of a large network, you won't have time to write code. Nor should you get down to this level of detail. Let's assume you're an employee in a Fortune 500 company. It's likely that the network staff will number in the hundreds. In this case, your job will take on a different dimension, and you won't have to undertake many of the tasks described so far. The most effective managers of larger networks are those who hire the best people they can find, pay them well, support them with the user community, and stay out of their way!

You have to keep your skills up-to-date, while juggling your duties. In the industry, it's a known fact that network administrators raise their salaries and their opportunities by moving from company to company. Many companies don't promote from within, so it's important that your skill set be up-to-date in case you find that ideal position on an Internet job site.

The various resources available for keeping your skills up-to-date and exploring new knowledge related to information technology are abundant. In terms of reference and hands-on books alone, there's a great deal of information related to networking and computer technology published every year.

You should try to make room in your network budget for the purchase of resource books. Or, as a last resort, you need to spend some of your own hard-earned cash and take some time to read. The fact that you've become the greatest Novell Net-Ware guru on the planet will do you little good if your company decides to migrate to the Microsoft networking platform.

Keeping Your Skill Set Up-to-Date

There are many ways to keep your network skills and knowledge of networking up-to-date. Online courses, training courses in your city (from training companies and colleges and universities), and books that provide hands-on training present different learning environments. Yes, your job keeps you busy, but you have to ensure that your skill set will allow you to keep your job or move up the career ladder. Pursuing industry certifications such as those offered by Sun, Microsoft, and other software vendors offers you a context for learning a new body of technical information. Professional certifications also look good on your resume in terms of promotions and seeking other employment opportunities.

Strategies for Supporting Users

Without network users, there would be no need for network administrators. So your job is to keep your users happy—a job that most network administrators accept with alacrity.

Users, however, are not always reasonable. After all, they're a snapshot of the human race and, as we know, not all humans are reasonable. As an administrator, you have certain charges laid on you, such as required network standards and behaviors. If a user calls on you to violate those basic charges, you have to be able to say no, escalate the user's request to someone who can grant an exception to the rules, or (in rare cases) escalate the issue because you see potential security breaches or behavior that exposes the organization to liability or other dangers.

The bottom line is that your users are your customers. If you have a dissatisfied user community, your life as a network administrator will be quite unpleasant. On the other hand, if your users are happy with your work, that work will be much more pleasant. The following list provides some tips on how to work with and relate to your network users:

▶ Never get angry with a user, even if he is senselessly venting on you. The user's anger can come from a variety of sources, ranging from frustration at not getting his work done to a wholly unrelated argument with someone else.

▶ Stop and listen to the user when he complains. It's way too easy to interrupt a user in midsentence and announce that you've got a solution to the problem. If you take the time to listen to a user's complaint, you might discover that the problem extends beyond the computer per se; he might be upset that the software won't automate certain functions.

▶ After you've listened to the user, take a second and think about what the most appropriate response should be. It's all well and good for you to know that the user's IP configuration is incorrect and that changing the subnet mask will resolve the problem, but do you have to explain it? For most users, the answer is no; all they want is a functioning network, and they don't care what's behind it. So your response to the user should be based on a now or later fix: If it's a 5–10 minute fix, suggest that you can do it now; on the other hand, a long fix means that you have to defer the repair if the user needs the machine and can limp it along until you fix it properly.

Above all, take time to get to know your users and their needs. Don't make haste with this part of your job. Take your time, and remember the old saw, "Hasty climbers have sudden falls."

When users experience problems on a network, the root cause of those problems almost always boils down to three possibilities: user errors, software problems, and physical connectivity problems. Although network administrators have received a bad rap of always blaming the user for the problem, establishing policies that provide a set of rules for behavior on the network can alleviate a lot of problems. Let's look at some issues related to establishing policies for network use.

Establishing Network Policies

Providing end user training and written policies related to network use can negate a lot of potential problems on the network. Build some sort of educational opportunity for your users into your overall plan for your network implementation and management.

Documentation that the users can read and refer to as they use the network can cut down on their errors. A brief and concise manual that explains basic network logon and resource access can be a real help to your users.

The manual also gives you an opportunity to establish written policies for network use; for example, you might establish rules that prohibit downloading software from the Internet or playing CDs from home. Both of these rules can reduce the risk of virus infection, and prohibiting downloads means that local hard drives remain clean. (A user can fill up her own hard drive with junk pretty fast if she has a high-speed Internet connection and some free time on her hands.)

Establishing user policies for your company's network not only provides a set of rules for the network users but allows you to assume (although users aren't always going to follow all the rules) that network client machines will only be running software that's appropriately licensed and correctly configured and that important user files are stored in the appropriate place so they can be periodically backed up.

Although everyone is aware of the often-overused anecdote that accompanies the word "assume" when an assumption proves to be wrong, at least assuming that computers have been configured in a particular "standard" way allows you to concentrate on other issues when attempting to troubleshoot network problems.

Summary

In this hour, we viewed a typical day of a network administrator. We looked at some ideas for staying organized and managing that elusive commodity called time.

Q&A

Q. *What's the one thing you can count on as you tackle a network administrator's typical day?*

A. You have to work with your end users. Handling their requests and problems in a polite and efficient manner makes your job easier. Also be advised that you have to constantly rework your daily task list to accommodate "network crises" and lesser network problems. Stay flexible!

Q. *What are two important aspects of succeeding as a network administrator?*

A. Staying organized and keeping your skill set up-to-date are important aspects of succeeding as a network administrator. Use a system, such as a calendar program, to keep your schedule manageable. Also, take every opportunity you can to learn new things and upgrade your personal knowledgebase.

Q. *What's a good approach to cutting down on user error on the network?*

A. Provide your network users with a list of rules related to using the network. Also, find different avenues of providing user training or end user tips to your user base. That helps cut down the one-on-one training you have to provide to a user who doesn't understand how to use a particular network application.

HOUR 24

Where Are Networks Going from Here?

What You'll Learn in This Hour:

▶ The growth of Linux
▶ The likelihood of universal wireless "hot spots"
▶ The computing "cloud"
▶ The convergence of advanced technologies

We've covered a lot of territory these past 23 hours. I hope you've found this time well spent. For the final hour, we'll look into the crystal ball in an attempt to foresee what's on the horizon for computer networks.

Continued Growth of Linux

Both private companies and government have increasingly looked to Linux as an alternative to vendor-specific products that have been a mainstay of the industry. Linux provides an open standard for development and interoperability of computer operating systems. The pluses of using open source software platforms have been mentioned several times in this book, which are the reasons for adopting Linux. It's an open, nonproprietary platform that doesn't require proprietary hardware (although some flavors of Linux only run on certain vendor hardware products).

Linux is making inroads in commercial and governmental installations. According to a survey published in Wikipedia, Linux's market is growing rapidly, and the revenue of servers, desktops, and packaged software running Linux is expected to exceed $35.7 billion in the near future.

Smaller companies often look for platforms that are easy to install, configure, and support. There's sometimes an attitude of "if it isn't broken, don't fix it." This means that companies may still be using the same network and service platforms they've used since their businesses were first computerized. For example, many NetWare installations around the world are using older software.

Some large institutions haven't made a move to the PC platform and are still maintaining cumbersome and costly legacy mainframe systems. Again, some institutions just haven't seen a compelling reason to turn their operations upside down to embrace a new technology.

Nonetheless, the trend is for an increased use of Linux. It currently holds around 13% of the server market. In addition, the XO laptop project of One Laptop Per Child is creating a huge market for Linux. The project's goal is to provide a Linux-based laptop to several hundred million school children in developing countries.

Nationwide Variation of Wi-Fi: WiMax

Several communications companies have announced a plan to create a nationwide wireless network called WiMax. The goal is to extend the range of the current 802.11 Wi-Fi technology to more than a square mile from the cell phone tower. It will provide fast connections to the Internet and operate at around 15 megabits per second (Mbps).

Headed up by Sprint, and under the company Clearwire, WiMax is intended to saturate the United States with cell towers to, as the marketing ads claim, "...turn the core of North America into one, big hot spot." By 2010, it plans to have the services available to about half the U.S. population.

This plan is a logical and perhaps inevitable evolution of mobile, wireless networks. Its realization will spur growth and the proliferation of mobile wireless interfaces in more end user devices, such as PDAs, gaming machines, digital cameras, smart meters, perhaps dipsticks in gasoline tanks, and yes, perhaps that wireless toaster we joked about earlier.

This network system will change the playing field in the wireless industry. AT&T and Verizon will be affected, as will Comcast and Time Warner. The latter CATV companies have no comparable wireless network strategy. In addition, several major enterprises are investing in this plan, including Google, Intel, and interestingly, Comcast and Time Warner.

We're at the tip of the iceberg with Wi-Fi and user machines. Worldwide shipments of electronic products with wireless capability totaled about 1.7 billion in 2008. By 2012, shipments are expected to total 2.3 billion, and this figure is a conservative estimate.

Computing with Clouds[1]

One of the current buzzwords being bandied about is "cloud." We've used an icon of a cloud in several figures in this book, partially to make the point that users don't care—nor should they be concerned—with the operations inside a network cloud.

Today, the term cloud still conveys this idea, but it goes further. The cloud will eventually be viewed as an immense set of services that will be offered to users. The services will go beyond conventional email and web servers; they'll expand beyond YouTube, Facebook, and blogs.

The basic idea of the cloud is simple: Offload work from users' devices onto thousands of servers that will operate in the clouds. This work includes not only software applications, such as spreadsheets, word processing, and file management, but also services such as simulation models, and packages for taking care of users' databases, photographs, and movie libraries. In essence, and ideally, the cloud will become a technologically advanced, yet benevolent Big Brother.

Rationale for the Clouds

Presently, many organizations don't use their computing facilities to their capacity. It's estimated that about 7,000 large corporate data centers exist in the United States. As an average, only 6% of their server capacity is used. Some centers are no longer using some of their servers. Other centers don't even know what's running on them! The cloud takes over these responsibilities.

In addition, many companies—especially small businesses—don't have the size or economies of scale to warrant a data center. Once again, the cloud becomes a virtual corporate data center for these companies.

Examples of Emerging Clouds

In 2006, Amazon, the online retailer, started Amazon Web Services (AWS), which allows customers to "rent" computer time and software, as well as storage space. AWS is a good example of the features of a cloud. First, because of a huge server farm, a customer is provided scalable capacity, with AWS-provided computing power during spikes of usage. Furthermore, the fees are based on usage. Also, the cloud servers provide extensive redundancy and backup features. In addition, AWS and similar clouds provide a range of security services.

---

[1] Some of the facts and figures cited in this part of the hour are sourced from "A Special Report on Corporate IT," The Economist, October 25, 2008.

Google is also moving to cloud services. Although the company wouldn't confirm *The Economist's* estimates, it's said that Google is operating more than three dozen data centers, which contain more than two million servers. As well, Microsoft is investing billions of dollars into server clouds and is adding up to 35,000 servers per month to its systems.

Potential Problems and Opportunities with Clouds

If the ideas behind clouds sound too good to be true, that's because they may be. The main problem with a company relying on clouds for its IT is that it must rely on clouds for its IT. I don't mean to be flippant, but it's a sobering notion to realize our sacrosanct data—the essence of our professional existence—is beyond our control. A full commitment to the cloud requires a huge leap in trust and faith.

Yet, are you and I any better prepared or more competent to manage and back up our company's data than, say, Google or Amazon? Are we better attuned to protect the privacy of our organization's information? Only you and I (and our company's officers) can answer these questions.

Nonetheless, I recommend that you and your staff delve into the "cloud." It's becoming a force in the industry, and you may find the economics of a virtual IT just too compelling to pass up. If so, you can put this book into the trash can (please don't!), because most of the networking tasks will be moved to that nebulous cloud. But it still behooves a company to understand the interworkings of the cloud, even if the cloud providers want to make the cloud opaque to customers.

Computers, Bioengineering, and the Clouds

Beyond the immediate horizon of three or four years into the future, if we try to detect longer visions in our crystal ball, some fantastic scenarios might come forth—perhaps apparitions! One example is the emerging technology of protein-based computers.

Efforts began in the 1990s to create libraries of programmable DNA parts, a discipline called synthetic biology. The goal is to create general components that can be used in more than one DNA application.[2] These plug-and-play parts could be like a generic capacitor used in electrical hardware circuits, or a generic perpetual calendar routine used in accounting software packages. Researchers have dubbed this technology "BioBricks."[3]

---

2 W. Wayt Gibbs, "Synthetic Life," Scientific American, *May 2002, p. 75–81. And "Life 2.0," The Economist, September 2, 2006, p. 67–70.*

[3] *Ibid., "Life 2.0," p. 67.*

The first efforts have focused on assembling Boolean logic gates in certain microbes, those that could digest dangerous chemicals, such as TNT or carcinogens. The microbe not only locates the substance but glows as it does so, thus signaling it has found a land mine or a dangerous part of a land fill. The systems can operate inside living cells, deriving their energy from their hosts. Some of them can move and reproduce.

In addition to the TNT and carcinogen "sniffers," other early synthetic biology devices are made of artificial amino acids and remove heavy metals from waste-water. Later systems remove plaque from arterial walls. And some perform binary logic! This application is of great interest to the scientists because of its relationship to computer architectures. Let's examine this part of the technology in more detail.

At the simplest level, a protein (coded by another gene) is input into a distinct section of DNA to produce (say) a Boolean NOT operation. An inverter gene produces a protein *output* if it has no input and, conversely, produces *no output* if it receives input—just like a Boolean NOT gate on a computer. It's that simple and that extraordinary.

It's also complex. Researchers believe it will take many years to refine this process to allow the creation of building blocks of biologic binary circuits, the vital combinations of Boolean gates that make up the architecture of computers. The task is daunting. For example, the engineers must cope with the fact that their living machines will likely mutate as they reproduce.

Nonetheless, extensive research is being conducted on building computers made of "natural" parts. Already, brain surgeons have placed conventional computers inside humans' brains to fix problems and abet other operations. Some scientists are banking that implants of wireless devices into the brain are only a matter of time—giving a new meaning to "head set."

Fantastic? Certainly. Unrealistic? Not necessarily. Viewing the progress we humans have made with computers and networks in the past three decades, we should not close our minds to these possibilities. It may well be that the convergence of WiMax, computing clouds, DNA tailoring, and brain bioengineering will propel us into yet more fanciful networks.

As an anonymous source once said, "In the past, the present was judged to be an improbable future." That's a fine thought to keep in mind about the future of computers and networks.

Glossary

As networking terminology changes, so do glossaries. This glossary doesn't claim to define everything; nothing can. However, web glossaries (such as www.webopedia.com) offer frequently updated definitions of current computer and networking terms.

By the Way

adapter card   A hardware component in a computer used to support attached devices.

addresses   Identifiers placed in packets (protocol data units, or PDUs) to identify the source and destination nodes for the PDU.

American Standard Code for Information Exchange (ASCII)   A convention for using the binary numbers (0 and 1) to represent letters, numerals, and special notations, such as ESC.

application programming interface (API)   A software facility that permits a user's application to communicate with another piece of software. Also known as function or library calls.

applications   The end user's software, such as email, word processors, video players, audio players, and photo editors.

ARPA (Advanced Research Projects Agency)   A U.S. Department of Defense establishment that is responsible for creating the Internet.

asymmetrical bandwidth   A network link that provides different capacity (in bits per second, or bps) in each direction (up link and down link).

asynchronous systems   Systems, such as networks, that don't use a common clock for synchronizing their signals between network nodes.

Asynchronous Transfer Mode (ATM)   An international standard describing how to create small packets and route them through a wide area network (WAN).

autonomous system (AS)   A collection of Transmission Control Protocol/Internet Protocol (TCP/IP)-based networks that a company or organization administers.

best practices   A term to describe tested and proven behaviors leading to effective operating procedures.

bits per second (bps)   The capacity of a network or communications channel based on how many bits per second are sent across the channel.

Bluetooth   A wireless network standard designed to connect low capacity nodes.

Border Gateway Protocol (BGP)   An Internet route discovery protocol as well as a tool for establishing peering relationships between Internet service providers (ISPs) and Internet Exchange Points (IXPs).

bridge   (a). A local area network (LAN) device that connects network nodes. (b). A machine acting as a central relay point on a star network topology using MAC addresses.

broadband network   A high-capacity network (more bits per second) available from telephone, cable TV, and satellite companies.

broadcast network   An arrangement in which one node in a network sends data to all other nodes.

bus network   A network topology consisting on a serial link connecting all nodes.

bytes   A string of seven or eight bits.

cell   Used in two contexts: (1) In wireless networks, a cell is a geographical area covered by a specific radio antenna; (2) In data networks, it's a small packet (53 bytes) that Asynchronous Transfer Mode (ATM) systems use.

central processing unit (CPU)   The overall hardware controller of a computer.

checksum   A method for detecting corrupted data.

ciphertext   Data that has been encrypted.

Classless Inter-Domain Routing (CIDR)   A method of altering the IP address format to permit the use of additional addresses.

cleartext   Data that has not been encrypted.

client/server   A network in which a central computer called a server performs a variety of services to the attached computers, which are called clients. The servers play a lead role in these operations.

communications protocol   A set of rules by which computers must communicate with each other.

computer network   A connection through a physical medium of two or more computers.

datagram   A discrete unit of data (also called a packet).

DHCP (Dynamic Host Configuration Protocol)   An Internet protocol used to dynamically assign IP addresses to network nodes.

digital signature   A method using pubic key procedures for proving an identity.

digital subscriber line (DSL)   A high-capacity link operated by local telephone companies.

direct sequence spread spectrum (DSSS)   A wireless technology in which sender and receiver privately communicate with an agreed-upon code to cipher and decipher the traffic.

disk mirroring   A process in which data is placed on more than one disk.

DNS Security Protocol (DNSSEC)   An Internet protocol that guards against receiving invalid DNS information from servers.

Domain Name System (DNS)   Internet standards and procedures for (a) registering reserved Internet names and (b) correlating an IP address with the name.

DS (digital signaling)   A special term that describes communications lines that use digital signaling techniques and a specific convention (developed by AT&T) for encoding the signals.

encapsulation   Placing the contents of one frame or packet in the data field of another frame or packet.

Ethernet   A local area network (LAN) standard published by the Institute of Electronic and Electrical Engineers (IEEE).

extranet   A private computer network.

fault tolerance   A hardware setup where components are duplexed. There are two of each device.

firewall A security feature on a network that filters unwanted traffic from entering a network or a computer.

FireWire A high-speed interface published by the Institute of Electronic and Electrical Engineers.

firmware A special type of software that is rarely (if ever) changed.

frames A unit of data into which packets or datagrams are encapsulated. The most common example is the Ethernet frame, which contains a packet/datagram in its user information field.

frequency hopping spread spectrum (FHSS) A wireless technology in which the sender and receiver communicate with each other by frequently changing (hopping) frequencies.

FTP (File Transfer Protocol) A widely used Internet standard that defines procedures for exchanging files between computers.

function calls A software command invoking the execution of other software. Sometimes called library calls.

grooming On a communications link, adding, combining, separating, and dropping payloads from different users.

groupware An application that a community of users shares.

high availability Clustering multiple computers for backup purposes.

host A general (and vague) term describing a hardware device that is attached to a network. Some vendors use the word to describe a computer; others use the word to describe a server.

hot swapping Replacing disk drives while the system is up and running.

hub A machine acting as a central relay point on a star network topology.

hybrid network A network supporting both wire-based and wireless connections.

hyperlink A reference to another part of a document, a different document, or a different site on the Internet.

hypertext Text that allows users to link the text to other images or other websites.

Hypertext Markup Language (HTML) Code that defines the content and look of web documents.

Hypertext Transfer Protocol (HTTP) An Internet standard for sending and receiving linked hypertext files.

IMAP4 (Internet Message Access Protocol, version 4) A widely used Internet email standard.

inner-network interface (INI) The communications interfaces(s) between network providers' equipment within the same network.

Internet The public computer network.

Internet Packet Exchange (IPX) A proprietary protocol developed by Novell.

interworking Connecting network nodes together so they can communicate and exchange data with each other.

intranet A private computer network.

IPSec (IP Security Protocol) A set of Internet standards that define means to protect the integrity of user data in an Internet Protocol (IP) packet.

ISP (Internet service provider) A commercial organization that provides access to the Internet, such as AOL.

IXP (Internet Exchange Point) An organization that controls Internet routing nodes, which form the backbone of the Internet.

kernel The basic, key part of an operating system (OS).

killer app   A software application of such consequence that it affects the operations of an organization or a network.

Layer 2 Tunneling Protocol (L2TP)   An Internet standard to extend PPP capabilities across networks.

leased lines   Those communications links that are rented from communications carriers, such as AT&T.

link   A communications channel, such as a copper wire. This is not to be confused with a web link, which is a form of an address.

local area network (LAN)   A network that's designed for connecting devices located close together. Usually a private network.

logical connection   Network actions that permit the transfer of data between computers, usually the execution of software routines.

logical protocol   Conventions in software for sending and receiving traffic on the physical media.

malware   A nickname for software and or packets that can do harm to a user's computer system.

media   The links (channels) in a communications network.

Media Access Control (MAC)   Layer 2 of a local area network (LAN).

MIB (Management Information Base) A database containing information about managed resources in a network, such as Ethernet connections. Usually accessed by the Simple Network Management Protocol (SNMP).

MIME (Multipurpose Internet Mail Extensions)   An Internet standard that defines and identifies different types of files, such as video, text, and graphics.

modem   From modulator/demodulator, a device that converts binary, digital signals into analog signals at the sending site and performs a reverse operation at the receiving site.

motherboard   The central circuit board in a computer.

multicasting   The sending of traffic from one network node to three or more nodes.

multiplexing   Sharing a communications link with more than one user.

Multiprotocol Label Switching (MPLS) A wide area technology using labels (instead of addresses) to identify and forward traffic.

Network Address Translation (NAT) An Internet protocol that allows private IP addresses to be reused by translating them into fewer public IP addresses.

network architecture   The logical and physical structure and behavior of a computer network.

network card   The hardware inside a computer that's attached to a physical port, such as a USB.

network interface card (NIC)   See network card.

networking   Used in two contexts: (1) Operating a device attached to a network, or (2) Learning how to build and operate a network.

network-network interface (NNI)   The communications interface(s) between network providers' equipment between networks.

node   A generic term to denote a machine, such as a computer or router, that is attached to a network.

Open Systems Interconnection model (OSI)   A widely used representation of the major functions of a computer network, and how these functions are related to each other.

operating system (OS)   The central set of software on a computer, which directs the actions of all other components.

packet   A self-contained piece of data, including a header with destination and source addresses. Also called a datagram.

paging   A process in which software is swapped into and out of computer memory.

payload   The part of a packet or frame containing user data.

peering   An arrangement between Internet ISPs and Internet Exchange Points (IXPs) to allow the transport of traffic between these parties.

peer to peer   A network in which all nodes play equal roles in the interactions.

permanent virtual circuit   One or more communications lines in a network that are linked to each through switches or other cross-connect devices. The links may be shared with many users, but each user is pre-allocated access to the end-to-end facility and guaranteed a certain amount of bandwidth. Thus, the service mimics a leased line.

physical connection   The hardware and physical channels of a network.

physical protocol   The conventions for using wiring, plugs, and antenna, as well as the physical signals on these media.

plain old telephone service (POTS)   A nickname for conventional telephone service.

Point-to-Point Protocol (PPP)   An Internet standard for authentication and negotiating services between two network devices.

Point-to-Point Tunneling Protocol (PPTP)   An extension to Point-to-Point Protocol (PPP), used to transmit PPP packets through networks.

POP3 (Post Office Protocol, version 3)   A widely used Internet email standard.

port   Used in two contexts: (1) A physical interface on a computer, and (2) An Internet identifier associated with a specific software process, such as email or domain names.

prefixes   The use of parts of the IP address to provide address aggregation.

private key   An encryption/decryption key, known only to its creator.

protocol   An agreement on how to exchange data between two or more devices; usually documented in a standard.

protocol converter   A computer that translates and converts protocols to allow two or more computers that use different procedures to communicate with each other.

protocol data unit (PDU)   A generic term to describe any self-contained unit of data, such as a packet, a frame, a datagram, or a cell.

public key   An encryption/decryption key known to the public.

quality of service (QOS)   The measurement and provision of a certain level of service (such as response time and throughput) by a network provider to a user.

RAID (redundant arrays of inexpensive disks)   A method of providing backup for data and software.

replay   Capturing data, modifying or replicating it, and resending it to the legitimate receiver.

residential broadband   A somewhat inaccurate term to describe a high-capacity link between a network provider and a residence, or an office.

resource records (RRs)   The entries in a Domain Name System (DNS) database. The most common RR is the correlation of a domain name to an Internet Protocol (IP) address.

ring network   A network topology that forms a concentric link between nodes.

route filtering   The operation by a router in which possible routes to a destination are chosen or not chosen.

router   A machine acting as a central relay point on a network.

Secure Shell (SSH)   A security login protocol found on UNIX and Linux operating systems.

Secure Socket Tunneling Protocol (SSTP)   An extension to PPP, which allows remote access data to pass through a firewall.

Secure Sockets Layer (SSL)   An Internet protocol used for authentication.

security certificate   A means to establish secure communications between two parties.

server   A general term to describe either software or hardware that provides support services to user computers, such as email and print operations.

server operating systems (SOS)   Software that operates in a server. Also called a network operating system (NOS).

SMTP (Simple Mail Transport Protocol)   A widely used Internet email standard.

SNMP (Simple Network Management Protocol)   An Internet standard that defines the structure and use of network management messages.

socket   Used in two contexts: (1) A physical interface inside a computer, or (2) an Internet identifier, consisting of an Internet port number, an IP address, and a protocol ID.

SONET (Synchronous Optical Network)   An advanced digital, optical transport technology, usually implemented inside core networks.

star topology   A physical network arrangement in which a central connection point, such as a hub or router, acts as a relay unit (a switch) between the attached computers.

subnetwork   A part of a full network, distinguished by separating the physical network into logical subnets by configuring nodes with various IP addresses.

switch   A machine acting as a central relay point on a star network topology.

synchronous systems   Systems, such as networks, that use a common clock for synchronizing their signals between network nodes.

T1   A general term to describe a range of digital communications links offered by long-distance companies and local telephone companies.

TCP/IP (Transmission Control Protocol/Internet Protocol)   Used in two contexts: (1) A general term to describe a range of Internet standards and protocols, and (2) TCP: A Layer 4 protocol that provides end-to-end traffic integrity; IP: A Layer 3 protocol used to forward packets containing IP addresses.

time-division multiplexing   Sharing a communications link with multiple users by taking turns using the link.

topology   The physical shape of a network, such as a ring or star.

traffic engineering (TE)   The configuration and tuning of hardware and software to manage (engineer) traffic.

Trojan horse   A hidden piece of software, such as a virus, that is triggered by an event, such as a date.

trunk   A term used by telephone personnel to describe a communications link or channel.

UDP (User Datagram Protocol)   An Internet Layer 4 protocol that's used in place of Transmission Control Protocol (TCP) if users don't need traffic accountability or can't tolerate the overhead of TCP.

uniform resource locator (URL)   An identifier that correlates a hyperlink to a domain name.

USB (Universal Serial Bus)   A standard physical interface on computers.

user-network interface (UNI)   The communications interface(s) between a user's equipment and a network provider's equipment.

virtual circuit/path IDs   Identifiers placed in Asynchronous Transfer Mode (ATM) protocol data units (PDUs) to identify the payload (user data, control data).

virtual private network (VPN)   A public network designed in such a way (with privacy and security safeguards) that it appears to the users as a private network.

virus   A piece of code that damages software or files.

VoIP (Voice over IP)   A set of Internet standards that define procedures for transporting digital voice traffic in Internet Protocol (IP) packets.

wardriving   A nickname for roaming an area and tapping into someone's wireless network.

wide area network (WAN)   A network connecting devices that are not located close together. A WAN is often implemented as a public network, such as the Internet.

Wi-Fi   A wireless networking standard designed to interconnect low to high capacity nodes.

wireless access point   A device used to connect wireless nodes and relay traffic among these nodes.

Wireless Equivalent Privacy (WEP)
A security protocol used in wireless networks, typically those employing Wi-Fi standards.

Wireless Protected Access (WPA)
A security protocol used in wireless networks, typically those employing Wi-Fi standards.

workgroup   A set of computers that share resources among themselves.

Index

J-K-L

L

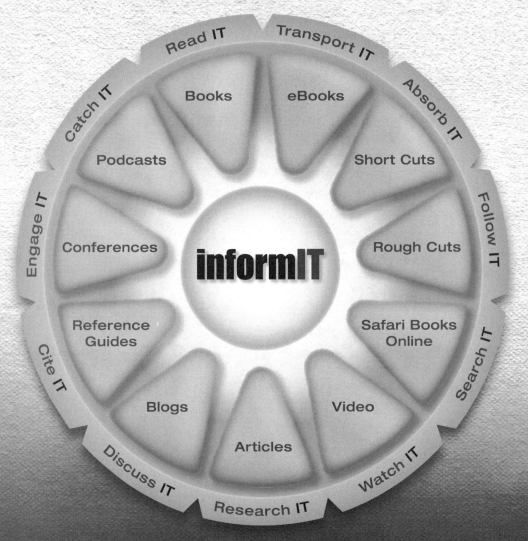

LearnIT at InformIT

Go Beyond the Book

- Read IT
- Transport IT
- Absorb IT
- Catch IT
- Books
- eBooks
- Short Cuts
- Podcasts
- Follow IT
- Engage IT
- Conferences
- **informIT**
- Rough Cuts
- Reference Guides
- Safari Books Online
- Search IT
- Cite IT
- Blogs
- Video
- Discuss IT
- Articles
- Watch IT
- Research IT

11 WAYS TO LEARN IT at **www.informIT.com/learn**

The digital network for the publishing imprints of Pearson Education

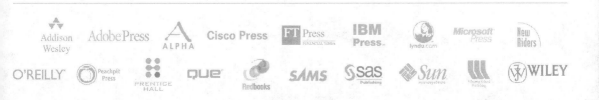

FREE Online Edition

Your purchase of **Sams Teach Yourself Networking in 24 Hours** includes access to a free online edition for 45 days through the Safari Books Online subscription service. Nearly every Sams book is available online through Safari Books Online, along with more than 5,000 other technical books and videos from publishers such as Addison-Wesley Professional, Cisco Press, Exam Cram, IBM Press, O'Reilly, Prentice Hall, and Que.

SAFARI BOOKS ONLINE allows you to search for a specific answer, cut and paste code, download chapters, and stay current with emerging technologies.

Activate your FREE Online Edition at www.informit.com/safarifree

> **STEP 1:** Enter the coupon code: VGNSSZG.

> **STEP 2:** New Safari users, complete the brief registration form.
> Safari subscribers, just log in.